Law 101

Law 101

*Everything You Need to Know About
American Law*

Fifth Edition

JAY M. FEINMAN

OXFORD
UNIVERSITY PRESS

OXFORD
UNIVERSITY PRESS

Oxford University Press is a department of the University of Oxford. It furthers
the University's objective of excellence in research, scholarship, and education
by publishing worldwide. Oxford is a registered trade mark of Oxford University
Press in the UK and certain other countries.

Published in the United States of America by Oxford University Press
198 Madison Avenue, New York, NY 10016, United States of America.

Library of Congress Cataloging-in-Publication Data
Names: Feinman, Jay M., author.
Title: Law 101 : everything you need to know about American law / Jay M. Feinman.
Description: Fifth edition. | New York, NY : Oxford University Press, [2018]
| Includes bibliographical references and index.
Identifiers: LCCN 2017052995 | ISBN 9780190866327 (hardback) |
ISBN 9780190866334 (updf) | ISBN 9780190866341 (epub)
Subjects: LCSH: Law—United States—Popular works. | BISAC: LAW / General. |
LAW / Administrative Law & Regulatory Practice. | LAW / Constitutional.
Classification: LCC KF387 .F45 2018 | DDC 349.73—dc23
LC record available at https://lccn.loc.gov/2017052995

1 3 5 7 9 8 6 4 2
Printed by Sheridan Books, Inc, United States of America

To Leah and Bryan, Keith and Allie,
and, more than ever, Carole

Contents

Contents

Law is everywhere. Check the news any day and you'll hear about a notorious criminal trial, a massive lawsuit, or a new constitutional claim.
And it all seems so complicated. Why are there legal technicalities that
trip up the police and allow criminals to get off? Why does litigation take
so long and cost so much? How do the courts figure out how the words
of the Constitution apply to situations the framers never dreamed of?

Lawyers are trained to understand issues like these, and there are
plenty of resources to help them. The library at my law school has more
than a million volumes and innumerable online resources in which
lawyers can find statutes, judicial opinions, and learned commentary on
the law. This book is for everybody else. *Law 101* is a basic explanation
of the rules and principles that lawyers and judges use. The premise of
the book is straightforward: It's not easy to decide legal questions, but
anyone can acquire a basic understanding of what the questions involve.

Each of the substantive chapters of the book covers one of the basic
subjects that every lawyer learns during the first year of law school: constitutional law, civil rights, civil procedure and the litigation process,
torts, contracts, property, criminal law, and criminal procedure. In each
chapter you will learn the fundamental principles that underlie the subject, acquire a legal vocabulary, and see how the rules are applied in
ordinary and unusual situations. (If you want simple definitions of even
more legal terms, consult this book's companion volume, *1001 Legal
Words You Need to Know*.) The book not only tells you about the law—
more importantly, it engages you in the process of lawmaking by asking
you to think about the tough questions and troubling cases that lawyers
and judges face. You will have some fun along the way as well, because
the situations the law deals with are always interesting and sometimes
amusing or outrageous.

After reading this book, when you hear about controversial legal
issues you will have a better sense of the background and the complexity
of the issues and you will be better able to make your own judgments
about what the law should be. You also will be better prepared to think
about the legal problems that you may encounter in everyday life, from
owning a home to suing someone to asserting your constitutional rights.
If you ever have considered going to law school, *Law 101* will give you
a taste of what it is like. And if you are a student, either in law school

or elsewhere, it will give you the big picture of basic legal subjects that otherwise can be hard to obtain.

Although I am a lawyer and law professor, writing and revising this book have been as much of an education for me as I hope it will be for its readers. I have had to rethink many subjects that are not my specialties, and I have freshly examined areas I have studied for years. I am very grateful to all of those who helped me in the process. Carl Bogus, Dennis Braithwaite, Ed Chase, Kim Ferzan, Beth Hillman, Greg Lastowka, Thomas LeBien, Earl Maltz, Stanislaw Pomorski, Mike Sepanic, Rick Singer, Allan Stein, and Bob Williams gave me excellent comments. Elizabeth Boyd, Sheryl Fay, Nicole Friant, Amy Newnam, and Beth Pascal provided helpful research assistance. Chris Carr and Bill Lutz gave early support. Rutgers Law School and its deans have provided an environment in which work of this kind could be done. Most of all, thanks to John Wright, who made it happen.

Law 101

There Are No Secret Books

You Can Understand the Law

Americans are fascinated by the law. And why not? The law is important, intellectually challenging, and sometimes outrageous. Consider some cases that have made front-page news:

- Stella Liebeck, seventy-nine years old, bought a cup of coffee at the drive-through window of a McDonald's in Albuquerque, New Mexico. As she placed the cup between her legs to remove the lid to add cream and sugar, she spilled the coffee, scalding herself. Liebeck's injuries sent her to the hospital for seven days for burn treatment, including skin grafts, so she sued McDonald's, alleging that the coffee was dangerously hot. A jury awarded her $160,000 to compensate her for her injuries and $2.7 million to punish McDonald's, an amount the jury calculated was equal to two days of coffee sales for McDonald's. (The trial judge later reduced the punitive damage award to $480,000.) Was this an outrageous example of a tort system run amok, or a fair judgment for an injured victim against a wrongdoer? See Chapter 5.

- James Obergefell and John Arthur met, fell in love, and established a decades-long committed relationship. After John was diagnosed with ALS, or Lou Gehrig's disease, a debilitating, progressive illness with no cure, they wanted to marry before James died. They flew from their home in Ohio to Maryland, where same-sex marriage was legal, and were wed. After John died three months later, James could not be listed as the surviving spouse on John's death certificate because Ohio did not recognize same-sex marriage. James sued, and the Supreme Court held that the Fourteenth Amendment required states to issue marriage licenses to same-sex couples and to recognize such marriages performed in other states. How do the justices know what the Constitution means in cases like these? See Chapter 3.

- Ferguson, Missouri, police officer Darren Wilson approached Michael Brown, an African American teenager, following the robbery of a convenience store; a struggle took place between Brown and Wilson and then Brown fled. Witness accounts were in conflict about just what happened next, but in the end Wilson shot the unarmed Brown at least six times, killing him. A grand jury investigated and refused to indict Wilson for homicide. Brown's death and the grand jury's decision contributed to the spread of the Black Lives Matter movement. When can a police officer use deadly force in arresting a suspect? See Chapter 8.

Most of the law is not about important cases like the constitutional protection of same-sex marriage or dramatic cases like Michael Brown's shooting. Law penetrates our everyday life in many ways. Critics charge that in recent years we have become plagued with "hyperlexis"—too much law and too many lawyers—but law has pervaded our society from the beginning. Even before the Pilgrims landed in Massachusetts they formulated the Mayflower Compact, a legal document that governed their settlement of the new world. In colonial times, legal regulation of the economy, public conduct, and social morality was at least as extensive as it is today. Common human failings such as fornication, drunkenness, and idleness were legally—and frequently—punished, and laws closely regulated economic affairs, prescribing the size of loaves of bread and the time and place at which goods could be sold. Ordinary litigation provided an occasion for public gathering, with great orations by the lawyers and much comment by the public. Today the law affects us individually when we rent apartments or own homes, marry, drive cars, borrow money, purchase goods, belong to organizations, go to school or work, and obtain health care and collectively when the government taxes, regulates the airwaves and cyberspace, polices crime, and controls pollution.

For all our endless fascination with the law, it is hard for most people to learn much about its substance. The law is so complex and voluminous that no one, not even the most knowledgeable lawyer, can understand it all. Moreover, lawyers and legal scholars have not gone out of their way to make the law accessible to the ordinary person. Just the opposite: Legal professionals, like the priests of some obscure religion, too often try to keep the law mysterious and inaccessible.

But everybody can learn something about the law. That is what *Law 101* is for. It explains the basics of the law—the rules, principles, and arguments that lawyers and judges use. Not all the law is here; there is just too much law for anyone to learn more than a few pieces of it here and there. That's one reason that most lawyers specialize, so that they can learn in depth the law of medical malpractice in New Jersey or federal tax law relating to corporations, for example. But all lawyers do know pretty much the same things when it comes to basic subjects and basic concepts, because they all go through a similar law school experience.

The public seems to be morbidly fascinated by law school as much as by law. Books and movies from *The Paper Chase* to *Legally Blonde* have fed the folklore of the first year of law school as an intellectually stimulating but grueling and dehumanizing experience. Because the first year of law school is the near-universal training ground for lawyers, this book focuses on the substance of what law students learn there as the core of knowledge that is useful and interesting to nonlawyers as well.

The first-year curriculum in nearly every American law school looks alike. A few topics are fundamental, and this book explores those topics. Constitutional law involves the structure of government (Chapter 2) and personal liberties protected from government action (Chapter 3). Civil procedure concerns the process of litigation (Chapter 4). Tort law concerns personal injuries (Chapter 5). Contract law is the law of private agreements (Chapter 6). Property law governs relationships among people with respect to the ownership of things (Chapter 7). Criminal law defines wrongful conduct for which the state can deprive a person of life or liberty (Chapter 8). Criminal procedure prescribes the process of criminal adjudication and the rights of defendants (Chapter 9).

Nearly every law school offers courses in constitutional law, contract law, and the rest, and the courses taught in different schools resemble each other to a considerable degree in the materials used and the topics covered. Schools in New Jersey, Iowa, and California all teach basic principles of national law, often using the same judicial opinions and statutes. If you attend law school after reading this book, you will find much of the first year will be familiar to you. Every course is taught by a different professor, however, and every professor has a different perspective. Some of those differences in perspective are trivial, but some are crucial. One professor may be a political liberal, another a conservative. One may favor economic analysis as a key to understanding the law, while another takes a natural law approach. Each of these differences in perspective, and the many others that occur, leads to a very different understanding of what the law is. So while law students and lawyers all understand the same law in principle, they understand it in different ways.

This book has a perspective, too. It couldn't be any other way. The perspective of this book is informed by much of the best scholarship about the law. Some of the elements of the perspective are widely accepted, and others are more controversial. The perspective can be summed up in a few insights about the law, as follows.

Law is not in the law books. Books are one of the first things that come to mind when we think about law: fat texts almost too heavy to lift; dust-covered, leather-bound tomes of precedents; law libraries filled with rows and rows of statutes and judicial opinions. While books tell us a lot about the law, they are not the law. Instead, law lives in conduct, not on the printed page; it exists in the interactions of judges, lawyers, and ordinary citizens.

Think, for example, about one of the laws we most commonly encounter: the speed limit. What is the legal speed limit on most interstate highways? Someone who looked only in the law books might think the answer is 65 mph, but we know better. If you drive at 65 mph on the New Jersey Turnpike, be prepared to have a truck bearing down on you, flashing its lights to get you to pull into the slow lane. The speed limit according to drivers' conduct is considerably higher than 65. And legal officials act the same way. The police allow drivers a cushion and never give a speeding ticket to someone who is going 66. If they did, the judges would laugh them out of traffic court. As a practical matter, the court doesn't want to waste its time with someone who violated the speed limit by 1 mph, and as a matter of law, the police radar may not be accurate enough to draw that fine a line anyway. So what is the law on how fast you can drive? Something different than the books say.

To understand the law, then, we have to examine events as they occur in the world. We can generalize from those events and create theories and concepts to inform our understanding of the law, but the touchstone is always the world and not the idea. One way this is done in law school is by focusing on individual fact situations that give rise to litigation and on the judicial opinions that resolve the situations, known as *cases*. Each of these cases starts out as a real-world event, such as Stella Liebeck's suit against McDonald's or the killing of Michael Brown by Officer Darren Wilson, and becomes the vehicle for thinking about many related events in a way that allows us to go back and forth between the particular fact situation and a general principle of law. This book follows that model and uses many interesting cases to explore legal principles.

Law is not secret. Along with the mistaken notion that the law resides in the books goes the equally mistaken idea that law is secret, or at least inaccessible to the ordinary person. To understand and apply the law at the advanced, technical level that lawyers do requires professional knowledge, but to understand the basic substance of the law does not. Law reflects life. The principles and issues embodied in the law are not different from those that we experience in other aspects of our lives. Contract law, for example, is a commentary on the way people make, interpret, keep, and break their promises in commercial and noncommercial settings. Few nonlawyers can describe the objective theory of contract formation or the Statute of Frauds (you will be able to after you read Chapter 6), but they have thought a lot about contracts and promises. If you cross your fingers when you make a promise, does it mean that the promise doesn't count? If you promise to take your children to the movies, are you off the hook if an important business meeting comes up in the meantime? What about if you just don't feel like it? If your newly purchased television doesn't work, can you return it to the store? And so on.

These are the kinds of issues that we all confront every day. The law provides a different forum for the discussion of these issues and the exploration of the principles, and the basic ideas involved are wholly accessible to the nonlawyer.

There are no simple answers. Law reflects life, and life is complicated. Therefore, legal problems defy simple solutions.

Life is complicated in two ways. First, things are often messy, so it is hard to define a legal issue and construct an appropriate solution. Think about the speed limit. If we formulate a clear rule, in this instance "driving faster than the speed limit is a crime," we will inevitably end up with exceptions, such as "a parent rushing a desperately ill child to the hospital may exceed the speed limit." If we formulate a fuzzy rule— "drive at a speed that is reasonable under the circumstances"—we will engender arguments in every case about how the rule should apply.

Second, life is complicated because we often are of two minds about an issue. We would like to have clear legal rules to ensure consistency, fairness, and predictability. But we want to make room for the equities of individual cases in which the application of a rule would produce an unfair result, in order to relieve a particular party of the hardship of the rule.

Politicians often would like us to think that there are simple answers to tough legal questions. Over the past few years we have become accustomed to sound-bite politics and simplistic ideologies that assert that all our problems can be solved by cutting down on frivolous litigation, getting tough on crime, making people responsible for their actions, or adhering to some other slogan. From the perspective used in this book, it's just not so.

Law is a battleground of political conflict. The complex questions with which law deals and our conflicting responses to them are the stuff of political controversy. This is not politics in the Republican–Democratic, electoral sense, but a struggle over social resources and social values just the same. At stake in legal decisions are the most fundamental kinds of questions with which any society has to grapple: Who gets what? Who lives and who dies? What is right and what is wrong? Everyone can see this in major constitutional issues like the abortion controversy, but it applies to all other legal issues, too. Should fast-food chains be liable for obesity-related illnesses because they promote and sell super-sized portions of fattening foods? We have to see all legal decisions like this as political in a broad sense.

People make the law. Often, the law appears to be part of the natural order of things. The law and legal decisions can be seen as inevitable, based on immutable principles of justice, hardly the product of human action at all. Lawyers and judges speak as if the law itself were acting, free from their intervention: "The law requires that . . . " or "The precedents determine a result. . . . " Nonsense. Law is made by people, and "the law" or "the precedents" never control anything; we control them. All this view does is let a small group of people—the privileged, the politically powerful, and the legal professionals—control the legal system while they deny their responsibility for doing so. Whether the issue is abortion, manufacturers' liability, or the enforceability of handshake agreements, all of us—not just the lawyers and judges—have to decide what we think is a fair and useful result.

This book strips away the mystery of the law to allow the nonlawyer to understand the rules of law and the principles and conflicts that are behind them. It doesn't tell you how to be your own lawyer. You won't learn how to file for divorce, sue in small claims court, or draft your own will. Other books convey that kind of advice; this one deals with issues that are more important, if less immediate. It explores the big issues that are fundamental to law, not the mechanics of particular transactions. Later, whether you use a how-to manual or go to a lawyer to deal with a legal matter, you will have a better sense of what is going on behind the rules and mechanics. And there is an important difference between this book and other law books, whether professional treatises for lawyers or how-to manuals on will drafting: This one is fun to read. The invented children's author Lemony Snicket wrote, "Books about the law are notorious for being very long, very dull, and very difficult to read." Not *Law 101*. Like the law itself, this book is full of puzzles, challenges, interesting tidbits, thought-provoking questions, and intellectual stimulation.

Each chapter is organized in question-and-answer format. The questions provide guideposts to the development of the chapter, and they make it possible to read selectively by dipping into particular topics of interest. At many points there are more questions than answers, and issues are left unresolved. Students of the law—and now you are one of them—experience this frequently and find it very frustrating. But that's the way it has to be. The law doesn't clearly answer some questions, and some issues are never finally settled. The courts cannot decide everything; figuring out the just solutions to hard problems is the right and duty of every informed person. After reading this book, you should be in a better position to participate in the process.

2

The Supreme Law of the Land

Constitutional Law

People who don't know anything about civil procedure or property law can still recall the basic elements of constitutional law from their eighth-grade civics class: separation of powers; checks and balances; judicial review; due process and equal protection of law; freedom of speech, religion, and press. And if they can't remember what they learned in the eighth grade, the news will remind them of the continuing significance of constitutional law. Is abortion constitutionally protected? How about same-sex marriage? Do corporations have free-speech rights?

Everything the government does is bounded by the Constitution. Constitutional law defines the relations between the president and Congress and between the federal government and the states, and it regulates the government's ability to assess taxes, to build highways, to maintain and deploy the armed forces, and to print stamps. Moreover, every hot issue seems to become a constitutional question. Once it was the constitutionality of slavery or of laws establishing maximum hours and minimum wages for workers; now it is abortion, LGBT rights, and campaign financing. In the aftermath of the 2000 election, even who should be president became a constitutional issue, in the litigation resulting in the Supreme Court's decision in *Bush v. Gore*. So constitutional law—how our government is organized and what it can and cannot do—is the place to begin our exploration of American law.

What Is Constitutional Law?

Constitutional law involves the interpretation and application of the U.S. Constitution and each state's constitution (more on state constitutions shortly). Drafted in 1787, the U.S. Constitution contains fewer than 4,400 words, divided into seven short parts called articles. The Bill of Rights (the first ten amendments to the Constitution) was added in 1791, and only seventeen more amendments have been added in the more than two centuries since. It wouldn't take you long to do what few Americans do—read the whole Constitution, front to back.

It seems that constitutional law ought to be easy to understand. But despite the Constitution's simplicity—or perhaps because of it—what the Constitution means and how it should apply are the most hotly debated topics of the law. And constitutional law is unique among all the bodies of law we will consider in this book, for four reasons.

First, other bodies of law work together. Property law creates rights in things like land and refrigerators, and contract law prescribes how to transfer those rights to another person. Tort law defines the right of an injured person to recover damages from a wrongdoer, and civil procedure establishes the process by which the victim can recover. But constitutional law has a different subject matter and a different status than the other fields of law. Constitutional law doesn't address relations among individuals the way property, contract, and tort law do. Instead, it defines the structure and function of the government and the relationships between the government and individual citizens. It also defines the relative powers of the national government and the state governments and prohibits the government from taking certain actions, such as those that infringe on freedom of religion. In defining and limiting government powers, constitutional law is superior to every other body of law. The Constitution proclaims itself to be "the supreme Law of the Land." Any state or federal law on any topic—contracts, criminal punishment, campaign contributions, or public schools—that conflicts with the Constitution is invalid.

Second, other bodies of law are based on a mix of statutes and judicial decisions that provide a wide range of sources for rules, principles, and arguments. Contract law, for example, began as a common law subject determined by judges and has been overlaid by legislation. To decide a contracts case, a court can look to a rich variety of sources, from old English precedents to modern state statutes. Constitutional law is different. All constitutional decisions ultimately refer to a single, narrow source: the text of the Constitution with its amendments.

The necessary reference to a single text makes constitutional law so challenging because of the infinitely broad range of situations that the text must cover. When the constitutional text addresses a narrow issue and does so specifically, we have little problem in figuring out how to apply the text; more often, the text is vague and the cases that it covers are much more diverse, so we have to decide what the text means and what result follows from it in a particular case. Sometimes, by universal agreement, the words mean something other than what they appear to mean. The First Amendment states that "Congress shall make no law respecting an establishment of religion, or prohibiting the free exercise thereof," but even the most ardent strict constructionist understands that the amendment also applies to the president and the courts. Other times the words demand extensive interpretation. Does the constitutional command that no state may "deny to any person within its jurisdiction the equal protection of the laws" mean that a state university cannot give a preference in admissions to African American students in order to diversify its student body?

Third, constitutional law, more obviously than other areas of law, raises fundamental political issues and value choices. One of the themes of this book is that every body of law and every legal decision implicates important values; tort law, for example, forces us to make important choices about to what extent people must take account of the harm they may cause to other people. But in constitutional law, the value questions are more readily apparent and therefore are more controversial. If all law is politics to some extent, constitutional law is more explicitly political than other bodies of law. There are very few simple or noncontroversial issues in interpreting and applying the Constitution.

Fourth, in other areas of law the processes of making and applying law seem obvious and appropriate. Legislatures and courts formulate principles of law, and courts apply those principles in deciding individual cases. In constitutional law the decision process also is clear, but whether it is appropriate is much more contested. In other areas of law the power of the courts is taken for granted, even if the correctness of the results they reach may not be. In constitutional law, by contrast, the central issues are why judges have the power to be the final arbiters of constitutional law and what theories of constitutional interpretation they should use in interpreting and applying the Constitution.

When the constitutional text requires interpreting, the courts do so, especially at the federal level. If necessary, cases are taken to the top, to be heard by the nine justices of the U.S. Supreme Court. But the Supreme Court justices are appointed, not elected, and once appointed they serve for life, without ever being subject to review again. If constitutional law involves fundamental political issues, why can those issues be decided for a democratic society by such an undemocratic institution? Moreover, the more overtly political institutions of government such as Congress resolve political issues by consulting constituents, being lobbied by interest groups, looking at opinion polls, and openly debating the pros and cons. How does the Supreme Court decide hot political issues when it apparently is insulated from the political process?

These four distinctive features of constitutional law generate the subject matter discussed in this chapter. The most basic issues concern the structure and authority of the federal government. The ratification of the Constitution created the national government and dictated its organization and powers. Constitutional law first specifies how the federal government is organized into three branches—legislative, executive, and judicial—and what each branch, and the federal government as a whole, can do. In concept, at least, the federal government is a government of both limited and supreme powers—limited to those powers granted it by the Constitution but supreme within its sphere. Accordingly, defining the powers of the national government also defines the principles of federalism, or the relationship between the national government and the states. (The powers of both national and state governments also are limited by the constitutional guarantees of individual liberty, especially in the Bill of Rights and the post–Civil War amendments, which are discussed in Chapter 3.) Running through all of these particular topics is the issue of constitutional interpretation. The federal courts, especially the Supreme Court, are the authoritative interpreters of the Constitution. How do they determine what the constitutional text means when applied in a particular case?

We usually think of the U.S. Constitution when we think of constitutional law, but each state has its own constitution and therefore its own body of constitutional law, too. The state constitutions are in many respects like the federal Constitution, as they establish the structure of the legislative, executive, and judicial branches and include bills of rights. But state constitutional law differs from federal law in important ways.

Most state constitutions are much longer and more detailed than the federal Constitution. The Alabama constitution, for example, is more than 600 pages long—about twice as long as this book. The New Jersey constitution of 1947, a modern, reform constitution, is still about three times the length of the U.S. Constitution.

Several factors contribute to the length of state constitutions. The national government is a government of enumerated powers, possessing only the authority granted to it under the Constitution, typically in vague language. The states, on the other hand, inherently have general authority to govern, so state constitutions limit rather than grant power, and the limitations often are stated very specifically. State constitutions also often contain provisions that are not particularly "constitutional," in the sense of being directives about fundamental issues of rights or government organization. Some of these provisions address topics of particular concern to a state; Idaho has constitutional provisions on water rights and livestock, and New Mexico on bilingual education.

Others are simply matters of detail that someone thought belonged in the constitution; the California constitution contains guidelines for the publication of court opinions. Finally, the national Constitution can be amended only through a cumbersome process and has been amended only seventeen times since the adoption of the Bill of Rights in 1791. State constitutional amendments generally can be proposed by the legislature, a constitutional commission, or citizens' petition and can be adopted by referendum. As a result, state constitutions are often amended; the Alabama constitution, for example, has been amended over nine hundred times. Indeed, state constitutions can and frequently are even replaced altogether; the current Georgia constitution is its tenth.

The bills of rights in state constitutions also are more detailed and are in some ways more important than the federal Bill of Rights. Instead of being added on to the main body of the constitution as in the federal Constitution, state bills of rights typically come first. This tradition dates from the earliest state constitutions that contained such well-known documents as the Virginia Declaration of Rights, a model for the Bill of Rights in the U.S. Constitution. These early documents included provisions guaranteeing the rights of the people and also hortatory statements of government principle, such as the recommendation in the Pennsylvania Declaration of Rights that the legislature consist of "persons most noted for wisdom and virtue." Today state bills of rights look more like the federal Bill of Rights but add to it in two important ways. They often contain protections that are similar to those in the federal Bill of Rights but are more detailed. The Louisiana constitution, for example, prohibits "cruel or unusual punishment," a restriction analogous to the Eighth Amendment's prohibition of "cruel and unusual punishment," but it also bars "excessive" punishment, a requirement that the Louisiana Supreme Court has interpreted to mean that criminal penalties must be proportionate to the offense. And they express many rights not guaranteed by the federal Constitution; eleven constitutions expressly state a right of privacy, which the Supreme Court has found implicit in the Bill of Rights (as described in Chapter 3), and thirty-nine states guarantee access to a legal remedy for persons who suffer a legal injury. State courts have applied these rights to strike down caps on the damages that can be awarded in personal injury cases as a violation of the right of access to the courts, to compel the state to provide special funding for poor urban school districts, and to establish a right to same-sex marriage long before the U.S. Supreme Court did, among other things.

The statement of rights in state constitutions that are broader than those granted under the U.S. Constitution has led to what Justice William Brennan labeled "the new judicial federalism." For a long time lawyers and the public at large looked mostly to the federal courts for the protection of individual rights. Since the 1970s, however, there has been a surge of interest in attention to state constitutional law as an independent source for the definition and potential expansion of rights. Since then state courts have been actively engaged in applying state constitutions to situations both like and unlike those addressed by the federal courts.

Protection against unreasonable search and seizure, for example, is a right common to federal and state constitutions. In a 1988 case the U.S. Supreme Court ruled that a person has no reasonable expectation of privacy in garbage bags left out for collection, so it did not constitute a violation of the Fourth Amendment when the police searched the garbage for evidence of a crime (*California v. Greenwood*). When the same issue came to the New Jersey Supreme Court shortly thereafter in *State v. Hempele* (1990), the New Jersey Supreme Court believed that a person does have a reasonable expectation of privacy in trash. The court recognized the Supreme Court's contrary decision but in rather grandiose language pointed out the independent responsibility of state courts: "[A]lthough that Court may be a polestar that guides us as we navigate the New Jersey Constitution, we bear ultimate responsibility for the safe passage of our ship. Our eyes must not be so fixed on that star that we risk the welfare of our passengers on the shoals of constitutional doctrine."

Why Do We Need Constitutional Law?

This seems like an odd question. We have become so used to constitutional law that it is obvious why we need it: to organize the government and to protect civil liberties. And whether or not we need it, we have it; the Constitution is there, and it is the foundational document of our political system.

Nothing in the law is inevitable or necessary, though. Other nations manage to have a democratic political system and abundant civil liberties without our form of constitutionalism. Great Britain, for example, has neither a written constitution nor judicial review of legislation. When we think about whether we need constitutional law, the real question is what our brand of constitutional law does for us.

To accomplish together the things we cannot accomplish individually, we constitute and support a government to act on our behalf. Government facilitates collective action, enabling us to pool our resources to build schools, hire teachers, and make a system of public education available to everyone, for example. Government also provides security, protecting us from criminals, unscrupulous merchants, manufacturers of dangerous drugs, and foreign terrorists.

Government, to do all these things, must be strong. It needs the power to tax us to pay for the schools, to regulate drug companies, to fine crooked merchants, to put robbers in jail, and to maintain an army and navy. Such a powerful government presents a problem in itself. How do we make sure that the government won't tax us beyond our means, impose unreasonably burdensome regulations on small businesses, imprison the wrong people, or use the army to repress dissent?

One way we check the power of government is to make it a democratic government. The people control a democratic government, so the government cannot do something the people don't want or that infringes on their rights. But even if democracy is effective and the people have real control over the government (which some may question in modern America), there is a potential problem. An essential element of constitutional law is protecting the rights of minorities and individuals against attack by the majority. Constitutional law not only protects the integrity of the democratic process, but it protects minorities, protesters, dissidents, and eccentrics from the democratic process.

Constitutional law grapples with this conflict between empowering and limiting government. It deals with questions such as: How is the government organized? How much authority does it have? What processes does it have to follow in exercising that authority? What areas of people's lives are free from intrusion by the government? Constitutional law is not alone in considering these issues, and it never resolves them finally, but it provides a process for struggling with them.

But how does it do this? It may be helpful to think of constitutional law as a process. Constitutional law provides a language and a forum for the debate of important issues. The language of constitutional law begins with the text of the Constitution and expands to the precedents that interpret it and the principles that can be drawn from it. Important social and political issues are habitually framed in this language: separation of powers, federalism, free speech, due process. Lawyers would like to think that this is a peculiarly legal language spoken only by professionals, but in fact constitutional debate is carried on not only by courts and lawyers but also by other government officials, interest groups, and the public at large.

Constitutional debate goes on in this language in many places, but our constitutional tradition has designated the courts—especially the U.S. Supreme Court—as the forum that can resolve the debate authoritatively. The Court is hardly nonpolitical, but it operates at a greater distance from immediate political influence than other branches of government because its judges have a limited function and they serve for life. The Court does not settle all matters for all time, but the arguments made before it and its decisions in constitutional cases play a significant role in structuring the analysis and resolution of major controversies.

Take as an example some highlights and lowlights of the Constitution's encounter with race in America. In the heated controversy over slavery that led up to the Civil War, a slave named Dred Scott brought an action in federal court alleging that he had become free as a result of residing with his master in Illinois and the Wisconsin Territory prior to their return to the master's home in Missouri. Illinois was a free state, and slavery was prohibited in the territory north of latitude 36°30′ by the Missouri Compromise of 1820; Scott argued that once he set foot in a state and territory where he was legally free, he could not be kept in slavery when he returned to Missouri, a slave state. Slavery was an issue of overwhelming importance for the nation with immense political, moral, and economic dimensions, but in *Scott v. Sandford* (as Dred Scott's case was styled in the Supreme Court, also commonly known as *The Dred Scott Case*), the issue was framed in constitutional terms.

In an 1857 opinion by Chief Justice Roger Taney, the Court held that blacks such as Scott were not "citizens" within the meaning of Articles III and IV of the Constitution, and he therefore could not bring a lawsuit in federal court; even more remarkably, the court determined that the Missouri Compromise was unconstitutional. In Taney's view, at the time of the framing of the Constitution blacks were "considered as a subordinate and inferior class of beings" not included within the Declaration of Independence's claim that "all men are created equal" and thus not within the class of persons who, as citizens, could sue in federal court. And even though Congress had carefully crafted the Missouri Compromise as one in a series of political judgments that balanced the interests of North and South, it had exceeded its constitutional authority in doing so. Once the settlers of a territory organized their own government, Congress could no longer legislate for the territory.

The *Dred Scott* case illustrates the nature and limits of constitutional law. Slavery had been a highly charged issue since the founding of the nation, embodied in compromise provisions in the Constitution itself and the subject of debate in the Congress, the courts, and the country at large. As in *Dred Scott*, the debate dealt with substantive constitutional issues and was carried on in constitutional language as well as in moral, political, and economic terms. What was Congress's authority to legislate concerning the slave or free status of territories and newly admitted states? How far could a state go in prohibiting slavery or in effectively preventing the travel of masters and slaves through its borders?

Were blacks members of the constitutional community who could sue in federal court?

The debate in constitutional terms spilled outside the courtroom as well. Abraham Lincoln and Stephen Douglas clashed over *Dred Scott* and the nature of constitutional authority in their famous debates during the Senate campaign of 1858. Douglas affirmed the finality of the Court's decision: "[W] hen the decision is made, my private opinion, your opinion, all other opinions must yield to the majesty of that authoritative adjudication." Lincoln argued that the other branches of government could offer their own interpretation of the Constitution: "If I were in Congress, and a vote should come up on a question whether slavery should be prohibited in a new territory, in spite of that *Dred Scott* decision, I would vote that it should."

This dispute went to a central element of American constitutionalism—whether the Supreme Court is the final authority on constitutional interpretation. A half-century before *Dred Scott* the Supreme Court had proclaimed itself the last word on constitutional interpretation, and the political system had acquiesced. However, the political reaction to *Dred Scott* demonstrated the limits of the Court's role. Chief Justice Taney apparently hoped that the *Dred Scott* decision would resolve the national controversy over slavery once and for all. But what the political branches could not do in the Missouri Compromise and the Compromise of 1850 the judicial branch could not accomplish through its decision. Instead of bringing resolution, *Dred Scott* only inflamed the passions that shortly would lead to war.

Despite the failure of the Supreme Court to settle the slavery issue through constitutional adjudication, the race problem was still seen as a constitutional issue after the Civil War. New constitutional provisions—the Thirteenth, Fourteenth, and Fifteenth Amendments—were believed to be the vehicles for ending slavery, preventing racial discrimination, and ensuring political participation by blacks. The Fourteenth Amendment was especially important, drawing on concepts in the original Constitution and the Bill of Rights to guarantee newly freed slaves citizenship (overruling *Dred Scott*), the privileges and immunities of citizens, due process of law, and equal protection of the laws. These Reconstruction Amendments both empowered government to eradicate the vestiges of slavery and limited government's ability to discriminate or interfere with the lives of its citizens.

The interpretation of these provisions over the succeeding century and a half has not been uniform either in principle or in result. In two famous cases, for example, the Court first allowed racial segregation of railroad cars (*Plessy v. Ferguson*, 1896) and subsequently prohibited racial segregation in schools (*Brown v. Board of Education*, 1954). Without rehearsing this long and complicated story, note that, as with *Dred Scott*, in court and in the public arena, the debate about race has been carried on with the aid of these constitutional principles. Defining "equal protection of the laws" under the Fourteenth Amendment—ascertaining what equality means and what government may or must do to create equality or to prevent or remedy inequality—has been a central inquiry in the debate about race. May the government favor minority contractors for highway projects? May a college give preference to black applicants to enhance the diversity of its student body?

For questions like these, the debate is partially carried on through constitutional discourse, and part of the answer comes through court decisions. The debate spills outside the courtroom, however, and outside the bounds of constitutional law, to be influenced by the legislatures, the electoral process, the media, and public sentiment.

Constitutional law, therefore, provides a vocabulary and a process for dealing with important issues. It is neither the only vocabulary nor the only process, but it has been an important and familiar one, if ever-changing, for more than two hundred years.

How Does the Supreme Court Decide What the Constitution Means?

In applying the Constitution, the Supreme Court defines and limits the powers of the government. But what limits the Court? Suppose the Court declared that from now on it would tell Congress how much to spend on building highways, or suppose it announced that every American was required to attend a Roman Catholic Church every Sunday? What prevents the Court from usurping the rightful powers of the other branches of government or of the states, or from trampling on the rights of the people through outrageous decisions?

As these absurd hypotheticals suggest, ultimately the Supreme Court is constrained by political realities. If the Court tried to direct Congress to spend money on highways or to force people to go to church, the resulting uproar would drown out the words of the Court's opinions. Because the Court cannot coerce compliance with its decisions, its constitutional authority is supported by our culture's tradition of respect for judicial authority and the rule of law. This respect is supported by the belief that in applying the Constitution, the justices of the Supreme Court are not simply expressing their own preferences about what the law ought to be. Rather, the Constitution itself directs their decision. Something in the text or the means of its interpretation controls or limits what the Court can do in a particular case. Just as the Constitution as interpreted by the Court regulates the authority of the rest of the government, the Constitution limits the authority of the Court itself.

The problem, though, is that the constitutional text is short and vague, yet the Court has to use it to decide a huge array of cases. Article I, section 8, clause 3, for example, empowers Congress "To regulate Commerce with foreign Nations, and among the several States, and with the Indian Tribes." How does the Court know if this means Congress in enacting Obamacare could require individuals to purchase health insurance? (The Court said Congress could not do so under the commerce clause but could establish a tax penalty for failing to buy insurance.) Or consider the abortion case *Roe v. Wade*. How did the Court conclude that the Constitution gives a woman an essentially unconstrained choice to have an abortion in the first trimester of her pregnancy but that it also allows the state to regulate or prohibit abortion as the pregnancy progresses? Or think about *Brown v. Board of Education*, the 1954 case that ordered the desegregation of public schools. Today virtually everyone agrees that the decision was correct and a landmark in the development of social justice in America. But how could the Court conclude that segregated schools were prohibited by the Fourteenth Amendment's equal protection clause when the Congress that passed the amendment also authorized segregated public schools in the District of Columbia?

The Constitution nowhere mentions health insurance, abortion, segregation, or schools. Yet the Court has to decide cases dealing with these and thousands of other subjects. A theory of constitutional interpretation is crucial to constitutional law, but the Constitution does not provide a guide to its own interpretation. Accordingly, constructing such a theory has been a major concern of judges and scholars.

It would be easy to interpret the Constitution if its meaning were clear from the text itself. Unfortunately, that's not the case. Most constitutional provisions are vague, like the commerce clause. Saying that Congress may regulate commerce "among the several states" just doesn't tell us whether mandating the purchase of health insurance is included in Congress's interstate commerce power. Moreover, sometimes we come to understand that the text doesn't mean what it says anyway. The First Amendment states that "Congress shall make no law . . . abridging the freedom of speech," but all constitutional lawyers agree that this constitutional prohibition applies to the president and the courts as well, even though this isn't specifically stated. Because words never have meaning by themselves, we need a way to interpret them.

The major struggle over theories of constitutional interpretation is between those judges and scholars who believe that the Constitution should be narrowly interpreted only according to the intent of the framers or the understanding of its provisions at the time of adoption and those who assert that we have to look beyond those intentions and understandings. The former theory, that the Constitution has a "changeless nature and meaning," as Justice David Brewer wrote (*South Carolina v. United States,* 1905) is known as *originalism* or *interpretivism*; the latter is known as *nonoriginalism* and is sometimes described as the idea of a *living Constitution.*

For originalists, adhering to the original understanding of constitutional provisions is mandated by the structure of the Constitution and keeps judges from running amok. The framers of the Constitution, acting on behalf of the people, delegated powers to the federal government. The power of judicial review is one of those powers. But no part of the government, including the courts, may exceed the scope of the powers that have been delegated to it, so the Supreme Court always must abide by the intent of the framers in making its decisions.

This adherence to the original understanding is more than a legal necessity based on the structure of the Constitution, originalists argue; it is a practical necessity as well. Original intent provides a firm basis for constitutional decisions. As Justice Scalia, one of the most prominent originalists, wrote, "The originalist at least knows what he is looking for: the original meaning of the text. Often—indeed, I dare say usually—that is easy to discern and simple to apply." Once the Court goes beyond this basis, it necessarily must resort to something other than the determinate understanding of the framers—something such as a political, economic, or philosophical theory as to what a just result would be in the case. But there are many such theories available—liberal, conservative, and otherwise—and a justice has no basis for choosing among them other than his or her own preferences. This ability to choose raises the specter of activist judging, of the justices superseding the decisions of the Congress or the states simply on the basis of their own personal preferences—a "judicial Putsch . . . [that] robs the People of the most important liberty they asserted in the Declaration of Independence and won in the Revolution of 1776: the freedom to govern themselves," as Justice Scalia warned in *Obergefell v. Hodges* (2015), the case that recognized a constitutional right to same-sex marriage.

The concept of originalism as a solid source of constitutional law is as attractive as the idea of a text with plain meaning, but nonoriginalist judges and scholars have identified problems with the concept. There is an initial problem of our ability to render a historical judgment about original intent or understanding. Reference to "the intention of the framers" suggests that there existed a definable group of framers and that we can determine their intentions with a high degree of certainty. But who are the framers? The original Constitution was drafted, negotiated, and voted on in a convention composed of delegates from different states with different points of view and then ratified by the members of thirteen state legislatures and conventions. The Bill of Rights was drafted in the First Congress and then submitted to the states for ratification. Subsequent amendments were drafted by later Congresses and ratified by still more state legislatures. Whose intent are we to focus on: the drafters of the provision at issue, others who participated in the debate at the convention or in the Congress, or members of the ratifying legislatures?

The difficulties of ascertaining historical intention have led some originalists to shift focus from the intention of the framers to the general understanding of a constitutional provision at the time of its enactment, what Justice Scalia described as "the intent that a reasonable person would gather from the text of the law." The search for original understanding therefore presumes that we can comprehend the framers' world and apply that comprehension to our own world. But nonoriginalists point out the difficulty of achieving that comprehension. Originalism presumes that historical intent is a fact, like a physical artifact waiting to be unearthed, but it is often hard to dig up the truth about an event two hundred years in the past. Historians know, moreover, that an understanding of the past is always shaped by our own views. It is impossible to achieve knowledge of the past unfiltered by our understanding of the present; how can we pretend not to know what we do know about what has happened over the past 200 years? Moreover, any historical understanding we do have must be applied to vastly changed circumstances. When the authors and ratifiers of the First Amendment thought of freedom of speech and freedom of press, they could only have in mind some idea of freedom of speech and press—literally—because speaking and printing were the only forms of communication available. How do we translate that understanding to the regulation of, for example, readily accessible pornography on the Internet or pervasive commercial advertising on television?

In dealing with social changes of this magnitude, the Court cannot simply ascertain and apply an original understanding that could not actually have been held. Instead, perhaps the Court should look more broadly for the original principles motivating a particular constitutional term, a set of provisions, or the Constitution as a whole. The problem with a strict originalism may be that it looks too narrowly for the intention behind a provision. Some originalists and nonoriginalists suggest instead that it is possible to constrain the Court's interpretation of the Constitution through the development of principles that arise from the text.

Consider the due process clauses of the Fifth and Fourteenth Amendments, which state that no person may be denied life, liberty, or property without due process of law. Assume that we can tell that at the time of enactment people held some specific ideas about the meaning of the clauses. Here we can even refer to the rest of the Bill of Rights to suggest the content. Liberty includes physical liberty, and the government may not take someone's liberty away without a trial by jury in which the defendant is allowed to be represented by counsel, to confront witnesses, and so forth. But the due process clauses would be superfluous if all they did was to restate the protections of the Fourth, Fifth, and Sixth Amendments. The clauses logically must state a more general principle about the right of Americans to be protected from government interference. "Liberty" in this more general understanding means the right to be left alone to carry on one's daily life and personal affairs, and that liberty interest may only be invaded by the government when it has an important basis for doing so. Thus in determining and applying the meaning of the due process clause, the Supreme Court can refer both to the narrower meaning—the right to a jury trial—and the broader meaning—the right to be free from government interference. The broader meaning may be particularly useful as the Court faces cases that the framers would not have considered because the technology or social conditions that present them had not yet been developed.

Two problems inhere in this approach, however. First, principles such as the right to be left alone may have even a weaker historical pedigree than attempts to establish a narrower original intent. All the problems of reconstructing a historical intention are magnified when the Court tries to establish a general understanding of a constitutional provision. It is as if the Court were to ask the framers not just "What did you understand the due process clause to mean?" but also to engage them in dialogue about "What broader conceptions, including those you may never have explicitly considered, lay behind your thinking?" This inquiry is unmoored from historical intention and sets the Court loose to try to attach its own meaning to the constitutional provision without being bounded by original understanding.

Once the Court begins down this path, the second problem becomes apparent. For any constitutional provision, it is possible to state principles at different levels of generality as inhering in the provision. The decision in a particular case will depend on the level of generality at which the Court states the controlling principle. The difficulty is that every principle, whether broad or narrow, is developed by the Court based on its own view of what constitutes a sensible reading of the provision at issue. The Court's view is informed by the text, its history, its subsequent interpretation, and contemporary political and social realities. The risk, of course, is the problem with which constitutional interpretation began; in formulating its view, nothing checks the Court except its own good judgment and, ultimately, political realities.

In the end, the choice between originalism and nonoriginalism and among their many variations is a choice based on political theory: What is the nature of the Constitution, why does it command obedience, and what is the role of the Court in interpreting it? These are difficult questions to resolve, and history does not answer them for us. Indeed, constitutional historians argue that the framers themselves were not originalists. Lawyers and statesmen in the late eighteenth century did not hold a conception of fundamental law as the positive enactment of a legislative body, such as a constitutional convention, whose understanding in enacting the law should guide its interpretation. And as Justice Kennedy wrote, the authors of the Constitution and its amendments may have intended it to be subject to change:

> The generations that wrote and ratified the Bill of Rights and the Fourteenth Amendment did not presume to know the extent of freedom in all of its dimensions, and so they entrusted to future generations a charter protecting the right of all persons to enjoy liberty as we learn its meaning. When new insight reveals discord between the Constitution's central protections and a received legal stricture, a claim to liberty must be addressed. (*Obergefell v. Hodges*, 2015)

Does this leave constitutional interpretation at the point where we simply say that it's all up to the justices' points of view and that they can read into the Constitution their own political views and personal preferences? Yes and no. "Yes," in the sense that no plain meaning of the text, historical evidence, or objective principles determine their decisions. Constitutional interpretation inevitably involves an act of choice by a Supreme Court justice among many alternatives, and, as with choices elsewhere in life, the judge will choose based on his or her sense of what the right answer is. And "no," in the sense that a justice is not completely free to reach any decision on any basis he or she wants. Justices are constrained by the ways the constitutional text has been understood historically and by the political and legal culture.

This brings us back to the idea that constitutional law is as much a language and a process as a body of rules and rights. The words of the Constitution and the ways it has been understood, interpreted, and argued about inside and outside the courts provide the language the justices must use in interpreting and applying the Constitution. Constitutional law provides a way of framing issues and expressing arguments. It is possible to say many different things and remain within the constitutional tradition, but, as with natural languages, some things cannot be said because the words are unavailable or because they seem improper or inappropriate. The Court in the *Dred Scott* case in 1857 could use constitutional terms and constitutional history to declare that blacks were a "subordinate and inferior class of beings" who could not be citizens of the United States, but a court today could not do the same thing. A court today could, however, rule in favor of or against affirmative action because either result would be within the scope of accepted constitutional discourse; even if we would not agree with the decision or would find it "wrong," we would recognize it to be at least arguable in a way that a modern-day *Dred Scott* decision would not be.

When it is taken seriously and pursued in good faith, constitutional interpretation becomes a model of principled debate on important social issues. It can be conducted at one level removed from immediate political controversies, making it easier to consider consequences, construct principles, and analogize to other situations—the kinds of things the legal process is best at. In addition to persuading others, constitutional analysis can be a way of examining one's own assumptions and beliefs. Too often, of course, constitutional debate is not carried on at this level. Instead, it becomes one more vehicle for the expression of preconceived beliefs. Because the Constitution is subject to varying interpretations, justices and others can select the interpretation that best fits the conclusion they wish to reach without engaging in a serious process of interpretation.

Where Does the Supreme Court Get the Authority to Interpret the Constitution?

The issue of how the Supreme Court interprets the Constitution is vitally important because of the Court's power of judicial review. In most cases, the Court has the final say on what the Constitution means and how it applies in a particular case. (Every court, federal and state, has the responsibility and the authority to render decisions on constitutional issues, but all of those other decisions can ultimately be reviewed by the U.S. Supreme Court.) We have become so used to judicial review that it seems a natural, inevitable, and even necessary part of our government structure. But note how sweeping the power is. The president, Congress, state legislatures, governors, state courts, state and federal administrative agencies, public officials, and all ordinary citizens are subject to the commands of the nine justices on questions of constitutional law. At the time of the drafting of the Constitution, a power this broad was unknown anywhere else, and even today it is unusual among judicial systems around the world.

Remarkably, the power of judicial review is not given to the Supreme Court in the Constitution itself. Article III states that "The judicial Power of the United States, shall be vested in one supreme Court, and in such inferior Courts as the Congress may from time to time ordain and establish," and it extends that power to "all Cases, in Law and Equity, arising under this Constitution" and to other categories. These provisions are organizational and jurisdictional. They create the Supreme Court, but "supreme" means only "highest," designating a place in the hierarchy but not the Court's authority. The power to hear cases arising under the Constitution is likewise a grant of jurisdiction to hear certain kinds of cases but not a grant of authority to exercise constitutional review in hearing them. Article VI states that "This Constitution, and the Laws of the United States which shall be made in Pursuance thereof . . . shall be the supreme Law of the Land." This provision does not tell us either that the Constitution takes precedence over other "laws of the United States"—in other words, that the Constitution is superior to acts of Congress—nor that the Supreme Court, rather than the Congress, the president, or the states, has the authority to conclusively determine what the Constitution means.

The power of judicial review was established by the Court's decision in the 1803 case of *Marbury v. Madison*. Constitutional scholars, by consensus, regard *Marbury* as the most important case the Court ever has decided, and its story bears retelling. As with so many important legal events in our own time, the story involves important personalities, partisan politics, and a little intrigue to go along with the law.

Toward the end of George Washington's presidency, national politics came to be dominated by two groups: the Federalist Party, which elected John Adams president and controlled the Congress from 1796 until 1800, and the Democratic Republican Party (predecessor of today's Democratic Party), which would gain a majority in the Congress and elect Thomas Jefferson in 1800. When it became apparent to the Federalists that they would lose control of the executive and legislative branches, they moved to consolidate their power in the judiciary. President Adams nominated his secretary of state, John Marshall, to be chief justice. The Federalist Congress also passed legislation to increase the number of lower federal judges, reduce the number of members of the Supreme Court (to prevent the incoming Republicans from filling a vacancy), and authorize forty-two new justices of the peace in the District of Columbia.

In the last days of his administration, President Adams nominated faithful party members to the new positions, and the Senate confirmed them. On the night before Jefferson was to become president, John Marshall—still serving as secretary of state for the last month of Adams's term—performed the secretary's traditional duty of affixing the Seal of the United States to the commissions of the new judges. Through inadvertence, a few commissions were not delivered to the new officeholders that night, and the next day the newly inaugurated President Jefferson directed his secretary of state, James Madison, to withhold the remaining commissions, including one belonging to the soon-to-be-famous William Marbury, who had been appointed as a justice of the peace.

Marbury sued for his commission, bringing what was known as a writ of mandamus in the Supreme Court. (A writ of mandamus is an order from a court to a government official directing the official to perform some duty of his or her office.) Although he brought his action in 1801, the new Republican Congress had abolished the 1801 and 1802 terms of the Supreme Court, and therefore the case was not decided until 1803. Finally, the Court decided the case in an opinion by Chief Justice Marshall who, consistent with the ethical sensibilities of the time, saw no conflict between his roles as participant in the drama and judge of its resolution.

In deciding *Marbury*, Marshall and his Court faced a dilemma. If Marshall failed to rule that Marbury was entitled to his commission, he would be acquiescing in an assumption of power by the executive branch, contrary to his Federalist principles and his belief in the need to assert the power of the judiciary. But the authority of the Supreme Court was not yet well established, so if he ordered that the commission be delivered, Jefferson and Madison might simply refuse to comply, undermining the authority of the courts. Marshall's ingenious response was to sidestep the controversy by claiming the power of judicial review for the Court but exercising it in a way that denied Marbury his commission.

Marshall's opinion for the Court first held that Marbury's appointment was complete when his commission was signed by the president. At that point the secretary of state's duties in sealing and delivering the commission were ministerial details, and failing to carry them out did not affect Marbury's status. Next, because Marbury had a right to his commission, the appropriate remedy under law was mandamus directed to the secretary. The catch arose at the third step. Was the Supreme Court the proper forum in which to seek this remedy?

Article III granted the Supreme Court original jurisdiction (i.e., the authority to hear cases in the first instance) in cases in which a foreign diplomat or a state was a party; in all other cases, it had only the authority to hear appeals from lower courts. The Judiciary Act of 1789 had expanded the Court's original jurisdiction to include the power to issue writs of mandamus against federal officials. Marbury asserted that the Court had jurisdiction of his suit against Madison under the Judiciary Act. In the opinion's tour de force, Chief Justice Marshall ruled that the Judiciary Act had impermissibly extended the Court's original jurisdiction beyond that granted by Article III and therefore the Court could not grant relief to Marbury because it did not have jurisdiction of the case. This satisfied the immediate concerns of the Republicans, but the great significance of the case lay in the Court's assumption to itself of the final authority to determine if the Judiciary Act or any other act of Congress was constitutional. Thus the opinion ceded the immediate issue while profoundly enhancing the Court's authority.

For Marshall, whether the Court had the power to review the constitutionality of legislation was an easy question. The people created the Constitution to be fundamental, supreme, and permanent law. Part of the constitutional scheme is that the federal government is a government of limited powers. The branches may exercise only the authority that the people have delegated to them in the Constitution. Therefore, any act that is contrary to the Constitution or beyond the powers enumerated in it is void. Article III's grant of limited jurisdiction was exclusive, so Congress had no constitutional authority to expand the Court's jurisdiction to include mandamus actions.

So far, so good. The key comes at the next stage of the argument. The Constitution is fundamental law, so it is *law*, and the interpretation and application of law is the traditional domain of the courts.

> It is emphatically the province and duty of the judicial department
> to say what the law is. . . . So if a law be in opposition to the
> constitution; if both the law and the constitution apply to a
> particular case, so that the court must either decide the case
> conformably to the law, disregarding the constitution; or
> conformably to the constitution, disregarding the law; the court must
> determine which of these conflicting rules governs the cases. This is
> of the very essence of judicial duty.

Thus Marshall neatly concludes the syllogism. The Constitution is law. Courts interpret law. Therefore courts interpret the Constitution. But what was obvious to Marshall was not obvious to others. The law that the courts traditionally interpret and the law embodied in the Constitution may be two entirely different things. If the Constitution is fundamental law, perhaps it should not be treated the same as ordinary statutes and cases. Precisely because it is fundamental, constitutional interpretation might just as easily be left to the other branches of government. Congress can make a judgment about the constitutionality of a statute when it enacts one, as with the Judiciary Act, and it would not be obviously inconsistent with the constitutional scheme for the courts to consider that judgment to be definitive.

Despite the lack of logical rigor in *Marbury v. Madison*, it was the first strong pronouncement of the principle of judicial review. Although the Court exercised sparingly its power to declare congressional enactments unconstitutional in the decades after *Marbury*—it didn't invalidate another federal statute until the *Dred Scott* case in 1857—the power had been asserted and initially acquiesced to by the other branches. Or perhaps it was *because* the power was exercised sparingly that it took root, since the Court was frequently under attack in the early years of the nineteenth century.

The Court consolidated its power of judicial review by asserting a similar authority over state law. In 1810 the Court first invalidated a state statute in *Fletcher v. Peck* on the grounds that the statute, an attempt to rescind title to land that had been fraudulently conveyed, violated the contract clause. Then in *Martin v. Hunter's Lessee* in 1816, another case involving a land dispute, the highest court in Virginia ruled for one party but the U.S. Supreme Court, on appeal, ruled differently. The Virginia court refused to obey the Supreme Court's mandate, asserting that it could decide the issue for itself and that the federal Judiciary Act, which granted appellate jurisdiction to the Court, was unconstitutional. When the case returned to the Supreme Court, the Court, in an opinion by Justice Joseph Story, reasserted its constitutional authority. In adopting the Constitution the states had ceded some of their sovereignty to the federal government. The federal judicial power included all cases involving constitutional interpretation, and the supremacy clause made the federal law preeminent. Finally, in *Cohens v. Virginia* (1821) the Court extended its power to encompass the review of state criminal proceedings. Unless state proceedings were subject to review in the federal courts, the states could thwart federal law and policy by punishing individuals who asserted valid constitutional rights.

Thus by the end of John Marshall's tenure as chief justice in 1834, the foundation had been laid for Supreme Court review of the constitutionality of the acts of state and federal legislative bodies and executive officials. Since then it has been recognized that the Court's power to interpret the Constitution is immense. That power is, however, neither unique nor unlimited. Every major public official takes an oath of office pledging to uphold the Constitution and therefore is required to interpret it in the performance of his or her duties. A senator weighs the constitutionality of a bill in deciding whether to vote for it, the president decides whether ordering drone attacks on terrorists is within his constitutional authority as commander-in-chief, and even a police officer on the beat decides whether frisking a suspect is constitutional. To that extent, the real question is not who interprets the Constitution but whose interpretation counts the most.

Throughout American history, presidents and other officials have asserted their independent authority to determine what the Constitution requires and to act on those determinations. Thomas Jefferson regarded the idea of "judges as the ultimate arbiters of all constitutional questions" to be "a very dangerous doctrine indeed, and one which would place us under the despotism of an oligarchy"; because he considered the Sedition Act of 1798 to be unconstitutional, he exercised one of the powers granted to the president by the Constitution and pardoned defendants convicted under it, even though the act had been applied and upheld by the court. Abraham Lincoln famously denounced the *Dred Scott* decision, which held that blacks were not citizens, declaring that it would not bind him as a member of Congress or president. Recent presidents, especially George W. Bush, have issued many *signing statements* when signing bills into law that challenge the constitutionality of provisions of the bills and assert their intention not to enforce them. Today some scholars argue for a revival of *popular constitutionalism*, in which the political branches of government have more of a role in interpreting the Constitution.

When the Court and other branches come into conflict in interpreting the Constitution, however, the Court generally triumphs. Consider two illustrations of attempted and potential resistance and its ultimate futility. The Court's decision desegregating public schools in *Brown v. Board of Education* was met in many southern states by official and unofficial resistance. Some southern legislatures, for example, enacted resolutions "nullifying" the decision and tried to avoid its effects by schemes such as refusing to fund desegregated schools. In *Cooper v. Aaron* (1958), the Court rejected all of these efforts and reasserted the principle of *Marbury*, that "the federal judiciary is supreme in the exposition of the law of the Constitution, and that principle has ever since been respected by this Court and the Country as a permanent and indispensable feature of our constitutional system." The southern states' defiance of the Court's power was so challenging to the constitutional order that all nine justices took the extraordinary step of attaching their names to the opinion individually.

In the Watergate era, the courts were faced with a number of cases arising from the investigations into the illegal activities of President Nixon and his cronies. In *United States v. Nixon* (1974), for example, the Court held that the courts, not the president, could determine whether evidence sought by the Watergate special prosecutor was validly subject to the president's claim of executive privilege. More remarkable than the Court's pronouncement was President Nixon's acceptance of it. Even though the chain of events would lead to his resignation in disgrace, the president could not challenge the established practice of judicial review.

Since the Constitution covers the entire scope of government affairs, judicial review could conceivably encompass every aspect of government, and the logic of *Marbury v. Madison* suggests that the Court should engage in constitutional review of any case. Nevertheless, the Court has concluded that as a matter of constitutional requirement or judicial prudence, there are some issues that are committed to Congress or the president without judicial review. The Court is limited in what it can do as a practical matter as a judicial body and as a political matter in assessing its responsibilities relative to the other branches, so it refrains from deciding *political questions.*

To take an example, there was a spate of litigation during the Vietnam War that sought to declare the war illegal because Congress had never formally declared war, or to prevent the government from prosecuting some parts of the war such as the bombing of Cambodia. Following *Marbury*, one might consider this a straightforward issue of constitutional interpretation. Does the Constitution require Congress to declare war before the president commits troops, or may the president conduct and Congress fund an undeclared war? But would deciding that question engage the Court in policymaking of the kind that is only or best left to the other branches of government? If so, it is a nonjusticiable political question that the courts cannot decide. Although none of the cases reached the Supreme Court, the lower courts held in these cases—and in subsequent cases involving President Reagan's military engagement in El Salvador and the first Persian Gulf war—that decisions about war and peace were committed to the president and the Congress.

What Powers Does Constitutional Law Give to the Rest of the Federal Government?

The Supreme Court has the power to review state and federal legislation to determine if the laws are constitutional. The federal court system also has jurisdiction over many nonconstitutional cases including ordinary civil cases arising under federal statutes or involving citizens of different states and criminal cases such as bank robbery, drug offenses, and other violations of federal law. What does constitutional law say about the powers of the other branches of the federal government—the legislative branch (the Congress) and the executive branch (headed by the president)?

Recall the basic question with which constitutional law struggles. How do we empower a government to do what we cannot do for ourselves, while making sure that it does not become so strong that it threatens our liberties? The Constitution's answer grew out of a particular historical situation.

The framers of the Constitution responded to the widespread perception that the government created under the Articles of Confederation was too weak. Under the Articles, Congress had no power to tax, to issue a single national currency, or to control trade. There was neither a strong executive—at that time the president was a member of Congress with limited powers—nor a federal court system. Conflict between the states was widespread, with one state imposing tariffs on goods imported from another, and the national government's inability to repay the huge Revolutionary War debt precipitated a financial crisis. Accordingly, the national government under the Articles was widely perceived to be a failure.

The problem was the inadequacy of the federal government to deal with the situation, so the response was obvious and was adopted by the constitutional convention of 1787: Give greater powers to the national government, powers that would be sufficient for it to control conflicts among the states, order the nation's financial affairs, raise and pay an army, and conduct foreign relations. But that only answered part of the basic question. The framers also were deeply concerned that the new national government might invade the proper province of state governments or threaten the basic rights of the people. Therefore, the federal government was conceived as a government of expanded but limited authority, having only the powers "enumerated" in the Constitution itself. Implicit in the constitutional structure and made explicit in the Tenth Amendment, the concept of *enumerated powers* stated that "The powers not delegated to the United States by the Constitution, nor prohibited by it to the States, are reserved to the States respectively, or to the people." And the new government could exercise its powers only through a system we know as *checks and balances* or *separation of powers*. A majority could not run roughshod over the interests of the states or the rights of the people because legislation had to come out of a bicameral legislature and be acceded to by the president. To add a final degree of protection against an overly powerful national government, the specific guarantees of the Bill of Rights were drafted by the First Congress and adopted in 1791.

The government lived up to these expectations in the first years under the Constitution. The new government addressed the most pressing issues of the time and the most fundamental requirements of a nation. The First Congress created the essential government departments—State, War, Treasury, the Post Office, the office of Attorney General, and a system of federal courts—and dealt with important economic issues, including imposing taxes, chartering a national bank, taking a census, establishing a monetary system, and creating patent and copyright laws. Up until the Civil War, though, the size of the government was still minuscule.

But look at what has happened to this government of limited, enumerated powers. Ask someone today what "the government" is and they are likely to think first of the national government. The president is often described in the media as "the most powerful person in the world." Congress legislates on nearly everything, from the protection of endangered species to taxes on imported goods. The federal bureaucracy, two million strong, collects taxes, administers Social Security and Medicare, reviews the safety and effectiveness of pharmaceuticals, manages more than half a billion acres of federal lands, and spends three and a half trillion dollars each year. The states, meanwhile, do important things such as operate public schools and maintain the roads, but their activities seem dwarfed by the presence of the federal government.

Every step of the transformation of this government of enumerated powers—from one of tiny scope and limited influence to one that penetrates virtually every aspect of modern life—has been sanctioned through interpretations of the Constitution. The ways in which it did so illustrate how the Constitution is interpreted and applied. The vague constitutional text covers situations unforeseen at the time of its drafting, and the Supreme Court has to respond both to the text itself and to changing political, economic, and social values in considering the appropriate scope of government power. The basic elements of the story are, of course, a tremendous expansion of the power of the federal government, relying on broad interpretations of the enumeration of powers in the constitutional text and balancing of the authority of the executive and legislative branches, and the federal government and the states, resulting in more a sharing of powers than a separation of powers.

The fundamental grants of government authority are given to Congress in Article I, section 8, in seventeen specific clauses and one general clause. "Specific" is not the same as "limited," however. The government's powers under section 8 include the powers to "lay and collect taxes," "borrow money," "declare War," and "raise and support Armies"—and, in the residual authority clause 18, "[t]o make all Laws which shall be necessary and proper for carrying into Execution the foregoing Powers, and all other Powers vested by this Constitution in the Government of the United States."

Consider as an example of the expansion of federal power and the sharing of power among the branches the ways in which the legislative or executive branches have attempted to exercise power under the commerce clause and how the Supreme Court has responded by weighing the constitutionality of the exercise.

Article I, section 8, clause 3, gives Congress the power "[t]o regulate Commerce with foreign nations, and among the several States, and with the Indian Tribes." Under the Articles of Confederation the federal government had little power either to regulate interstate or international commerce or to prevent individual states from interfering with it. The commerce clause was designed to correct this situation, enabling the federal government to exercise authority over the national economy internally and externally. The breadth of this power depends on the interpretation of the term "Commerce . . . among the several States." This could be read simply to prevent interstate conflicts of the kind that prevailed under the Articles where, for example, one state taxed goods brought in from another. Instead, Congress has used the commerce clause as an authorization to extend federal regulatory power throughout the economy and to place a corresponding limitation on state power. The Supreme Court has usually acquiesced in this assertion of authority, with occasional notable exceptions.

Like so many other constitutional principles, the scope of the commerce clause was first broadly defined in an opinion by Chief Justice John Marshall. In *Gibbons v. Ogden* (1824), the New York legislature had granted Robert Fulton (the inventor of the steamboat) and a partner the exclusive right to operate steamboats on New York waters, and Fulton had franchised a portion of this monopoly to Ogden. Gibbons began to operate a competing steamboat line between New Jersey and New York under a federal statute, and Ogden sued to enjoin Gibbons from infringing on his franchise. The Supreme Court held that New York's grant of a monopoly conflicted with an act of Congress concerning the licensing of ships, and therefore it was void because of the supremacy clause. Nevertheless, Marshall took the occasion to expound on the power of the national government under the commerce clause.

Marshall identified three elements of Congress's power over interstate commerce and broadly defined each of them. First was commerce. Ogden's counsel argued that "commerce" meant only traffic, or things moving from one state to another, which would exclude navigation. For

Marshall, traffic was only a part of commerce: "Commerce, undoubtedly is traffic, but it is something more, it is intercourse. It describes the commercial intercourse between nations, and parts of nations, in all its branches."

The next term to be defined was "among the several states." "Among" did not mean merely "between," according to Marshall. "A thing which is 'among' others is intermingled with them; therefore commerce among the states cannot stop at the external boundary line of each state but may be introduced into the interior." Congress had no power to regulate commerce that occurred wholly within a state, but whether an activity was wholly within a state was measured by its effects, not its physical presence. Even if an activity was carried on entirely within the borders of a single state, if it affected commerce beyond the borders of the state, it was interstate commerce.

The final step was to define "regulate." Marshall determined that "This power, like all others vested in Congress, is complete in itself, may be exercised to its utmost extent, and acknowledges no limitations, other than are prescribed in the constitution itself."

Thus the Court concluded that Congress had constitutional authority to regulate commercial activities that had effects beyond the borders of a single state. But the definition of this authority by the Supreme Court could come only in response to congressional assertion of the authority and challenges to it, and for a half century after *Gibbons v. Ogden*, the Court had little occasion to further consider the definition.

In the following half century—from 1887 to 1937—the Court took a narrower tack even as Congress attempted to exercise the commerce power more vigorously. This was the era of bigness, with the rise of U.S. Steel, Standard Oil, and other new concentrations of wealth and economic power. Congress and state legislatures acted to control the new economic powers, but as the Court became more conservative, it became less willing to acknowledge legislative authority over commerce. In defining the scope of the commerce clause, it abandoned Marshall's focus on the effects of commerce and adopted a formal, definitional approach. Marshall had decided in *Gibbons v. Ogden* that commerce was more than traffic, but in an 1895 case the Court came close to saying that commerce was only traffic. Congress had enacted the Sherman Antitrust Act to control the new monopolies of major industries. In *United States v. E. C. Knight* the Court limited the Sherman Act by a narrow interpretation of the scope of Congress's power under the commerce clause. The American Sugar Refining Company had acquired a monopoly of the sugar industry, controlling more than 90 percent of the country's sugar production. But, the Court said, the federal government could not constitutionally regulate this monopoly because it was a monopoly of manufacturing, not commerce: "Commerce succeeds to manufacture, and is not part of it. . . . The fact that an article is manufactured for export to another State does not itself make it an article of commerce."

The Supreme Court's conservative interpretations of the commerce clause reached their most extreme when the Court struck down some key pieces of New Deal legislation designed to bring the country out of the Great Depression. In *Schechter Poultry Corp. v. United States* (1935), for example, the Court struck down the central element of the plan for economic recovery, the National Industrial Recovery Act. Among other things, the act empowered the president to enforce codes of competition approved by local trade associations. *Schechter Poultry Corp.* concerned the code of competition for the poultry industry in New York City. Poultry undoubtedly was produced in mass quantities, shipped in interstate commerce, and had important national economic effects. The act attempted to regulate the sale of poultry, however, and this was beyond the scope of the commerce clause. In language reminiscent of *E.C. Knight*, the Court defined commerce narrowly: "So far as the poultry here in question is concerned, the flow in interstate commerce had ceased. The poultry had come to a permanent rest within the State."

The Court's invalidation of the New Deal legislation presented a challenge to the other branches of government, and, after President Franklin Roosevelt's resounding reelection victory in 1936, he took up the challenge. FDR proposed his famous court-packing plan, under which he would have been authorized to appoint one new justice to the court for each current justice who was seventy years old and had served on the court for ten years. Adoption of the plan would have enabled him to appoint six new justices to create a solid liberal majority that would uphold New Deal legislation.

The debate over the court-packing plan was fierce, and it clearly demonstrated the ambiguities of the Court's constitutional role. Progressives were outraged by the Court's ability to thwart the will of an overwhelming popular majority and saw the plan as a means of reining in an undemocratic institution. But the Court had many defenders, even among those who did not agree with its decisions; if there was more to constitutional law than simple politics, the Court had to be immune from this kind of direct political intervention in its decisions.

In the end the court-packing plan failed in Congress but still influenced the Supreme Court. By the middle of 1937 middle-of-the-road Justice Owen Roberts became a more consistent upholder of regulatory legislation, and over the next few years the notoriously conservative "Four Horsemen" (James McReynolds, Willis Van Devanter, Pierce Butler, and George Sutherland) retired, to be replaced by justices appointed by Roosevelt and more sympathetic to his legislative program. The result was a shift in interpretation of the commerce clause to a standard of near-total deference to congressional power, evocative of Marshall's emphasis on effects, which remained in place until very recently.

In *Wickard v. Filburn* (1942), for example, the Court specifically referred to Marshall's analysis of the commerce power in *Gibbons v. Ogden*. The secretary of agriculture fined Filburn, a small farmer, $117.11 for growing 239 bushels of wheat over his allotment, even though he intended to use the wheat exclusively on his own farm and not sell it in commerce, interstate or otherwise. Whether the activity was production or manufacturing on the one hand, or marketing and distribution on the other, was irrelevant; the issue for the Court was the effect on commerce, not the character of the activity. The key to determining the scope of Congress's power under the commerce clause was whether the regulated activity would have an effect on interstate commerce, even if it was not interstate commerce itself. If Filburn grew and consumed his own wheat, he would not buy wheat on the market. If many small farmers did the same, their cumulative decisions would have a substantial effect on the national market in wheat, so it would affect interstate commerce and therefore was a proper subject for congressional action.

For a half century following the New Deal transformation, the Supreme Court acquiesced in nearly every application of the commerce power by the Congress, including legislation setting minimum wages and maximum hours of work, prohibiting racial discrimination in places of commerce, regulating the sale of food, and criminalizing loan sharking, among many others. In *Hodel v. Virginia Surface Mining and Reclamation Association* (1981), Justice Rehnquist summarized this history and suggested that "one of the greatest 'fictions' of our federal system is that the Congress exercises only those powers delegated to it" and "the manner in which this Court has construed the Commerce Clause amply illustrates the extent of this fiction." As new appointments shifted the majority on the Court, a *new federalism* emerged that limited Congress's power under the commerce clause for the first time since the New Deal.

In 1990 Congress enacted a statute making it a federal crime to possess a gun within 1,000 feet of a school. Alfonso Lopez was charged under the statute for carrying a handgun into his high school, and he moved to dismiss the indictment on the basis that enactment of the statute was beyond any of the enumerated powers of Congress. The government defended the statute as an exercise of the commerce power; possession of a gun in a school zone may result in violent crime, the costs of violent crime are substantial, and the presence of guns in schools threatens the learning environment, which results in a less productive citizenry, so possession of a gun in a school zone may substantially affect interstate commerce. The Court, in an opinion by Chief Justice Rehnquist, rejected the government's position, holding that the possession of a gun in a school zone was not economic activity, unlike the growing of wheat in *Wickard v. Filburn*, and so it was not within the scope of the commerce clause. Particularly in the absence of congressional findings about the burden that carrying guns imposed a special burden on interstate commerce, if this statute was held valid almost any other statute would be constitutional too, including those that invaded subjects traditionally within the province of the states, such as crime, education, and childrearing (*United States v. Lopez*, 1995).

The strength of the new federalism became clear in 2013 when the Court considered the constitutionality of the Affordable Care Act (ACA), popularly known as Obamacare, the signature health insurance reform of the Obama administration (*National Federation of Independent Business v. Sebelius*, 2012). The most controversial provision of the act was the "individual mandate," which required individuals either to maintain health insurance coverage or to pay a penalty on their income taxes for failing to do so. In an unusual lineup for the Court, four conservative justices joined Chief Justice John Roberts in holding that the mandate was outside Congress's commerce clause power, and four liberal justices joined Roberts in holding that the mandate was constitutional under Congress's power to tax.

The individual mandate was designed to address some of the economic problems of the health insurance market. For example, hospitals sometimes are required to provide treatment whether their patients have insurance or not; to pay for that treatment, the hospitals pass on the costs through higher rates in other cases, and insurers who pay those rates pass on the costs to their customers. Also, the ACA prevented insurers from denying coverage to people with preexisting conditions, which could encourage people to wait until they are sick to buy insurance, again increasing the cost of insurance to everyone. Therefore an individual's decision to maintain coverage had an effect on the market for health insurance and the cost of the health care system overall, a system that everyone will use at one time or another. Because of this effect, the government argued, the ACA was much like the regulation of wheat growing in *Wickard v. Filburn* and was constitutional because it regulated activity that had a substantial effect on interstate commerce.

Chief Justice Roberts disagreed. The Constitution grants the federal government the power to "regulate commerce," but that presupposes that there is commerce to be regulated. The individual mandate does not regulate commercial activity. "It instead compels individuals to *become* active in purchasing a product, on the ground that their failure to do so effects interstate commerce." *Wickard* was different because the farmer was involved in growing wheat—an activity, not an inactivity—which had an effect on the market for wheat. The analogy that often was used in debate about the case, to which Roberts alluded in his opinion, was that Congress can regulate the sale of vegetables but it cannot compel everyone to purchase vegetables because doing so would increase vegetable consumption, which would increase heath and decrease obesity, thereby lowering health care costs.

Although the individual mandate was beyond the commerce power, Roberts did uphold it as within the government's taxing power. The ACA designated the payment uninsured individuals must make as a "penalty," not a "tax," but it is to be collected by the IRS through the income tax system. Under the taxing power, the activity/inactivity distinction of the commerce clause was irrelevant, and it resembled other tax incentives, such as the mortgage deduction that encourages the purchase of a home.

Commentators had much to say about Chief Justice Roberts' opinion beyond its constitutional analysis. The normally conservative Roberts further limited the scope of the commerce clause but used another route to uphold this landmark piece of legislation. Some viewed it as an exercise in overall judicial restraint, drawing fine lines and narrowly construing precedents. Others, reflecting on the controversies about the early New Deal Court, wondered if the opinion was partially motivated by a concern for the Court's role; the opinion limited the commerce power but avoided striking down a major and politically controversial piece of legislation.

The president's specific powers under the Constitution include acting as commander-in-chief of the armed forces; appointing ambassadors, judges, and executive officials with the advice and consent of the senate; and recommending and vetoing legislation. Moreover, although Congress possesses only the "legislative Powers herein granted," the Constitution states that "The executive Power shall be vested in a President," which suggests, and the Supreme Court has held, that the president has all powers normally exercised by a chief executive even if those powers are not specifically enumerated in the Constitution. Within the scope of the president's powers, the president's authority is expansive. For example, in 2002 Congress enacted a statute permitting citizens born there to have their place of birth designated on their passports as "Jerusalem, Israel." The Supreme Court invalidated the statute as infringing on the president's sole authority to recognize the sovereignty of foreign nations (*Zivotofsky v. Kerry*, 2015).

The president's enumerated and general executive powers are great but neither unlimited nor independent of the powers of Congress. Debates about the scope of federal power and of the president's executive authority are most intense in times of crisis. The extent of the government's power to defend the nation and the president's role as commander-in-chief have long been controversial, and the controversy intensified after the terrorist attacks of September 11, 2001.

The Constitution grants to Congress the powers "to declare war" and to finance and regulate the armed forces, and it designates the president as "Commander in Chief." Congress and the president therefore can act together, when Congress declares war, which the president then carries out. Congress has declared war only six times in the nation's history, beginning with the War of 1812 and most recently during World War II; the Civil War and Korean War were among the many undeclared wars. More often Congress fails to formally declare war but in some other way authorizes the president to send troops into combat. Following the September 11 attacks, Congress passed an Authorization for the Use of Military Force resolution enabling the president to use the armed forces against those responsible for the attacks and to prevent future acts of terrorism; presidents since then have used that resolution to justify not only the invasions of Afghanistan in 2001 and Iraq in 2003 but also military action there and in a dozen other countries.

The president also often takes military action without congressional approval or seeks approval after action is taken; by one account, that has happened more than 130 times, beginning with President Adams's use of the navy to capture French ships that had attacked American merchant vessels and extending at least through President Clinton's ordering an air campaign to stop ethnic cleansing in Kosovo. Presidents have justified actions like these by their inherent power to defend the nation against attacks, by the need to protect Americans caught in conflicts abroad, and by obligations to international organizations such as the United Nations and NATO.

How far the president's power as commander-in-chief extends when he acts without Congressional authorization has been the most controversial issue. One approach was suggested in the Steel Seizure Cases during the Korean War. President Truman ordered the seizure by the federal government of the nation's steel mills to maintain production in the face of a threatened strike. The Supreme Court held that in the absence of Congressional authorization (indeed, in the face of Congress's refusal to authorize seizure to settle labor disputes), Truman had no such authority as commander-in-chief or under his general executive power. Concurring in the result, Justice Robert Jackson suggested a flexible, functional test for analyzing presidential power that has been frequently cited. When the president acts pursuant to congressional authorization, his power is greatest; when he acts contrary to the express or implied will of Congress, his power is at its lowest; when he acts on an issue Congress has not addressed, relying on his independent powers as president, he operates in "a zone of twilight," where the scope of his power depends "on the imperatives of events and contemporary imponderables" (*Youngstown Sheet & Tube Co. v. Sawyer*, 1952).

Congress also has tried to rein in the president's power through the War Powers Resolution of 1973, enacted over President Nixon's veto as a response to the controversy over the Vietnam War. The resolution requires the president to consult with Congress when sending troops into combat situations and to withdraw forces after sixty days unless Congress has approved. Whether the resolution unconstitutionally restricts the president's power has never been tested, and probably never will be, because it raises political questions the Supreme Court has been reluctant to take up. In the meantime, presidents have sometimes respected the resolution and sometimes not; President Clinton used it when he sent troops to restore Haitian president Jean-Bertrand Aristide after a coup in 1994 but failed to do so when he ordered air strikes against Al Qaeda bases in Sudan and Afghanistan in 1998.

The power to make war also can conflict with constitutionally protected civil liberties. During the Civil War, President Lincoln suspended habeas corpus to enable the indefinite detention of those hindering the war. When Supreme Court Justice Roger Taney issued a writ of habeas corpus ordering that a Confederate sympathizer named John Merryman be brought to court or released, Lincoln directed the military officers holding Merryman to ignore the order, claiming the constitutional authority to act when Congress was not in session. Taney did not pursue the matter, and subsequently Congress endorsed the suspension of the writ, as the Constitution permits it to do.

Following the September 11 attacks, American forces seized combatants and others believed to be tied to Al Qaeda (including American citizens) and detained them both in the United States and at the naval base in Guantanamo Bay, Cuba. The administration of President George W. Bush claimed that the resolution authorizing military force and, perhaps more importantly, the president's inherent powers as chief executive and commander-in-chief authorized a broad series of actions beyond the control of peacetime law and beyond the review of the courts. His Justice Department issued a legal opinion that stated: "In wartime, it is for the President alone to decide what methods to use to best prevail against the enemy." Accordingly, he initially claimed the constitutional power to order the torture of prisoners to obtain intelligence even though Congress had prohibited such action in its adoption of the United Nations Convention against Torture; after extended publicity, the Justice Department withdrew its opinion and the president disavowed that claim. The administration also claimed that prisoners held at Guantanamo Bay and even U.S. citizens designated as "enemy combatants" were beyond the reach of the courts. (After September 11, the government also expanded its use of wiretapping, interception of email, and other electronic surveillance; those measures presented issues under the Fourth Amendment and are discussed in Chapter 9.)

In a pair of cases in 2004, the Supreme Court rejected those claims, asserting that the president's powers were limited even during the war on terror and that the courts had the authority to determine the scope of those powers. Particularly because of the extent of control of Guantanamo Bay by the United States, the federal courts had jurisdiction "to determine the legality of the Executive's potentially indefinite detention of individuals who claim to be wholly innocent of wrongdoing" (*Rasul v. Bush*, 2004). Yaser Hamdi, an American citizen seized in Afghanistan for having fought with the Taliban, likewise was entitled to receive notice of the basis for classifying him as an enemy combatant and to contest the claims before a neutral decision maker. The president, pursuant to the congressional resolution, could designate a citizen as an enemy combatant and order his detention, but even an enemy combatant could not necessarily be held indefinitely, and not without being given due process (*Hamdi v. Rumsfeld*, 2004).

In response to *Rasul* and *Hamdi*, Congress enacted the Detainee Treatment Act of 2005 and the Military Commissions Act of 2006 to prescribe procedures for the review of detainees' status and to restrict review by the courts of the military's decisions on detainees, specifically excluding habeas corpus actions. In *Boumedienne v. Bush* (2008), the Supreme Court declared that the procedures and restrictions were unconstitutional. The Constitution provides that habeas corpus may be suspended by Congress only "when in Cases of Rebellion or Invasion the public Safety may require it," and the statutes neither hewed to the requirements of the suspension clause nor provided procedures that were an adequate substitute for habeas corpus. A detainee whose fate was being determined by a military commission could have a "representative" who was neither a lawyer nor even the detainee's advocate, the evidence presented by the government would be presumed valid, the detainee could have access only to unclassified portions of the evidence, and he could present only limited, "reasonably available" evidence of his own.

The post-9/11 cases are especially dramatic, but they illustrate a more general point. The powers of the president and Congress always are limited by the commands of the Bill of Rights. For example, Congress may not enact statutes that impose on religious liberty (discussed in Chapter 3), and it may not impose restrictions on the use of property that so diminish its value that they constitute a taking of the property (discussed in Chapter 7).

What Powers Do the States Have Under Constitutional Law?

The story so far has been the creation of a national government strong enough to correct the weaknesses of the government under the Articles of Confederation, the limitation of the powers of that government by the doctrine of enumerated powers, and the subsequent expansion of its powers through broad interpretation of specific grants of authority such as the commerce clause. But what about the states? The states existed before the national government was created, and state delegates drafted and ratified the Constitution. As the power of the federal government has expanded, how do the states fit into the constitutional scheme?

As with every other issue of constitutional law, the answer to this question is not simple. The text of the Constitution says little about state authority, explicitly granting few powers to state governments and explicitly placing few limits on federal authority vis-à-vis the states. As times have changed and the federal and state governments have asserted their authority in different ways, the Supreme Court has struggled to define the areas in which each may properly operate.

Even though the Constitution doesn't say so, federalism—the idea that governmental power is shared by state and national governments—is a basic postulate of our constitutional system. The federal government is a government of enumerated powers, exercising only those powers specifically granted to it in the Constitution—though we have seen that that limitation is often more theoretical than real, given the Supreme Court's acquiescence in the expansion of federal authority. The states, on the other hand, are assumed to exercise the general *police power*, or the power to do all of the usual things that governments do. The courts have developed a substantial body of law on the meaning of the enumerated powers of the federal government (such as the commerce power), but there is no comparable body of law on the authority of state governments, because their powers are general rather than enumerated. The Constitution does not specify the general authority of state governments because it doesn't have to—everyone understood the concepts at the time of the drafting, as we do today from current political situations and the necessary implication of the constitutional structure.

It should be easy to reconcile state and federal powers. The states have general authority, while the national government has limited authority specifically enumerated in the Constitution. The Tenth Amendment makes clear that the authority of the states extends beyond that of the national government: "The powers not delegated to the United States by the Constitution, nor prohibited by it to the States, are reserved to the States respectively, or to the people." But the Constitution also contains a supremacy clause, in Article VI, section 2: "This Constitution, and the Laws of the United States which shall be made in Pursuance thereof . . . shall be the supreme Law of the Land; and the Judges in every State shall be bound thereby, any Thing in the Constitution or Laws of any State to the Contrary notwithstanding." Thus the states have general authority, and the federal government has limited authority, but within its authority the federal government is supreme. So how are the courts to draw the line between federal and state authority?

For a long time, from the post–Civil War years to the beginning of the New Deal, the Supreme Court tended to limit federal authority in favor of state authority. This approach was a corollary of the Court's conservative approach (discussed earlier), which limited the scope of federal powers under the commerce clause and other provisions. The concept was called *dual sovereignty*. Both the national and state governments had their proper sphere of authority, and neither could invade the other's sphere. Frequently the Court would invalidate congressional enactments by finding that the statute in question was beyond the federal government's enumerated powers or that it invaded the powers of the states. In *Hamner v. Dagenhart* (1918), for example, the Court held that a federal law prohibiting the shipment in interstate commerce of goods produced with child labor exceeded the commerce power, and in *Keller v. United States* (1909) it ruled that a federal prohibition on houses of prostitution invaded the states' police power.

The concept of dual sovereignty and the broad scope for state authority it entailed has faded. The possibility of clearly distinguishing between areas of sovereignty was more congenial to the nineteenth-century mind than to legal thinkers of the twentieth and twenty-first centuries, and, after FDR, the Great Depression, and the New Deal, the Court was more willing to acquiesce in the expansion of federal authority. Today the allocation of authority between the national and state governments is controlled by the doctrine of *preemption*, including the puzzling effect of *dormant* federal powers. Where the federal government acts, it preempts state law that actually or potentially conflicts with the federal law. And sometimes where the federal government has not acted but could act—where its power is dormant—state legislation also is barred.

The preemption of state law that is inconsistent with federal law is easy to understand as an operation of the supremacy clause. Where the Federal Arbitration Act says that parties to a contract can agree to submit a dispute to arbitration notwithstanding any contrary provision of state law, a California statute that attempted to invalidate such an agreement is preempted (*Southland Corp. v. Keating*, 1984). The difficult question is to what extent state and federal laws that are not obviously inconsistent still conflict to such an extent that the state law must fall. Sometimes the Supreme Court will be deferential to the concerns of federalism and interpret the statutes to avoid a conflict; at other times the Court will be more sensitive to national interests, particularly where it perceives a need for national uniformity. In *Cipollone v. Liggett Group, Inc.* (1992), the Court held that federal law on cigarette labeling preempted state tort liability for failure to warn of the dangers of smoking. But in *Altria Group, Inc. v. Good* (2008), it concluded that a federal statute did not preempt a state fraud claim against cigarette manufacturers for deceptively advertising that "light" cigarettes were less harmful. In both cases, the Court focused on Congress's express and implied intent in enacting the law; in *Cipollone* the state law conflicted with the federally required health warning on cigarettes, but in *Altria Group* the state law was aimed at deceptive advertising, not the health effects of smoking. Unless Congress has demonstrated "a clear and manifest purpose" to preempt state law, the state's police power remains intact.

Federal law can preempt state law even in the absence of an actual conflict where Congress has occupied the field subject to regulation. This is a matter of interpretation of how far Congress originally intended to go. Where the issues are of national interest or require national uniformity—as with the regulation of Indian tribal affairs, immigration, or the migration of birds throughout the country—the Court is likely to read federal statutes as preempting the field.

Perhaps the fuzziest area of preemption doctrine concerns cases within the powers of Congress in areas within which Congress has not yet legislated. Does the dormant power not yet exercised prevent the states from acting in the meantime? Early advocates of a strong national government argued that the ability of states to legislate on matters having effects beyond their borders was a major weakness of the government under the Articles of Confederation, which the commerce clause and supremacy clause were intended to cure. Accordingly, states could not act within areas covered by the federal commerce power, although they might legislate in other areas that would have some incidental effect on commerce. Others took a narrow view of the federal power, arguing that state legislation was preempted only where it actually conflicted with federal enactments.

The resolution of this issue began in the 1850s and was definitively formulated in a series of cases from the New Deal forward. The test is sensitive to concerns of federalism. States ought to be permitted to legislate in response to local needs, but they should not be permitted to interfere with the flow of commerce among the states. The Court balances the state's local interests in enforcing its legislation against the burden and discrimination imposed by it on interstate commerce. Thus a state may protect its interest in safe highways by enacting maximum height and weight limits for trucks on its roads, even if few trucks can meet the limits, because the ban was imposed equally on trucks used within the state and going through the state (for example, *South Carolina State Highway Dept. v. Barnwell Bros.*, 1938), but it may not ban extra-long tractor-trailers where the terms of the ban exempted many in-state truckers (as in *Kassel v. Consolidated Freightways Corp.*, 1981).

One other aspect of the constitutional allocation of authority between the national government and the states deserves mention. The states have independent constitutional status and general police power, while the federal government has only enumerated powers, so there are things the federal government cannot direct the states to do. The federal government could not, for example, tell a state where to locate its capital, as it tried to do when Oklahoma was admitted to the Union (*Coyle v. Smith*, 1911). But as the federal government and the federal budget have grown, Congress has devised a mechanism for getting the states to do what it wants without directly commanding them. Congress establishes federal spending programs administered through the states but conditions a state's participation on its compliance with specified conditions. For example, the Twenty-first Amendment ended prohibition and gave the states near-total authority over the sale of alcoholic beverages. Because of the states' authority, arguably the amendment bars Congress from enacting a national minimum drinking age. In 1988, however, Congress enacted a statute that withheld a portion of federal highway funds from a state unless the state had a minimum drinking age of twenty-one. As a practical matter, this was equivalent to a national requirement because every state depended on federal funds to build and maintain its roads. Could Congress do indirectly what it could not constitutionally do directly? Yes, Chief Justice William Rehnquist said for a majority of the Court, because controlling highway funds was within the Congress's spending power and the drinking age was related to safe travel on interstate highways (*South Dakota v. Dole*, 1987).

As with Congress's commerce clause power, *NFIB v. Sebelius* (2013) drew limits on this use of congressional action in relation to the states— the first time the Court had held a Congressional spending condition unconstitutional. The ACA extended the Medicaid system for providing health care to low-income Americans by requiring states to cover residents within 133 percent of the poverty line; the federal government would pay 100 percent of these costs until 2016 and would decrease its payments to 90 percent thereafter. Chief Justice Roberts' opinion concluded that this measure crossed the line from encouraging the states to participate in Medicaid to coercing them to do so. He characterized the threat of cutting off all Medicaid funds for failing to comply with the new program as "a gun to the head" of the states, because Medicaid was so well entrenched and constituted such a large portion of the budget of the states that they could not bear to lose the funds.

Amazon Order Number: 113-6363807-6784225
Shipment Number: 2486623

SKU	Title
KCC-U-1284-001606	Law 101: Everything You Need to Know About American Law, Fifth Edition

Returns Policy:
For issues with your order, please contact us prior to initiating a return.
For general returns, initiate a return through your order on Amazon, and you will receive a prepaid return bel.

Return Notes:
Please include your Order ID: (Pull from Order info). We are not responsible for issuing a refund if the em is unidentifiable.
If the return is no fault of FirstClassBooks, the cost of the return label will be subtracted from your refund
Keep the tracking information for your shipment until your refund is completed
Please do not mark the item "Return or Sender" or "Refuse."
In all cases the book must be returned in the condition advertised or received. If the book was received in orse condition than advertised you must notify us prior to the return.
Please note used access cards will not be accepted for returns
Orders returned after 30 days may not receive a refund.

How to contact us:
Go to Your Orders.
Find your order in the list.
Select Problem with order.
Choose your topic from list displayed
Select Contact seller.

2486623

TO REORDER YOUR UPS DIRECT THERMAL LABELS:

1. Access our supply ordering web site at **UPS.COM**®
   or contact UPS at 800-877-8652.

2. Please refer to label #0277400801 when ordering.

3

First Freedoms

Constitutional Rights

The basic issue of constitutional law is how to create a government strong enough to do what we want it to and yet limit the power of that government so that it can't do what we don't want. One of the main things we don't want the government to do is to invade our "rights." What is meant by "rights" changes over time, of course, but we have become used to the idea that there are certain things the government can't do to us.

For the first century and a half of our constitutional history, the primary concern of constitutional law was with the issues of government structure discussed in the last chapter: what powers the Constitution gives to the federal courts, Congress, and the president and how the federal powers limit the authority of state governments. Since the middle of the twentieth century, more of the action in constitutional law has been concerned with defining individual rights, and it is to that area that we now turn.

What Rights Does Constitutional Law Protect?

Every constitutional right is grounded in one or more provisions of the text of the Constitution. One way of learning about these rights is to refer to the provisions one by one—the First Amendment guarantee of free speech, the Second Amendment right to bear arms, and so on—and consider the rights that emanate from them. But it is easier to understand the rights if we separate them into two groups.

The first group of rights is *process rights*. These rights are about the procedures the government must follow—how the government must behave when it acts with respect to an individual or, sometimes, a group. The second group of rights is *substantive rights*. These rights define the areas of individual freedom that the government cannot invade regardless of the procedures it follows. Although the line between process rights and substantive rights isn't a particularly sharp one, the distinction is helpful.

A couple of examples suggest the difference between process and substantive rights. If you are receiving Social Security benefits, the government can't just take them away because some bureaucrat believes you are no longer entitled to them. Before your benefits can be cut off, your constitutional right to due process guarantees that you must receive notice of the government's claim and must have the opportunity to present your arguments about the issue at a hearing. This is a process right. On the other hand, if the government wants to force you to attend a Catholic Mass, the constitutional issue is one of substance, not process. Even if the government gives you notice and a hearing, it cannot infringe on your substantive constitutional right to choose your own religion.

Process rights include the right to "due process of law," found in the Fifth and Fourteenth Amendments, and the right to "equal protection of the laws," from the Fourteenth Amendment. Due process means that the government must follow fair procedures in taking action with respect to an individual. The difficult question is figuring out what process is due in a particular case. If someone is charged with a crime for which he or she could be executed, the matter is obviously more serious than the threatened termination of Social Security benefits, so the Constitution in that instance would impose more procedural requirements. Often, though, determining when someone is entitled to due process and what procedures are required is a more complex issue.

The constitutional law of equal protection has expanded greatly since the middle of the twentieth century, first as a result of the civil rights movement and then because of claims for equal treatment from members of groups other than racial minorities, such as women, ethnic groups, and LGBT people. Equal protection requires that the government treat similarly situated people the same; for example, as the Supreme Court held in *Brown v. Board of Education*, a state can't treat black children unequally by sending them to separate schools from white children. That seems obvious to us now, but most equal protection claims are more controversial. Who is entitled to equal protection: Latinos? Transgender people? Physically challenged people? And what does it mean to treat different people and different groups equally?

Substantive rights are more varied than process rights, but at a very general level, they can be described as serving one or two purposes. One purpose is allowing people to participate fully in the affairs of society, including the political process. For example, freedom of speech and freedom of the press contribute to open political discourse and democratic government. The other purpose is allowing people to protect their well-being and personal integrity and to develop and express their individuality. Freedom of speech also permits personal expression, for example, and the right to choose and practice one's own religion furthers personal growth.

One other note about constitutional rights in general before turning to the details of particular rights: The Bill of Rights—the first ten amendments—was added to the Constitution shortly after its adoption as a means of further protecting individuals against the threat of the newly powerful federal government. By its terms and under the common understanding of the time, the Bill of Rights protected people only against actions of the federal government, not the states. After the Civil War the Thirteenth, Fourteenth, and Fifteenth Amendments were added to the Constitution; these abolished slavery, ensured voting rights, guaranteed equal protection, and extended due process requirements to the states. Although the amendments did not themselves explain the relationship between their provisions and the freedoms expressed in the Bill of Rights, eventually the Supreme Court adopted an approach known as *selective incorporation*. The Fourteenth Amendment does not apply all of the Bill of Rights protections to the states wholesale; instead, the Court examines each provision and selectively incorporates the most important ones into the Fourteenth Amendment. The standard the Court arrived at was to adopt "principle[s] of justice so rooted in the tradition and conscience of our people as to be ranked as fundamental . . . [and] implicit in the concept of ordered liberty." Applying this standard, the Court eventually brought nearly all of the provisions of the Bill of Rights into the Fourteenth Amendment and so rendered them binding on the states.

What Is Due Process?

The Fifth Amendment, which applies to the federal government, states that "No person shall . . . be deprived of life, liberty, or property, without due process of law." The Fourteenth Amendment adds "nor shall any State deprive any person of life, liberty, or property without due process of law." Most of the key terms in these two clauses—"liberty," "property," and "due process"—are vague. A knowledge of history, culture, and judicial authority, and extensive debate about the values of our society, are needed to get us close to a meaning. But by reading the text itself we can begin to understand the due process clauses.

The due process clauses suggest that all persons have rights to something known as "life, liberty, or property." The government cannot take away any of those rights unless it observes "due process of law." This concept contains both a prohibition on government action and by implication an authorization of government action. The clauses explicitly, if vaguely, state what the government cannot do—deprive someone of life, liberty, or property without due process. They also imply what the government can do—deprive someone of life, liberty, or property if it does so with due process.

This is obvious but important. We know that the government can deprive someone of life, liberty, and property. A state can imprison a criminal, confiscate his gun and his getaway car, and even execute him. The government has tremendous power—even over the life and death of its people. But the power is limited by the due process clauses. Before it imprisons someone, for example, the government must allow a fair trial, a right of appeal, and an attorney for the accused if he needs one. Due process is designed to ensure that government policies and rules of law are carried out fairly and consistently. (Due process requirements in criminal proceedings are discussed in Chapter 9.)

As our initial reading of the clauses indicates, there are two issues that arise when a right of due process is asserted. First, is the interest asserted a right to life, liberty, or property that is within the protection of the Fifth or Fourteenth Amendment? Second, if the right is worthy of protection, how much protection does it get—that is, how much process is due?

While life has not figured much in interpretations of the due process clauses, liberty and property have to a much greater degree. The right to *life* arises most often in death penalty cases. It also figures by implication in abortion cases. In *Roe v. Wade*, for example, the Supreme Court held that a fetus is not a person within the meaning of the due process clauses because as used in the Constitution the term "person" does not refer to a fetus. Thus a fetus does not have due process rights.

Liberty in the constitutional sense obviously includes physical freedom, so it limits the ability of the government to imprison people for crimes. Liberty also includes physical restraints besides incarceration in prison. When the state seeks to have a child removed from the custody of its parents and declared a ward of the state or to commit a mentally ill person to a psychiatric institution, it is attempting to restrain their liberty, and the due process clauses require that it observe fair procedures in doing so.

Constitutional liberty also includes the freedom to engage in activities besides physical movement. The Supreme Court has said that liberty, for due process purposes, denotes "not merely freedom from bodily restraint but also the right of the individual to contract, to engage in any of the common occupations of life, to acquire useful knowledge, to marry, establish a home and bring up children, to worship God according to the dictates of his own conscience, and generally to enjoy those privileges long recognized . . . as essential to the orderly pursuit of happiness by free men" (in *Board of Regents v. Roth*, 1972, quoting *Meyer v. Nebraska*, 1923). Thus if a state wishes to take a child away from its parents, the child has a liberty interest because he or she will be placed in foster care or a state home, and the parents also have a liberty interest, the interest in the autonomy of their family.

Property obviously includes tangible property. The government cannot use or seize your property without a fair procedure. Property rights also are protected by the Fifth Amendment's mandate that the government may not take property without *just compensation*. In the exercise of its power of *eminent domain*, the government can condemn your property and take it for a public purpose, such as when building a highway through your land, but it must provide a hearing and it must pay for the land. (Eminent domain is discussed in Chapter 7.)

Property ordinarily means things that are important to own, including intangible property. Does a state employee have a property interest in her job, for example, or a recipient of Social Security disability payments a property interest in his benefits, that give rise to due process rights?

In the 1960s and 1970s it became more apparent that many of the most important things in society no longer took a physical form but were intangible interests created by the government: licenses, entitlement programs, public contracts, government jobs, and so on. In a 1970 case, *Goldberg v. Kelly*, the Supreme Court held that New York could not terminate a welfare recipient's benefits without first providing him an evidentiary hearing. In other cases the Court held that a prisoner's interest in being granted parole on specified conditions, a state college professor's interest in continued employment, and customers' expectation of continued service by a public utility were all sufficient property interests to trigger due process protections.

In a series of cases beginning in the mid-1970s, however, the Court limited the expansive possibilities of this analysis. Due process is required only where someone has an entitlement, and an entitlement is defined as something already possessed, as distinguished from an expectation of future benefit. Thus a prisoner does not have a due process right in determining whether he is eligible for parole, although he may have a due process right if the state attempts to revoke a parole already granted. To decide whether something was an entitlement or an expectation, the Court would look to the state law that created the interest in the first place. Therefore, a student has a right to a hearing before being suspended from school because under state law students are expected to attend school, but a government employee may not have a due process right to a hearing before being fired if the state law defines his right of continued employment as a mere expectation.

Assuming that someone has a life, liberty, or property interest, the second issue that arises in due process analysis is what process is due before the government can infringe that interest. In the Anglo-American tradition, the first thing lawyers think of in terms of due process is a trial. The paradigm for giving someone due process is, therefore, something that looks like a trial, including notice of the issues, a chance to present evidence and arguments, the opportunity to cross-examine witnesses or otherwise dispute the government's evidence, the right to be represented by an attorney, and an impartial decision maker who will give reasons for her decision.

But should a trial-like proceeding be constitutionally required every time the due process clauses are invoked? Are the due process values equally important in a capital crime, the revocation of Social Security benefits, or a suspension from school, so that in each case the person affected is entitled to a full trial, a lawyer, and an appeal? There is also a concern for efficiency; if the government had to provide a full trial every time it affected a liberty or property interest, the system would grind to a halt.

In *Mathews v. Eldridge* (1976), the Supreme Court defined a three-factor balancing test to determine how much procedure is required in a given situation. First, what is the interest of the person who will be affected by the government action? The stronger the interest, the more process is required; a mentally ill person who may be involuntarily committed to a mental institution for an indefinite period is entitled to more procedure than a driver whose license is being suspended for three months—who is, in turn, entitled to more procedure than a student who is being suspended from school for three days. Second, how great is the risk of making an erroneous decision, and how much would that risk be reduced by expanding the procedures? In cases in which no facts are left to be decided—the automatic suspension of a driver's license after a third conviction, for example—additional procedures would not be of much help, but where many facts and legal issues are in dispute—say, whether a driver was intoxicated—more procedures would reduce the risk of error. Third, how important is the government's interest in taking the challenged action, including the administrative or financial burden required to use more extensive procedures? Providing a full trial for every change in Social Security benefits status would impose a huge cost on the federal government.

Consider how this test applies in the case of schools punishing their students. Suppose the principal of a Columbus, Ohio, high school wants to suspend a student for ten days for being involved in a lunchroom fracas that damaged school property. Because Ohio has created a system of compulsory and free public education, a constitutionally protected property interest is involved, and therefore due process is required. But how much process is due? Is the principal allowed to suspend the student simply on the report of a teacher who witnessed the events, does the principal also have to get the student's side of the story, or is the student entitled to a full hearing including being represented by a lawyer? Does the procedure have to come before the student is suspended, or is it enough that there is a review of the decision after it is made?

The Supreme Court addressed these issues in *Goss v. Lopez* (1975). Because of the importance of attending school and the stigma attached to suspension, the student has an important interest in not being suspended without a good reason that has been fairly determined. Even principals acting in good faith can make mistakes if they act after hearing only one side of the story and without giving the student an opportunity to rebut the charges or explain his conduct. It does not cause much delay or expense for the principal to call the student in and ask for an explanation before meting out a suspension; requiring a full hearing, however, would impose undue expense and burden on school administrators.

In some cases, however, even this much process is not due. If a teacher wants to give a student detention for acting up in class, does she have to provide him with an opportunity to be heard first? Of course not. And sometimes more process is due. If the school wants to suspend the student for an entire school year, the student's interest in attending school and in preventing an erroneous decision is much greater, so a fuller process is required, perhaps even including a trial-type hearing with the opportunity to be represented by counsel and to present and cross-examine witnesses.

Does Constitutional Law Require That Everyone Be Treated Equally?

No, it doesn't. But it does guarantee everyone "equal protection of the laws." What's the difference?

The Fourteenth Amendment, originally adopted during Reconstruction to deal with the vestiges of slavery in the South, forbids a state to "deny to any person within its jurisdiction the equal protection of the laws." (After the amendment's adoption an equal protection principle applying to the national government was read into the due process clause of the Fifth Amendment.) The equal protection clause has been the source of a tremendous expansion of rights since the middle of the twentieth century. The civil rights movement and the other antidiscrimination battles it spawned have been litigated primarily on the basis of the equal protection clause.

In three respects, the equal protection clause does not guarantee that everyone be treated absolutely equally. First, like all other constitutional provisions, the equal protection clause limits government discrimination but not private discrimination. The Constitution prohibits a state from discriminating against black people, but it has no power over the actions of private individuals; a white supremacist group is not constitutionally required to admit black members. However, the equal protection clause does indirectly regulate private conduct. When a private person exercises a right created or enforced by the government, the Court will view it as if the state itself were acting. In *Shelley v. Kraemer* (1948), for example, a landowner sued to enforce a restrictive covenant in his neighbor's deed that prohibited the sale of the neighbor's home to a black person; the homeowner was effectively prevented from engaging in the discriminatory behavior because any court decision enforcing the covenant would constitute discriminatory "state action" in violation of the equal protection clause. Also, many actions of private individuals and businesses are controlled by state and federal civil rights laws. To further the equality principle of the Fourteenth Amendment, state legislatures and Congress have enacted laws that prohibit discrimination on the basis of race, gender, national origin, sexual orientation, or some other bases in hiring, in providing access to public accommodations such as restaurants, and so on.

Second, "equal protection *of the laws*" means that when the government passes a law, creates a program, or engages in an activity, it must treat people equally under the relevant law. But the government does not have to go out of its way to initiate programs that would correct inequalities that people otherwise suffer. The government may not discriminate on the basis of race, for example, but it is not constitutionally required to enact legislation to cure private discrimination (although Congress has done so anyway).

Third, and most important, the government can "discriminate" by putting people into groups and treating the groups differently if it has a legitimate reason for doing so. If you retire at age sixty-six you collect Social Security benefits, but if you retire at age forty-six you don't. A state university charges lower tuition to state residents than to out-of-staters. The federal and state governments make these kinds of distinctions in every activity they perform, treating people or groups differently. The equal protection clause does not require that the government treat everybody the same, but it does require that the government treat everyone who is *similarly situated* the same. For equal protection purposes, this means that the people or groups in question must be in about the same position with respect to the relevant government policy.

Remember that the basic issue of constitutional law is giving the government enough power while setting limits on the exercise of that power. The equal protection clause prescribes a particular kind of limit. We want the government to be able to further the public interest, and that requires it to use classifications that advantage some people and disadvantage others. But we don't want those advantages and disadvantages to be distributed on the basis of characteristics that do not advance the public interest or that are morally repugnant.

The need for this kind of limit on government action is particularly apparent where government policy discriminates against a minority group. Under our system, the majority rules, but not too much; electoral majorities can impose their will on minorities, but not when it has a particularly disadvantageous, disempowering, or stigmatizing effect. Creating racially segregated schools, for example, didn't advance the purpose of providing a good public education for all children; it undermined that purpose because of the tendency of the black schools to receive inferior resources from the white majority and because of the stigma attached to racial segregation. Segregated schools also offended our notions of fairness and equality; geography, academic merit, or even wealth can affect what kind of school a child attends, but race shouldn't have anything to do with it.

The picture is further complicated because the courts are the government institution authorized to enforce the equal protection clause. If the courts are too aggressive in reviewing legislation on equal protection grounds, they can become too powerful, by invading the province of the legislature and making judgments about which classifications best serve public needs. If they are too deferential to legislative judgments, they fail in their constitutional duty to provide equal protection and they allow the other branches to become too powerful.

The Supreme Court responds to these concerns by giving more deference to some legislative decisions and less to others, depending on who or what is being discriminated against. (And, of course, depending on the ideological orientations of the justices and the political atmosphere at a given time.) Classifications that arise out of ordinary government regulation of economic affairs are not particularly suspicious, as long as the classification used seems reasonable in light of the government interest to be advanced. In those cases the Court will give only a cursory review by looking for a *rational relationship* between the classification and the government interest and probably will uphold the program. On the other hand, some classifications have been regarded as especially suspicious—those that discriminate on the basis of race, national origin, or some other *suspect class*, for example, or that burden the exercise of a constitutionally fundamental right such as free speech. In those cases the Court will take an especially hard look at the legislative distinction (called *strict scrutiny*) and probably invalidate it. If the case lies somewhere in between, so will the Court's review, called, appropriately, *intermediate review*.

The rational relationship test is applied to most ordinary economic or regulatory legislation. One of the functions of government is to regulate all sorts of economic affairs, from controlling advertising to providing retirement benefits. In making these regulations, the legislature (and the executive branch in carrying out legislation) must make classifications between groups (such as drawing a line at age sixty-six for retirement benefits). If the courts were to second-guess the legislative or executive judgments in each of those cases, the judicial branch would in effect become the most powerful branch of the government. Instead, the Supreme Court has concluded that in reviewing ordinary legislation like this under the equal protection clause, its task is limited to asking two questions: Is the legislation directed at a legitimate government objective? Is it rationally related to achieving that objective? If the answer to both questions is "yes," the legislation complies with the equal protection clause.

As a practical matter, when the Court applies the rational relationship test it usually upholds the challenged government action. In the Court's view, the legislature is entitled to tremendous deference to decide what classifications are appropriate in enacting ordinary legislation of this sort. Accordingly, the Court typically accepts or even infers a legitimate end for legislation and requires only the most minimal connection between the end and the classification used. The few exceptions involve cases in which the classification demonstrates "animosity toward the class of persons affected," as the Court said in *Romer v. Evans* (1996). In that case, for example, the Court invalidated an amendment to the Colorado constitution prohibiting state or local governments from enacting laws to protect against discrimination on the basis of sexual orientation, because the amendment "classifies homosexuals not to further a proper legislative end but to make them unequal to everyone else. . . . A State cannot so deem a class of persons a stranger to its laws."

The opposite of the rational relationship test is strict scrutiny. The equality principle of the Fourteenth Amendment has two core areas of application: When government action is directed against a *suspect class*, such as African Americans whom the amendment originally was intended to protect, or when government action invades a *fundamental right* in a discriminatory manner, the Court will engage in strict scrutiny in reviewing the action's compliance with the equal protection clause. Instead of deferring to the other branches of government, the Court will determine for itself whether the classification is necessary to promote a compelling governmental objective. Most of the time, when the Court uses strict scrutiny the challenged government action is held invalid.

The suspect classifications with the longest history are, of course, race and similar categories such as national origin. When a government action distinguishes people on the basis of their race, the action is inherently suspect in light of the nation's history of slavery and racism. Accordingly, the Court will closely examine the action to see if the racial classification is really necessary to achieve a compelling government objective and will almost always invalidate such a classification. Indeed, only in the notorious Japanese internment cases did the Supreme Court uphold an explicit discrimination against minority races, where it permitted the government to remove Japanese Americans from the Pacific Coast states during World War II and imprison them in internment camps. (In the 1980s, decades after the war had ended, the Japanese Americans who had been convicted of violating the internment orders had their convictions vacated, and Congress issued an official apology for the action.)

Strict scrutiny also is applied when a government classification discriminates against a constitutionally fundamental interest. Some fundamental interests are expressed in the Constitution itself, such as the right to free speech; others have been found by the Court to be implicit in the constitutional scheme, such as the right to travel from state to state. When a government classification burdens some people in the exercise of a fundamental interest, the Court will strictly scrutinize the classification to determine if it is necessary to achieve a compelling government interest. If it is not—and in most cases it is not—the classification is held to violate the equal protection clause. For example, the Court has invalidated, as undue burdens on the right to travel, one-year residency requirements for voting (*Dunn v. Blumstein*, 1972) and for receiving welfare benefits (*Shapiro v. Thompson*, 1969).

Finally, there are classifications that are not as invidious as suspect classifications but are at least questionable, and there are interests that do not have the constitutional status of fundamental interests but are nonetheless important. These intermediate classifications and interests provoke, naturally enough, an intermediate level of review. Here the Court does not examine the relationship between the government interest and the challenged classification as closely as it does with a suspect class or fundamental interest, nor is it as deferential as with ordinary economic regulation. Classifications based on gender are the prime example of an intermediate class; in the Court's view, sex discrimination does not bear the opprobrium or the history of oppression of racial discrimination, but it is sufficiently questionable that it demands closer examination than ordinary legislative classifications. Because sex discrimination falls in this intermediate category, the decisions are much less predictable. For example, the Court struck down a Utah law that provided that women reached the age of majority at eighteen but men at twenty-one, so that parents had to support their sons longer than their daughters, on the basis that the longer period was designed for males to receive an education so they could better support a family (*Stanton v. Stanton*, 1975). However, it upheld a California statute that made it statutory rape for a male to have sexual intercourse with a minor female, even though there was no corresponding prohibition of a female to have intercourse with a minor male, because of the state's interest in preventing the unique harm to women that follows from illegitimate pregnancies (*Michael M. v. Superior Court*, 1981).

This three-tiered scheme of equal protection analysis provides an orderly start to the concept, but tough issues remain. Consider one of the most important recent issues under equal protection doctrine: "affirmative action," as it is called by its proponents, or "reverse discrimination," as it is called by opponents. The issues are simple to state but difficult to solve: Does the equality principle embodied in the Fourteenth Amendment demand formal equality, so that the government may never use racial distinctions? Or does it permit the government to consider history and context to make racial distinctions to correct racial inequality? The equal protection clause originally was adopted to protect minority interests. Proponents of affirmative action argue that taking remedial measures to benefit minorities who traditionally have been discriminated against and have been less powerful politically is consistent with the clause's original purpose and, in fact, is necessary to erase the effects of discrimination. Moreover, affirmative action that, for example, increases diversity in schools benefits everyone by providing role models for minority students and enriching the educational environment for all students. Opponents of affirmative action argue that the proper application of the equal protection clause is to prohibit all forms of discrimination using suspect classes such as race and gender, whether they advantage or disadvantage a particular group. Affirmative action that favors members of minority groups unfairly burdens others who have not contributed to discrimination and themselves become the objects of unfair discrimination.

As usual, we can begin with some relatively easy cases. In the school desegregation cases, school districts were found to have deliberately discriminated among students on the basis of race. To remedy the effects of segregated schools, it may be necessary to take race-conscious actions, by assigning teachers and students to schools on the basis of their race. This kind of affirmative action is remedial; the only way to remedy proven, intentional discrimination is to use race as a category.

Suppose, however, that the government voluntarily undertakes affirmative action without a proven history of discrimination. Here shifting majorities on the Court and the varied contexts from which the cases arise have produced a variety of approaches. In 1990, for example, a 5–4 majority of the justices held that the Federal Communications Commission policy favoring minority owners of radio or television stations was constitutional (*Metro Broadcasting, Inc. v. Federal Communications Commission*), but in 1995, Justice Thomas, who was appointed in 1991, joined the four *Metro Broadcasting* dissenters to hold that the federal government's policy of favoring minority contractors on highway projects was not (*Adarand Contractors, Inc. v. Pena*).

An area in which affirmative action has been hotly contested is higher education. In *Regents of the University of California v. Bakke* (1978) the justices issued six separate opinions, with no single opinion commanding a majority of the Court; Justice Powell cast the deciding vote and his opinion became regarded as controlling, even though no other justice entirely agreed with his reasoning. He concluded that a public university could not set aside seats in its class especially for members of a minority group, it could consider the race of applicants in making individualized admissions decisions, and an affirmative action program that did so would be subject to strict scrutiny.

In the decades following *Bakke*, universities used a variety of affirmative action programs. In 2003 the Court revisited the issue in a pair of cases involving admissions to the University of Michigan's law school and undergraduate college. In *Grutter v. Bollinger* the Court upheld the constitutionality of the law school's affirmative action program, and in the companion case of *Gratz v. Bollinger* it struck down the college's program. The Court repeated that racial classifications are subject to strict scrutiny requiring that they be "narrowly tailored to further compelling government interests." The university's compelling interest was the same in each case, "to obtain the educational benefits that flow from a diverse student body," an interest that the Court acknowledged to be valid. In furthering this compelling interest, the law school engaged in a wide-ranging, individualized review of every applicant's potential contribution to the diversity of the law school community, considering factors such as extensive community service and experience in business or other fields as well as race. The college, on the other hand, used a point system for admissions under which minority applicants automatically received one-fifth of the points necessary for admission, which had the practical effect of guaranteeing admissions for minimally qualified minority applicants. Different majorities of the Court found that the law school program was narrowly tailored to meet its goal, consistent with the requirements of *Bakke* and therefore constitutional, but the college program was not.

After *Grutter* and *Gratz,* the University of Texas responded to the problem of an insufficiently diverse student body by adopting an admissions plan under which 75 percent of the entering class was taken from the top 10 percent of Texas high schools and 25 percent was taken according to an admissions index that used diversity as one factor. Abigail Fisher, a white student, was rejected under this plan and sued, claiming that the use of race as a factor was impermissible.

In *Fisher v. University of Texas* (2013, 2015), Justice Kennedy, writing for the Court, reaffirmed that colleges have a compelling interest in a diverse student body. Because racial classifications were subject to strict scrutiny, however, the university needed to show that the use of race was necessary to achieve diversity. After reviewing the steps the university took to define and achieve its goal of diversity, the Court concluded that its plan was narrowly tailored and there were no available and workable alternatives to achieve that goal.

How Does the Constitution Protect Freedom of Speech?

The Bill of Rights was adopted to make clear that the new national government lacked the power to infringe the rights of the people. Included in the First Amendment to the Constitution was what may be the most fundamental of those rights: "Congress shall make no law . . . abridging the freedom of speech, or of the press." Freedom of speech acts as the guarantor of the other rights, permitting open political debate and challenges to government authority.

The free speech clause was little used for more than a hundred years, until government repression at the time of World War I sparked the first flurry of free speech cases. Since then the Supreme Court has developed a body of First Amendment jurisprudence that significantly protects speech. Often in times of stress—the era of McCarthyism in the 1950s is a prime example—that protection has waned, but protection of free speech in the United States is still broader than in any other country.

Judges and scholars have developed several theories of free speech to explain and guide the legal developments. The theories are important: Why we protect free speech may determine what we protect and how we protect it. The classic view is that freedom of speech permits a "marketplace of ideas" in which different versions of truth and good contend for the greater number of supporters. This view received its foremost expression in Justice Oliver Wendell Holmes Jr.'s dissent in *Abrams v. United States* (1919), a prosecution of anarchists for publishing leaflets calling on the "workers of the world" to strike in opposition to the United States' intervention against the Bolsheviks during the Russian Revolution. A majority of the Supreme Court affirmed the convictions of the leafletters (who were sentenced to up to twenty years in prison), but Holmes, joined by Justice Louis Brandeis, dissented, arguing "that the ultimate good desired is better reached by free trade in ideas—that the best test of truth is the power of the thought to get itself accepted in the competition of the market."

The most important "marketplace" in which ideas are contested is the political realm. In a democracy, free debate about public issues, government policy, and candidates for office is essential to self-governance because it informs citizens, inculcates public values, and provides a forum for criticism of the government. Protection of political speech is, therefore, at the core of the First Amendment, even if it does not define its entire scope.

The marketplace of ideas approach may be too limited because it attends only to the instrumental effects of free speech in reaching better political decisions. Therefore, another theory argues that freedom of speech has an independent value in affirming the dignity and promoting the development of individuals. Protecting the speech of every person demonstrates that every person's voice potentially is valued in society and allows everyone to learn and grow through participating in public discourse.

Whether we follow one theory or the other, or some combination of the two, we face a difficult task in defining the content of the First Amendment's free speech guarantee. "Speech" takes many forms: expressing a political opinion, using a racial epithet, shouting "Fire!" in a crowded theater, publishing a scurrilous story about a movie star in a supermarket tabloid, or making false promises in an advertisement, to name only a few. Speech, for First Amendment purposes, also has come to include some nonverbal expression: burning an American flag, picketing, contributing to a political campaign, or making an obscene gesture. Which of these forms of "speech" are protected by the

First Amendment from government intrusion, and how far does the protection extend?

The First Amendment protects speech, and speech has to be carried on by a speaker. Who counts as a speaker for First Amendment purposes? Ordinarily this is an easy question. Someone orating from a soapbox, carrying a picket sign, or publishing a web page is surely a speaker. But what if that someone is not a real person but is a corporation? Corporations, labor unions, and similar associations long have been subject to special restrictions on their communicative activities. In the controversial case of *Citizens United v. Federal Election Commission* (2010), the Court broadly extended First Amendment protection to corporate expenditures.

In 2008 Citizens United, a nonprofit corporation, produced a film critical of Hillary Clinton, then a candidate for the Democratic presidential nomination, and also produced television ads promoting the film. Federal election laws limited the ability of corporations to spend funds for "electioneering communications" like these within thirty days of a primary election. The Court held that "The First Amendment protects more than just the individual on a soapbox and the lonely pamphleteer," as Chief Justice Roberts said in concurrence; it also protects corporations, including modest nonprofits, mom-and-pop businesses, and ExxonMobil. The government argued that corporate expenditures may have outsize influence and may lead to the corruption of public officials or at least the appearance of corruption, but the Court dismissed those concerns, noting that all speakers derive their financial resources from the economic marketplace and are entitled to participate in the marketplace of ideas.

Oddly enough, the government itself is not a speaker for First Amendment purposes, so expressive actions by the government are not subject to free speech restrictions. Citizens' speech contests in the marketplace of ideas, where persuasive ideas and opinions will triumph over unpersuasive ones. There is a different check on government speech, however—the political and electoral processes themselves. Therefore, a city could display monuments in a public park honoring the victims of September 11, commemorating a historic granary, and commemorating the city's first fire station, among others, while refusing to permit the erection of a religious organization's monument setting forth the group's tenets of faith; the city as speaker could choose what it wished to express and not express (*Pleasant Grove City v. Summum*, 2009). Even what seems like personal expression authorized by the state is government speech; the Texas motor vehicles department could refuse an application from the Sons of Confederate Veterans for a specialty license plate displaying a Confederate battle flag while approving plates that featured the slogan and logo of Rotary International and plates with the slogan "Get It Sold with RE/MAX" (*Walker v. Texas Division, Sons of Confederate Veterans*, 2015).

One of the most important principles of constitutional law was established, bizarrely enough, in a footnote of a Supreme Court opinion. Chief Justice Harlan Stone's opinion in *United States v. Carolene Products Co.* (1938) included the now legendary footnote 4, asserting a special constitutional status for certain rights, including freedom of speech. Footnote 4 stated that the presumption of constitutionality that the Court ordinarily gives to legislation may have a narrower scope "when legislation appears on its face to be within a specific prohibition of the Constitution such as those of the first ten amendments." Constitutional rights within the Bill of Rights, therefore, were given a "preferred position" over other rights. This preferred position is to be effectuated through "more exacting judicial scrutiny" of government attempts to control speech, and that is exactly what has occurred in the area of protected speech.

The preferred position of free speech restricts the power of state and federal governments to prohibit or limit constitutionally protected speech in a number of ways. First, the government generally may not impose prior restraints on speech; that is, it may not prohibit speech in advance, even where it constitutionally could punish the speaker after the fact. Second, it may not limit speech based on its content. Third, the government may limit the time, place, and manner of speech but only in cases in which it has a compelling interest in doing so, adopts the least restrictive means of limiting the speech, and does so by a regulation that is neither too vague nor overly broad.

The prohibition on prior restraints of speech may be the strongest limitation in the First Amendment. Suppose during a time of war a former government employee intends to interfere with the conduct of the war by revealing information that is critical of government policy (as Daniel Ellsberg, a former national security employee, did during the Vietnam War in the Pentagon Papers case). If the information might undermine support for the war and conceivably even help the enemy, the government may want to obtain an injunction to prevent the harm before it occurs. Moreover, an injunction requires only an expedited hearing in front of a judge, and if the employee violates the injunction, he can be punished for contempt. The injunction, therefore, is a better remedy for the government than would be a criminal punishment for revealing the information.

But the free speech clause was designed to deny the government what is best for it. The earliest understanding of free speech in English and

American law was a prohibition on prior restraints. The government could punish a person for saying or printing something that was seditious, blasphemous, or otherwise prohibited, but it could not censor the statement or prohibit in advance its publication. That principle has been carried over into modern First Amendment jurisprudence under the doctrine prohibiting prior restraints. Government generally cannot keep speech out of the marketplace of ideas, even when it can punish the speech subsequently. The singular exception, which the Court recognized in the Pentagon Papers case, is the disclosure of something like troop movements in time of war or other speech that "must inevitably, directly, and immediately" present a similar peril.

The Supreme Court has allowed prior restraints in two areas, however: obscenity and commercial advertising. The Court has not been clear on the distinction here, but it may be based on the smaller significance of delay in publication and the lower status of the speech in these areas. Imposing a prior restraint on a matter of political debate could keep an important opinion or fact out of the marketplace of ideas at a crucial moment, but there usually is less time pressure on the distribution of obscene materials or on advertising.

The second kind of protection for speech is a prohibition on government regulation of the content of speech. Except in the most unusual circumstances, government regulation of speech must be *content-neutral*. That is, the government may not favor or disfavor the expression of one point of view over another. As Justice Thurgood Marshall wrote, "But, above all else, the First Amendment means that government has no power to restrict expression because of its message, its ideas, its subject matter, or its content."

Consider in this context the highly controversial issue of flag burning. While protesting the policies of the Reagan administration during the 1984 Republican National Convention, Gregory Lee Johnson unfurled an American flag, doused it with kerosene, and set it on fire. While the flag burned, Johnson and other protesters chanted, "America, the red, white, and blue, we spit on you." Johnson was convicted under a Texas statute that prohibited the intentional desecration of the flag and was sentenced to one year in prison and a $2,000 fine.

Johnson ignited not only a flag but a storm of national controversy. His appeal (*Texas v. Johnson*) came to the Supreme Court in 1989. By a five-to-four majority, the Court invalidated Johnson's conviction because the statute was a content regulation in violation of the First Amendment. As the attorneys for the state admitted, Johnson's conduct was meant to be expressive—to communicate an idea—and he was prosecuted for doing so. The state argued, however, that it had an interest in preventing breaches of the peace that might occur because people would be upset by the flag burning and in "preserving the flag as a symbol of nationhood and national unity." The first argument failed because there was no evidence that the flag burning was likely to produce imminent lawlessness; even if that might have been the result, prosecution of Johnson for the probable violence might create an unconstitutional "heckler's veto," in which the anticipated reaction to constitutionally protected speech can be used as a basis for suppressing the speech. The second argument failed because it was a direct regulation of content. As the majority wrote, "If there is a bedrock principle underlying the First Amendment, it is that the Government may not prohibit the expression of an idea simply because society finds the idea itself offensive or disagreeable. We have not recognized an exception to this principle even where our flag has been involved."

The requirement that government regulation of speech be content-neutral even restricts its ability to control or punish speech that may be offensive or false. The Asian American members of the rock band The Slants had chosen the ethnic slur as their name to "reclaim" it and drain it of its denigrating power. The federal Patent and Trademark Office refused to register the band's name as a trademark because it violated a law against trademarks that disparaged or brought into disrepute people or groups. The Supreme Court overturned the government's decision, remarking, "Speech that demeans on the basis of race, ethnicity, gender, religion, age, disability, or any other similar ground is hateful; but the proudest boast of our free speech jurisprudence is that we protect the freedom to express the thought that we hate" (*Matal v. Tam*, 2017). In another case Xavier Alvarez had lied about playing hockey for the Detroit Red Wings and having married a Mexican starlet—"Lying was his habit," the Court said—but the lie that brought his case to the Supreme Court was his public claim that he had received the Medal of Honor (*United States v. Alvarez*, 2012). That lie was criminally punishable under the Stolen Valor Act, and Alvarez was prosecuted. The government argued that false speech was valueless, contributing nothing to the marketplace of ideas and public debate. The Court refused to create an exception to the principle of content neutrality for false speech. Certain kinds of false speech can be prohibited or punished, such as speech that is defamatory or that has adverse consequences, such as making false statements to a public official. But content-based restrictions are presumed to be invalid because "our constitutional tradition stands against the idea that we need Oceania's Ministry of Truth," as in George Orwell's novel *1984*.

While the government cannot regulate the content of speech, it can regulate the time, place, and manner of speech and other expressive conduct. Does freedom of speech mean, for example, that someone is free to expound their views over a loudspeaker at midnight in a residential neighborhood, or that a group can parade down the middle of a street during rush hour to protest traffic policies? Certainly not. The government can impose reasonable restrictions on the way speech is communicated without censoring its content.

There is a problem, however. Time, place, and manner regulations can act as a subterfuge for content regulation. If a municipal ordinance requires that anyone wishing to use a loudspeaker get permission from the chief of police, the chief's exercise of discretion in deciding who to permit to use a loudspeaker, as well as where and when, could be used to discriminate against some types of content. To avoid this problem, the Court has developed standards for time, place, and manner regulations that follow from the preferred position given the right of free speech. First, as the Court said in *United States v. O'Brien* (1968), "the incidental restriction on alleged First Amendment freedoms [must be] no greater than is essential to the furtherance of [the government's] interest." This is often stated as the *least restrictive alternative* test. In regulating the time, place, or manner of expression, the government must use the least restrictive alternative means of serving its interest to avoid unnecessarily limiting free speech. A city has an interest in preventing littering, but it may not advance that interest by banning all distribution of handbills and leaflets, when a less restrictive alternative would be to prosecute people who actually throw papers on the streets.

Second, the regulation must not be overly broad. If the regulation is drafted too broadly, it could prohibit protected speech or regulate content to too great an extent. In *Houston v. Hill* (1987) the Court invalidated an ordinance making it unlawful to "interrupt any policeman in the execution of his duty." While the government could prevent interference with police officers, it could not do so through a prohibition that also would punish some protected speech.

Third, the regulation must not be overly vague. A vague statute does not put people on notice as to what they can and cannot do, so they might limit their First Amendment activities in fear of prosecution. And a vague statute puts too much discretion in the hands of government officials to license, limit, or prosecute under it, raising the possibility that officials might exercise their discretion in a constitutionally impermissible manner.

Suppose someone blackmails you, threatening to reveal a dark secret from your past unless you pay her off. Or suppose a publisher wants to distribute a magazine filled with child pornography. Can he do so with impunity and claim the protection of the First Amendment? Most people agree that some speech should receive full constitutional protection and some should not. The problem is figuring out where to draw the lines.

To define fully protected, partially protected, and unprotected speech, the Court begins with the theories of the First Amendment. From the marketplace of ideas perspective, speech or communicative conduct has value primarily because it is part of a public debate. Speech that does not contribute to public debate does not deserve the same level of protection as speech that does contribute. Advocates of regulation argue that, for example, pornographic pictures do not add anything to public discourse. Other kinds of speech simply cause harm without contributing to debate, or the harm they cause vastly outweighs any contribution they make. Threats by blackmailers pose a threat to the social order much greater than any value the statements have. The same may be said from the self-expression point of view; even though many forms of speech are important means of self-expression, some (such as blackmail) are not, and in others (child pornography) the harm of the speech outweighs the value of permitting the expression.

One form of unprotected speech that is so obviously not entitled to constitutional status that it rarely appears in the cases is speech that is part of an act the law traditionally would consider criminal. When a robber says "your money or your life" or a corporation issues a fraudulent prospectus in connection with a stock offering, the speech expresses no opinion on a matter of public importance but is merely the functional equivalent of the robber sticking his hand in your pocket and taking your wallet.

Speech that is part of criminal conduct is an easy case. Other forms of unprotected or less protected speech present more difficult definitional and line-drawing problems. Commercial speech, speech that may give rise to liability for defamation or other torts, obscenity, and incitement to illegal activity receive some First Amendment protection but not as much as other more traditionally protected forms of speech.

Commercial speech includes advertisements, use of trade names, solicitations of clients by lawyers, posting of "For Sale" signs on houses, distribution of general consumer information, and similar activities for which there primarily is an economic motivation. The Supreme Court first declared that commercial speech is entitled to First Amendment protection in 1976 when it struck down a Virginia statute that prohibited pharmacists from advertising the prices of prescription drugs (*Virginia State Board of Pharmacy v. Virginia Citizens Consumer Council, Inc.*). Speech is not disqualified from protection because the speaker's interest is economic; union members involved in a labor dispute have an economic interest, but their speech had long been protected. Individual consumers seek good products at low prices, and the public at large benefits from well-informed decisions by consumers, so there is a strong interest in the free dissemination of information and ideas in the commercial as well as the political realm.

That interest is strong enough to accord commercial speech First Amendment protection but not as strong as the interest in other types of speech. Some types of commercial speech can be prohibited altogether, including false and deceptive advertising. This category shows how much less protection commercial speech gets. The Court upheld a Texas statute that prohibited optometrists from practicing under trade names; although there was no proof that optometrists had used trade names to deceive consumers, the risk that they might was enough to support the regulation. Nondeceptive commercial speech is entitled to more protection, but because the government has a legitimate interest in regulating some of that speech—to reduce excessive drinking through the regulation of beer advertising, for example—how much is not always clear. The Court has struck down a variety of restrictions on advertising alcoholic beverages, upheld prohibitions on advertising lotteries and casino gambling, invalidated a ban on billboard advertising of tobacco products, and split on state laws that limit the ways in which lawyers and other professionals can solicit clients.

Defamation is a tort that imposes liability for making false and derogatory statements that injure someone's reputation. Therefore, if someone falsely states that a senator has been improperly influenced to support a piece of legislation by donations from a corporation, or if a newspaper publishes a false article to that effect, the senator may sue for damages to her reputation. (For these purposes, First Amendment freedom of the press is treated under the same standards as freedom of speech.) But there is a problem here. The First Amendment encourages commentary on public affairs, including criticism of the government and its officials. If the law of defamation is too generous in providing a remedy to public officials and others, citizens would be much more cautious in voicing their criticisms, and the marketplace of ideas would be diminished. Yet the interest in protecting one's reputation is still valid. How do we balance the two?

The Supreme Court addressed this dilemma in *New York Times Co. v. Sullivan* (1964), a case arising out of the civil rights movement. The police commissioner of Montgomery, Alabama, sued the *New York Times* over an advertisement alleging police brutality in Montgomery and soliciting support for the civil rights movement. Although the advertisement was false only in a few minor respects, under Alabama law it was defamatory and the *Times*, as publisher, was liable even though it had published the ad without knowledge of the misstatements. The Supreme Court reversed the judgment, however. There is a "central meaning of the First Amendment," wrote Justice William Brennan for the Court, that includes "a profound national commitment to the principle that debate on public issues should be uninhibited, robust, and wide-open, and that it may well include vehement, caustic, and sometimes unpleasantly sharp attacks on government and public officials."

To protect this central meaning, the Court gave constitutional protection to some forms of speech that would constitute common law defamation. Otherwise, defamation actions could be used as a tool to chill the expression of opinions. Advocates of unpopular views would be afraid of being punished for getting the facts wrong, or that a jury unfavorable to their view would decide against them, or simply of the cost of litigation and therefore would be reluctant to express their opinions—what the Court referred to as "self-censorship." A statement about a public official is constitutionally protected unless the official could prove that it was false and was made with "actual malice," which the Court defined as "knowledge that it was false or with reckless disregard of whether it was false or not." Under this standard, most public comment and all good-faith journalistic judgments—including the publication of the advertisement by the *Times*—would be constitutionally privileged; only defamation made with malice is constitutionally unprotected.

The same interest in public debate protects speech that otherwise might give rise to liability for other torts. Members of the Westboro Baptist Church picketed the funeral of Lance Corporal Matthew Snyder, a Marine who had been killed in the line of duty in Iraq. The church members believed that God hates the United States for tolerating homosexuality, particularly in the military, and they frequently picketed military funerals and similar events with signs reading "Thank God for Dead Soldiers," "God Hates Fags," and other repulsive sentiments. Snyder's father sued the church members for the tort of intentional infliction of emotional distress, claiming that their outrageous conduct caused him extreme emotional harm and intruded on a private affair. The Supreme Court recognized that the picketing was hurtful, but it was done peacefully on a public street and involved "matters of public concern," the protection of which "is at the heart of the First Amendment's protection." Even speech that causes pain as in this case is protected from tort liability "to ensure that we do not stifle public debate" (*Snyder v. Phelps*, 2011).

Obscene speech (which includes writing, pictures, movies, and live actions) is outside the scope of the First Amendment, so government action to restrict or prohibit obscenity is not subject to the same heightened scrutiny as protected forms of speech. The Supreme Court most often has assumed that obscenity is unworthy of protection, rather than justified the point. In a case involving the restriction of adult theaters, however, it offered a few reasons: Because there may be some connection between obscene material and crime, the state may regulate the former in the hope of preventing the latter. Further, the presence of obscenity in the community injures the community as a whole by polluting the public environment and by intruding on unwilling recipients. In terms of the theories supporting the protection of free speech generally, material that is truly obscene contributes neither to public debate about significant issues nor (in the middle-class sensibilities of the justices) to legitimate personal growth or self-expression.

While the Court has long held the view that obscenity is unprotected, it has had much more difficulty in drawing the line between unprotected obscene speech and protected nonobscene speech. *Hustler* magazine may be a mix of penetrating social satire and harmless entertainment to one person but a disgusting appeal to animal lust to another. Perhaps the most famous definition of any legal concept came from Justice Potter Stewart, who said he could not define what it means to be obscene but "I know it when I see it" (*Jacobellis v. Ohio*, 1964). But in addition to their private predilections, the justices have formulated a series of tests to try to determine what is obscene, and the substantial disagreement among the justices shows how hard it can be to give specific meaning to general constitutional propositions.

The most recent test articulated by the Court came in *Miller v. California* (1973). The test for obscenity has three parts:

(a) whether the average person, applying contemporary community standards, would find that the work, taken as a whole, appeals to the prurient interest; (b) whether the work depicts or describes, in a patently offensive way, sexual conduct specifically defined by the applicable state law; and (c) whether the work, taken as a whole, lacks serious literary, artistic, political, or scientific value.

The first part of the test distinguishes between a "shameful or morbid" interest in sex (a prurient interest) and "normal, healthy sexual desires," as the Court said in a later case. This element essentially defines a decision-making procedure. States have wide latitude to describe what constitutes unprotected obscenity by defining "contemporary community standards" in a statute or ordinance and then leaving it up to a jury to determine whether a particular book or adult movie, for example, violates the standards. The state also can define the relevant community;

there is no constitutional requirement that a national community be used or even that any particular community be defined in advance for the jury. So the producer of a film might be subjected to different standards in, say, the laid-back, anything-goes community of Hollywood and a straight-laced village in the Bible Belt. The community standards test is particularly problematic for materials published on the Internet that reach every community in America. In reviewing the Child Online Protection Act's attempt to prevent children from viewing obscene material on the Internet, only a plurality of justices upheld the statute's use of community standards; as Justice Breyer noted in his concurrence, by using local community standards, "the most puritan of communities" would be able to effectively prohibit the dissemination of material nationwide (*Ashcroft v. American Civil Liberties Union*, 2002).

The second element is similarly vague, but the Court in *Miller* helpfully provided a few examples of patently offensive sexual conduct: "(a) patently offensive representations or descriptions of ultimate sexual acts, normal or perverted, actual or simulated, (b) patently offensive representations or descriptions of masturbation, excretory functions, and lewd exhibitions of the genitals." Of course, the examples are filled with ambiguity: Where is the line between a thoughtful and expressive description of masturbation, a description of masturbation fit for a trashy novel, and a patently offensive description of masturbation?

Finally, the third element explicitly looks to the value of the work. If a book has serious literary, artistic, political, or scientific merit, it is not obscene. This judgment, unlike the first two, is not made with reference to a local community's standards. If, for example, a group of distinguished critics find a book to have literary value, it is not obscene under the third element even if no one in a local community agrees.

One related type of unprotected speech is sexually explicit material containing pictures of children that might not be obscene under *Miller*. Because the state has an unusually strong interest in protecting children from sexual exploitation, in *New York v. Ferber* (1982) the Court unanimously held that a state could criminalize the distribution of materials containing sexual performances by children under the age of sixteen. The prohibition on distribution accomplishes the state's goal indirectly, by creating a tremendous disincentive to use children in this way in the first place. Virtual child pornography involving sexually explicit, computer-generated images of children is protected, however, because the connection between the images and harm to actual children is remote (*Ashcroft v. Free Speech Coalition*, 2002).

Another form of unprotected speech is speech that incites violence. The story begins with Holmes's remark that "The most stringent protection of free speech would not protect a man in falsely shouting fire in a theater and causing a panic." Words, in such a case, "have all the effect of force." The issue in any particular case is whether the words create "a clear and present danger" of harm.

The metaphor of a crowded theater is powerful, but the issue has arisen most often in cases in which a speaker advocates an act directed against the government. First during World War I and the Red Scare of 1919–1920, then during the McCarthyism of the 1950s, and up to the present governments have prosecuted their opponents for such potentially dangerous speech. Despite Holmes's limitation of unprotected speech to speech that carries a clear and present danger, the Supreme Court was all too willing to exclude a variety of forms of political expression from the protection of the First Amendment.

During the First World War era, the government prosecuted persons who opposed the war effort, radicals sympathetic to the Russian revolutionaries, and other political dissidents. The prevailing doctrine was the "bad tendency" test, under which words that could be seen as tending to produce a bad result were unprotected, even if in the context the bad result was extremely unlikely to come about. In *Abrams v. United States* (1919), for example, Abrams and his cohorts scattered leaflets on the streets of New York denouncing the U.S. role in opposition to the Russian Revolution and calling for a general strike in response. They were convicted under a wartime act that punished resistance to the war effort, and despite the absurdity of the prospect that their leafleting would lead to massive unrest, resistance, or interference with wartime production, the Court upheld their conviction. Holmes dissented:

> [W]e should be eternally vigilant against attempts to check the expression of opinions that we loathe and believe to be fraught with death, unless they so imminently threaten immediate interference with the lawful and pressing purposes of the law that an immediate check is required to save the country.

In the 1950s the Court employed a balancing version of the clear and present danger test that weighed the gravity of the harm threatened against the likelihood of its occurrence. In *Dennis v. United States* (1951) defendants were convicted of conspiring to organize the Communist Party of the United States, the goal of which was to overthrow the government by force. Because the harm threatened (violent overthrow) was great, even though the defendants were improbably far from achieving it, their speech was unprotected incitement under the First Amendment. In *Yates v. United States* (1957), on the other hand, Communist Party officers were convicted only of advocating and teaching the need for the violent overthrow of the government. Unlike in *Dennis*, their conduct was directed at the teaching of doctrine, not the organizing of action, so they could not constitutionally be convicted.

Finally, in 1969 in *Brandenburg v. Ohio* the Court rejected the bad tendency and balancing approaches in favor of a standard that limited unprotected speech to speech that imminently threatened unlawfulness. The Court held that it would be unconstitutional "to forbid or proscribe advocacy of the use of force or of law violation except where such advocacy is directed to inciting or producing imminent lawless action and is likely to incite or produce such actions." Racist speech made during a rally of hooded, gun-toting Ku Klux Klan members was protected because it was not "preparing a group for violent action." Advocacy of any idea is protected speech, and advocacy of any action is protected unless it was made with the intent to cause a violation of the law and it is very likely to do so.

As during World War I, the Red Scare of the 1920s, and the McCarthyism of the 1950s, the First Amendment has been under stress because of the threat of terrorism since the attacks of September 11, 2001. The need to increase security against future attacks and the prospect of a war on terrorism of indefinite duration against shadowy enemies within and outside the United States pose new challenges for free speech and other civil liberties. One sign of the maturation of our understanding of the importance of constitutional protections even in wartime is that government overreaction has been limited, compared to earlier eras. As legal scholar Geoffrey Stone pointed out, Eugene Debs, who had received almost a million votes as the Socialist Party candidate for president in 1912, was arrested, tried, and convicted during World War I for obstructing army recruitment, but it was implausible to consider an analogous prosecution of Democratic presidential candidate Howard Dean in 2004 for opposing the Iraq War. After the July 7, 2005, subway bombings in London, British prime minister Tony Blair proposed new laws that would make "condoning, glorifying or justifying" terrorism a crime and that would enable the government to shut down mosques used "for fomenting terrorism." No comparable measures were seriously considered in the United States, and they would surely be unconstitutional under the *Brandenburg* test.

First Amendment protections are never entirely secure, however, particularly in times of crisis. The Bush administration proposed and Congress quickly enacted the USA PATRIOT Act to expand the government's investigative powers, the administration asserted new executive powers in wartime (discussed in Chapter 2), and, immediately after 9/11, it detained thousands of noncitizens without specific evidence of their ties to the terrorists. The PATRIOT Act was followed by other statutes that expanded the powers of the National Security Agency to monitor communications in secret, and the Obama administration used those powers aggressively. Yet the resilience of the civil liberties tradition was demonstrated by the controversy these measures generated among the public, in Congress, and in the courts. Professor Stone aptly quoted Justice Louis Brandeis, who wrote in *Whitney v. California* (1927) "fear breeds repression" but "courage is the secret to liberty."

How Does the Constitution Protect Freedom of Religion?

Americans think of freedom of religion as one of our most important liberties, and it is. The Constitution contains three provisions on religious liberty. Article VI provides that "no religious test shall ever be required as a qualification to any office or public trust under the United States." At the time of its drafting this was an extraordinary innovation; it was common in England and throughout the colonies to require that office holders swear their belief in a particular religion as a requirement of public office. The First Amendment contains two clauses that speak to different components of freedom of religion: "Congress shall make no law respecting an establishment of religion, or prohibiting the free exercise thereof. . . . " The two religion clauses are referred to as the *establishment clause* and the *free exercise clause*. (As with the free speech clause, although the religion clauses expressly limit the power of the Congress they have been applied to all activities of government, federal and state.)

At a basic level, the establishment clause and the free exercise clause have been interpreted to protect religious liberty in different but complementary ways. The establishment clause prevents the government from establishing a state religion or using the powers of the government to support a particular religion, and the free exercise clause prohibits the government from intruding on individual religious choices. By forbidding state support of religion, the establishment clause gives greater latitude to an individual's exercise of religious choice, and by committing religious belief and practice to the realm of individual choice, the free exercise clause reduces the possibility that religion will become an area of state power.

The Supreme Court noted the interaction of the establishment clause and the free exercise clauses in *Hosanna-Tabor Evangelical Lutheran Church and School v. Equal Employment Opportunity Commission* (2012). Cheryl Perich, a teacher at a church school, developed narcolepsy and took a disability leave. When she tried to return to work the school told her that she had been replaced. When she threatened legal action the school revoked her "call" to teach and terminated her. The Equal Employment Opportunity Commission sued on her behalf, claiming retaliation in violation of the Americans with Disabilities Act. The Court recognized a "ministerial exception" to the Act, under which the government could not intervene in the hiring and firing of a church's ministers, including "called" teachers at a religious school. Such intervention would violate the establishment clause because it would involve the government in ecclesiastical decisions and would violate the free exercise clause because it would limit a religious group's right to shape its faith through the appointment of its clergy.

Freedom of religion is so fundamental to our understanding of the American way of life that it may be surprising that the Supreme Court dealt with few religion cases until the middle of the twentieth century. By then, of course, the role of government had vastly expanded; states as well as the federal government regulated, intervened in, and financially supported a host of activities that previously had been wholly committed to the private sector. In doing so, the potential conflict between the establishment clause and the free exercise clause became apparent. If a state provides special education services to students in a religious school, isn't it supporting an establishment of religion? But if it does not, is it abridging the free exercise of religion by parents whose beliefs compel them to send their children to religious school?

To resolve conflicts like this we might think of the religion clauses as motivated by some guiding principles about the relationship between the government and religion. As usual in complex areas of the law, the principles won't necessarily be consistent or provide clear guides to deciding all the cases, but they can get us started.

A first principle is that religion is a realm of voluntary choice. A person can choose the faith she wishes to observe or can choose not to observe any faith at all. The state may neither compel nor encumber that choice. And support of religious institutions must be voluntary. Like the marketplace of ideas in the free speech area, there must be a marketplace of faith and practice, in which religions flourish or wither depending on their ability to attract supporters, free of state encumbrance or support.

A second principle is that religion and government are two separate spheres. This principle is broader than the prohibition on the establishment of a state religion. The government should avoid involvement or entanglement in religious affairs entirely. The strongest application of this principle is that the state may not use tax dollars to fund religious institutions or religious activities.

A third principle is that the government should be neutral as to religion. It should not favor or disfavor one religion over another, nor should it give preferences to religious activities over nonreligious activities, or vice versa.

All of these principles have circulated through the Supreme Court's attempts to interpret the religion clauses. The Court focuses separately on the establishment and free exercise clauses, and the standards used to evaluate government action under each clause have changed over time.

The establishment clause has an indisputable core meaning: The government may not establish an official religion. This seems like an obviously correct principle to us, but many other countries have official religions, even liberal democracies such as the United Kingdom. A corollary to that principle is that government may not provide its support to religious institutions by providing financial aid, public services, or official endorsement. As Justice Black explained in *Everson v. Board of Education of Ewing Township* in 1947, "In the words of Jefferson, the clause against establishment of religion by law was intended to erect 'a wall of separation between church and State.'" More recently, Justice Stevens emphasized "the impact of religious strife on the decisions of our forebears to migrate to this continent, and on the decisions of neighbors in the Balkans, Northern Ireland, and the Middle East to mistrust one another. Whenever we remove a brick from the wall that was designed to separate religion and government, we increase the risk of religious strife and weaken the foundation of our democracy" (dissenting in *Zelman v. Simmons-Harris*, 2002).

Under this standard, some cases are easy. The state cannot aid an established church, so if a Baptist church burns down, state funds cannot be appropriated to rebuild it. But as the fire is burning, can a municipal fire department put out the fire, or would that be using tax money and public employees to aid religion? The answer obviously is that the fire department can provide the same level of service to a religious institution as to a nonreligious institution. The relevant legal category when the fire alarm rings is not "church" but rather "building on fire," so extinguishing the fire doesn't breach the wall of separation, even though tax dollars are being used to aid a religious activity. Putting out a fire doesn't entangle the state in religious matters or violate the state's neutrality toward religion.

The Court has said that "the line of separation, far from being a 'wall,' is a blurred, indistinct, and variable barrier, depending on all the circumstances of a particular relationship" (*Lemon v. Kurtzman*, 1971). Harder cases involve the many ways that government supports or otherwise influences social institutions and community life. It defined the bounds of permissible government activities in *Lemon v. Kurtzman*, describing when government activity that affected religion did not violate the establishment clause: "First, the statute must have a secular legislative purpose; second, its principal or primary effect must be one that neither advances nor inhibits religion; finally, the statute must not foster an excessive entanglement with religion." The purpose-effect-entanglement test provides some guidance but has been difficult to apply. (Some scholars have said the *Lemon* test was appropriately named.) Most of the justices on the current Court have criticized the *Lemon* test without expressly repudiating it. As Justice Scalia noted, "When we wish to strike down a practice it forbids, we invoke it; when we wish to uphold a practice it forbids, we ignore it entirely" (*Lamb's Chapel v. Center Moriches Union Free School District*, 1993).

Since the late 1990s, a majority of the Court has emphasized the neutrality principle rather than the possibility of entanglement or the perception of state endorsement of religion. In a world of pervasive government benefits and services, the government does not violate the establishment clause by providing financial support or other aid to religious entities on the same basis as it does to others. Where a state university used the proceeds of a student activities fee to fund student publications, it was prevented by the establishment clause from discriminating against religious publications; in funding those publications, it was not endorsing a viewpoint or aiding religion but only treating religious and nonreligious groups the same (*Rosenberger v. Rector and Visitors of the University of Virginia*, 1995).

One area that has generated a large number of cases is public aid to nonpublic—principally religious—schools. Applying the *Lemon* test, the Court held the state could not pay for textbooks in secular subjects in religious schools but it could lend textbooks for secular subjects to religious school students, and it could not pay the salaries of teachers of secular subjects but it could provide public school personnel for speech and hearing tests at nonpublic schools and remedial and guidance services to religious school students at neutral sites. With its new emphasis on neutrality, the Court has upheld sending public school teachers to parochial schools for remedial instruction of disadvantaged children and a program that loaned library books, computers, and other educational materials to nonpublic schools.

The most contentious issue has concerned school voucher programs, in which the state provides financial aid to students that can be used to pay tuition at nonpublic schools. Ohio enacted a voucher program for the city of Cleveland under which parents could enroll their children in any school and receive tuition aid according to financial need. In fact,

96 percent of the schools receiving benefits from the program were parochial schools. Nevertheless, a majority of the Court, in an opinion by Chief Justice Rehnquist, held that the program did not violate the establishment clause (*Zelman v. Simmons-Harris*, 2002). Looking at Cleveland's entire system of public education, not just the voucher program, he regarded the program as "neutral in all respects toward religion." Justice Souter in dissent argued that the issue was the voucher program, not the entire education system, and the program was not neutral, because it allowed the use of tax money "for teaching the covenant with Israel and Mosaic law in Jewish schools, the primacy of the Apostle Peter and the Papacy in Catholic schools, the truth of reformed Christianity in Protestant schools, and the revelation to the Prophet in Muslim schools."

Another area of continuing controversy has involved public displays of religious significance. The core of the establishment clause, of course, is that the government may not sponsor or promote religious activities, but the Supreme Court has allowed governments to permit or engage in activities that less obviously endorse one religion. Legislative sessions and other public meetings long have opened with a prayer, and the Court has interpreted the establishment clause in line with that historical practice, even upholding invocations that are explicitly sectarian and given only by Christian ministers in a town (*Town of Greece v. Galloway*, 2014). In a number of cases the Court evaluated holiday displays on public property under what became known as the "plastic reindeer doctrine." Placing a nativity scene on the steps of a county courthouse constituted a government endorsement of religion in violation of the establishment clause, but a holiday display including a Christmas tree, a menorah, and a sign celebrating a "Salute to Liberty" or a Christmas display including plastic reindeer pulling Santa's sleigh did not because it was a celebration of the holiday season (*Lynch v. Donnelly*, 1984; *Allegheny County v. ACLU*, 1989).

The display of the Ten Commandments has become the most controversial type of public display with a potentially religious message. In 2005 the Supreme Court addressed the issue in a pair of cases. In *McCreary County v. ACLU of Kentucky* the Court concluded that the display of the Ten Commandments in county courthouses, first by themselves and then, to forestall litigation, accompanied by other historical and religious texts, had a religious rather than a secular purpose. In placing one of the exhibits, for example, county officials noted that the Kentucky House of Representatives had once adjourned with a Christian flourish "in remembrance and honor of Jesus Christ, the Prince of Ethics." Although the counties claimed a secular purpose of emphasizing the historical significance of the Ten Commandments as the basis of our laws, in light of the nature of the display and their statements and actions the Court regarded that claim as a sham. In *Van Orden v. Perry*, on the other hand, a different majority of the Court (with Justice Breyer providing the deciding vote in each case) upheld the display of a Ten Commandments monument on the Texas State Capitol grounds. The monument was one of seventeen monuments and twenty-one historical markers on the grounds representing the state's political and legal history, and it had been placed by a secular organization forty years earlier and thus outside the scope of the current controversy over the Ten Commandments, so it need not be read as a state endorsement of religion. Not every display of a religious symbol violated the establishment clause; as the Court noted, its own courtroom included a depiction of Moses holding the tablets among a frieze depicting other lawgivers. The Ten Commandments have historical significance as a source of law and morality, and in evaluating their display, context is crucial.

The basic principle of the free exercise clause is as clear as the basic principle of the establishment clause. As Justice Robert Jackson said in *West Virginia State Board of Education v. Barnette* (1943):

> If there is any fixed star in our constitutional constellation, it is that no official, high or petty, can prescribe what shall be orthodox in politics, nationalism, religion, or other matters of opinion or force citizens to confess by word or act their faith therein.

Barnette involved a West Virginia statute that required all schoolchildren to recite the Pledge of Allegiance to the Flag. The Barnette children were expelled from school because, as Jehovah's Witnesses, their religious convictions prevented them from paying homage to a graven image. In its decision—on Flag Day, June 14, 1943—the Court held the statute violated the free exercise clause. The state could not punish the Barnettes for acting in a manner required by their conscience.

The *Barnette* principle, that government may not compel acts of conscience, is well established and has been applied in other situations, forbidding, for example, mandatory prayer (vocal or silent) or Bible reading in school. But most free exercise disputes involve acts of religious conscience that violate laws not directed at the acts themselves or that disadvantage the actor from receiving a government benefit. Suppose, for example, that a person's religion takes literally the biblical injunction of "an eye for an eye" so that, having been partially blinded in an automobile accident, he pokes out the eye of the other driver. Can he be prosecuted for following the dictates of his religion?

The justices have disagreed about the standard to be applied to decide cases like this. In *Sherbert v. Verner* (1963) the Court devised a balancing test. If a challenger showed that a law substantially burdened the free exercise of her religion, the government must offer a compelling interest that justified the law. The Court would then balance the burden on free exercise against the government interest and the extent to which it would be harmed by exempting the challenger. In *Sherbert* the Court struck down a rule that denied unemployment compensation benefits to a Seventh-Day Adventist who refused to work on Saturday. The rule imposed a significant burden on her religious exercise, and the state's interest—to prevent fraudulent claims—could be served in other ways.

In *Employment Division v. Smith* (1990), however, a changed Court held that "generally applicable, religion-neutral laws that have the effect of burdening a particular religious practice need not be justified by a compelling governmental interest"—even if the law has the incidental effect of burdening a particular religious practice. If a law is not directed at religious practice and applies to all persons equally, it does not violate the free exercise clause. In *Smith*, drug rehabilitation counselors who were fired because they used peyote in a religious ceremony were not entitled to state unemployment benefits because they violated a rule that was neutral as to religion and of general application to all workers.

The balancing test of *Sherbert v. Verner* seems much more accommodating to religious liberty than the *Smith* test, but the Court has been markedly unwilling to invalidate legislation on a free exercise basis under either test. Under *Sherbert*, for example, it upheld the requirement that an Amish employer participate in the Social Security system despite religious objections, refused to grant an orthodox Jewish officer an exemption to the Air Force's ban on wearing nonuniform clothing, including a yarmulke, and upheld the provision of the tax laws that denies tax-exempt status to schools that discriminate on the basis of race, even if the discrimination is religiously motivated. In fact, the Court has held in only a few situations that the free exercise clause exempts individuals from generally applicable laws because of their religious convictions. One type of case involves an involuntary profession of belief, as in the flag salute cases such as *Barnette*; those cases involve free speech claims as well as religion claims. A second type of case concerns employment situations, as in *Sherbert* and *Smith*. Following *Sherbert*, the Court held that a state is required to exempt persons from at least some of the conditions for receiving unemployment compensation benefits if they cannot satisfy the conditions because of religious convictions, and in *Hosanna-Tabor Evangelical Lutheran Church and School v. EEOC* the Court used the free exercise clause and the establishment clause to grant religious institutions an exception from employment discrimination laws in the hiring and firing of their clergy. A third type of case involves laws that on their face discriminate against religious institutions; for example, the Court struck down a Missouri state program that reimbursed nonprofit groups for purchasing playground surfaces made from recycled scrap tires but expressly excluded churches or religious schools from the program (*Trinity Lutheran Church of Columbia v. Comer*, 2017). The final exception is the singular case of *Wisconsin v. Yoder* (1972). There the Court held that Wisconsin could not require Amish parents to send their children to school beyond the eighth grade in violation of their religious beliefs. The Court later characterized this decision as resting not only on the free exercise clause but also on the expanded right of privacy, which is discussed in the next section. The state's compelling interest was in assuring the development of adolescents as citizens and members of society, but the combination of formal schooling through the eighth grade and the training Amish children received at home and in their community was deemed to satisfy the state's interests.

What Other Rights Are Protected by the Constitution?

The Constitution protects many other important rights. Some of the protections are now archaic. The Third Amendment prevents the government from ordering that homeowners provide quarters for soldiers in peacetime, or in wartime except as provided by law, but it has been a very long time since the government has even tried. Other protections have only recently been defined. It was not until 2008 that the Supreme Court definitively interpreted the Second Amendment to guarantee an individual's right to own guns. The Second Amendment's unusual structure had generated much debate because, like few other constitutional provisions, it contained both a prefatory clause ("A well regulated militia, being necessary to the security of a free state") and an operative clause ("the right of the people to keep and bear arms, shall not be infringed"). Did the prefatory clause modify the operative clause, so the right to bear arms applied only to those in the militia? In *District of Columbia v. Heller* (2008) the Court ruled that the right was an individual right unrelated to militia service, so a District of Columbia law banning the possession of handguns was unconstitutional.

The constitutional provisions that protect individual rights are vague, but the conduct they protect is usually reasonably related to the text of the particular constitutional provision that authorizes the protection. For example, where the First Amendment protects freedom of speech, it is not too hard to see how that can be expanded to encompass nonverbal communicative acts such as burning an American flag.

But what about some of the more unusual and controversial liberties that the Supreme Court has decided are protected by the Constitution? Where does the Constitution guarantee the right to obtain an abortion, to engage in sexual behavior, to purchase contraceptives, or to travel from state to state?

The answer is: everywhere and nowhere. Beyond the specific protections of provisions such as the First Amendment and the due process clause, the Supreme Court has defined constitutional protection for a variety of fundamental rights, including the right to travel, the right to vote, and the right of access to the courts. The Court also has recognized a right of privacy as inherent in the Constitution and in our system of "ordered liberty"; the right of privacy includes the right of parents to care for their children, the right to control one's sexual activity and reproduction, and the right to make medical decisions. These rights protect a range of personal actions and intimate associations that are otherwise not protected by particular constitutional provisions. The most controversial of these, of course, is a woman's right to choose to have an abortion.

The Constitution doesn't mention privacy, travel, or sexual activity. Where do the Supreme Court justices find a textual basis for these rights?

Over a series of cases, the Court has concluded that particular constitutional guarantees of liberties are sources of "emanations" or "penumbral rights" that are not found explicitly in the text. Different justices emphasize different sources, but the most prominent include the following:

- The First Amendment protects freedom of expression. To properly exercise that right, people need to be able to study, learn, and be exposed to ideas as they choose.

- The First Amendment also protects the freedom to associate to achieve political objectives. Freedom of association can be effective only if a person has a right to keep his or her associations and activities private.

- The Fourth Amendment limits the government's powers in the criminal process by, for example, prohibiting the police from searching a person's belongings without a warrant or an emergency. This rule is designed to prevent intrusive police behavior, but the behavior is intrusive in large part because people have a penumbral right to personal privacy.

- The Ninth Amendment states: "The enumeration, in the Constitution of certain rights, shall not be construed to deny or disparage others retained by the people." There is considerable historical dispute about the meaning of the amendment, but some justices have interpreted it as assuming the existence of fundamental rights not specified elsewhere in the Constitution.

When the Court puts together all of these individual rights, the whole is greater than the sum of its parts. The extension of these textually based rights creates a new right of privacy, grounded in a vision of personhood read into the Constitution when it is understood as a whole. As constitutional scholar Laurence Tribe notes, it is not clear if the right of privacy is a "unitary concept" or a "bag of unrelated goodies." However it is framed, it has generated some of the most ringing statements of human freedom ever made by the justices. To quote them indicates the importance of the constitutional right of privacy.

> Justice Louis Brandeis in dissent in *Olmstead v. United States*, 1928:
> The makers of our Constitution undertook to secure conditions favorable to the pursuit of happiness. . . . They conferred, as against the government, the right to be let alone—the most comprehensive of rights and the right most valued by civilized men.

> Justice James McReynolds in *Meyer v. Nebraska*, 1923:
> Without doubt, liberty denotes not merely freedom from bodily restraint but also the right of the individual to contract, to engage in any of the common occupations of life, to acquire useful knowledge, to marry, establish a home and bring up children, to worship God according to the dictates of his own conscience, and generally to enjoy those privileges long recognized at common law as essential to the orderly pursuit of happiness by free men.

> Justice John Paul Stevens in dissent in *Meachum v. Fano*, 1976:
> I had thought it self-evident that all men were endowed by their Creator with liberty as one of the cardinal unalienable rights. It is that basic freedom which the Due Process Clause protects, rather than the particular rights or privileges conferred by specific laws or regulations.

The two most important early cases establishing the right of privacy are *Meyer v. Nebraska* (1923) and *Pierce v. Society of Sisters* (1925). In *Meyer* the state of Nebraska, in a burst of nativist fervor, had forbidden the teaching of foreign languages before the eighth grade. In *Pierce* the state of Oregon required all students to attend public schools. In both cases the Court struck down the legislation as interfering with "the calling of modern language teachers, with the opportunities of pupils to acquire knowledge, and with the power of parents to control the education of their own." In a companion case to *Pierce* the Court applied its holding to nonreligious private schools, demonstrating that the basis of the decision was not freedom of religion but a broader right to be free of state control in making personal decisions.

Meyer and *Pierce* demonstrated the importance of parental concern for their children's education. This is a part of a broader interest in family relations, including marriage, that is part of the right to privacy. In *Loving v. Virginia* (1967) the Court invalidated a Virginia law that prohibited marriage between blacks and whites, and in *Boddie v. Connecticut* (1971) it held that a Connecticut law that required applicants for a divorce to pay a filing fee could not be applied to poor people who could not afford to pay. Both cases illustrate how the right of privacy has developed. In each case the Court identified another doctrinal ground for the decision (equal protection in *Loving* and due process in *Boddie*), but in each case the opinions also recognized that marriage is a fundamental right, so the state cannot unduly restrict a person's ability to get into or out of a marriage.

A more recent pair of cases demonstrates how the Court has developed the right of privacy and how the thinking of the justices can change in a relatively short period of time. Michael Hardwick was charged with violating Georgia's sodomy law by committing a sexual act with another man in his bedroom. In *Bowers v. Hardwick* in 1986, the Court held that the law was constitutional. Justice White's majority opinion defined the issue as whether there was a fundamental constitutional right to engage in homosexual conduct, found that the proscription of homosexual acts had "ancient roots," and declined to extend the right of privacy that far. In 2003, however, a different majority of the Court reached a different conclusion. In *Lawrence v. Texas*, Justice Kennedy's opinion criticized the historical basis of *Bowers*, noted changing public attitudes toward homosexuality and the need for sexual autonomy (including a controversial reliance on sources of international law), and held that *Bowers* was wrongly decided and should be overruled. Justice White had incorrectly stated the issue as the right to engage in homosexual acts, where the real issue is the constitutionality of statutes that "touch upon the most private human conduct, sexual behavior, and in the most private of places, the home." "Liberty," according to Justice Kennedy, "protects the person from unwarranted government intrusions into a dwelling or other private places. In our tradition the State is not omnipresent in the home. . . . Liberty presumes an autonomy of self that includes freedom of thought, belief, expression, and certain intimate conduct." Accordingly, John Lawrence and Tyron Garner, the defendants who were convicted under a Texas statute criminalizing homosexual acts, were "entitled to respect for their private lives. The State cannot demean their existence or control their destiny by making their private sexual conduct a crime."

The challenges of defining individual rights and determining the proper role of the courts in applying them were sharply posed in the series of cases concerning same-sex marriage. In 1996, as some states were considering legalizing same-sex marriage, Congress enacted the Defense of Marriage Act (DOMA), part of which defined "marriage" to exclude same-sex marriages. The definition controlled the application of more than a thousand federal laws, including the tax law. Edith Windsor and Thea Spyer were married in Canada, a marriage recognized by their state of residence, New York. Spyer died and left her entire estate to Windsor, who was unable to claim the marital exemption from the federal estate tax because of DOMA, so she paid the tax and sued for a refund.

In *United States v. Windsor* (2013), Justice Kennedy's opinion for the Court majority first noted that marriage has traditionally been a subject of state, not federal, law, and by recognizing same-sex marriage, New York conferred on gay people "a dignity and status of immense import" and "enhanced the recognition, dignity, and protection of the class in their own community." DOMA, by contrast, "seeks to injure the very class New York seeks to protect." "The avowed purpose and practical effect of the law . . . are to impose a disadvantage, a separate status, and so a stigma" on those who enter into same-sex marriages. Accordingly, the statute was unconstitutional as "a deprivation of the liberty of the person protected by the Fifth Amendment to the Constitution," a liberty that was made even more specific and "better understood and preserved" by the Fourteenth Amendment's guarantee of equal protection. That liberty "withdraws from Government the power to degrade or demean the way this law does."

Justice Scalia issued a scathing dissent that posed sharply the issue of the Court's role:

This case is about power in several respects. It is about the power of our people to govern themselves, and the power of this Court to pronounce the law. Today's opinion aggrandizes the latter with the predictable consequence of diminishing the former. . . . The Court's errors on both points spring forth from the same diseased root: an exalted conception of the role of this institution in America.

He excoriated the vagueness of the constitutional support for the majority's opinion. Was it about federalism, suggesting that DOMA had invaded the states' traditional power to regulate marriage? Or was it about equal protection, although the majority suggests that equal protection only makes some other grant of liberty more specific? Or was it about a penumbral right through the due process clause, a right the majority refrained from invoking?

Then came *Obergefell v. Hodges* (2015). James Obergefell and John Arthur met, fell in love, and established a decades-long committed relationship. In 2011 John was diagnosed with ALS, or Lou Gehrig's disease, a debilitating, progressive illness with no cure. James and John wanted to commit to one another and marry before John died. They flew from their home in Ohio to Maryland, where same-sex marriage was legal; they were wed in a medical transport plane sitting on the tarmac because it was too difficult for John to move. He died three months later. Because Ohio did not recognize their marriage, James could not be listed as the surviving spouse on John's death certificate, rendering them, as the Supreme Court said, "strangers even in death." James sued to be shown as the surviving spouse on John's death certificate.

The Supreme Court held that the Fourteenth Amendment's due process clause and equal protection clause required states to issue marriage licenses to same-sex couples and to recognize such marriages performed in other states. Justice Kennedy drew four principles from the Court's privacy cases:

A first premise of the Court's relevant precedents is that the right to personal choice regarding marriage is inherent in the concept of individual autonomy.

A second principle in this Court's jurisprudence is that the right to marry is fundamental because it supports a two-person union unlike any other in its importance to the committed individuals.

A third basis for protecting the right to marry is that it safeguards children and families and thus draws meaning from related rights of childrearing, procreation, and education.

Fourth and finally, this Court's cases and the Nation's traditions make clear that marriage is a keystone of our social order.

Applying these principles, he concluded that the historical discrimination against gay people could not be squared with the contemporary understanding of liberty:

The limitation of marriage to opposite-sex couples may long have seemed natural and just, but its inconsistency with the central meaning of the fundamental right to marry is now manifest. With that knowledge must come the recognition that laws excluding same-sex couples from the marriage right impose stigma and injury of the kind prohibited by our basic charter.

Four justices dissented, principally on the basis that the majority stepped beyond its judicial role. Chief Justice Roberts recognized that there were strong arguments in favor of Obergefell's position but found them to be irrelevant:

This Court is not a legislature. Whether same-sex marriage is a good idea should be of no concern to us. Under the Constitution, judges have power to say what the law is, not what it should be. . . . The majority's decision is an act of will, not legal judgment. The right it announces has no basis in the Constitution or this Court's precedent.

Justice Scalia was characteristically blunt:

Today's decree says that my Ruler, and the Ruler of 320 million Americans coast-to-coast, is a majority of the nine lawyers on the Supreme Court. . . . This practice of constitutional revision by an unelected committee of nine, always accompanied (as it is today) by extravagant praise of liberty, robs the People of the most important liberty they asserted in the Declaration of Independence and won in the Revolution of 1776: the freedom to govern themselves.

The area in which perhaps the broadest expansion of the right to privacy has come, and the area in which it has generated the most heat, is in reproductive rights. *Meyer* and *Pierce* concerned the government's power to control people's minds; the reproductive rights cases, like *Bowers* and *Lawrence*, concern the government's power to control a person's body.

Two cases in the 1960s and 1970s transformed the right to privacy and brought the Court full force into the area of reproductive rights. In *Griswold v. Connecticut* (1965) the executive director and the medical director of Planned Parenthood were convicted of giving advice to married couples on contraceptives, in violation of a Connecticut statute that forbade the use of contraceptives or the giving of advice on them. The defendants were allowed to raise in defense the right of married persons to use contraceptives, a right that the Court found not in a particular constitutional text but in the "penumbras [of specific guarantees of the Bill of Rights], formed by emanations from those guarantees that help give them life." The Court described the right to privacy in marriage as "older than the Bill of Rights—older than our political parties, older than our school system. Marriage is a coming together for better or for worse, hopefully enduring, and intimate to the degree of being sacred. . . . [I]t is an association for as noble a purpose as any involved in our prior decisions." Such a right, the Court concluded, was fundamental in a free society and could not be invaded by so broad a government regulation.

Griswold was followed by *Eisenstadt v. Baird* (1972), which made clear that the right to privacy in the area of reproduction was not limited to married couples. The defendant in *Eisenstadt* was convicted of violating state law by providing contraceptives to an unmarried woman. In overturning the conviction, the Court stated:

> Yet the marital couple is not an independent entity with a mind and heart of its own, but an association of two individuals each with a separate intellectual and emotional makeup. If the right to privacy means anything, it is the right of the *individual*, married or single, to be free from unwarranted governmental intrusion into matters so fundamentally affecting a person as the decision whether to bear or beget a child.

Griswold, Eisenstadt, and other contraceptive cases were a novel extension of the privacy doctrine but not too controversial in themselves. The storm broke in 1973 when the Court decided *Roe v. Wade* and concluded that the right of privacy is "broad enough to encompass a woman's decision whether or not to terminate her pregnancy." Subsequently the Supreme Court faced dozens of abortion cases, and the lower courts hundreds of cases, as states and the federal government struggled over accommodations, evasions, exceptions, and outright challenges to the Court's decision. And, of course, the ferment spilled outside the courtrooms into electoral politics, large demonstrations, picketing of abortion clinics, and even the murder of physicians who provided abortions to their patients.

Let's begin with a quick summary of the abortion rights cases in the Supreme Court. Most constitutional rights issues require the Court to weigh the interest of the affected individual against the interest that the government asserts in attempting to regulate the individual's conduct. In *Roe* the Court identified three interests. The woman's interest in deciding whether or not to terminate the pregnancy is an aspect of the interest in personal autonomy that extends from *Meyer* and *Pierce* through *Griswold* and *Eisenstadt*. The state has two interests in affecting that decision: Because abortion is a medical procedure, the state has an interest in seeing that the procedure is performed under conditions that ensure the patient's safety. The state also has an interest in protecting the fetus.

Because the decision to continue or terminate a pregnancy entails basic questions about control of a woman's life, the Court considered it to be a constitutionally fundamental right. Therefore, the state could regulate that right only if it had a compelling interest in doing so and if its regulations were narrowly tailored to achieve that interest. The state's interest in protecting the health of the mother is not compelling during the first trimester of pregnancy; until that point, the risks of abortion are less than the risk of normal childbirth. After the first trimester, the state may regulate abortions in a manner reasonably calculated to protect the mother's health by, for example, requiring that the procedure be performed by a qualified person in a licensed facility. Because the Court concluded that a fetus is not a person either for purposes of the Fourteenth Amendment or for other legal rules, the state's interest in protecting the fetus also is not compelling at the early stages of the pregnancy. When it becomes viable (i.e., capable of living outside its mother's womb) in the last trimester, however, the state has "logical and biological" justifications for protecting the fetus. Therefore, during the last trimester of the pregnancy, the state's compelling interest allows it to constitutionally prohibit abortions unless the life or health of the mother is endangered by continuing the pregnancy.

After the *Roe* decision, the legislatures in many states still attempted to restrict or regulate the right to abortion. The Court responded by applying the interest analysis in numerous cases. For example, the state could advance its interest in protecting the mother's health by requiring that abortions be performed only in hospitals or clinics that met specified safety standards, but it could not require that abortions be performed only in full-service hospitals; the former but not the latter requirement was reasonably designed to protect the mother's health. Although the government was required to honor a woman's right to an abortion, it was not required to enhance the exercise of the right; the federal government, for example, constitutionally could refuse to use Medicaid funds to pay for abortions.

Over the next twenty years, especially as the composition of the Court changed, the structure of the *Roe* interest analysis wavered. Finally, in *Planned Parenthood v. Casey* (1992), the Court seemed to settle the fundamental issue of abortion rights, at least for a time, as a plurality of the Court reaffirmed that the right to choose an abortion was fundamental but suggested that the compelling interest test leading to a trimester analysis in *Roe* might be abandoned in favor of a test that asked whether the state regulation imposed an "undue burden" on the woman's right. Unlike *Roe*'s trimester analysis, the undue burden test is heavily fact-intensive; the test directs courts to examine whether a state restriction on abortion has the purpose or effect of placing a substantial obstacle in the path of a woman seeking an abortion. In *Casey* itself, for example, a mandatory twenty-four-hour waiting period between the time a woman discussed the abortion with a physician and the procedure itself was held to not unduly burden her choice because the lower court had found only that it was particularly burdensome on some women, not unduly burdensome on all women. However, a requirement that a woman certify that she had notified her husband that she was to undergo an abortion was held unconstitutional because of extensive findings that the possibility of domestic violence or psychological abuse by the husband would deter many women from seeking an abortion. Similarly, in *Stenberg v. Carhart* (2000) the Court applied the principles of *Casey* to hold that Nebraska's ban, except in narrow circumstances, on certain late-term abortion procedures that the legislature described as "partial-birth abortion" was unconstitutional because it lacked an exception for the health of the mother and imposed an undue burden on the woman's choice of an abortion procedure. In *Whole Women's Health v. Hellerstedt* (2016) the Court struck down a Texas statute that required physicians performing abortions to have admitting privileges at a nearby hospital and that required abortion facilities to meet the same standards as ambulatory surgical centers. The statute would have forced many abortion providers to close and many women to be denied effective access to abortions; for example, 2 million women of reproductive age would live more than fifty miles from an abortion provider, and 750,000 would live more than two hundred miles from an abortion provider. This would place an undue burden on the right of Texas women to choose an abortion with little or no corresponding benefit in improving women's health and safety.

The abortion issue has generated hundreds of judicial opinions and pieces of legislation, political controversy, philosophical debate, and angry rhetoric. It would be impossible to review all of the law on the topic, much less the other dimensions of the issue. But because abortion is such a controversial topic, it is a good vehicle to summarize two of the most important points about constitutional law covered in this and the previous chapter.

First, where does the right to an abortion come from? More generally, how does the Court determine what the Constitution means? To those who argue for "strict construction" or "judicial restraint," this whole process seems like an unprincipled power grab. It's bad enough when the Court stretches the meaning of a single constitutional phrase, but here the justices seem to be slapping together a series of unrelated provisions to come up with the authority to declare as constitutional law their personal preferences about a controversial issue, unfettered by any particular constitutional text. In doing so, the unelected justices thwart the will of the democratic branches of government on issues such as protecting the rights of an unborn fetus.

This argument has some appeal to it. Surely there is nothing in the Constitution that spells out the right of privacy or the consequences for particular legislation such as abortion regulations. But that brings us back to the issue of the proper method of constitutional interpretation with which our discussion of constitutional law began. There is nothing in any provision of the Constitution that tells the Court how to decide a case. What the Court has done in creating the right of privacy is the same thing it does in other areas: It tries to make sense of the constitutional scheme, which inevitably involves interpreting specific provisions of the text, weighing one portion of the text against another, and considering judicial interpretations along with social, political, and economic developments subsequent to the adoption of the Constitution. In this area the Court has defined the common core of freedoms it sees as essential to our form of political community. The justices have not always agreed on the content of that core, but they generally have agreed that the process of attempting to establish it is a valid one.

Justices Sandra Day O'Connor, Anthony Kennedy, and David Souter, in the central opinion in *Casey*, engaged in this process of constructing an understanding of the Constitution. They tried to define what general principle underlay all of the previous privacy cases and concluded that

Our precedents "have respected the private realm of family life which the state cannot enter." These matters, involving the most intimate and personal choices a person may make in a lifetime, choices central to personal dignity and autonomy, are central to the liberty protected by the Fourteenth Amendment.

Accordingly, the abortion decision is so "intimate and personal" that the state cannot simply impose its view of the choice on a pregnant woman.

But this is antidemocratic, isn't it? In a sense, it is. That's what constitutional law is all about. The will of a temporary majority, the sentiments of the moment, a vote in the legislature, cannot upset basic constitutional guarantees. In determining the content of those guarantees, though, the Court is not free to ignore the sentiment of the moment; the Court's view of what rights are fundamental can be shaped by the temperament of the times as to what rights are fundamental.

That leads to the second point. Is constitutional law really law, or is this just a form of politics in which the judges enact their personal preferences? The issue was posed sharply by Justice Harry Blackmun's opinion in *Casey*. After pointing out the basic conflict between the majority and dissenting justices over whether *Roe* should be overruled, the author of the Court's opinion in *Roe* closed with an unusual personal statement:

> In one sense, the Court's approach is worlds apart from that of the Chief Justice and Justice Scalia [who dissented in *Casey*]. And yet, in another sense the distance between the two approaches is short—the distance is but a single vote.
>
> I am 83 years old. I cannot remain on the Court forever, and when I do step down, the confirmation process for my successor well may focus on the issue before us today. That, I regret, may be exactly where the choice between the two worlds will be made.

Blackmun was right in raising the political process of nomination and confirmation of justices as an essential element of the making of constitutional law. But he also pointed out what was remarkable about *Casey*:

> Make no mistake, the joint opinion of Justices O'Connor, Kennedy, and Souter is an act of personal courage and constitutional principle. In contrast to previous decisions in which Justices O'Connor and Kennedy postponed reconsideration of *Roe v. Wade*, the authors of the joint opinion today join Justice Stevens and me in concluding that "the essential holding of *Roe v. Wade* should be retained and once again reaffirmed."

Why was this considered an act of personal courage? All three were appointed by conservative Republican presidents (O'Connor and Kennedy by Reagan and Souter by George H. W. Bush). The O'Connor and Kennedy appointments were hailed by conservatives as presaging a shift away from liberal activism toward greater conservatism. (Souter's judicial politics were perceived as unknown to moderate at the time of his appointment.) And Kennedy was a devout Catholic. Yet all three ended up supporting abortion rights, not as a matter of personal preference but, as Blackmun said, "of constitutional principle."

What are we to make of this? Obviously, constitutional decision making is not all a matter of personal preference and political choice.

But surely it is part of that as well; even though these three justices favored abortion rights, on other issues they were noticeably more conservative than their liberal predecessors of the Warren Court era. The three justices were not bound by the constitutional text or the prior decisions of the Court; they could have read the text differently and concluded that *Roe* was wrongly decided, as Rehnquist and Scalia did. But they felt themselves to be bound by what they concluded was the correct interpretation of the Constitution and by the Court's prior decisions. They found in the prior privacy decisions a broad principle of personal liberty, and they concluded that the principle supported the continued application of a woman's right to choose expressed in *Roe*.

4

Your Day in Court

The Litigation Process

Litigation is the part of the legal system that people think of first. *See you in court. Don't make a federal case out of it. I'll take this all the way to the Supreme Court.* It is also the most complex part of the system. Some litigation is simple, such as a landlord-tenant dispute in small claims court. But much of litigation is vastly complex—armies of lawyers using arcane forms to fight about peripheral issues at great expense. How can lawyers make things so complicated? Does it have to be that way? The answers lie in the subject that law students find to be the most alien to their experience—civil procedure.

What Is Civil Procedure?

Litigation is the legal system's mechanism for resolving disputes between private parties; *civil procedure* is the body of law that structures the mechanism.

Litigation begins with a dispute between two or more people, companies, or institutions. Any kind of dispute can get the process going: an automobile accident, a broken contract, a sexual harassment claim by an employee, a civil rights claim against the government. If the disputants cannot settle their problem themselves, they can hire lawyers to negotiate, threaten, or otherwise try to resolve the dispute. If that doesn't work either, then it's off to court.

In the olden days, the king of England would sit and "hold court"; that is, he would sit in a public square, courtyard, or other open space and, among his other royal duties, dispense justice. John Doe, one of the king's subjects, would come complaining that Richard Roe, a neighbor, had injured Doe's ox, causing it to go lame. The king would summon Roe, hear what they each had to say, and decide whether Roe had to pay for the damage to the ox. (Doe and Roe are the traditional names for fictitious or anonymous litigants. The plaintiff in the famous abortion case *Roe v. Wade* followed this convention in styling herself Jane Roe, to conceal her true identity.) Over time, because the king had to issue royal proclamations, keep ambitious noblemen in line, fight wars, and do the other things kings do, he became too busy to hear all of his subjects' individual disputes, so he delegated the authority to do so to some of his royal officials. Over even more time, those officials institutionalized their function and became judges conducting litigation in courts.

This little story tells us much of what we need to know about litigation. Litigation is a process of authoritative dispute resolution by the government. People with problems present their arguments to officials empowered by the government to hear their arguments and resolve the dispute. By playing out some of the details and implications of the story, we can get a more complete understanding of civil procedure and the litigation process.

First, Doe doesn't have to go to court, and most of the time, people like Doe won't go to court. Maybe the ox isn't that badly injured and Doe doesn't want to be thought of as a disputatious person, so he decides to forget the whole thing. Or he talks to Roe and they reach an amicable understanding that Roe will let Doe borrow his ox when he needs it. Perhaps he wants to sue but he can't take time away from farming to travel to the king's court.

Even today, litigation is a rare event. People suffer many harms and indignities in everyday life, but relatively few of them end up in litigation. Litigation is an expensive, time-consuming, and emotionally draining process that is reserved for cases of real significance, measured in both social importance and money. The lawsuits discussed in this chapter and elsewhere in the book are only the tip of the iceberg of the social problems that the litigation process could address.

Second, litigation in countries under the influence of English law, including the United States, is an adversary process. The contending parties are in control of the process. Doe decides whether to bring his case before the king in court and what to say when he gets there. Roe has the opportunity to present his own facts and argument. The king's job is to listen to both and then decide.

Today the system is much more complicated, but it still is essentially adversarial. Civil litigation is a contest between the parties, and the lawyers for the parties have the primary role in shaping the litigation. The lawyers decide whom, where, and when to sue, what legal issues to raise, how to investigate the facts, and what witnesses and other evidence to present. The judge is the referee who makes sure that the lawyers follow the rules of the game and ultimately decides the case or supervises a jury in its decision of the case. The pure model of the adversary system is never entirely observed in practice, however. Especially in recent years, as the volume of cases has mounted and courts have become more crowded, judges have become more inclined to manage the cases in front of them by trying to narrow the issues, encourage settlement, and generally move things along.

Third, litigation always involves both finding facts and making or applying legal policies. When the king hears Doe say that Roe injured the ox, that's not the end of the story. Roe responds that he borrowed the ox from Doe but the ox appeared to be slightly lame when he borrowed it, even though the injury may have worsened when the ox stepped into a hole in Roe's field. The king has to decide when the ox was lamed and, if Roe did it, whether one who borrows an ox is responsible for an accidental injury to the borrowed animal. The same is true in every case today.

Fourth, civil litigation is not the only form of governmental dispute resolution. If Roe borrows Doe's ox and never returns it, Doe could ask the king to make Roe return it or pay for it; we would think of that as a civil action. But when the king hears the story, he might also take matters into his own hands and send Roe to jail for stealing the ox; that would be a criminal action. A dispute between two people, when the government's only role is to provide the system for dispute resolution (the courts), is civil litigation; typical remedies in civil cases are judgments for money damages or an order to do something (such as return the ox). When the government pursues the action and the potential sanction includes a fine, imprisonment, or even capital punishment, it is criminal litigation.

Finally, when the English king held court individually and decided his subjects' disputes himself, there was little need for rules about who could bring a complaint or what process they had to observe. The king was the fountainhead of justice and the principal authority figure in the realm, so if subjects had problems, they could simply go to him and present their stories. As courts became institutionalized, matters became more complicated. Today, courts would be overwhelmed if people simply walked in and voiced their complaints. To cope with this situation, legislatures and courts have devised rules to govern the litigation process. The main body of those rules is known as the law of civil procedure, which regulates every step of the civil litigation process from beginning to end.

Civil procedure is often the most difficult subject for law students to learn because it is so foreign to them. Everyone knows a little about promises, accidents, and ownership, so they can begin to understand the basics of contract law, tort law, and property law. But civil procedure is uniquely lawyers' law. This chapter tries to explain this alien body of civil procedure in the context of an account of the goals and values of procedural rules and litigation systems. There is a big picture here, involving basic values that we want the systems to serve. If you keep the big picture in mind—beginning with the simple hypothetical about Doe and Roe—the details are easier to digest.

Why Do We Need Civil Litigation and Civil Procedure?

The complaints are voiced in the news, on social media, and in political campaigns: Too much litigation. Too many lawyers. Everyone is getting sued for everything. No matter if you win or lose, it will cost you a fortune.

Much of the complaining is about the substantive law and not civil procedure or the litigation system. Commentators are concerned that tort law has gotten out of hand, for example. But a lot of the criticism is directed at procedural law and the lawyers and judges who implement it. Too cumbersome, too expensive, and too time-consuming. Does it have to be this way?

Go back to the beginning: Problems arise between people; many of the problems go away by themselves, and others are solved through negotiation, economic pressure, or other informal means. But there remains a residuum of disputes that the parties cannot solve for themselves. The litigation process provides a mechanism for resolving those disputes.

Consider what happens in subcultures in which litigation is unavailable. Among drug dealers, for example, disputes and claims of right are likely to be settled with drive-by shootings. But even aside from the threat of violence, the presence of unresolved grievances corrodes the public's sense of social order and well-being. In a fair, well-ordered, smoothly functioning society, problems get solved and injustices get corrected.

We don't need a complex, adversarial litigation system to resolve these disputes, however. We could adopt a much cheaper, simpler procedure—a judge could simply flip a coin to decide who wins. Or the judge could decide in favor of the party who slipped him the largest bribe. That system could resolve many more problems at a much lower cost. But a judicial system based on chance or corruption violates two of our fundamental beliefs about fairness: The courts should render decisions based on rules of substantive law that are fair, and they should do so after observing a fair process.

The first task of civil procedure, then, is to implement substantive rules of law and the values and policies on which they are based. When a legislature or court announces a rule of law, the rule acquires authority simply by virtue of being the law. People respect the law and usually obey it without the threat of sanctions for failing to do so. But litigation provides both a backup mechanism for those cases in which people do not conform their conduct to the requirements of the law and a forum in which the values and policies underlying the law can be articulated, reinforced, and worked out in new situations. Although no procedural system does this perfectly, a good system will reduce the possibility of error by removing the barriers to a focused decision-making process.

Civil procedure has a second task, too. We are offended by a dispute resolution system based on chance or corruption because it violates our understanding of fair process. Civil procedure has an independent value in creating a litigation process that conforms to our concepts of fairness. A fair procedural system provides a public affirmation of our belief in justice under law. It also affirms the dignity of the individual litigants and of others like them. Litigation, like electoral politics, is an arena in which individuals can assert their values and the significance of their own interests. "Having your day in court" is a cherished American tradition. The role of civil procedure is to make sure that the day in court is a meaningful one.

Under an adversary system as developed in the United States, fair process has several essential components. Parties to litigation must have an opportunity to adequately develop the facts and law in support of their cases and to present the relevant facts and legal arguments to the decision maker. In the typical case, the parties must have a right to have a jury determine the facts of the case. The jury and judge must be neutral to both parties, must listen to their evidence and arguments, and must decide the matter solely on the basis of the evidence and arguments presented. The parties must be able to have the adjudication reviewed for error by an appellate court and to have serious errors corrected. After review, the decision must have finality, so the parties cannot be subjected to endless relitigation of the same issues.

Finally, civil procedure has a third task. In order to be fair, civil procedure must be efficient. Too much fair process, like too much of any other good thing, is counterproductive. If litigants had unlimited opportunities to present their cases, litigation would become unbearably cumbersome, time-consuming, and expensive. Moreover, the litigation system is a social resource that the government provides to individual citizens. There is undeniable benefit to individuals and the society as a whole from a fair and effective litigation process, but how much justice can we afford? Accordingly, procedural rules have to balance the benefits of better process against the burdens of expense and delay.

Where Do Court Cases Come From?

Let's take a case and follow it through the litigation process. Litigation is so diverse that no case is typical, but the facts of this one are pretty ordinary. (The result was not, however; as we will see later, this case ended up in the U.S. Supreme Court.)

Harry and Kay Robinson and their two children, Eva and George, were moving from New York to a new home in Arizona. As they were driving their year-old Audi 100 LS along Interstate 44 in Oklahoma en route to Arizona, their car was struck from behind by a Ford Torino driven by a drunk driver going around 90 to 100 mph. The impact of the collision crushed the rear end of the Audi, jammed the doors shut, and punctured the car's gas tank. The Robinsons' car burst into flames, and Kay Robinson and the two children were severely burned.

It may be a little surprising that the Robinsons did not sue the drunk driver who struck their car. Instead, they sued Audi AG, the German company that manufactured the car; Volkswagen of America, Inc., the U.S. company that imported Audis; Seaway Volkswagen, Inc., the dealer in New York from whom they bought the car; and World-Wide Volkswagen Corp., the regional distributor that had sold the car to Seaway. This turn of events helps us think about how disputes make their way into the court system.

The first steps in initiating litigation are to recognize that there is a problem and that the problem is potentially subject to legal resolution. In the case of the Robinsons' potential suit against the drunk driver, it's easy to take those steps. The Robinsons suffered a severe injury. They knew, as we all do, that there is a legal remedy for injuring someone else by driving carelessly.

The Robinsons' suit against the Audi defendants is less obvious. It requires a little more knowledge of the law and the situation to recognize that they might have a suit against the manufacturer and sellers of the car for a product defect that exacerbated their injuries. Perhaps those issues arose only when they consulted a lawyer who was experienced in auto accident litigation.

There is a very general point here. As Professor Marc Galanter, one of the most thoughtful scholars of the litigation process, has said, there is "a vast sea of events, encounters, collisions, rivalries, disappointments, discomforts and injuries" in the world, but only when the victim recognizes the possibility of legal resolution does the event become a potential lawsuit.

A victim's recognition that a potential legal dispute exists is only the first step. It must be worthwhile to incur the costs of the legal process rather than using alternative means of dispute resolution or forgetting the whole thing. In the Robinsons' case, the obvious suit against the drunk driver probably was unattractive because the driver had little or no insurance or assets to pay a judgment. People seldom litigate just to establish a principle; unless there is something to be gained, they will not spend the time and they will be unable to find a lawyer to invest in the litigation.

Even if there is a potential recovery, alternative means of dealing with the problem may be better. Especially if an auto accident is relatively minor, the injured party will settle with her own or the other driver's insurance company rather than sue. Even when they have a viable cause of action and a good chance to get a money judgment, homeowners often do not litigate against their neighbors and businesses do not litigate against their suppliers; the bad feelings generated are not worth the dollars recovered.

In an increasing number of consumer disputes, parties are required by the terms of a form contract to submit their disputes to arbitration rather than litigate. Websites, banks, and other businesses attempt to avoid litigation altogether through these terms. In arbitration, procedures are more limited, there is no jury, and one arbitrator or a panel of arbitrators who are not judges decide the case. Whether businesses should be allowed to preempt litigation in this way is a controversial aspect of contract law discussed in Chapter 6.

An important element of the decision to pursue litigation is the victim's ability to obtain a lawyer to pursue the matter. One way or another, lawyers have to be paid by the parties. In serious personal injury cases like the Robinsons', even victims of moderate means can get the best lawyers, because the lawyers commonly will take the case on a contingent fee basis, under which they are paid a percentage of the eventual recovery. In other cases, though, many otherwise meritorious claims will never be brought because the potential recovery for the lawyer is too small and the client can't pay the lawyer directly.

One massive study of civil litigation tried to attach some numbers to this process of filtering out potential cases. The figures vary widely depending on the type of case and the people involved, but here are the rough results. First take a roundup of, say, 10,000 bad experiences of all kinds—a slip on a neighbor's icy sidewalk, a new toaster that breaks, a landlord's failure to provide enough hot water to a tenant. The injured party in 1,000 of these incidents will see herself as the victim of a wrong caused by some other person (the neighbor, the manufacturer of the toaster, the landlord). Of these people, 700 will complain to the wrongdoer about the problem; the other 300 will let it go. The wrongdoer will reject the claim in 450 of the cases, and the victim will go see a lawyer in about 100 of those cases. The lawyer will file a case in court in 50 cases. The parties will settle 25 to 35 of those cases, the court will dispose of most of the rest without a trial, and perhaps 2 or 3 cases will go to trial, and only one of those will be a jury trial.

The Robinsons made it through these filters. They found a lawyer willing to take their case, and the lawyer assessed the potential legal theories and identified defendants who might be held liable and who would be able to pay if they were. Probably the lawyer found that the driver who hit them had no insurance or assets or too little to pay for their injuries, and he contacted Audi, who refused to settle the case for an adequate amount, so he decided it was time to sue.

Where Can a Lawsuit Be Brought?

Two kinds of considerations are involved when a lawyer decides where to bring a suit. The first is a legal issue: Which courts have the authority to hear the case? The second is a strategic issue: In which court is it most advantageous to litigate? We deal with those issues in the next few sections.

The law of civil procedure frames the first issue as involving *jurisdiction*. Jurisdiction, translated from the Latin, means "to speak the law." Anyone can speak the law, but only a court with jurisdiction can speak the law authoritatively. If a court does not have jurisdiction, or legal authority over the parties and the case, it cannot lawfully hear the case, and any decision it reaches is not valid or binding on the parties.

To lawfully adjudicate a case, a court must have both *subject matter jurisdiction* and *personal jurisdiction*. Subject matter jurisdiction empowers a court to hear the kind of case at issue, and personal jurisdiction permits the court to exercise authority over the parties to the dispute. For a court to hear the Robinsons' case, therefore, it must have power over tort claims arising out of automobile accidents (subject matter jurisdiction) and power to compel the defendants to litigate before the court, and, if the Robinsons win, to pay a judgment (personal jurisdiction).

Three states have a logical relationship to the accident and the parties that makes them obvious places to bring suit. The accident occurred in Oklahoma. The Robinsons had purchased their Audi in New York from Seaway Volkswagen, one of the defendants, and they were still legal residents of New York at the time of the accident. And they were on their way to establish a new legal residence in Arizona. Therefore, they might logically have brought suit in the courts of Oklahoma, New York, or Arizona. (We restrict our analysis to American courts; it is possible but unlikely that they would have sued in Germany, the home of Audi.)

Every state has a set of courts called *courts of general jurisdiction* that are empowered to hear most kinds of civil cases, including tort, contract, and property claims. These are the basic-level trial courts that hear the bulk of the state's judicial business. Usually the subject matter jurisdiction of courts of general jurisdiction is unrestricted; the state constitutional provision or statute that gives them authority is expressed in broad language, giving them "original jurisdiction in all civil, probate, and criminal cases, except as otherwise provided herein," as the Colorado constitution provides. By tradition, the general jurisdiction courts of different states have different names. In Arizona, the Superior Court is the court of general jurisdiction; in Oklahoma, it's the District Court; and, strangely enough, in New York the general jurisdiction court is known as the Supreme Court. (In New York, the highest court in the state, which is known practically everywhere else as the state's supreme court, is called the Court of Appeals.) Every state also has courts of limited jurisdiction, such as a family court, whose subject matter jurisdiction is limited to divorce and child custody issues, a probate court, with jurisdiction limited to inheritance matters, and a small claims court, which has jurisdiction only over cases involving relatively small dollar amounts.

Another traditional division of courts is into *law* and *equity*. As the royal courts became more rigid and bureaucratic in the thirteenth century, frustrated litigants turned to the king as the fount of justice. The king assigned his right-hand man, the chancellor, to provide more flexible justice in cases in which the law courts would not. Over time the chancellor's exercise of discretion itself became institutionalized in a *court of chancery* or, because its goal was fairness, of *equity*.

The existence of two competing judicial systems became a point of conflict in the struggles between the crown and Parliament and, later, between the crown and American colonists, for whom the equity courts were a symbol of royal authority. Beginning in the nineteenth century, the conflict faded as law and equity merged into a single system. Today, equity remains important as a distinctive set of remedies and procedures. When a litigant seeks an *injunction* (a court order compelling someone to do or not do something) rather than money damages, for example, it is an equitable matter. Injunctions are available in some private cases when the legal remedy of damages is inadequate, as when one business seeks to enjoin another from illegally using its trademark. They also are used in civil rights cases and similar public litigation; the desegregation of schools in the South through the 1950s and 1960s was ordered by federal courts exercising their equitable powers. One final, important consequence of the distinction is that, in equity, the judge decides the case without a jury.

The Robinsons also have to sue in a court that has personal jurisdiction over the potential defendants. In most cases personal jurisdiction is easy. Suppose first that they want to sue the driver of the Ford that hit their car. They certainly can do so in Oklahoma, the state in which the accident occurred, because committing a tort in a state provides a basis for jurisdiction. If the Ford driver lives in Texas, the Robinsons can sue him there, because a person always can be sued in the state in which he or she has legal residence. But the personal jurisdiction issue is trickier when the defendants have a less obvious relationship to the state in which the suit is brought and when they are corporations, not people, for whom it is harder to pin down where they are and where they act. Which courts, then, have personal jurisdiction over Audi, Volkswagen, World-Wide, and Seaway?

This issue has been addressed in a series of confusing U.S. Supreme Court cases dating back more than a century and featuring *World-Wide Volkswagen Corp. v. Woodson*, as the Robinsons' case was called when it reached the U.S. Supreme Court in 1980. To make it simple, think about why we feel comfortable if the Robinsons sue the Ford driver in Oklahoma or in his home state of Texas. In either of those cases, the driver can't really complain that it is unfair for the court to exercise jurisdiction over him. In each case, there is a sufficient connection between the driver and the forum state (the state in which suit is brought) so that it seems fair to make him defend an action brought in the forum state's court. It doesn't seem unfair to require someone to litigate in a state in which he is involved in an accident, and it certainly isn't unfair to require him to litigate in his home state. And, in each case, the forum state has a legitimate interest in adjudicating the dispute. Oklahoma ought to be able to try cases involving accidents on its highways, and Texas should have the power to decide actions against its residents.

The Supreme Court distilled this sense of fairness into a constitutional requirement in the case of *International Shoe Company v. Washington* (1945). The due process clause of the Constitution limits the ability of a state to exercise personal jurisdiction by requiring that the defendant have "minimum contacts" with the forum state, so that requiring him to defend there does not offend "traditional notions of fair play and substantial justice." (This really makes first-year law students crazy; the court creates an intensely complicated body of law and ostensibly grounds it in a concept like "fair play" that everyone should be able to understand.)

The Robinsons attempted to sue the four Volkswagen defendants in Oklahoma, but the Supreme Court said that an Oklahoma court could properly assert jurisdiction only over the manufacturer, Audi, and not the distributor or dealer, World-Wide and Seaway. Audi sells its cars in a national market, so it has contacts with every state and should reasonably expect to be subject to a suit when one of its cars malfunctions in any state. It obtains the benefits of doing business everywhere, so it must accept the responsibility of being sued anywhere. World-Wide and Seaway, however, sell cars only in the New York area. Although they could foresee that some of their customers would drive to Oklahoma, it would be constitutionally unfair to require them to go there to defend suits in the absence of any other contacts between them and that state.

When Can You Make a Federal Case Out of It?

The Robinsons brought their case in the District Court in Creek County, Oklahoma, part of the Oklahoma state court system, but they could have "made a federal case out of it" by bringing suit in the federal courts. The United States has a court system parallel to the state court systems. Like most state systems, the federal judicial system has trial courts (called the U.S. District Courts), intermediate appellate courts (called the U.S. Courts of Appeals, or sometimes the Circuit Courts, from the days when Supreme Court justices "rode circuit" to hold court in different places), and a highest court (the U.S. Supreme Court). The system is geographically organized, with, for example, a U.S. District Court for the Northern District of Oklahoma and a U.S. Court of Appeals for the Tenth Circuit, hearing cases from Oklahoma, Colorado, Kansas, New Mexico, Utah, and Wyoming.

Although the federal court system looks pretty much like the state systems, on the issue of jurisdiction the systems are fundamentally different. In the state courts, jurisdiction over the kind of case (subject matter jurisdiction) is usually easy because the trial courts have general jurisdiction over most kinds of cases, but jurisdiction over the defendant (personal jurisdiction) is subject to the constitutional limitation of sufficient contacts with the state such that it is fair to assert authority over the defendant. In the federal courts it is just the opposite. Personal jurisdiction is unrestrained by constitutional due process requirements; even though the district courts sit locally, they are all part of a national system that can assert jurisdiction over defendants. (By court rule, however, federal district courts assert personal jurisdiction over defendants only to the same extent as the courts of the states in which they sit.) Subject matter jurisdiction is much trickier, though, because the federal courts are courts of limited jurisdiction; they have authority only to the extent that the Constitution and the Congress have granted it to them. So unlike the state courts, the federal courts only hear cases in particular categories.

If each state has a judicial system, why do we need a set of federal courts at all? The framers of the Constitution and the Congresses that enacted enabling legislation had two reasons for establishing federal courts. First, some cases involve important national issues that should be decided by judges of the U.S. government rather than of any particular state. Second, Americans always have been a bit parochial, so the framers wanted to provide a neutral forum for, say, New Yorkers who had to litigate in Oklahoma. Each of those reasons resulted in a particular kind of authority for the federal courts, known respectively as *federal question jurisdiction* and *diversity jurisdiction*. (In addition, there are a few other classes of cases given to the federal courts, such as *admiralty* cases, which involve maritime affairs, and suits in which the U.S. government is a party.)

The first type of federal subject matter jurisdiction is federal question jurisdiction. Under the Constitution and statutes, the power of the federal courts extends to cases arising under the Constitution, federal statutes, and federal administrative rules. Federal courts hear cases involving the whole range of federal law, including the environmental laws, Social Security, Food and Drug Administration regulation, and violations of constitutional rights. Sometimes, as with civil rights, the states also have jurisdiction over these issues; a claim that a shopping mall is infringing on free speech by preventing leafleting can be brought in state or federal court. In other cases, the federal courts have exclusive jurisdiction; only a federal court, for example, can hear a bankruptcy case or a patent claim. The federal courts are believed to be in a better position than the state courts to develop expertise, to make the law more uniform, and to consider national interests in the interpretation and application of federal law. In addition, many federal laws are unpopular when applied to local controversies, and vesting federal courts with jurisdiction over them makes it more likely that the laws will be enforced free of local prejudice and political interference. Through the 1950s and 1960s, for example, the federal courts were primarily responsible for enforcing civil rights laws in recalcitrant Southern states.

Diversity jurisdiction is designed to prevent prejudice against out-of-state litigants. The framers wanted to avoid bias by local judges and juries against litigants coming from other states, or at least to allay the fears of out-of-staters about the possibility of bias. Diversity jurisdiction also permits many economically important cases—those involving large commercial transactions between companies from different states, for example—to be heard in the federal courts.

Where to sue initially is the plaintiff's choice, but the concern for local prejudice underlying diversity jurisdiction has historically been so great that defendants are given a similar choice through a doctrine known as *removal*. If the plaintiff brings the action in state court, an out-of-state defendant can remove it to federal court, as long as the federal court would have had jurisdiction in the first place. That way a New York defendant, for example, can avoid the prejudice that might result if sued by an Oklahoman in an Oklahoma state court, by removing the case to the U.S. District Court in Oklahoma.

The two traditional requirements for diversity jurisdiction are a sufficient amount of money at stake in the case and diversity of citizenship between the parties. The amount in controversy requirement is a simple one; the plaintiff's claim has to be worth more than a minimum amount set by Congress to be brought in federal court. The diversity of citizenship requirement is more interesting. In most cases, to establish federal jurisdiction there must be complete diversity; that is, the plaintiff and the defendant must be from different states, and if there is more than one plaintiff or defendant, all of the plaintiffs must be from different states than all of the defendants.

This is the key to the Robinsons' case. The Robinsons claimed that the gas tank on their Audi was defective and caused the fire that injured them, so they sued Audi and Volkswagen of America, the manufacturer and importer of the car. If the gas tank was defective, Audi and Volkswagen were the ones responsible, and they certainly had the assets to satisfy any judgment against them. So why did the Robinsons also sue World-Wide Volkswagen, the regional distributor of Audis, and Seaway Volkswagen, the dealer from whom they bought the car? The answer is a strategic choice made by their lawyer using the law of diversity jurisdiction. The Robinsons had not completed their move from New York to Arizona, so they were still citizens of their former home, New York, for diversity purposes. Audi was a German company and Volkswagen of America was a New Jersey corporation, but World-Wide and Seaway were both New York corporations. Bringing them into the case destroyed complete diversity, which meant that the case could not be heard in federal court. Of all the possible forums—state and federal courts in New York, Oklahoma, and possibly Arizona—the Robinsons' lawyer decided the best place to sue was in state court in Creek County, Oklahoma, then considered one of the most sympathetic jurisdictions for personal injury plaintiffs in America. With World-Wide and Seaway in the case, the defendants could not remove the case to federal court in Tulsa, which was much less attractive from the Robinsons' point of view.

Although the Robinsons' lawyer made the correct calculation about destroying diversity jurisdiction—an issue of subject matter jurisdiction—he ran up against the law of personal jurisdiction. Seaway and World-Wide challenged the ability of the Oklahoma state court to assert jurisdiction over them, and the U.S. Supreme Court agreed, holding that it would be unfair to force the New York distributor and dealer to litigate in Oklahoma. With the New York defendants out of the case there was complete diversity, so Audi and Volkswagen could and did remove the case to federal court, where a jury found that the speed of the car that struck the Robinsons' Audi, and not a defect in the gas tank, was the cause of the fire.

Cases like the Robinsons' cause some critics to question whether diversity jurisdiction is still necessary or useful. Today, the critics argue, diversity is more commonly used as a lawyer's tactic than a protection for out-of-state defendants. Local prejudice against out-of-staters has declined to a considerable extent, so the value of fair process no longer requires a neutral federal forum. Moreover, federal courts apply the same substantive law as state courts and draw their judges and jurors from about the same locales as the state courts, so the differences between the two forums have diminished. We could, they say, eliminate diversity jurisdiction and reduce the workload of the federal courts—though this would, of course, increase the burden on the state courts.

As we can see from the Robinsons' case, where a plaintiff can sue and where he or she should sue often are two different questions. Under the jurisdictional rules, a plaintiff may have a choice of courts: state or federal, New York or Oklahoma. Choosing among those forums is a strategic issue for the plaintiff's lawyer. A lawyer simply may choose to litigate at home, in the jurisdiction where the plaintiff lives and the lawyer practices, and the only decision to be made is state or federal court. One court system may be more expeditious than another; in some urban areas, the wait to go to trial may be six years in a state court and two years in a federal court, or the difference may be as great in neighboring state jurisdictions. As with the Robinsons, the probable composition of the jury may differ from one court to another. The rules of civil procedure may be more attractive for one reason or another; often the federal discovery rules are broader and more efficient than comparable state rules. The quality of the judges may differ as well; there is a traditional belief that federal judges are of higher quality, at least in some respects, than state judges, and, again, judges in one jurisdiction may be better regarded than those across the river or down the road.

If You Can Sue in Different Places, What Law Will Apply in Each Place?

One consequence of having different state court systems and a parallel federal system is that different bodies of law potentially apply to a single case. The Robinsons brought their case in Oklahoma state court. If they had gone to federal court instead, would the federal court have applied different law to determine if the Audi's gas tank was defective? Or if they sued in New York, would New York's tort law have applied to the case instead of Oklahoma's law? Because the law varies from place to place, issues like these often determine the outcome of the case, so it is essential that civil procedure have ways to resolve them.

Some kinds of conflict between the law in different jurisdictions are easily resolved. Generally, a court applies its own rules of procedure, whatever substantive law applies to the case. Also, when a state court has a case involving federal law, it applies the federal law, including federal court decisions interpreting the law, because the Constitution makes federal law "the supreme law of the land." Conversely, a federal court follows state law on all substantive issues. Therefore, a federal court in a diversity case applies the same principles of tort law, contract law, and so on as would be applied if the case were in state court.

A more complex kind of interjurisdictional conflict is between two bodies of state law. Suppose Oklahoma holds manufacturers strictly liable for defects in their products but New York holds them liable only when they have been negligent in making their products. (For more on products liability, see Chapter 5.) Can the Robinsons avoid the New York rule by suing in Oklahoma? This issue falls within the area of law known as *conflicts of law* and requires a choice between the law of competing jurisdictions.

The law of conflicts of law is among the messiest areas in the entire body of the law. Its uncertainty tortures students, and its complexity often baffles courts. The reasons for this confusion illustrates something very basic about law.

Until about the middle of the twentieth century, the law of conflicts of law was composed of what purported to be relatively clear rules based on territorial notions of sovereignty and justice. For example, a tort case would be governed by the law of the jurisdiction in which the accident occurred; an accident in Oklahoma would be controlled by Oklahoma tort law whether the case was tried there or in New York. Similarly, a contract dispute would be governed by the law of the state in which the contract was made. Unfortunately, many transactions have a multistate character. What law governs an action by the Robinsons, who purchased a car in New York that was made in Germany and that was involved in an accident in Oklahoma? Did the relevant wrongful act occur when the car was made, sold, or burst into flames? Is it fair to subject Audi to the tort rules of fifty different states, including some states in which it may not even sell cars? Moreover, courts became uneasy about applying the law of another state that conflicted with their own rules. As the courts grappled with these issues, they created counterrules and exceptions to the rules that generated confusion and ultimately much criticism.

Judges and scholars were very successful in criticizing the old rules but less successful in formulating new ones. The results in particular cases have become unpredictable in many states, as courts abandon the old rules in favor of flexible standards requiring them to weigh and balance a multiplicity of factors. And many jurisdictions never came on board, implicitly or explicitly clinging to the older rules. As a result, things are different but not necessarily better.

The lesson from all this is that clear, rigid legal rules are often not what they appear to be. They either produce injustice as they are applied to varying fact situations or they demand interpretations and exceptions—yet interpretations and exceptions cause complexity and uncertainty. Broad, flexible legal rules, on the other hand, give the courts great discretion, and discretion produces conflicting decisions and uncertain rules, which is another form of complexity and injustice.

How Does a Lawsuit Begin?

A lawyer begins a suit by preparing and filing with the court a document known as a *complaint* in which, as its name suggests, the *plaintiff* (the person who is suing) complains that the *defendant* (the person who is being sued) violated his legal rights and asks the court for a remedy. (The law doesn't require that a lawyer file the complaint or otherwise represent the plaintiff. Anyone can represent himself—the term for this is *pro se*, Latin meaning "for oneself." As a practical matter, though, outside of small claims court a lawyer is a necessity.) Attached to the complaint is a *summons*, a document from the court that summons the defendant to respond to the charges. The plaintiff must cause *service of process* on the defendant by having a copy of the complaint and summons delivered to the defendant by a sheriff, process server, or mail, depending on the rules of the court in which the case is filed.

The complaint begins to define what the litigation is about. In the Robinsons' case, for example, the complaint would state

- who the Robinsons and the Audi defendants were,

- that the Robinsons had purchased an Audi from Seaway Volkswagen,

- how the Audi had been involved in an accident,

- how the Audi was defective,

- that the defect caused injuries to Kay Robinson and the children, and

- for those reasons, the Audi defendants ought to pay the Robinsons money.

This information serves several purposes. First, it lays the basis for the jurisdiction of the court. By stating that this case involves an automobile accident that occurred in Oklahoma, the complaint makes clear that the case can be brought in Oklahoma District Court. Second, it notifies the defendants that they are being sued and why they are being sued. Adequate notice to the defendants enables them to hire lawyers and to begin to think about the basis on which they will contest the plaintiffs' claims. Third, it frames the issues of fact and law that will be involved in the case and, by implication, the issues that will not be involved. By going through the elements of the cause of action—why the plaintiffs claim they are entitled to relief because of what they allege the defendants did wrong—the complaint tells the parties and the judge what will be relevant to the ultimate decision in the case. On the facts, for example, the speed of the Robinsons' car and the other car involved in the accident will be relevant, because excessive speed rather than a defect in the Audi may have caused the fire, so both parties may want to investigate and, at trial, present proof about the speed of the cars. Whether the defendants defrauded the Robinsons by advertising the car as having a high-fidelity sound system when it actually had a cheap, tinny system is not relevant, though, because that claim has nothing to do with the accident. The parties should know not to investigate or present proof about the sound system; if they try to do so anyway, the judge will know to stop them.

Traditionally, the complaint and other pleadings were the exclusive means of defining the issues in the case for the parties and the court. Judges required that a lawyer plead the facts underlying the claim specifically and precisely. If a lawyer failed to do so—if, for example, the Robinsons' lawyer misstated Audi's corporate name or failed to specify how exactly the defect occurred—the case would be thrown out of court. Because this hypertechnicality conflicts with the goals of serving the values of the substantive law and providing fair process, judges have relaxed the pleading requirements, and the process of defining the issues in the case begins with the complaint but continues through the discovery and pretrial stages of the case.

As an illustration of this flexibility, if a lawyer makes a mistake in pleading or discovers new information that reveals a pleading to be incomplete or incorrect, the court usually allows the pleading to be amended to correct the error or account for the new information. The Robinsons originally sued only Volkswagen of America, Seaway, and World-Wide, but subsequently they amended their complaint to add Volkswagen AG, the German corporation who they thought was the manufacturer; when they learned through formal discovery that Audi AG, a different German company, was really the manufacturer of the car, they amended again to substitute Audi for Volkswagen. Indeed, the rules on amending pleadings are so liberal that a party usually can amend at or after trial, so that the pleadings match the proof presented at trial. As long as the defendant has fair notice of the basics of the case, justice is served by focusing on the substance rather than the lawyer's technical compliance with pleading rules.

This does not mean that there are no limits on pleading, however. Everything in a pleading has to be grounded in fact and stated in good faith, and, depending on the jurisdiction, either the party must swear to its truthfulness or the attorney filing the pleading must sign it. The Federal Rules, for instance, require an attorney to sign a pleading and attest to the fact that she has concluded, after reasonable inquiry, that the pleading is well grounded and that she is acting in good faith and without improper motivations in filing the pleading. If a statement in a pleading is false or frivolous, the court can impose penalties on the party or on the attorney. The vigorous application of rules such as this creates an incentive for attorneys to be careful in drafting and investigating the accuracy of pleadings.

What Can the Defendant Do to Respond to a Lawsuit?

Someone first receives official notice that he is being sued by receiving the plaintiff's complaint and an accompanying summons from the court. The summons typically directs the now-defendant to answer the complaint, but the defendant actually has a number of different ways of responding to being sued.

First, the defendant can simply ignore the whole thing. If the defendant in a criminal case fails to answer a summons or appear for trial, the police can go out and arrest her. Not so in a civil case. If World-Wide Volkswagen receives the Robinsons' complaint and summons in the mail and doesn't do anything in response, the police won't come and drag the company's president into court. But that doesn't mean that anyone can just ignore a complaint. The sanction for failing to respond to the complaint is that the plaintiff can get the court to enter a *default* against the defendant. A default prevents the defendant from subsequently entering any defenses on the merits of the case, and the plaintiff can proceed to get a *default judgment* that concludes the case against the defendant and then can attempt to enforce it like any other judgment.

Sometimes a defendant may take the chance of ignoring a complaint and having a default judgment entered against it because the defendant doesn't think the plaintiff will be willing or able to enforce the judgment. Suppose the defect in the Audi had not caused serious injuries but had required only a minor repair costing $200. If the Robinsons had for some strange reason sued for this small amount, World-Wide might have ignored the suit, figuring that either it wouldn't be worth the money to hire a lawyer in Oklahoma to defend a suit for such a small amount, or the Robinsons wouldn't bother to go to New York to try to collect it. Ordinarily, though, if it is worthwhile for the plaintiff to sue, it is worthwhile for the defendant to respond, so the defendant will do something other than ignore the complaint and risk a default.

The second tack the defendant can take is to raise an objection to being sued that is unrelated to the merits of the case. The objection takes the form of a *motion to dismiss*. A motion is a formal request to the court, here to get rid of the case without ever reaching the substance of what happened.

Some of these objections are trivial. A defendant can say that there was a technical defect in the form of the summons or in the method of service of process, sending the complaint and summons by mail, for example, when personal service is required. If the plaintiff can cure the defect, in this case by personally serving the defendant, then the objection may delay the case but doesn't halt it altogether. If the plaintiff cannot cure the defect because the defendant is unavailable to be served, then the defendant's strategy may prevent the case from going forward at all.

A more important basis for a motion to dismiss is that the court lacks jurisdiction over the defendant or the case. Recall that a court can render a binding judgment only in a case where it has jurisdiction, or authority over the subject matter of the case and over the parties. If the defendant demonstrates that the court lacks jurisdiction, the court has no power to do anything other than officially recognize its lack of jurisdiction by dismissing the case. This is effectively what World-Wide Volkswagen and Seaway Volkswagen sought in the Robinsons' case. Arguing that the Oklahoma state court had no personal jurisdiction over them because they had no contact with the state other than the fortuity that the

Robinsons' drove their car there, World-Wide and Seaway asked to be let out of the case without having to defend on the merits.

The third move the defendant might make is to challenge the legal sufficiency of the plaintiff's complaint. This procedure was classically known as a *demurrer* and is today more commonly referred to as a *motion to dismiss for failure to state a claim* or *failure to state a cause of action*. In such a motion to dismiss, the defendant argues that even if all of the facts that the plaintiff alleges are true, there is no legal basis for holding the defendant liable to the plaintiff. The motion therefore tests the strength of the plaintiff's legal argument without getting into the facts underlying the dispute.

Suppose, for example, that Oklahoma tort law states that the manufacturer of a defective product is strictly liable to a consumer who is injured by the product, but the distributor of a product who did not manufacture it is not liable to the consumer. Seaway Volkswagen could move to dismiss the Robinsons' action against it for failure to state a claim. Even if the Audi was defective and the defect contributed to their injuries, under the law Seaway, the retail dealer, is not liable to the Robinsons. Seaway is in the same position as if the Robinsons had sued Ford or Google; whatever the facts of the case, the law provides no remedy against this defendant.

If the defendant has no basis for making a motion to dismiss the complaint, or if any motions to dismiss fail, the defendant finally has to meet the complaint on the merits of the case. The defendant does this by filing a pleading called an *answer*, which, obviously, answers the allegations made in the plaintiff's complaint. The defendant can meet the plaintiff's allegations in three ways, by saying "no" (denying that the allegations are true), "I don't know" (disclaiming knowledge about the allegations), or "yes, but" (admitting the allegations but stating facts that would provide a defense to the plaintiff's claims).

Ideally, a defendant might like to deny everything the plaintiff said in its complaint, thereby hiding all the information the defendant has about the case and putting the plaintiff to the trouble of proving every piece of information it needed to establish its claim. In former times and in a few jurisdictions today, the defendant could accomplish that through a *general denial*, which places into contention every allegation in the complaint. Most courts no longer permit a general denial, though, because in most cases it subverts the purposes of the pleadings and the goals of the procedural system. The pleading process is designed to help identify and narrow the issues that are in dispute. If the defendant, through a general denial, controverts an allegation that it knows to be true, an issue that could be excluded is raised unnecessarily. From the system's point of view this is inefficient and shows a discouraging lack of candor.

Sometimes the defendant will admit that the essential elements of the plaintiff's complaint may be true, but the defendant will argue that the complaint doesn't tell the whole story. If so, in its answer, the plaintiff can raise an *affirmative defense*. A defense introduces a new factor that eliminates or reduces the defendant's liability even if all of the elements of the plaintiff's claim are established. If, for example, the Robinsons' accident had occurred ten years earlier, Audi could raise as an affirmative defense the statute of limitations, which requires that suits be brought within a prescribed time period.

Often the defendant doesn't know whether some of the plaintiff's claims are true. When the Robinsons allege that they suffered serious injuries in the crash and incurred large medical bills, Audi can neither admit nor deny the claims, because it has not yet seen their medical records. In that case, the rules of civil procedure permit the defendant to say, in effect, "I don't know." This puts the issue into dispute and the plaintiff has to come up with its proof. Of course, the desire to promote candor and to define the disputed issues through the pleadings requires that the defendant really not know if the plaintiff's allegation is true, and courts often extend that requirement to force the defendant to engage in a reasonable degree of investigation to ascertain the truth. If, for example, the allegation concerns some facts about what the defendant itself did, the defendant cannot profess lack of knowledge; if the Robinsons allege that an Audi brochure described the 100 LS as "the safest car on the road," Audi cannot disclaim knowledge of what was in its own brochure when a simple check of its files would turn up the truth. Once again, the goal of the process is to efficiently define what the parties are really disputing about and what they can agree on.

What If There Are More Than Two Parties to a Lawsuit?

Usually we think of a lawsuit as involving two people, the plaintiff and the defendant. But as we can see from the Robinsons' suit, even an ordinary action may involve multiple parties—in that particular case, four plaintiffs (Kay and Harry Robinson and their two children) and four defendants (Audi, Volkswagen of America, World-Wide Volkswagen, and Seaway Volkswagen). Moving from the paradigm of a bipolar suit between two parties litigating a single issue to a more complex action involving several parties and several issues presents a challenge for the procedural system, but the way the system handles more complex cases tells us a lot about modern civil procedure.

A vague but effective principle governs courts' ability to hear cases involving multiple parties and multiple claims: A court has great discretion to do what is most consistent with substantive justice, fair process, and efficiency. Often it is best to resolve a number of related disputes in a single case, even if it involves bringing in other parties and different claims. By doing so, the parties do not have to duplicate effort, waste time, and risk inconsistent results by litigating the same or similar issues over and over in different forums. At the same time, a court can separate out issues or parties if bringing in other parties or claims would make the case too confusing or create an undue risk of prejudice to someone.

Plaintiffs usually can sue together if their claims arise out of the same events and involve common issues of law or fact. Harry and Kay Robinson and their two children were all injured in the same accident, so they brought suit in one action, represented by one lawyer. It would be grossly inefficient and possibly unfair to require each of them to sue Audi separately. Even if the plaintiffs don't bring their actions together, the court has the option of consolidating the actions on the defendant's request, or even on its own initiative. Eighteen thousand cases against Eli Lilly & Co. arising out of problems with the antipsychotic drug Zyprexa were consolidated in the federal court in Brooklyn; having all the plaintiffs in one court facilitated settlement of the case. The courts have considerable authority to try to work out an appropriate way of dealing with these cases, even if they are filed in different courts.

Now think about the defendants' side of the litigation. The Robinsons sued Audi, the manufacturer; Volkswagen of America, the importer; World-Wide Volkswagen, the distributor; and Seaway Volkswagen, the dealer. The same principle applies as with plaintiffs. Some or all of these defendants are potentially liable because of the same set of events: the manufacture and sale of an Audi with an allegedly defective gas tank that injured the Robinsons in an accident. Because the trial will be pretty much the same for all of the defendants, it is most efficient to have everything heard at once. In fact, if the Robinsons had wanted to sue the driver of the car that struck them, they could and probably would have brought that claim in the same suit. In that case, however, not only would there be different evidence and argument about each of the defendants' liability, but the claims could vary as well. If the facts were different from those in the actual case, by bringing suit the Robinsons could be saying that either the negligence of the other driver caused the harm or a defect in their Audi caused the harm; they are permitted to bring all the potentially liable defendants into court and let the evidence fall where it may. (In the actual case they argued that the other driver was negligent and that the defective gas tank made their injuries more severe than they would have been otherwise.)

If a plaintiff chooses not to bring in all of the potentially liable parties, the initial defendant may do so. Suppose the Robinsons for some reason decided to sue only Seaway, the dealer from whom they brought the car. Seaway could have *impleaded* Audi—brought Audi in as a defendant—on the theory that either by contract or as a matter of law the manufacturer has to pay any damages for which the dealer is held liable due to a product defect. Seaway could also have brought in the driver of the other car, claiming that it was his negligence that was responsible for some or all of the Robinsons' injuries.

In addition to involving multiple parties, lawsuits often involve multiple claims. This is obviously the case when the Robinsons sue the Audi defendants on a products liability theory and the other driver for negligence, but it can get even more complicated. One species of claim is called a *counterclaim*, in which the defendant sues the plaintiff back. If the driver of the other car was injured in the accident, when the Robinsons sue him he will respond with a counterclaim against them, alleging that their negligence was liable for his injuries. This is so obviously connected to their claim against him that the courts require him to bring it in the same action; if he doesn't, he cannot subsequently bring a different suit for his injuries. In other cases the counterclaim is not so intimately connected to the events at issue that it must be considered at the same time, but the defendant may bring it because the parties are in court and litigating anyway. Suppose immediately after the accident Harry Robinson, not having been seriously injured, jumps out of his car and shouts, "You maniac, look what you've done," and punches the other driver in the face. Either in the Robinsons' suit or in a separate suit, the other driver can bring a claim for battery for being punched. Even though relatively little of the evidence overlaps their claim for the accident and his claim for the punch, the counterclaim can be brought in the original action. But because it would unduly complicate trials if defendants had to bring as counterclaims all claims they might have against the plaintiff, no matter how loosely related to the main event, the driver can save his battery claim for another time.

One other type of claim occurs when defendants begin fighting among themselves. Suppose that after the accident the Audi catches fire and injures the Robinsons and the driver of the other car. The Robinsons name Audi and the other driver as defendants in their action, saying that the driver's negligence caused the action and the product defect made it worse. The driver may file a *cross-claim* against Audi, alleging that his own injuries occurred because the defective Audi caught fire. The cross-claim is just like a new action except it is between defendants and can be tried with the main action.

What If There Are Many Parties to a Lawsuit?

Sometimes there are so many parties—usually on the plaintiff side, occasionally on the defendant side—involved in a single lawsuit that the court treats them as a group rather than individually. This type of suit is known as a *class action*, because the individual parties represent many members of a class of people like them who are, as the law says, "similarly situated." That is, the other class members share the same grievance.

Suppose that the Robinsons had financed the purchase of their car through Volkswagen's in-house finance company, they believe that the finance company had overcharged them by miscalculating the interest rate on the loan, and other customers of the finance company believe they have been overcharged in the same way. If there are a hundred, a thousand, or a million such cases, it may be more manageable to have the cases tried as a class action in which the issue of overcharging can be determined once for all the plaintiffs. In a class action, the Robinsons can bring a class action on behalf of themselves and the other customers; as class members, the other customers do not actually participate in the conduct of the litigation and probably do not even know about it, but they will be bound by its outcome.

The numbers involved in class actions range from the large to the spectacular. A hog farm alleged to emit noxious odors was sued by a class of 450 nearby property owners. Volkswagen's falsified pollution test results for its "clean diesel" cars resulted in a class action involving 475,000 vehicle owners. Five million merchants were in the class that sued MasterCard and Visa for antitrust violations.

By allowing plaintiffs to bring class actions, courts attempt to balance the conflicting goals of civil procedure. The ultimate goal, of course, is to carry out the policies and values of the substantive rules of law. Especially when many individual plaintiffs each have relatively small claims, this can be done only through a class action. A borrower may pay a few dollars more when the finance company miscalculates the interest rate. Because of the small size of the claim and the expense of litigation, it isn't worthwhile for any one borrower to sue. The collective loss of all borrowers, though, is very large. By bringing one suit for all of the borrowers, a class action makes sure that the law against misrepresenting interest rates is carried out and the people who are injured by the wrongful conduct are compensated.

Aggregating claims in a class action where it would be impracticable to join all the claimants also serves the value of operating the litigation system efficiently. A class action always involves at least one issue of law or fact that is common to all the claims, such as whether the interest rate was miscalculated. Examining and deciding that issue once is more efficient than doing it over and over in different cases. Where the facts or law applicable to each claimant differ too much, however, efficiency is not served by a class action. Even if a thousand other Audis like the Robinsons' were involved in accidents in which a defective gas tank allegedly caused a fire following a crash, those cases would be less suitable for class-action treatment because the evidence about the specific facts of the accidents and the resulting injuries would be so different.

Because most class members do not participate in the litigation, class actions also implicate special fairness concerns. All members of the class will be bound by its result, so courts are required to give absent class members adequate notice of what is happening, allow them the opportunity to opt out of the class action and sue on their own, and make sure that the class representatives and their lawyers provide fair representation for the interests of the absent members.

Because of their massive scale and because the potential cost to the defendant of an adverse judgment is so great, class actions often are settled rather than tried. Indeed, sometimes class actions are brought with the purpose of being settled; the plaintiffs' lawyers and the defendants will negotiate and arrive at a settlement before or shortly after the case is filed, without ever really expecting to go to trial. In these cases, the court has a heightened obligation to scrutinize whether the case is appropriate for a class action and whether the proposed settlement is fair.

The law on class actions is very complicated and hotly disputed. Some courts seize on class actions as an effective means of disposing of large numbers of claims in a relatively expeditious manner; even though a class action can be complicated and cumbersome, it is still better than thousands or tens of thousands of individual cases. Other courts are more reluctant to use the device in very large cases, believing that the farther away one goes from the traditional paradigm of adjudication—a well-defined dispute between two adverse parties—the less well equipped a court is to deal with the problem. And many businesses are hostile to class actions, viewing them as a bludgeon used by plaintiffs' lawyers to coerce massive settlements and generate huge fees.

How Do the Parties Discover the Facts About Their Case?

This is handled through a process called, naturally enough, *discovery*.

It's easy to find out some of what a party needs to know during litigation. The Robinsons, for example, know the speed at which they were driving before the accident and how extensive their injuries were. Audi, on the other hand, knows how the fuel tank was designed and built. But each of them wants information that the other has—the Robinsons want to know about the fuel tank, and Audi wants to know about the accident and the injuries.

It would be possible to proceed to trial without each party finding out in advance what the other knows. That was the traditional common law system, in which the facts were only minimally developed through the pleadings and the parties had no other opportunity before trial to find out what the other knew. But modern civil procedure uses a more open system in which each party has an extensive opportunity to unearth all of the facts relevant to the litigation during the pretrial stage of the litigation. To obtain information that is in the adversary's possession, or that can be most easily obtained from the adversary even though it may be available elsewhere, a party can interview the other party under oath, called a *deposition*; submit written questions, called *interrogatories*; demand that documents or other physical evidence be produced; require the other party to submit to a physical examination; and ask the other party to admit the truth of facts relevant to the litigation.

A deposition is an oral examination of the other party or someone else with knowledge of the case. A deposition is like the examination of a witness at trial in that it is conducted by an attorney, a verbatim record is made, and the witness is under oath; the key differences are that the examination is not conducted in front of a judge and there is no cross-examination. Instead, a court reporter swears in the witness and records the testimony. By taking someone's deposition, an attorney can find out what that person knows in a flexible way; the answer to one question may open up a new line of inquiry. If the witness might testify in an adverse way at trial, the deposition pins down the testimony, allowing the attorney to develop contrary evidence or to use inconsistencies between the deposition testimony and subsequent testimony at trial. It also gives both attorneys a chance to assess how good the witness will be at trial—not only what she says, but how persuasive or credible she is.

The disadvantage of taking depositions is the expense. In a typical deposition, the attorneys for both sides will be present, running up their fees, and the court reporter must be paid, too. One way of reducing this cost is to submit written questions (interrogatories), to be answered under oath. All the attorney has to do is prepare and submit the interrogatories, not be present at a deposition; therefore, interrogatories can be much cheaper, especially because standard form interrogatories are often used for routine aspects of cases. No doubt Audi would submit to the Robinsons standard interrogatories used in every personal injury case, asking them to detail their injuries and medical treatment. Interrogatories also place on the adversary the responsibility of ascertaining the facts needed to respond to the questions posed. The disadvantage of interrogatories, though, is that they are inflexible and not spontaneous. The answers often are crafted by the attorney for the responding party to be responsive but not particularly forthcoming, cryptic, and narrowly drawn to give no more information than is absolutely necessary. Nor can an attorney follow up on the answer to one question by asking another; the attorney has to anticipate all the questions that might be asked and include them in the original set of interrogatories.

In connection with depositions or interrogatories, or in a separate request, one party can demand that the other produce documents or other evidence. The Robinsons can ask for all engineering reports and test results on the Audi's fuel tank, and Audi can ask for the Robinsons' medical records. Where someone's physical or mental condition is at issue in the case, one party can ask the court to require them to submit to a medical examination. And a party must disclose whether it has retained an expert to testify at trial and what the expert will testify about.

Finally, where one party believes that some facts are undisputed, that party can request the other to admit that they are true, narrowing down the issues to be tried. If Audi believes or has evidence to suggest that Harry Robinson was driving too fast, its attorney might request that the Robinsons admit that; if they know it to be true, they cannot deny that he was speeding and must enter the admission. That might not conclude the whole case—even though he was going too fast, the car still might not have been crashworthy—but at least it removes one issue at trial.

Pretrial discovery has significant advantages over a system of trial by surprise in achieving a fair and efficient process and in promoting the values of the underlying substantive law. Simply at a practical level, it focuses the recollection of witnesses at an early stage and preserves information that otherwise might not be available at the time of trial. Because it typically takes years for a civil case to come to trial, witnesses may forget details about events or may even die, and documents or other evidence may be lost or destroyed. Discovery comes well before trial, when recollections are fresher and evidence is more likely to still be available.

More important, through discovery the parties learn the contours of each others' cases and clarify which issues actually are in controversy. This helps the parties to prepare for trial and negotiate a settlement because it narrows down what is involved in a case and gives them a sense of the strength and weakness of each party's position. By finding out from the Robinsons that the accident occurred in a high-speed, rear-end crash, the Audi defendants may conclude that they do not have to invest resources in demonstrating the crashworthiness of the car in a low-speed, head-on collision. Audi also may learn how serious the

Robinsons' injuries are, that Harry was not driving carelessly, and that he would make a good witness at trial; those factors may convince Audi that there is a good chance of losing a large judgment at trial, and this might encourage them to settle the case. If they go to trial, the trial likely will be fairer if both parties have an adequate opportunity to evaluate in advance all of the relevant information.

Finally, discovery furthers the law's substantive values by making it possible to bring actions or assert defenses that could not be done in the absence of full discovery and by allowing the parties to bring out all of the evidence that might relate to the application of the relevant rules of law. The Robinsons would never know or be able to prove that their car's gas tank was defective unless they had access to the design notes, tests, and studies of Audi's engineers, and Audi might never know if the Robinsons contributed to the fire by carrying extra gas in cans in the trunk. (One of the best examples of this function of discovery occurs in medical malpractice cases. When a patient suffers harm as a result of an operation, she would never know if the harm was caused by the doctor's negligence unless, through discovery, she could obtain the medical records and take the testimony of the doctors and nurses present in the operating room.) Only when the parties discover and present at trial all of the evidence that bears on the case can the relevant rules of law be correctly applied.

These functions of discovery suggest that the scope of discovery—what information parties can discover and what tools they can use to obtain it—should be very broad, and in most court systems it is. The scope of discovery is limited by countervailing factors, however, the most important of which is the burden it can impose in time, inconvenience, and expense. Audi could overwhelm the Robinsons with detailed interrogatories about every aspect of the accident, Harry's driving record, their medical history, and so on and could compel each of them to appear for several days of depositions and medical examinations. To comply, they would have to consult their attorney, search their records, take time off from work, and go to the office of Audi's attorney to be deposed. The Robinsons, on the other hand, could conduct a fishing expedition in Audi's records. With little initial idea of what was wrong with the car, they could ask for all design studies, tests, engineering reports, complaints, and other documents potentially relevant, and Audi would be required to search its files to respond fully.

Overdoing it in discovery is a real risk because discovery is part of an adversarial process directed by the attorneys for each side. For the most part, the parties can submit interrogatories, take depositions, and request the production of documents without the court's permission.

Because things can get out of hand, though, courts have imposed limits and checks on the process.

First, the use of some discovery devices is limited by court rules. Medical examinations, for example, intrude on a person's privacy, so they can be required only when someone's medical condition is a major issue in controversy. If the extent of Kay Robinson's injuries are disputed, she can be required to submit to an examination, but an eyewitness to the accident could not be compelled to submit to an eye examination. Other rules limit the number of interrogatories that can be submitted or the number of depositions that can be taken without special permission from the court.

Second (and paradoxically), some courts under the lead of the federal system have opened up the discovery process. The Federal Rules of Civil Procedure now require parties to automatically disclose much of the information they have that is relevant to the litigation, including the names of persons having information and the issues that they know about, a copy or description of relevant documents or property, the amount claimed for damages and the evidence supporting the claim, and any insurance policies covering the potential damages. Requiring the parties to tell what they know at an early stage is designed to reduce the gamesmanship and burden associated with the discovery process.

Finally, even though most of the discovery process is driven by the attorneys themselves, the trial judge has the power to supervise it. Some devices, such as depositions above a stated number, may be used only with the judge's permission. And if one side objects to the other's discovery tactics—such as the nature of the questions asked in a deposition, the amount of requests for production made, or the proprietary nature of the information requested—that side can appeal to the judge for an order limiting the discovery.

What Else Happens Before the Trial?

Movies and television usually focus on the trial part of the litigation process. In fact, trials, in the relatively small proportion of cases in which they occur at all, come only at the end of a long process. Discovery takes up a large portion of the pretrial process, but the period before a case comes to trial is also filled with legal and factual research, negotiations between the parties, motions to the court on procedural or substantive issues, and other proceedings to move the case along.

Sometimes, as we have seen, a case can be terminated before trial by a dismissal—a decision by the court that even if the facts alleged are true, the plaintiff does not have a legally recognized cause of action.

That decision can be made on the pleadings alone. After the parties have begun to amass evidence about the case through the discovery process, a related event is known as *summary judgment*. ("Summary" in this sense means without a full trial.) One party can get summary judgment when the court determines that no facts are really in controversy (commonly referred to as *no genuine issues of material fact*), and when the undisputed facts indicate clearly that one party should win as a matter of law. The court can decide the whole case on summary judgment, ending the case altogether, or only part of it, reducing the issues to be tried or taking some party out of the case. In this way, the court can weed out cases and issues that are sure to be unsuccessful at trial, eliminating much expense, inconvenience, and delay; or, in the case of partial summary judgment, it can narrow the issues and thereby simplify the trial.

During the time before trial, as elsewhere throughout the adversary process, the parties play the dominant role in directing the litigation. But the increasing presence in the judicial system of more complex cases, expanded discovery, and the sheer bulk of litigation has caused judges to take a more active role in managing the litigation in the interest of promoting efficiency. Judicial management of the pretrial process takes several forms. Court rules and practices frequently specify that the attorneys must participate in a series of pretrial conferences designed to assess the status of the case, decide preliminary matters, and generally move the case along. At an early stage the judge might hold a discovery conference in which everyone agrees on a plan for the schedule and amount of discovery to be taken in the case. Closer to trial, many courts require a pretrial conference between the attorneys, the judges, and occasionally the principals in the case. Depending on the rules and customs of the jurisdiction and the proclivities of the judge, the pretrial conference may serve to finally prepare the case for trial, to encourage the parties to settle, or both. At the conference the attorneys will try to stipulate facts that are not in dispute, narrow down the issues remaining, present lists of the witnesses they intend to call, and agree on a schedule for the trial. If they cannot agree, the judge will decide those issues, and the judge also will resolve pending motions on evidence, witnesses, and other matters.

A major function of the pretrial process is to encourage the parties to settle the case before it gets to trial. Especially in busy court systems, where judges are under considerable pressure to conclude as many cases as possible, the judge may use the pretrial conference as an occasion to persuade, cajole, and pressure the attorneys to settle the case before trial. Many jurisdictions have instituted mandatory programs of alternative dispute resolution. Before going to trial, either all cases or cases below a certain dollar amount are referred for mediation, arbitration, or a mini-trial. These proceedings usually take place before a single mediator, a panel of attorneys, a magistrate, or a judge. In arbitration, for example, the attorneys present abbreviated versions of their cases and the arbitrators render a decision on who is liable and in what amount. The arbitration is not binding, and therefore a party can still opt to proceed to trial, but the process has a significant effect in keeping cases from going that far. The arbitration gives the parties and their lawyers an independent assessment of the strength and weaknesses of their cases. The Robinsons may think they have an airtight case worth millions, for example, but if the arbitrators find for the defendants, or give the Robinsons only a small award, it may serve as a reality check and deter them from proceeding to trial. Even if both parties don't accept the arbitration award, it may provide a reference point for settlement negotiations. And a bird in the hand is worth two in the bush; the parties may prefer to take a somewhat unsatisfactory arbitrator's decision rather than wait what may be years to take the uncertain risk of a trial.

With or without judicial intervention or formal alternative dispute resolution, most cases that have made it this far—from half to three-quarters, depending on the jurisdiction and the nature of the case—settle before trial. In small cases the potential litigation costs are greater than the likely return from pursuing the case to the end. If the Robinsons were involved in just a fender bender, the other driver (or his insurance company) would rather pay a small claim than pay their lawyers to try the case. In larger cases, the uncertainty about how the case might come out, the risk of losing big, and the delay and expense of going to trial often favor taking a settlement rather than taking a chance at trial. Not all cases settle, though. The lawyers may hold such differing views of the case that they can't agree on a settlement value. Or they may have other objectives in mind; one party may want to establish a legal principle or may want to build its reputation for litigating to the bitter end, as when an insurance company aggressively defends small cases to deter policyholders from bringing future claims.

What Happens at Trial?

Television, movies, and news reports justifiably focus on trials as the most exciting and important part of the litigation process. Even though only a tiny fraction of civil cases ever go to trial, the trial is the central event in litigation, looming over the rest of the system. And even though its antecedents date back many centuries, to the time of the English king sitting in court dispensing justice, the modern trial is a unique American institution.

Two key features control the trial process. First, the trial is the most intense manifestation of the adversary system; the lawyers for the parties shape the trial, and each side tries to do so in the way most favorable to its position. Second, in most civil cases the parties can choose to have the case tried before a jury; the importance of the jury is crucial for civil procedure and even substantive law. Both of these features are controversial. A trial is supposed to be a search for truth, and an adversary battle before an untutored jury may not be the best way to find the truth. In thinking about what goes on at trial, an important issue is how we balance the search for truth and the desire for efficiency with the historic functions of the adversary system and the jury. (The trial as an adversary proceeding is discussed in this section. The discussion of the jury follows in a later section.)

No trial is typical. The trial of a tort claim arising out of a slip-and-fall case or a contract case about a bank loan may involve only a few witnesses and be over in half a day. A more complex products liability dispute like the Robinsons' or a securities fraud case might require many witnesses, including experts, and last several weeks. The trial of some extremely complex matters like an antitrust claim or a class action may go on for months. Nevertheless, every trial has the same basic structure, a structure determined by its adversary nature.

Consider what might have happened at the Robinsons' trial. If the parties choose to have their case tried by a jury, the first step is to select the jury. Once the jurors are seated and the judge has given them an introduction to what will happen, the Robinsons' attorney makes an opening statement, explaining the case as he sees it: who the parties are, how the accident happened, how seriously the Robinsons have been injured, and why the Audi defendants are legally responsible. Then the defendants' lawyers will have their turn to lay out their view of the case. In a case with multiple parties, all parties on one side might be represented by one lawyer, as the Robinsons were, or each party on a side might have its own lawyer. If Seaway Volkswagen believes that its legal position may be different from that of Audi, it may want its own lawyer; if that happens, each lawyer will have an opportunity to open.

After the opening statements the plaintiffs begin presenting evidence that supports their view of the case. (It is customary to talk about the plaintiff and the defendant, but all of this is really done by their lawyers.) The plaintiff always goes first because the plaintiff bears the *burden of proof*. The burden of proof reflects a basic principle of law: Under our system, no one is liable for anything unless there is a good reason to hold that person liable. Suppose that after the parties present their evidence, the jury determines that the evidence is equally persuasive in each direction; it is just as likely that the gas tank was defective as it is that the tank was not defective. Who wins? The defendant wins because the plaintiff has not met its burden of proof. The plaintiff must prove its case by a *preponderance of the evidence*, so that the judge or jury is persuaded that it is more likely than not—fifty percent plus one—that the plaintiff's version of the case is true. To impose legal liability on someone, it is not enough that they might have violated a rule of law; it must be probable—more likely than not—that they did so. (The preponderance of the evidence standard is much lower than the standard of proof used in criminal cases; because the imposition of a criminal penalty by the state is a more serious matter, criminal cases require the higher burden of proof beyond a reasonable doubt. See Chapter 9.)

After the plaintiff presents its evidence, it is the defendant's turn. Like the plaintiff's lawyer, the defense lawyer calls and examines witnesses to support its side of the case. When the defendant has finished, the plaintiff may have a chance to present rebuttal witnesses, addressing issues raised by the defense. When everyone has finished, each side makes a closing statement to the jury, summing up its case. Then the judge instructs the jury on the law, and the jury deliberates in private and returns its verdict. In a bench trial (a trial to the judge without a jury), of course, the judge does not need instructions on the law, and she may take some time instead of rendering her decision immediately.

The structure of the trial is relatively simple, but, as noted, conflicting values govern the trial process. Consider how the adversary nature of the trial may conflict with the search for truth and the desire to efficiently move things along.

In an adversary trial, the lawyers for each side do more than simply present evidence favorable to their client. Each lawyer—at least a good lawyer—tries to use the whole trial, from the opening statement through the examination of witnesses to the summation, to tell a coherent story about the justice of her client's claim on the facts and on the law. The Robinsons' lawyer paints a picture of a happy family moving to their new home whose life was shattered because Audi's engineers ignored the obvious danger of the gas tank design to save a few dollars in the production cost of the car; justice demands that the wrongdoers compensate their victims, meager though monetary compensation would be for the physical and emotional pain they have suffered. Audi's lawyer recognizes the tragic nature of the accident (though they may describe its consequences as much less severe than the Robinsons are making it out to be) but portrays how the engineers did the best that anyone could in making the car safe; making Audi pay when it could not have done anything better would just be looking for a deep pocket to pay for the Robinsons' loss.

Because the lawyers are adversaries in telling these two inconsistent stories of what happened and what should follow from it, everything that each of them does at trial is directed toward enhancing his own story and discrediting the opponent's story. The ethical rules that govern attorneys' conduct prohibit a lawyer from lying or knowingly instructing a witness to testify falsely, but the same rules require that the attorney be a zealous advocate for the client's position. The lawyer will present all of her evidence in the most favorable light, and she will attempt to cast doubt on her opponent's evidence. The attorney may also engage in other forms of gamesmanship, such as wearing the right clothes to make a favorable impression on the jury, making sure her clients and witnesses act pathetic, sincere, honest, or whatever other role they have been assigned in the story, interrupting her adversary's questioning from time to time just to disrupt his rhythm, and generally doing anything within the bounds of the law and legal ethics to seek an advantage.

What Evidence Can Be Presented at Trial?

The presentation of proof at trial is governed both by the law of civil procedure and the law of evidence. Civil procedure controls the order and method of presentation; evidence law determines what can be presented.

Most of the evidence at trial is presented through the testimony of witnesses, pretty much as depicted on television shows. The witness is sworn to tell the truth, the lawyer who called the witness asks a series of questions that guide the witness through her testimony, and the other party's lawyer can cross-examine, or ask other questions to test the witness's story. If one party's lawyer objects to a question that has been asked, she can ask the judge to prevent the witness from answering, or exclude the answer if it already has been given. Witnesses ordinarily testify from their own knowledge of the facts of the case, but *expert witnesses* go beyond their own knowledge and give opinions on the ultimate issues in the case—whether there was a reasonable alternative design for the Audi's gas tank, for example. Because of their unusual role, expert witnesses have to be qualified and screened by the trial judge. (For more on expert witnesses, see Chapter 5.)

The major difference between the presentation of evidence on television and in real courtrooms is the level of drama. Because of the availability of discovery, the mundane nature of most cases, and the requirements of the law of evidence, seldom does a witness suddenly reveal a "smoking gun" piece of crucial evidence, break down in tears, or confess to a crime. Most witness examinations are methodical, step-by-step recitations of detailed facts. Many people who watch real trials on television or in person quickly become bored, as the attorneys use a seemingly endless series of questions to establish all of the details of a case.

In addition to witness testimony, the presentation of evidence at trial may include the presentation of documents and physical evidence, such as what is left of the Robinsons' gas tank. Sometimes the attorneys or witnesses, particularly expert witnesses, will enliven their testimony with charts, drawings, models, computer animation, or videos in an attempt to clarify their testimony, be more persuasive, and maintain the jury's interest. The parties also may agree that some evidence is undisputed and stipulate to it, so it can be summarized for the jury instead of having to be presented by detailed witness testimony.

The law of evidence involves a balancing act. The court needs to allow the parties to develop their own cases, bringing in all of the evidence that might influence the judgment about what happened and how the case should come out. But the court also wants to operate efficiently, focusing on what is really important, and sometimes it wants to serve values other than simple truth-seeking.

Because the court does not want to waste its time on matters that don't have anything to do with the decision of the case at hand under the prevailing legal rules, the basic proposition of evidence law is that only evidence that is helpful in establishing a legal proposition involved in the case may be considered. This is the basis for the most common objection to the introduction of evidence: when one attorney claims that something is *irrelevant*. If the Robinsons try to have an expert testify that an Audi gas tank will explode if you put a blowtorch to it, the judge will exclude the evidence. Even though that evidence addresses the condition of a gas tank, it does not help very much in determining whether the gas tank was defective; any gas tank will explode if you set fire to it, but the issue in the case is whether the gas tank was too dangerous in a highway crash. Of course, Audi's lawyer must object to the evidence for the judge to exclude it; because the trial is essentially an adversary process, the judge only rules on evidentiary issues raised by the lawyers.

A similar principle motivates the other bit of evidence law many people have heard about—the inadmissibility of *hearsay*. Hearsay evidence is second-hand testimony, or the introduction of an out-of-court statement offered to prove the truth of the content of the statement. If the Robinsons can find a former Audi engineer to testify that he warned the company that the gas tank was unsafe, that would be probative, admissible evidence. But they can't bring in someone else to testify that she had sat behind the engineer on a bus and she heard him say that he had warned the company; that would be inadmissible hearsay. Her testimony is not as reliable as the engineer's, in part because Audi's lawyer would have no effective means of cross-examining her. If the engineer was on the witness stand, Audi's lawyer could ask who he told in the company and what exactly he said, in order to prove that the warning was not given to anyone who could do anything about it or that it was unclear, but the witness who overheard the engineer cannot testify to any of that.

In two circumstances, however, the law of evidence deliberately excludes relevant, potentially useful evidence. The first instance concerns evidence that may be more harmful than helpful in deciding the case. An example is *character evidence*, which is defined broadly as any evidence showing a person's general tendency to act in a certain way. Suppose some parts of Audi's cars other than the gas tank on the 100 LS are known to be poorly designed. The Robinsons certainly would like to introduce evidence of these other failures to suggest that Audi is a sloppy manufacturer and that this pattern of conduct raises the inference that they designed the gas tank on this car poorly, too. But the jury will not be allowed to hear this evidence because the danger that they will assume that Audi made a mistake here outweighs the value of the inference that can be drawn from its past conduct.

The second basis for excluding evidence is when the use of the evidence conflicts with some legal policy outside of evidence law. Here we clearly sacrifice the search for truth at trial to some other value. For example, *privileged information* is excluded. Audi may learn that Mrs. Robinson told her husband and her lawyer that she was faking her injuries, but they cannot call the husband or lawyer to testify to that statement. Even though that would be persuasive evidence of malingering, we think it is more important that people should be able to confide in their spouse and their lawyer without fear that the confidences will be made public than it is to get out all the facts in the course of litigation.

What About the Jury?

In addition to its adversary nature, the second key feature of the trial is the role of the jury as the decision maker. The Seventh Amendment to the U.S. Constitution and most state constitutions preserve the right to a jury trial in civil cases. If both parties agree, a case may be decided by the judge without a jury (called a *bench trial*), but in most cases, if either party wants a jury trial, he or she is entitled to it.

Everyone recognizes that the jury is central to the litigation process, but it is also the most controversial element of the entire litigation system. For some people it is a triumph of the democratic process, a bulwark of the people's liberty, and an effective device for determining the truth at trial; for others, it is an antiquated, inefficient institution that only introduces arbitrariness, uncertainty, and delay into the system.

The unique attribute of the jury is that it is composed of amateurs. Rather than have a highly trained, professional judge decide the Robinsons' case, we entrust that responsibility to a group of people who know little about the law and nothing about the facts of the case other than what they hear in the courtroom. This group must sift through the conflicting evidence to decide what really happened, understand the judge's explanation of the law (which often involves subtle concepts that baffle law students and divide judges), and put the facts and the law together to reach a result that is both just and in accordance with the law—all by unanimous or near-unanimous agreement. (In many jurisdictions, the traditional requirement of a unanimous verdict by a twelve-member jury has been reduced in favor of smaller juries—often six—and nonunanimous verdicts—usually by a supermajority of two-thirds or three-fourths.)

The jury's job is to hear the evidence, decide what happened in the case, listen to the judge's instructions on the law, and apply the law to the facts. In doing so, jurors bring to bear their own experiences, beliefs, and values, making the decision process to a degree an expression of community sentiment and not just a mechanical fact-finding process.

To serve these functions, juries should be representative and impartial. To ensure that they are representative, the court constructs the list of potential jurors from the rolls of registered voters, licensed drivers, and other sources designed to draw in a large segment of the community. Potential jurors are randomly summoned from this list to appear for jury duty. Many people view jury service to be more of an inconvenience than a civic responsibility and try to avoid serving, either by claiming a statutory excuse (often given to police officers, physicians, or the like), by asking to be excused because of some hardship (caring for small children or a sick relative, for example), or simply by not showing up. In the latter circumstance, of course, the court may discourage that kind of behavior by summoning the juror again or even issuing an arrest warrant.

More potential jurors are called than can be used on scheduled trials, because many are winnowed out before the jury is seated. This process is known as *voir dire* (the French legal term meaning "to speak the truth"), and it is designed to make sure that the jury is impartial. The judge or the attorneys ask the jurors a series of questions, collectively and individually, to ferret out which potential jurors might have knowledge or associations that might bias their judgment. In the Robinsons' case, a potential juror who knew the Robinsons or worked as an automotive engineer might be challenged by one of the attorneys and excused by the judge for *cause*, since there was an obvious reason why they might not be impartial in deciding the case. Typically the attorneys also each have some *peremptory challenges* that allow them to remove potential jurors without giving a reason. Much attorney folklore governs the exercise of peremptory challenges—the idea that small business owners don't give large damage awards in personal injury cases, for example—and recently the field has been taken over, at least in very important cases, by jury consultants, psychologists, or other supposed experts who study jurors' backgrounds, body language, and responses in voir dire to advise the attorneys on who would make a favorable or unfavorable juror in a particular case.

After the jury has heard the evidence and been instructed on the law by the judge, it retires to discuss the case (to *deliberate*) in secret. When the jury reaches a decision, it returns to the courtroom to render a verdict. Unlike a judge, a jury does not give reasons for its verdict, although sometimes the judge requires a *special verdict*, or responses to a series of questions about the case. (Was the gas tank defective? Was the Robinsons' car traveling at an excessive speed?)

The great question about the jury system is how well it works. Is the jury an effective fact-finding and law-applying institution that brings community sentiment to the process in a constructive way, or is it an arbitrary, inefficient anachronism that too often makes bad decisions? Because of the constitutional status of the civil jury right, the issue cannot really be debated in terms of doing away with the jury altogether, but it is played out in deciding how much power the law gives to the judge to control the jury.

The judge controls the jury in four ways. First, the judge limits what the jury can hear during the trial by applying the law of evidence (discussed earlier). Second, the judge limits the issues that the jury can consider; the usual formulation is that *issues of law* are for the judge to decide and *issues of fact* are the jury's responsibility. Third, the judge tells the jury what rules of law to apply in deciding the case and what those rules mean; the amateur jury has no way of knowing what the law is, so it is supposed to follow the judge's instructions. Fourth, the judge can take the case away from the jury before it decides, or even upset the jury's verdict after it is rendered, by granting one of several motions for either party. (The substantive law also controls the jury, of course. If the jurisdiction has enacted a cap on damages for pain and suffering, for example, any award by the jury in excess of the cap will be reduced.)

The law–fact distinction seems as if it ought to be simple: The judge has read the law books and is in the best position to determine what rules apply and what they mean—the issues of law—and the jury figures out what happened in the case—the issues of fact. The reality is more complex. Labeling an issue as "law" or "fact" is simply a way for the judge to determine which issues he is willing to allow the jury to decide. Broadening the fact category expands the jury's role, while broadening the law category narrows it. If the judge thinks an issue is too complex, very important, or potentially subject to misinterpretation, he will be inclined to take it from the jury and preserve it for himself. As long as the judge doesn't go too far in usurping the constitutional function of the jury, treating issues as matters of law is an effective jury control mechanism.

In the Robinsons' case, for example, determining whether Audi is liable involves issues of law and fact. Tort law frames the issues in this way: whether Audi owed the plaintiffs a duty, what the content of that duty was, and whether Audi breached the duty. The first two questions involve important issues of social policy, so the court treats them as matters of law. Whether Audi owes a passenger in one of its cars a duty and how much of a duty are the basic issues of tort law; deciding these questions has immense consequences for society at large. If Audi did not owe a duty to passengers, it would have much less incentive to manufacture safe cars. Conversely, if it owed a duty to compensate people who were upset by hearing about the accident on the television news, its liability would be overwhelming. The content of its duty is equally important. One of the great debates in tort law has been whether the manufacturer of a product should be liable for all injuries caused by defects in its products (called *strict liability*) or only where it has been careless in manufacturing the product (where it has been *negligent*). The outcome of this debate is so important that the court in a products liability case like this one will not let the jury resolve it. But the third question— whether the car had a defect, assuming that Audi would be liable if the car was defective—is different. This is by no means a simple question of fact, because it requires the exercise of judgment about whether the risks of the gas tank's design outweigh its benefits, but it is much less important for the decision of other cases. The judge therefore will label the breach of duty question as one of fact and leave it to the jury to decide.

If the jury's function is limited to finding the facts and applying the law to the facts, it must have some way of knowing what the law is and what they are supposed to do with it. At the end of the trial, the judge tells the jury what issues it has to decide and what law it should apply by giving *instructions*, or a *charge*. The judge explains, for example, what standard of conduct the law requires of an automobile manufacturer in making its product safe, how to determine whether a design is defective, for what kinds of damages Audi can be liable, how sure of their conclusions the jurors must be before reaching a verdict, and how they should conduct their deliberations. In most jurisdictions the courts promulgate standard jury instructions for different types of cases, so the judge doesn't have to make them up each time. Typically, though, each attorney also offers a set of proposed instructions, modifying the standard instructions to fit the individual case, suggesting issues that ought to be included or excluded, and shading the instructions to a particular view of the law. This is part of the adversary process, as each attorney tries to get the most advantageous instructions, and it is up to the judge to decide what is appropriate.

Jury instructions are another point at which the limits of jury trials become contested. Even in a relatively routine case such as the Robinsons', the judge's instructions can go on for an hour or more; in a complex case, the instructions can take even longer. And the instructions are necessarily complicated, dealing with sophisticated legal issues and open questions. It's difficult for a nonprofessional juror to assimilate this recitation of rules that even lawyers and judges might find complex or consider highly debatable. Thus even though the lawyers and judge may have spent hours carefully crafting each sentence of the instructions, the jurors may be left with an impression or a few basic ideas that don't accurately reflect the law they are supposed to apply.

The final method of jury control is one that goes to the heart of the allocation of authority between judge and jury. At key points before, during, or even after the trial, a party can ask the judge to take all or part of the case away from the jury and decide it himself. We have already seen how the judge can prevent the case from going to trial by granting a motion to dismiss the plaintiff's case because it doesn't state a legally supportable claim against the defendant, or by granting a motion for summary judgment because there are no major factual disputes and the law determines how the case should be decided on the undisputed facts. Once the trial has begun, the judge can also limit the jury's power and find for one of the parties by granting a *motion for directed verdict* during the trial or a *motion for judgment notwithstanding the verdict* after the jury has decided; the two motions often are referred to together as *motions for judgment as a matter of law*. Or, at the end of the trial, the judge can set aside the jury's verdict and order that there be a new trial.

The motions for judgment as a matter of law may be granted if the judge determines that there are insufficient facts to go to the jury or that only one result reasonably could follow from the facts. The two motions differ in their timing. A party may move for directed verdict after its opponent has presented all of its evidence. After the Robinsons conclude their case, Audi may move for a directed verdict in its favor if, for example, the Robinsons have not presented any evidence that it was possible to make a safer gas tank (if that is part of the legal standard), or because all of the evidence they have presented indicates that the gas tank was as safely designed as possible. Similarly, the Robinsons may move for a directed verdict after Audi concludes its defense if Audi has not successfully refuted their evidence that the gas tank was improperly designed. If either motion is granted, the court will enter judgment for the successful party. (Even though it is called a motion for directed verdict, the jury doesn't have to go through the formality of actually rendering the verdict that the judge directs them to—the judge does that for them.)

Judgment notwithstanding the verdict is even more remarkable. The presentation of evidence concludes, the judge instructs the jury and sends it out to deliberate, and the jury returns with a verdict. But then the judge concludes that the jury arrived at an answer that is wrong on the law or unreasonable on the facts, so he declares one party the winner notwithstanding the jury's verdict in favor of the other party. Procedurally, this motion is treated as if it were a delayed motion for directed verdict, and the judge may use it because there is a tactical advantage to delaying his decision to take the case away from the jury. If it is a close question and the judge grants a directed verdict, one party will probably appeal and the appellate court might reverse the trial judge, requiring a new trial. By waiting to see if the jury arrives at the "right" answer, the judge may avoid the need for a second trial; a jury verdict is more likely to be upheld than his grant of a motion.

Judgments as a matter of law present a striking conflict between the jury's central place in the trial process and the judge's power to control the jury. Because there were predecessors of these motions at the time of the drafting of the Constitution, the Supreme Court has held that they do not violate the Seventh Amendment right to a jury trial. Nevertheless, because the device threatens the core of the jury's function, courts have taken some pains to try to define when such a motion might be appropriate, and different courts disagree on how much a trial judge can intrude into the jury's domain.

Instead of entering judgment for one of the parties, the judge has the option of ordering a new trial to correct errors that occurred in the first trial. Of course, an appeals court also can order a new trial, but the trial judge knows firsthand what happened and, having the opportunity to evaluate the trial, may decide that some individual error, or the accumulation of a number of smaller mistakes, prejudiced the opportunity of the losing party to have a fair trial. Like motions for judgment as a matter of law, granting a new trial can invade the jury's province by making their verdict ineffective. The new trial is less invasive, though, because at least a second jury will get to hear the case. Nevertheless, new trials are not granted just because the judge disagrees with the jury's verdict. If the judge has made a substantial legal error in conducting the trial—improperly admitting or excluding important evidence or incorrectly instructing the jury, for example—he may correct the mistake by ordering a new trial. Other reasons to grant a new trial include misconduct by an attorney or juror, newly discovered evidence, or because the verdict is excessive. In the latter case the judge may offer the winning party a choice: Accept a different amount or go to trial again.

What Happens After Trial?

The trial isn't necessarily the end of the story. The losing party, or even a party who wins only part of what it wanted, can appeal the case to a higher court. Not every loser does appeal. The lawyer might decide that there is not a good enough basis for appealing, or the party might be unable or unwilling to invest more money in the litigation. But in every jurisdiction, a losing party at least has the right to consider having the case reviewed by an appellate court.

The larger court systems, like the federal courts and those of big states, have two layers of appellate courts. The first layer is the intermediate appellate court, called the Courts of Appeals in the federal system and various names in different states. (Smaller jurisdictions omit this layer.) The second layer is the highest court in the jurisdiction, such as the U.S. Supreme Court or the Oklahoma Supreme Court. If the disappointed litigant doesn't like the result in the intermediate appellate court, she may ask the highest court to hear the case. Usually, though, while the appeal to the intermediate court is mandatory (the court must hear the case), the appeal to the next level is discretionary (the court can decide whether or not it wants to hear the case). In the U.S. Supreme Court, the procedure of asking the court to hear the appeal is called petitioning for a *writ of certiorari* (a Latin term meaning "to be informed"); by issuing the writ, the higher court tells the lower court that it wishes to be informed about the case so that it can decide it. A court of last resort will take only an appeal that seems important to it, either because the case raises an important legal issue or because there is confusion among the lower courts about the proper resolution of the legal issue involved.

The appeals process is not designed to achieve a correct result or to guarantee a perfect process in the case. Instead, it tries to balance the fundamental values of the litigation process. An appellate court will correct errors in the courts below that substantially impinge on the fairness of the process or the effectuation of the values of substantive law that are involved, but it tries to do this relatively efficiently, by not interfering too much, causing undue delay, or preventing finality in the process.

Take as an example part of the appeal in the Robinsons' case. (Remember that there also were complex procedural issues in the case, resulting in the case moving through the Oklahoma courts to the U.S. Supreme Court and then up and down through the lower federal courts.) The jury returned a verdict for the defendants and against the Robinsons in the U.S. District Court for the Northern District of Oklahoma. The Robinsons appealed to the U.S. Court of Appeals, arguing in part that the trial judge had improperly excluded evidence that Volkswagen, the parent company, had known of the risks of the gas tank design. The trial judge had excluded the evidence under the theory that the knowledge could not be attributed to Audi, the manufacturer of the car and a subsidiary of Volkswagen. The court of appeals agreed that the knowledge could not be attributed to Audi and affirmed that part of the judgment but disagreed with the trial judge's ruling that the evidence could not be used against Volkswagen, so it sent the case back for a new trial against Volkswagen.

First consider when someone can appeal from the trial court. Here courts see the route to efficiency and finality in different ways. Most courts observe the *final judgment rule*, which, as its name indicates, permits the review only of actions of the lower court that are final, completely settling the matter before it. Under this approach, the Robinsons cannot appeal the exclusion of the evidence of Volkswagen's knowledge of the defect at the time the trial judge makes his ruling; they have to wait for the end of the case, when they have lost. This is seen as efficient because it prevents the Robinsons from delaying the trial while they appeal, it allows the appellate court to look at the whole case at once, including that particular error or any others alleged, and review of the ruling might never be necessary; if the Robinsons win, the appellate court will never have to consider the issue. Other courts allow an appeal at any time when a substantial right is implicated in the trial judge's decision. In this case, allowing an appeal of the evidentiary issue would have made it unnecessary to complete the first trial only to have a new trial ordered when the appellate court reversed.

Next consider what the court of appeals did not do. Because the appellate process follows the same adversary ideal as the rest of the system, an appellate court will only answer questions that it is asked. The court of appeals did not decide on its own whim that it wanted to look at the Robinsons' case after the trial court had finished; it had to wait for one of the parties to appeal. And once it had the case, it only could address issues that were brought to its attention by the parties and that were raised in the court below. It did not, for example, consider whether the jury instructions were proper, because neither party raised that issue. Nor would the court consider an issue that the losing party had failed to raise at trial. If the trial judge had admitted the disputed evidence, Audi could not object to its admissibility for the first time on appeal. As a matter of fairness and efficiency, the appellate court only considers matters brought to the trial judge's attention and developed in the limited record that it has in front of it. Nor does the court consider facts that were not brought before the lower court. And the court will only consider issues on appeal that make a difference in the outcome of the case. Audi, for example, could not appeal some ruling of the judge just because it wanted to get a pronouncement from the higher court on the law on that issue; Audi won, so the court won't waste its time considering issues that are not important to the resolution of the live controversy. (Once the Robinsons appeal, however, Audi can raise other issues in support of the judgment.)

Finally, think about how an appellate court reviews what happened in the lower court. If the issue brought before it is a question of law, the appeals court will usually be willing to use its own judgment as to the correct result. The exclusion of the evidence of Volkswagen's knowledge turned on a principle of law about the relationship between parent and subsidiary corporations. The appeals judges know that law as well as the trial judge does, so they will consider the matter afresh and give no deference to the trial judge's ruling. (Because of their loftier position, appeals court judges often think they know the law better. As the saying goes about the justices of the Supreme Court, they are not final because they are infallible, but they are infallible because they are final.) If the issue is one that involves the facts, however, the appellate court will be more circumspect. They see only a portion of the transcript of the proceedings in the lower court and the parties' attorneys' arguments. They have not heard the witnesses or considered all of the evidence, so they are in a weaker position to evaluate, say, whether the gas tank was defective. Accordingly, the appeals court will give more deference to a factual determination, especially if it is made by a jury and not overturned by the trial judge.

When all the appeals have been exhausted, the case is over. Even though the losing party may discover new evidence or come up with a new theory, it cannot go back to court and try again. Finality is an important element of the legal system, incorporated in the Latin phrase *res judicata*—"the thing has been decided."

5

Hot Coffee and Crashing Cars

Tort Law

Stella Liebeck, seventy-nine years old and a passenger in her nephew's car, bought a cup of coffee at the drive-through window of a McDonald's in Albuquerque, New Mexico. As she placed the cup between her legs to remove the lid to add cream and sugar, she spilled the coffee, burning herself. Liebeck sued McDonald's, alleging that the coffee was too hot, and a jury awarded her $160,000 to compensate her for her injuries and $2.7 million to punish McDonald's.

This is the most famous case of "lawsuit abuse" pointed to by advocates of tort reform as they seek to revamp our system of civil liability, which is known as tort law. Everyone knows that coffee is hot, and if you spill it, you can burn yourself. But no one is willing to accept the consequences of an everyday accident, say tort reformers. Instead, judges and juries have run amok in allowing plaintiffs to pass their misfortune on to someone with a deep pocket.

Meanwhile, defenders of tort law view Liebeck's case as evidence of how well the tort system works. McDonald's had received over 700 complaints about the temperature of the coffee it served and had settled many of these complaints. The company served its coffee at a temperature twenty degrees hotter than its competitors, a temperature that its managers admitted was too hot to drink right away and hot enough to cause burns. Liebeck was in the hospital for a week with third-degree burns requiring skin grafts. She initially was willing to settle the case for her medical expenses, but McDonald's refused. The jury figured that $2.7 million was the amount McDonald's made from two days of coffee sales, so it used that amount as the punitive damage award. The jury also found that Liebeck was partially responsible for her injuries because she wasn't careful, so it reduced the damages it awarded her accordingly, and the trial judge further reduced the punitive damage award to $480,000. Only after this case and the resulting publicity did McDonald's reduce the temperature of its coffee. Here the tort system worked, its defenders say; a wrongdoer was forced to compensate an injured victim and to remedy its dangerous conduct. The case also influenced other potentially dangerous conduct: The Wendy's chain reduced the temperature of its hot chocolate, served mostly to children.

For several hundred years, courts and legislatures have been working out tort principles that determine when someone is responsible for someone else's injuries. Proponents of the tort system say that cases like Stella Liebeck's show how well the system works and that any change ought to come through a continuation of the centuries-old process of step-by-step development. Tort reformers argue that things have gone too far, shifting responsibility away from individuals and imposing costs on blameless defendants, so that drastic legislative changes are needed. Before we can decide to either maintain or revamp the system, however, we need to understand what tort law is all about.

What Is Tort Law?

Tort law is easy to describe at a general level and hard to define more precisely. *Tort* comes from a Latin word meaning "twisted" or "turned aside," so a tort is an act that is turned aside from the standard of proper conduct—a wrongful act. If you punch your neighbor in the nose, run over a pedestrian by driving carelessly, or injure a customer by serving burning hot coffee, you have committed a tort. (Some torts, not discussed here, involve only economic harm and not physical injury, such as falsely accusing someone of being a crook or using fraud to induce them to enter into a financial transaction.) All of these are wrongful acts for which the victim can receive an award of money damages.

We can get a good sense of what tort law is about from these typical cases. Notice, however, that the descriptions are basically empty because they do not answer the fundamental question about tort law: If tort law sanctions wrongful conduct, how do we tell what conduct is wrongful? Does your neighbor commit a tort when he punches you in the nose? How about a driver who causes an accident while going under the speed limit but arguably driving too fast for the weather conditions? Does McDonald's commit a tort when it serves coffee that is hot enough to scald a customer?

Questions like these suggest two important features of tort law. First, some cases are easy to decide and some cases are hard. Judges, lawyers, and tort scholars use the easy cases to develop policies and principles that help them analyze the hard cases. (Sometimes it works in reverse as well; thinking about the hard cases provokes insights that make us rethink our answers to the easy cases.) Second, tort law is as much a process as it is a body of rules. An essential element of tort law is the application of very general principles—such as "everyone must use reasonable care not to injure someone else"—to particular cases, like an auto accident that occurs on a rainy night. The institutional structure through which the rules are applied—the litigation system in which responsibility is shared by judges and juries—is as important in tort law as the content of the rules themselves.

For a long time, the tort litigation system almost uniformly involved cases brought by an individual plaintiff against an individual defendant arising out of a single event. At most, small groups would be on one side of the litigation or the other; the driver and three passengers in a car would sue the driver of the other car who caused the accident, or a patient injured during an operation would sue the surgeon, the anesthesiologist, and the hospital. Those types of cases still dominate tort litigation, but in recent decades, cases involving many people injured by the same conduct, known as *mass torts*, have become more important. Some mass torts involve multiple injuries produced by a single accident, such as an explosion, or a single source, such as pollution from a chemical plant. Others involve multiple injuries produced by the same kind of conduct repeated over time, such as the use of asbestos or the sale of a dangerous drug. The results, of either kind, are dramatic: 6,000 victims of the September 11 tragedy, 13,000 cases involving the blood thinner Xarelto, and more than 800,000 asbestos cases.

Mass torts present several challenges to the system. One challenge is dealing with the sheer number of cases, which can move through the tort system like a pig through a python, creating a bulge of litigation that threatens to overwhelm the courts and delay the adjudication of other cases. Another problem is parceling out justice to victims with different injuries who sue at different times. Many defendants in mass tort cases resort to bankruptcy to escape the burden of liability, and the courts must then determine who gets what; if early plaintiffs are fully compensated, there may be nothing left for those whose injuries manifest later. And toxic torts—mass torts arising from exposure to dangerous chemicals, drugs, or other substances—pose unusual causation problems, because it may be difficult to tie the risk posed to particular injuries, which may have complex origins and which may arise long after exposure. Some of these problems are discussed in later sections of this chapter. In responding to the question "what is tort law?", however, the presence of mass torts means that the answer includes both a process for the adjudication of individual disputes and a system for addressing spectacularly large numbers of injuries as well.

Why Do We Need Tort Law?

Injuries occur every day. A driver falls asleep at the wheel and crashes into a tree. Someone trips down the steps. Surgical procedures are not always successful.

Very often, though, people are injured when someone else is responsible. A homeowner fails to repair cracks in his sidewalk and a passerby trips and falls. Physicians misdiagnose and mistreat patients. Passengers are killed in an apparently minor car crash because the gas tank ruptures and explodes. Or take one of the bizarre fact patterns that is a favorite of torts teachers: A train conductor pushes a passenger, causing him to drop a package; fireworks in the package explode, knocking over scales which fall on another passenger waiting at the other end of the platform.

What if we had no legal system to deal with injuries like these? First, people would have less incentive to avoid injuring other people. Sometimes injuries would occur intentionally; more often, the injuries would be accidental, because people would have less incentive to be careful. An auto manufacturer would have an incentive to cut back on safety measures if it knew it would not be liable for injuries that were caused by defective cars. Property owners might be less inclined to repair their sidewalks. Conversely, businesses and individuals who did act safely would be penalized for their good behavior because it is often more expensive to act carefully with no corresponding reduction in liability.

Second, the victims of accidents would be left to their own resources to pay for medical expenses, lost wages, property damage, and other consequences of injuries they suffer. For most victims the cost would be significant; for the unlucky few, the cost would be catastrophic. Stella Liebeck's misadventure with hot coffee, for example, would cost her tens of thousands of dollars in hospitalization and doctor bills.

Third, it just would not seem fair that people could freely inflict harm on other people, either intentionally or carelessly. The careless driver would get away with acting wrongfully if he did not have to pay for his actions, and the innocent victim would have to suffer the consequences.

We could take care of these problems in several ways other than a tort system. Wrongful behavior could be prosecuted criminally. Beefed-up enforcement of the traffic laws could make sure people drove carefully. Government bureaucracies could regulate in detail how cars and other products are manufactured, how people have to maintain their property, at what temperature coffee can be served in fast-food restaurants, and so on. The market and general reputation would help, too; consumers might only buy products that they knew to be safe, and people would not want to be thought of as careless. Victims of accidents could purchase their own insurance. If they could not afford to do so, they could be taken care of by government assistance or private charities.

In fact, we do use mechanisms other than tort law to take care of the problems that arise from injuries. The threat of criminal prosecution discourages people from punching each other, and the federal government requires that cars have air bags, seat belts, and other safety devices. Someone who is injured in a traffic accident may have medical insurance to pay for his treatment and disability insurance to make up for his lost income; if he doesn't, Medicaid, Social Security, and welfare payments may fill the gap. Some areas have been removed from the tort system, substantially or altogether. Workers compensation is the largest; in every state, workers who are injured in the course of their employment cannot sue their employers (with limited exceptions) but are instead covered by a state-run insurance program. Children who suffer adverse reactions to childhood vaccines can seek compensation from a federal trust fund instead of suing the manufacturer. After the September 11 disaster, Congress established an administrative procedure to compensate victims and their families as an alternative to suing the airlines and airports for failing to protect against terrorism, and 97 percent of the potential claimants were granted compensation.

Nevertheless, over several hundred years we also have developed a system of tort law to address injuries and wrongdoing. Tort law provides incentives for good conduct and disincentives for bad conduct, requires that wrongdoers compensate their victims, and serves our sense of justice. These are the three principal purposes of tort law: deterrence or incentives, compensation, and fairness. As a system for serving these objectives and dealing with the problem of injury, the tort system has three advantages over other mechanisms.

First, tort law permits private persons to take the lead in implementing its policies. All torts cases are brought by private individuals or businesses, not by the government acting as the prosecutor. (Sometimes the government is a party to tort cases, but then it is in the same position as any other plaintiff or defendant.) The federal and state governments establish court systems to referee disputes, but private parties drive the tort system by their complaints and defenses. Moreover, the system is self-financing. Plaintiffs' lawyers take cases on a *contingent fee* basis, under which they advance the costs of the litigation, their clients pay no fees up front, and they take a portion of the recovery if they win and nothing if they lose. Thus the tort system does not require a large prosecutor's office or administrative bureaucracy to formulate rules, investigate wrongdoing, and pursue complaints. Instead, pursuing the public purposes of tort law is left in the hands of private persons. Stella Liebeck and McDonald's, for example, not the Food and Drug Administration or the Consumer Products Safety Commission, drive the debate about how hot is too hot for coffee.

Second, most of tort law is made up of relatively general rules, such as a rule that an auto manufacturer has to make a car in such a way that it does not contain a defect rendering it unreasonably dangerous. What that means is fleshed out in the context of individual cases and can be hotly contested, but it does not require the law to specify in advance, in tedious detail, how a car must be built and what safety devices it must contain. Regulatory agencies like the National Highway Traffic Safety Administration do some of this now, but without tort law they would have to do much more. Indeed, because of the infinite ways in which accidents can occur, it would be impossible to lay out prospectively how someone must behave in every conceivable circumstance, and the generality of tort law enables us to evaluate behavior without having to do so.

Third, tort law links the deterrence and compensation policies to the objective of fairness by requiring that the compensation to the victim come from the wrongdoer. Once an injury has occurred, it seems right that the wrongdoer should be made to pay and the victim should be compensated. There is a neat symmetry to the mechanism that accomplishes both objectives at the same time. If the wrongdoer is criminally prosecuted, the victim still bears her loss; if the victim has her bills paid by insurance, her loss is compensated but the wrongdoer gets away without taking responsibility.

Whether tort law works as it is supposed to is currently one of the most controversial issues in the law. Businesses, doctors, and insurance companies, arguing that tort law is out of whack, have joined under the banner of *tort reform* to do away with some basic tort doctrines and cut back on many others. Consumer groups and trial lawyers have defended the system and argued for its expansion. Meanwhile, tort scholars from the left and right sides of the political spectrum have analyzed and debated the effectiveness of the system.

Tort reformers argue that the courts have gone overboard in serving the compensation policy of tort law and have lost sight of fairness and of the real-world consequences of their rulings. Increasingly, they assert, the overwhelming impulse of courts in making tort rules and juries in individual cases is to compensate the injured victim. In following this impulse, they have forgotten the need to prove the defendant was at fault before imposing liability. Judges have created rules that do not require a finding of fault before shifting the victim's losses to the defendant. Similarly, juries faced with a seriously injured individual and a defendant who is a large corporation or a wealthy, well-insured doctor are not inclined to listen to explanations of the reasonableness of the defendant's conduct in their search for a deep pocket to pay the victim's losses.

The consequence of these actions is a system of too much tort liability and the ever-present threat of even more. This imposes a "tort tax" on products and activities that raises the cost of many goods and services and removes others from the market altogether. A car, a power tool, and a ladder cost more because manufacturers are forced to include unnecessary safety devices or warnings. Physicians must practice defensive medicine by ordering additional tests that drive up the cost of health care, or they leave high-risk specialties such as obstetrics altogether.

Tort reformers also argue that the expansion of tort liability undermines personal responsibility. Because courts refuse to enforce some agreements limiting or disclaiming tort liability, consumers are unable to exercise choice as to the level of safety they are willing to pay for. More broadly, the increase in liability has contributed to a society in which people do not feel responsible for their own actions and all look for an excuse for their behavior and someone else to pay for their losses. In the "sue 'em" society, no one has to bear the consequences of his or her acts anymore. In response to these problems, tort reformers have succeeded in enacting some changes and have proposed even more. The goal, they say, is to restore balance to the system by making it harder for injury victims to get to court, harder to win if they get there, and harder to collect large damages if they do win.

Defenders of the tort system disagree with the tort reform diagnosis and remedy. They point out that the system has been a great success in improving the safety of the American people. Tort law has had a significant effect in providing incentives for safety, in areas from medical malpractice to the manufacture of defective products. The prospect of tort liability, for example, encourages manufacturers to research the potential dangers of their products and to develop safer products. Many dangerous products either have been taken off the market, restricted in use, or improved—examples include asbestos, children's clothing that is not flame-retardant, and cars that are not crashworthy. For many victims of personal injury, tort law provides the only source of compensation. While tort reformers repeat high-profile horror stories (only some of which are accurately reported), the broader story of the success of tort law has been less frequently told.

This success has been accomplished without juries going wild. In the overwhelming majority of cases, lay juries agree with professional judges about the outcome of cases and do not simply hunt for a deep pocket to pay for the plaintiff's loss. And the issue of personal responsibility is a complicated one; making the plaintiff assume liability for her conduct is often achieved only by letting the defendant not bear responsibility for his.

These are difficult issues to resolve, and they will be discussed more as the chapter explores the substantive rules of tort law. But let's take a look at two stories to get started on the process.

Professor Peter Bell relates an anecdote that gives a perspective on how businesses are affected by the presence of tort law. He tells of visiting Niagara Falls and coming upon a cluster of wooden steps, platforms, and bridges that allowed tourists to walk right down to the falls. When his daughter asked, "Daddy, is it safe down there?" he had two conflicting reactions: On the one hand, the structure seemed too fragile, but on the other hand, it had to be safe. His belief that it was safe did not rest on the likelihood that some government agency had inspected the steps, nor on the confidence that the owners would check them carefully because it was the right thing to do or would serve their business interests. Instead, Bell reports, "What made me think the structure was safe was my knowledge that the operators of the tour were aware that if they did not make damn sure the thing was safe, they would get their pants sued off."

Second, think about the problem of drug safety. Pharmaceutical manufacturers generally try to make safe drugs, because that is the responsible thing to do and because it is good business. But they are in business to make a profit, and that goal creates pressure to put or keep a drug on the market even if there are questions about its safety. The consumer's next line of defense is the Food and Drug Administration, which approves new drugs, requires warnings of potential risks, and orders products taken off the market when greater risks become known. But there are major gaps in the FDA process. At its best, the FDA relies on information from drug companies and cannot adequately evaluate every product risk. At its worst, as law professor and torts expert Carl Bogus wrote, a regulatory agency such as the FDA can be "captured, exhausted, besieged, ossified, demoralized, co-opted, and starved," subject to political influence and control by the companies it is meant to regulate. Even FDA officials concede the problem; Dr. David Graham, associate director of the FDA's Office of Drug Safety, asserted that the FDA "is incapable of protecting America." When companies' own incentives or FDA regulations fail, tort law steps in to fill the gap. Tort law does not provide easy answers, however. Deciding whether a manufacturer should be liable for making a dangerous drug involves balancing between those who are harmed by the drug and those who are benefited by it and evaluating what the manufacturer knew about the dangers, when it knew it, and what it should have done.

Is It a Tort When You Hit Someone?

Tort law is divided into three categories: intentional torts, negligence, and strict liability. An *intentional tort* is when the person causing the harm meant to do so. *Negligence* involves carelessness. *Strict liability* holds the actor responsible even though he did not mean to harm the victim and exercised care in trying to avoid the harm. Of these, the easiest category to understand is intentional torts, where the prototypical tort is known as *battery*.

When Biff punches George in the nose, pushes him down a flight of stairs, or gleefully runs him over with his car, it constitutes the intentional tort of battery. Battery protects the integrity of a person's body against intentional invasions. Providing a remedy for battery serves the policies of tort law. We want to deter Biff and people like him from punching others, and if George has to go to the doctor because of his injuries, it is fair that Biff compensate him for his loss.

Simple enough. But of course, the law is seldom that simple. Intentional torts are wrongful because the tortfeasor intended to cause harm to the victim. (*Tortfeasor* is an elegant legal term for someone who commits a tort; substitute "wrongdoer" if you like.) But what does it mean to intend harm? And what kind of harm is required?

Consider the case of *Garratt v. Dailey* (1955) from the Washington Supreme Court. Brian Dailey, a five-year-old boy, was visiting in the backyard of Ruth Garratt, an older woman. Brian moved a lawn chair that Ruth intended to sit in. When she tried to sit down, not noticing that the chair was no longer there, she fell to the ground and fractured her hip. The precise chain of events was in dispute. Ruth alleged that Brian deliberately pulled the chair out from under her as she started to sit down in it. The trial court found that Brian had picked up the chair, moved it a few feet, and sat down. When he discovered that Ruth was about to sit in the place where the chair had been, he hurriedly got up and tried to put the chair back, but he was not in time to prevent Ruth's fall.

Take Ruth's version of the events first. If Brian testifies that he didn't mean to hurt Ruth but only thought it would be funny to see her fall to the ground, does he have sufficient intent to make him liable for a battery? In everyday language, Brian did not "intend" to cause the harm that ultimately occurred—a broken hip. He didn't mean for it to happen, but from the law's viewpoint, he still intended to cause an unlawful contact (having Ruth fall) that is sufficient for a battery. His motive—what kind of harm he intended to accomplish—is irrelevant if he wanted to bring about the contact.

Now take the court's version of the events. Here Brian did not even intend that Ruth fall, but he still might be liable. Under the law, a person commits a battery either by purposely causing the harm or by acting with *substantial certainty* that the harm will occur. If Brian knew for sure (with substantial certainty) that Ruth would attempt to sit down where the chair had been—because she just brought over a plate of food and put it down on a picnic table in front of the chair, for example—the intent requirement is satisfied. We want to discourage conduct that is substantially certain to cause harm as much as conduct that is intended to cause harm, and we want to compensate the victims of that harm to the same extent; as between Brian and the injured Ruth Garratt, it is fairer that he (or his parents) should bear the cost of her injury than that she should.

The concept of harm is as broad as the concept of intent. A battery is committed when someone intentionally causes *harmful or offensive contact*. A broken hip from a fall or a bloody nose from a punch are easy cases of harmful contact, but severe injury like that is not required. A slight bruise or cut is more than enough.

The real expansion of liability for battery comes from the concept of offensive contact. If Ruth falls to the ground and is not injured at all, Brian still has committed a battery because the contact offends her dignity. When the law combines the concept of offensive contact with the idea that the only intent required is the intent to cause such a contact, it produces an expansive conception of battery. From the obvious case of a punch in the nose the law inevitably moves to making judgments about the appropriateness of all kinds of contact. If Joe gives Maria an unwanted kiss as a sign of affection, it is a battery. Indeed, the conception of bodily integrity is so strong that Joe commits a battery even if he kisses Maria while she is asleep and unaware of the kiss.

Not every intentionally harmful or offensive contact is battery, however. If the victim consents to the contact—if Maria consents to the kiss—it is not battery. This makes sense in light of the goals of tort law. We do not have the same interest in deterring harmful or offensive contact when the person agrees to the contact; he has, in effect, forfeited his right of compensation. Nor would it be fair to impose liability on someone who is only doing what another person has agreed to.

If someone consents to a certain bodily invasion, he does not necessarily consent to any bodily invasion, however. Professional football players consent to be hit in the course of a game, but they do not necessarily consent to any act of violence. When Booby Clark of the Cincinnati Bengals gave Dale Hackbart of the Denver Broncos a forearm to the back of the head while Hackbart was kneeling on the ground after a play was over, he may have acted so far outside the scope of the sport that he committed a tort (*Hackbart v. Cincinnati Bengals, Inc.*, 1979).

How is it determined whether consent has been manifested? Express verbal consent to what would otherwise be a battery is not required. Actions speak louder than words. By stepping onto the field, a football player implicitly consents to being hit. But implicit consent can be difficult to determine, an issue that arises in cases involving alleged consent to sexual contact, just as it does in the criminal law of rape. Consent can be manifested by conduct as well as by words. The difficult issues arise when there is a clash of perceptions about the presence and scope of consent. When a woman acquiesces to a man's sexual advances, is she really consenting? In these cases, the court must define what constitutes reasonable conduct in sexual situations by choosing between different interpretations of events.

The hypotheticals from sports and sexual situations suggest something else about intentional torts such as battery. These issues sharpen our understanding of the nature of tort law, but in practical terms, the tort of battery is not used very much. Not many injured athletes or victims of unwanted sexual contact bring civil suits against their injurers. Usually, not enough money is at stake to make it worthwhile. Even when there is the potential for recovery, the victim may not want to get involved in litigation for other reasons, such as its protracted nature and emotional toll.

Other intentional torts are used more often. One of the most commonly litigated is false imprisonment. This tort protects a person's freedom from movement in the same way that battery protects freedom from bodily invasion. Locking someone in a room against her will is a classic case of false imprisonment, as is threatening to injure her if she leaves an unlocked room. Conduct like that should be deterred, and it is unreasonable to expect the victim to risk bodily harm in resisting a credible threat.

Many interesting false imprisonment cases arise when a customer in a store is detained under suspicion of shoplifting. Consider *Coblyn v. Kennedy's, Inc.* (1971). Marius Coblyn, a seventy-year-old man, went shopping at Kennedy's, a store in Boston. While trying on a sport coat, he removed the ascot he was wearing and placed it in his pocket. After purchasing the sport coat and leaving it for alterations, and just prior to exiting the store, he stopped, took the ascot out of his pocket, put it around his neck, and knotted it. Just as he stepped out of the door, Goss, a store employee, confronted him and said, "Stop. Where did you get that scarf?" Goss then grabbed his arm and said, "You better go back and see the manager." Eight or ten other people were standing around and were staring at Coblyn, who agreed to return. As he and Goss went upstairs to the second floor of the store, he paused twice because of chest and back pains. After reaching the second floor, the salesman from whom he had purchased the coat recognized him and confirmed that he had purchased a sport coat and that the ascot belonged to him. As a result of the emotional upset caused by the incident, Coblyn was hospitalized and treated for a heart problem.

Coblyn successfully sued for false imprisonment. Even though Coblyn voluntarily returned to the store, Goss's actions were sufficient for the tort, which does not require that the defendant physically compel the victim to remain. Massachusetts, like many states, has a *shopkeeper's privilege* statute under which a store owner may detain a customer in a reasonable manner for a reasonable length of time if there are adequate grounds to believe that the customer has stolen something. The detention in Coblyn's case was reasonably brief, but it was not in a reasonable manner; Goss failed to identify himself as a store employee and unnecessarily grabbed the arm of an elderly man who showed no desire or ability to resist. Moreover, Goss had no reasonable grounds for detaining Coblyn; merely stopping and putting on his ascot as he left the store is insufficient evidence from which the reasonable person would conclude that he had stolen it.

Is It a Tort When You Injure Someone by Not Being Careful?

Although intentional torts such as battery and false imprisonment have the longest heritage and are the easiest to see as wrongful, the most common torts involve harm caused by carelessness, not intentional harm. This area of tort law is called *negligence*. When we say that someone has been negligent, we mean that they have injured someone by failing to act with reasonable care. The core idea of negligence is that people should exercise reasonable care when they act by taking account of the potential harm that they might foreseeably cause to other people. For example, a driver is negligent in talking on his cell phone and letting his attention drift from the road, causing an accident. A physician is negligent in misdiagnosing a patient's illness because she fails to order tests that are indicated by the patient's symptoms.

The tort of negligence is about as easy to understand as intentional torts such as battery. The defendant has acted wrongfully, not in meaning to cause harm but in acting without sufficient concern for the interests of others. We want to discourage that behavior and to encourage people to act carefully. The injured victim has suffered a loss, and it seems fair that the careless tortfeasor whose negligence caused the harm should bear the burden of that loss.

Liability for negligence is narrower than liability for intentional torts, however. Someone committing an intentional tort acts without justification; there is no legally justifiable reason to punch somebody in the absence of consent or self-defense. But the defendant in a negligence action is performing an activity—such as driving a car—that is basically acceptable and even useful. We just want to make sure that she performs the activity reasonably—not perfectly, but reasonably—so liability is imposed only for violating the rules of the road, figuratively and sometimes literally. Of course, putting a word like "reasonable" in a legal rule invites endless controversy, and much of the law of negligence is concerned with setting standards and devising a process to give content to the term.

In most everyday situations—driving a car, practicing medicine—people have a duty to exercise reasonable care. There are a number of traditional if controversial exceptions to the core idea of a duty of reasonable care. Each requires a judgment about whether it is good policy to make someone liable to someone else if they act carelessly.

First, some classes of wrongdoers are simply immune from liability for some types of negligence (and often from other torts as well, not just negligence). Historically the list of immunities was very broad: Spouses could not sue each other, nor could children sue their parents, charities could not be sued by the beneficiaries of their good works, and the government was immune from suit as well—the king could do no wrong. Immunities declined dramatically through the course of the twentieth century, and today they generally remain in two rough categories. For the federal government and most states, governmental immunity has been abrogated only in part. Statutes define when and for what the government may be sued. For example, a common exclusion is for a discretionary function; when the government does what only a government does, such as decide how many police to put on the street, it cannot be sued for acting negligently in making the decision. Otherwise, immunities and near immunities for particular classes of defendants have become a staple of the tort reform agenda. After Chicago and other cities sued gun manufacturers for flooding the market with guns that ended up in criminals' hands, Congress enacted the Protection of Lawful Commerce in Arms Act that immunizes gun manufacturers and dealers from suits for criminals' use of their products. Similarly, after high-profile suits were filed against McDonald's, lobbyists persuaded legislatures to immunize restaurants and other food companies from suits claiming they contributed to the national epidemic of obesity.

Second, the duty to prevent economic harm is much more limited than the duty to prevent physical harm. If a driver carelessly causes an accident that blocks the Lincoln Tunnel leading into New York, many people will be late for work and have their wages docked, some sales representatives will miss appointments and fail to close important deals, and the coffee shops in Manhattan that sell coffee and donuts to arriving commuters will lose business. The driver clearly has a duty of care to anyone physically injured in the accident, but is she also liable to all these people who suffer only economic injury because of the same act of carelessness? Generally not, because even though it is easily foreseeable that harm will occur, the scope of the potential liability is too great.

In some cases, however, there is a duty to prevent economic harm. One important class of cases involves large environmental disasters. When the *Deepwater Horizon* oil drilling rig owned by Transocean and leased to BP suffered an explosion that caused a blowout and spilled millions of gallons of oil off the Gulf Coast, some shore property owners suffered physical damage to their property when the oil washed ashore. Many more people suffered economic harm without physical damage, though. Fishermen couldn't fish, boat rental agencies couldn't rent their boats to tourists, motorists paid higher gasoline prices, and so on. Courts have to engage in tough line-drawing issues to determine to which of these parties BP and Transocean owed a duty of care.

A third limitation is that the duty to protect against emotional harm is less extensive than the duty to protect against physical injury. Upon hearing that her child has been run over by a car and killed, a mother suffers a severe emotional reaction that causes her to lose sleep, develop an ulcer, and have painful headaches. Is the driver liable to the mother for her suffering? (That is, did the driver owe a duty to the mother?) In a series of cases, courts have imposed liability for causing emotional harm, but they have also faced the difficulty of determining where to draw the line. Does it matter if the mother is standing next to the child when the accident occurs, sees it from across the street, or only hears about it later? Some courts hold that the mother can recover only if she is in the *zone of danger* within which she could have been physically injured as well; others allow her to recover for observing the accident at the time it happens but not if she hears about it subsequently. What if the mother grieves for her child but has no physical symptoms? What if the plaintiff is the child's grandmother? Second cousin? Best friend?

Finally, the exception to the general duty of reasonable care that seems most outrageous to the layperson states that a person has no duty to act affirmatively to prevent harm that might befall another person. A man sitting in a park, eating his lunch, watches as an unattended toddler crawls toward an unfenced cliff. Is the man obligated to be a Good Samaritan and get out of his chair, walk a few feet, and redirect the toddler? The common law's traditional answer is that he has no legal duty to act in this case, so he is not liable for failing to exert what every moral person would say is a reasonable effort to avert a tragedy.

The basis for this monstrous rule is twofold. First, the duty of reasonable care is imposed on those who enter into a course of conduct, not those who refrain from acting altogether. The law avoids imposing affirmative burdens on people—even modest burdens—because to do so impinges on their personal liberty. The benefits of preventing harm and compensating victims are outweighed by the unfairness of compelling an uninvolved person to act. Second, once we start down the path of imposing affirmative obligations, it is hard to know where to stop. (This is what lawyers call a *floodgates* or *slippery slope* argument: By deciding one case one way, we open the floodgates or start down the slippery slope that makes us decide many other cases the same way.) If the man sees that the fence around the cliff is broken but no toddler is in the area yet, is he obligated to call the authorities to report the need for repair? Is a strong swimmer required to go to the aid of a drowning child? How about a swimmer of modest abilities?

Fortunately, the actual position of the law is less severe than it first appears. Cases that involve a failure to act affirmatively are extremely rare because the world is populated with Good Samaritans. And the courts have fashioned exceptions to the rule. For example, when someone has entered into a course of conduct, he may not abandon it and leave someone else at peril. When two drinking buddies spend the evening together going from one bar to another, one of them can't leave the other unconscious, dangerously intoxicated, and lying in the street without seeking aid. Likewise, a person who comes upon the scene of an accident has no duty to stop and help direct traffic around the accident, but if she starts directing traffic, she must be careful in doing so.

A related limitation on the duty of care is that a tortfeasor is liable only to victims and for harm within the scope of the risk that made its conduct negligent in the first place. For want of a nail the shoe was lost, for want of a shoe the horse was lost, and so on up to the loss of the kingdom. Is the negligent blacksmith liable in tort for the loss of the kingdom? Courts have to draw the line at some point, holding that a negligent defendant is not liable for consequences that are too remote.

This point was made in a favorite case of law professors, *Palsgraf v. Long Island Railroad Co.* (1928), in an opinion authored by one of the great American judges, Benjamin Cardozo. Helen Palsgraf was waiting for her train on the railroad platform after buying a ticket to go to the beach. Another train arrived at the station, and two men ran to catch it. One of the men, carrying a package, unsteadily jumped aboard the train. A conductor on the train reached forward to pull him up while another conductor on the platform pushed him from behind. The conductors' pushing and pulling dislodged his package, causing it to fall on the rails. The package contained fireworks that exploded upon impact. The shock of the explosion knocked down some scales at the other end of the platform, which fell on the unlucky Palsgraf, injuring her.

Assume, as the court did, that the conductors were negligent in pushing and pulling the passenger carrying the package. If he had fallen from the train and been injured, the railroad unquestionably would have been liable. (The railroad is responsible for the acts of its employees, the conductors. This is called *vicarious liability*—liability through the acts of another person for whom the defendant is responsible.) The conductors' negligence also undoubtedly caused the injury to Palsgraf, so should the railroad also be liable for her injuries? The only difference in the two cases is that the harm to her occurred through an extended, bizarre set of circumstances. The courts engage in line drawing to determine when enough is enough.

What Does the Law Mean by Reasonable Care?

Oddly enough, unlike the definition of intent for intentional torts, the definition of reasonable care in the law of negligence pretty much follows the dictionary definition and ordinary understanding of "reasonable": the degree of care that makes sense and that is prudent, enough but not too much. In applying this definition, naturally, the courts tend to complicate matters.

One of the best-known attempts to define reasonable care came in the case of *United States v. Carroll Towing Co.* (1947). Because the defendants had negligently tied the *Anna C*, a barge, it broke free of its moorings, rammed a tanker, filled with water, and sank. During these events the "bargee," the sailor in charge of the barge, was absent from the *Anna C*. In the litigation concerning the property loss, the defendants argued that the damages they owed should be reduced because it was negligent of the bargee to leave the barge unattended.

Judge Learned Hand pointed out that there could be no rule prescribing exactly when the bargee had to stay on the barge unless he could procure a substitute. Sometimes it would be reasonable to leave the barge unattended and sometimes not:

Since there are occasions when every vessel will break free from her moorings, and since, if she does, she becomes a menace to those about her; the [bargee's] duty, as in other similar situations, to provide against resulting injuries is a function of three variables: (1) The probability that she will break away; (2) the gravity of the resulting injury, if she does; (3) the burden of adequate precautions. Possibly it serves to bring this notion into relief to state it in algebraic terms: if the probability be called P; the injury, L; and the burden, B; liability depends upon whether B is less than L multiplied by P: i.e., whether $B < PL$.

Thus whether there was negligence depends on the facts in a particular case. If a storm is brewing and the harbor is busy, P and L are proportionately larger than if the weather is calm and the harbor is empty. In the former case but not the latter, P times L will be higher than B, the relatively small burden of having the bargee remain beyond his normal working hours or get a substitute bargee.

In theory, the Hand formula can be applied to judge the reasonableness of conduct in any case. How much care is reasonable in the construction of a Little League baseball field, for example? Suppose the builders of the field decide that a fence four feet high is high enough in the outfield. Because the fence is 200 feet from home plate, only an unusual Little Leaguer could hit the ball farther than that. If a ball does clear the fence, it probably will fall harmlessly—although it might conceivably cause minor damage by breaking a window in a car parked nearby. Stranger things might happen, however. A major league slugger might take batting practice at the field and hit a dozen balls in a row out of the park, or a ball might hit a pedestrian on a soft spot on her head, causing serious injury or death. But all in all, the probability of harm (P) is low, the likely injury (L) is also low, and the burden of preventing harm (B)—by building a fence twelve or twenty feet high—is significant.

Now compare the Little League field to an ice hockey rink. The builders of a hockey rink always put up shatterproof glass around the ice to protect fans from flying pucks. Even though the cost of doing so (B) is high, the probability that someone will be hit by a puck (P) and the serious harm that might follow (L) are also high—much higher than the product of P × L in the construction of a baseball field. Therefore, the standard of reasonable care is higher for the builders of the rink.

The fundamental tort policies provide the logic behind the Hand formula. We want to encourage people to exercise caution, but how much? If every Little League field had to have a twelve-foot fence, the cost of the sport would rise significantly, perhaps even to the extent that it would be too expensive to continue. That doesn't seem right. Someone might be seriously hurt by a ball that sails over the fence, but that would be in the category of freak accidents—something like being struck by lightning—rather than a consequence of the carelessness by the builders of the field. On the other hand, when a risk is foreseeable and significant, such as being hit by a puck, we require the rink owner to protect against the risk or pay the consequences.

The Hand formula expresses the factors to be taken into account in determining if someone has been negligent, but it can't reduce the decision about reasonable care to simple arithmetic. First, most of the time people don't think in algebraic terms. The driver of a car, for example, does not usually calculate in any serious way the potential risks of her action. Second, even if people did engage in rigorous analysis using the Hand formula, they would find it difficult or impossible to attach figures to the variables. In many cases, the probability of accident and the extent of resulting harm are uncertain because accidents can occur in all sorts of ways. A pedestrian might get a bump on the head, or the ball might break a window and a piece of flying glass lodge in someone's eye. Finally, in any of these cases, how do we measure the value of the injury? Is the cost of medical treatment and lost wages an accurate measure of someone's injury, or do we have to take into account noneconomic factors, like the fact that a person losing an eye will have more difficulty playing tennis?

The Hand formula is at best a rough guideline and at worst misleading in its apparent simplicity. The law has developed another yardstick for measuring reasonable care that is more accessible to the normal layperson and to the average juror than the Hand formula: the *reasonable person*. To exercise reasonable care, all you have to do is act the way a reasonable person would act in the circumstances. Easy enough. But using the reasonable person standard to define what constitutes reasonable care is putting the rabbit into the hat. The reasonable person is a legal construct, not an empirical fact. In defining how the reasonable person would act, courts weigh the same tort policies that they do in applying the Hand formula or, for that matter, in determining whether a duty exists in the first place. Nevertheless, the reasonable person is omnipresent in the law of negligence, so it is useful to define his or her qualities.

The reasonable person is not any particular person or an average person. Instead, the reasonable person is the personification of the Hand formula, a hypothetical and superior individual who acts the way everyone should act all of the time. The reasonable person always looks before he leaps, never pets a strange dog, waits for the airplane to come to a complete stop at the gate before unbuckling his seatbelt, and otherwise engages in the kind of cautious conduct that annoys the rest of us. As one court put it, "This excellent but odious character stands like a monument in our Courts of Justice, vainly appealing to his fellow citizens to order their lives after his own example."

The reasonable person standard does give some latitude to real people by considering the circumstances in which the defendant whose conduct is being judged had to act. For example, the reasonable person is subject to the same physical disabilities as the actual person. The conduct of a blind person is judged according to the conduct of a reasonable blind person, not a reasonable sighted person. A blind person is not unreasonable in failing to see and avoid an obstacle in her path, but she is unreasonable in attempting to drive a car.

However, the reasonable person does not suffer from the same mental limitations as the defendant, as was established in the English case *Vaughan v. Menlove*, back in 1837. Menlove, a hapless landowner, piled hay in a dangerous manner that resulted in a fire. The fire spread and damaged a neighbor's property. Menlove argued that he used his best judgment in stacking the hay, but his judgment just was not very good. As his lawyer delicately put it, Menlove suffered from "the misfortune of not possessing the highest order of intelligence."

Too bad, said the court. The reasonable person standard means the reasonable person of ordinary knowledge and intelligence. Perhaps Menlove can't be blamed morally, but he can still be held responsible legally. By imposing liability the law encourages Menlove or others who might be responsible for him to exercise more caution in the future, maybe by not engaging in activities that pose a danger to others. If we took into account Menlove's dimwittedness, we would have to allow for all sorts of shortcomings—bad driving, slow reflexes, and ignorance, for instance. The result would be not one reasonable person standard, but as many standards as there are defendants. In this type of case, what happens throughout the law of negligence becomes very clear: We are defining a legal standard based on how we choose to apply the tort policies.

How Does a Plaintiff Prove That a Defendant Has Been Negligent?

In most cases a plaintiff tries to prove that a defendant has been negligent by using the same techniques that are used in any other trial (or in drawing any conclusion outside of a trial, for that matter). Direct evidence from eyewitnesses is the most compelling. The testimony of a bystander who saw a driver taking swigs from a whiskey bottle, talking on a cell phone, and speeding through a stop sign just before the driver's car ran over a pedestrian provides overwhelming evidence of the driver's negligence. But circumstantial evidence—indirect evidence from which the jury infers negligence—can be just as persuasive. If no one witnesses the accident but the police find a half-empty whiskey bottle and a cell phone with the connection still intact in the front seat of the car, the driver's blood alcohol reading is twice the legal limit for intoxication, and an accident expert testifies that tire marks indicate the driver did not brake before reaching the intersection, any jury would conclude that the driver was negligent.

Some negligence cases require distinctive rules of proof. One set of rules concerns the use of expert testimony. Ordinarily, it is the jury's task to decide the ultimate issue of whether the defendant acted negligently. Witnesses provide evidence relevant to that conclusion, but the witnesses are not allowed to suggest the conclusion to the jury. A police officer can testify that she found the whiskey bottle and telephone in the car, but she cannot then say that the defendant must have been driving carelessly. Some issues are more complicated, however, and require expert testimony, including expert opinions about the defendant's negligence, to aid the jury in reaching its decision.

Expert testimony is most often used in medical malpractice cases. If a surgeon leaves two clamps and three surgical sponges inside a patient after an operation, it is easy for the jury to conclude that the surgeon was negligent. Even though the jury may not know the precise procedure in the operating room to account for clamps and sponges before closing up the patient, common sense dictates that there must be some relatively simple means of preventing this kind of mistake. When the victim alleges that a physician was negligent in diagnosing an illness or carrying out a medical procedure, however, the jury needs help from a medical expert to assess the claim. In the movie *The Verdict*, for example, Paul Newman's client suffered brain damage because her doctors had administered a general anesthetic too soon after she ate, causing her to vomit into her anesthesia mask and stop breathing. In such a case, the lay jurors do not know enough about reasonable medical practice concerning the administration of anesthesia to say whether the doctors had been negligent, so they need an expert opinion to guide them.

Negligence is the failure to observe reasonable care, and since people ordinarily act reasonably, the plaintiff or defendant may introduce evidence of a *custom* that is relevant to the issue of negligence. In one New York case a tenant was badly cut when he fell through his shower door, which was made of ordinary thin glass that easily broke, leaving sharp edges. For at least ten years prior to the accident, landlords routinely used shatterproof safety glass or plastic in shower doors to prevent injuries like this. The custom of using safety glass was persuasive evidence for the jury of the landlord's failure to act as the reasonable landlord acts.

Does the reverse hold true as well? If the landlord proved that most apartments do not have safety glass in the shower, does adherence to that custom exonerate the landlord? Not necessarily. Custom is evidence of reasonable conduct, but it does not define what is reasonable conduct. If the jury finds that a few landlords use safety glass, or even that no landlords do but that safety glass is readily available at a cost that is not too high considering the probability of accidents and their severity, it may conclude that adherence to the custom is unreasonable and the landlord was negligent. The jury applies the Learned Hand formula or the reasonable person standard on its own, and the custom is not conclusive.

A statute can be even stronger evidence of negligence than a custom. Suppose a driver traveling at 60 mph in a 35 mph zone strikes a pedestrian. The fact that the driver may have been going too fast suggests negligence, but the fact that the driver violated the legal speed limit is even more compelling evidence of negligence. Courts often view statutes that prescribe standards of conduct as statements of public policy that should be recognized as defining reasonable care. The reasonable person does not violate the law, so a lawbreaker is by definition acting unreasonably. As usual, a clear rule like this needs some exceptions. If the driver was rushing a desperately ill child to the hospital, for example, exceeding the speed limit might be reasonable.

Once the plaintiff has proven that the defendant was careless, the causal link between the defendant's careless act and the plaintiff's harm is usually clear. A driver fails to stop at a red light and kills a pedestrian who has entered the crosswalk; if the driver had not failed to stop, the pedestrian would not have been killed. This is known as the *but-for* rule of causation: A tortfeasor is liable if the victim would not have been injured but for the tortfeasor's negligence.

But things can get more complicated. Suppose the pedestrian is crossing eastward at a four-way intersection. Two drivers, one heading north and one heading south, are each inattentive to the traffic lights; they both drive through their respective red lights and converge on the pedestrian at the same instant, crushing and killing her. (Read enough torts cases and you will find that stranger things have happened.) Under the but-for rule each driver escapes liability, because but for the negligence of the first driver, the pedestrian still would have been killed by the second driver, and vice versa. But that seems like the wrong answer. Tort law wants to deter both drivers from running red lights, and the pedestrian is just as dead. It seems unfair that both drivers are let off the hook and that the pedestrian's heirs go uncompensated because of the fortuity that each driver's negligence coincided with the negligence of the other driver. So the law adopts an alternative rule: If the tortfeasor's negligence fails the but-for test only because something else would have caused the harm anyway, he still is liable.

In some cases, courts allow statistical evidence as the basis for liability. Scientific proof is never exact, but it is often the best we can do. A chemical plant dumps toxic waste that pollutes a town's water supply; as a result, the incidence of an unusual type of cancer among residents increases dramatically. How can a victim prove that her cancer was caused by the toxic chemicals? If she proves that one person out of a thousand normally develops this cancer but fifty people out of a thousand in the town developed it, the court may conclude that proof is sufficient. Similarly, if a physician misdiagnoses a patient and the patient dies, the patient's heirs cannot prove absolutely that the physician's negligence caused the death, since the patient might have died even if he had received the correct diagnosis and treatment; the best treatment may not work in 100 percent of the cases. If the heirs prove that the doctor's negligence reduced the patient's chance of survival from 80 percent to 20 percent, however, they probably have satisfied their burden of proof.

What if the Victim Is Partly at Fault for an Accident?

A pedestrian ignores a "Don't Walk" sign and steps into an intersection where she is struck by a car going 20 mph over the speed limit. The driver was negligent in speeding and could have avoided the accident if he had been going at a safe speed. But the pedestrian also was negligent in not observing the sign, and her negligence contributed to her being injured. If the pedestrian sues, can the driver use her negligence to cancel out his negligence, so that he is not liable?

Tort law's traditional answer was yes. Even if the defendant is negligent, the plaintiff's *contributory negligence* prevents any recovery. The reason for this answer was never quite clear. Surely we want to encourage plaintiffs to act safely, and there is something unfair about forcing the defendant to compensate the plaintiff for an injury that is partly her own fault, but barring any recovery by the plaintiff may be too harsh. As a result, courts often limited the scope of the doctrine in one way or another.

The great majority of states have resolved this dilemma by abandoning contributory negligence in favor of *comparative negligence*. Under comparative negligence, the plaintiff's fault reduces but does not entirely eliminate the defendant's liability for the plaintiff's injury. The jury is assigned the task of quantifying the degree of fault, and the damages are based on the numbers they come up with. If the speeding driver is 80 percent responsible for the accident, the driver pays 80 percent of the damages and the pedestrian is left to bear 20 percent of the cost. Or if the inattentive pedestrian is hit by two speeding drivers, each of whom is equally responsible, they each pay 40 percent and she pays 20 percent. In the McDonald's coffee case, the jury decided that the plaintiff, Stella Liebeck, was 20 percent responsible for the accident because she wasn't careful enough in taking the lid off the coffee cup, so it reduced her compensatory damages from $200,000 to $160,000.

Comparative negligence has a pleasing symmetry about it, but the devil is in the details. The jury must quantify the unquantifiable, attaching precise numbers to a messy set of facts. Then the court must figure out what to do with the numbers. If the jury determines that the pedestrian is 51 percent responsible and the driver 49 percent, should she be barred from collecting anything because she is more at fault than he is? Suppose it is 50–50? How about if there are two drivers, each of whom is 30 percent at fault, and the pedestrian is 40 percent at fault? Then the pedestrian is more responsible than either of them separately but less responsible than both of them together.

States have adopted different rules of comparative negligence to take account of these possibilities. The basic split is between a pure comparative negligence system, under which the plaintiff can always recover some amount, even if the defendant is only 1 percent responsible, and various modified comparative negligence systems, under which the plaintiff can only recover if she is not as (50 percent) or more (51 percent) responsible than the defendant.

One other situation involving the plaintiff's contribution to the harm arises when the plaintiff engages in *assumption of the risk* of harm. If you go whitewater rafting, skiing, or skydiving, or even if you join a health club with workout equipment, you will be required to sign a *release* acknowledging that the sport has certain inherent dangers and absolving the owner or instructor of liability if you are injured. Are these releases, also called *disclaimers*, enforceable? Agreeing to assume a risk is just like agreeing to play a risky sport, which constitutes consent to injuries incurred along the way. Releases also reduce the cost of providing some activities, and without them, these activities might no longer be offered; a ski area that had to pay for all injuries on the slopes might be put out of business. But releases threaten to undermine the tort policies of incentives for safe conduct and compensation of the injured, and we suspect that people often do not really know or think about the consequences of releases when they enter into them or may not have much choice in the matter. Courts attempt to balance these considerations. A disclaimer of liability for an essential service is generally unenforceable; you cannot effectively agree not to sue your doctor if he injures you through his negligence. Liability releases in recreational activities like rafting, in which people do not have to participate unless they are willing to assume the risk, are more likely to be enforceable. Even there, however, a court will scrutinize a release to make sure that it brought home to the consumer the risk being assumed; a release prepared by a skydiving school by which a participant agreed to "waive any and all claims . . . for any personal injuries" was held not to bar a suit for negligence because it did not specifically mention negligence.

Assumption of the risk can be implicit as well as express. In a famous New York case, Murphy was injured when he fell while on a ride known as "The Flopper" at the amusement park at Coney Island. The Flopper was a moving belt angling upward on which passengers attempted to stand. Many of the riders, like Murphy, were unable to stand and were thrown back onto the padded floor or walls. The obvious fun of the ride, of course, apparent from its name and from simple observation, was to be thrown and see others thrown. Although Murphy signed no release, he took his chances by implicitly assuming the risk of injury.

If Someone Does Not Intend to Injure Someone Else and Acts With Reasonable Care, Can He or She Still Be Liable in Tort?

Absolutely. The third major area of tort liability, along with intentional torts and negligence, is *strict liability*—liability that is imposed even in the absence of intent to injure or negligence. Some activities are socially beneficial but are likely to cause harm even if they are carried out with reasonable care. When building a highway through a hilly area, the construction company needs to use explosives and the explosions might result in projectiles that damage nearby property. Even though the company places the charges carefully, it seems fair that the cost of the damage to the property should be shared by everyone who benefits from the highway, by imposing the cost on the company rather than have it be borne solely by the unfortunate owner of the nearby property.

One of the earliest strict liability cases was *Rylands v. Fletcher*, decided by the House of Lords in 1868. The defendants, mill owners, had built a reservoir on their property. Unbeknownst to them, the reservoir was built on top of an abandoned coal mine. The water in the reservoir broke through the abandoned mine and flooded the connecting mine of an adjoining landowner. Because the defendants did not know or have reason to know of the abandoned mine, they were not negligent in locating the reservoir where they did. But, the court said, some activities, like building a reservoir to hold a large quantity of water, are abnormally dangerous even if they are performed with due care. The activity is not so dangerous that it is illegal, but it is sufficiently dangerous that we make the actor liable without fault for all damages that flow from it. This encourages a heightened degree of care, and it imposes on the actor the duty to pay all of the costs associated with the activity. Accordingly, the defendants in *Rylands v. Fletcher* were liable even though they acted with reasonable care.

Strict liability is imposed especially for activities that are not only dangerous but are unusual for their locale. Consider the collection of water, as in *Rylands v. Fletcher*. A suburban homeowner who builds a small decorative pond as part of his garden will not be strictly liable if water escapes and floods his neighbor's basement (although he may be liable in negligence if he has not taken reasonable care to prevent the escape of the water). Collecting such a small body of water to decorate a garden is not unusual in the suburbs and not particularly dangerous. But the homeowner who builds a massive irrigation system to water her small suburban garden will be strictly liable; the irrigation system that would be appropriate and common in a rural area is out of place and excessively dangerous in a suburban development.

The problem, of course, is drawing the line. Holding water in a small, decorative pond in a suburban development is not abnormally dangerous; keeping a massive quantity of water in an irrigation system is abnormally dangerous. Keeping a cocker spaniel, no; keeping a lion, yes. How about a pit bull? A python?

When Is a Manufacturer Liable for Injuries Caused by Its Products?

Strict liability also is sometimes applied to impose liability on manufacturers of defective products that cause injury—what lawyers call *products liability*. The expansion of products liability was one of the great success stories of tort law in the twentieth century. Perhaps because of that success, it is also the area in which large corporations, insurance companies, and their lawyers have mounted one of the strongest attacks on the tort system. Today there is great debate about the extent to which products liability is or should be strict liability, some version of negligence, or a mixture of the two.

Begin with one of the landmark cases in the law of products liability. Gladys Escola, a waitress in a restaurant, was moving glass Coca-Cola bottles from their case to a refrigerator when one exploded in her hand.

Escola said that the bottle "made a sound similar to an electric light bulb that would have dropped. It made a loud pop." The bottle broke into two jagged pieces and inflicted a deep, five-inch cut on Escola, severing blood vessels, nerves, and muscles in her thumb and the palm of her hand.

If this case is governed by the ordinary rules of negligence, Escola has to prove that the bottling company failed to exercise reasonable care to prevent the explosion of the bottle that injured her. To establish the bottler's lack of reasonable care, Escola must prove two things: first, that there was something wrong with the bottle, either that there was a defect in the bottle itself or that it was filled at too high a pressure; and second, that the bottler acted carelessly in producing or failing to detect the problem, by, for example, buying an inferior grade of bottle, failing to inspect bottles properly, or not operating its filling machines correctly. Both of these can be hard to prove.

To prove that there was something wrong with the bottle, Escola first has to have the bottle, or what is left of it after the explosion. In many cases this will be a problem; in the actual case, someone swept up the pieces of the bottle and threw them away. Even if she has the pieces, it may be impossible to identify the cause of the accident from the fragments that remain.

Suppose, though, that Escola gets over the first hurdle and is able to determine that there was a defect in the bottle that caused the explosion. She still must prove that the bottling company was negligent in producing or failing to discover the defect. The bottling company will argue that it buys its bottles from a reputable manufacturer, organizes its production line in as careful a manner as other bottlers, uses high quality equipment, trains its workers, and inspects the bottles at appropriate points—that is, that it acts reasonably. The bottler may even concede that there may have been a defect in the bottle. There may be statistics showing that one out of 100,000 bottles will explode. But that is not the bottler's fault. As long as it has acted carefully, it is not liable under a rule of negligence.

At this point we might say the tort system has done its best and that Escola just has to suffer her loss in silence. Someone who focuses narrowly on identifiable fault as the exclusive basis of liability is inclined to stop there. The courts that developed the law of products liability, however, thought they could do better and so created the doctrine of strict products liability. The manufacturer is liable for marketing a defective product without any requirement that the plaintiff prove its negligence in doing so. The key to products liability is that the product is in "a defective condition unreasonably dangerous," to quote the awkwardly phrased but widely adopted formulation of the rule. A bottle that explodes is in a defective condition (something must be wrong with an exploding bottle) and unreasonably dangerous (the explosion might injure someone). Whether the unreasonably dangerous, defective condition was caused by negligent filling or a negligent failure to inspect during manufacture or was unpreventable doesn't matter. The bottler is strictly liable—liable even if it cannot be proven negligent.

The courts developed strict products liability for four basic reasons. First, in many cases the defect in a product is caused by the manufacturer's negligence but the negligence is difficult or impossible to prove. The physical evidence may be destroyed or inconclusive, or the information about the manufacturing process that is required to prove negligence may be uniquely within the control of the manufacturer. Second, negligence liability alone provides insufficient incentives to induce manufacturers to make safe products. When considering how much to invest in careful product design, manufacture, and quality control, a manufacturer should calculate the full cost of injuries caused by its products and figure those damages into the cost of the product. Imposing strict liability encourages manufacturers to go the extra mile to produce safer products, and in many cases, manufacturers are in a better position to minimize injuries than are the users of the products. Third, manufacturers typically represent their products to be safe, and the expectations of consumers created by those representations should be protected. Fourth, even if the manufacturer has acted reasonably, the victim of the product accident is still injured. If the cost of the injury is shifted to the manufacturer, the manufacturer will in turn distribute the loss among all of its customers. The cost of each product increases slightly so that each purchaser is in effect buying insurance against being the unlucky product user who otherwise would suffer a catastrophic loss. This form of loss distribution through strict liability is not simply a question of finding a "deep pocket," or someone who has enough money to bear the plaintiff's loss; instead, it makes the product bear its true cost, including the cost of the injuries it produces, and distributes the cost among all users of the product.

Strict products liability, therefore, is widely imposed for manufacturing defects, as when a Coke bottle is improperly made. Products can be defective in two other ways as well: when the product has a design defect and when the manufacturer fails to warn about a risk created by the product. The expansion of strict liability to these types of defects has been more controversial. From the 1960s into the 1980s, most courts adopted strict liability for design defects and sometimes for warning defects as well. Since then, there has been a more conservative reaction leading to a cutback in strict liability in favor of a narrower, negligence rule, such that a leading torts textbook captions its discussion of the subject "Development, Rationales, and Decline of Strict Products Liability."

A product has a manufacturing defect when it is not made the way it is supposed to be. With a design defect, by contrast, the product is made exactly as the manufacturer intended, but the problem is with the design of the product itself. This is the most controversial area of products liability, and the debate over the scope of liability plays out in defining the test for a design defect. Is a product defectively designed if it is more dangerous than users of the product ordinarily expect it to be (called the *consumer expectations test*)? Is it defectively designed if the dangers created by its design outweigh the benefits of the design (called the *risk-utility test*)? If the latter, how do we weigh the dangers and the benefits?

Under the consumer expectations test, a product has a design defect and strict liability is imposed on its manufacturer if the product is more dangerous than would be expected by the ordinary consumer. The widely followed Restatement (Second) of Torts endorsed the consumer expectations test, imposing liability when a product is "dangerous to an extent beyond that which would be contemplated by the ordinary consumer who purchases it, with the ordinary knowledge common to the community as to its characteristics." But courts found that the consumer expectations test by itself is not enough to evaluate defective designs; in many cases, for example, particularly involving complex products, consumers had no fixed expectations of safety. Therefore, the risk-utility test developed as an additional or alternative standard.

The risk-utility test balances the costs and benefits of the product. In determining whether a product is defectively designed under the risk-utility test, the court weighs the risks that the product poses to users against the benefits of the product to users and society at large. If the risks outweigh the benefits, the product is defective and the manufacturer is liable for the harm the product causes.

As it developed, the risk-utility test moved away from strict liability and became more like negligence. Courts that favor negligence treat the test very much like the Learned Hand formula for negligence, require the victim to prove that the harm produced by the product is greater than its utility, and sometimes also require that the victim demonstrate that there was a reasonable alternative design of the product that would have prevented the accident.

In weighing the risks and benefits of the design of a product, a manufacturer has to consider all of the normal uses of a product. This rule has produced a number of interesting cases involving the crashworthiness of cars. Drivers certainly don't want to be involved in accidents, but everybody knows that sooner or later many cars will crash. In designing cars, manufacturers have to recognize this fact and make a car that is to some degree crashworthy. Today many crash safety features, such as seat belts, airbags, and reinforced frames, are required by government regulations, but the need for them was first highlighted by products liability litigation and consumer advocates.

Most commonly, the risks of a product outweigh its utility when there is either an alternative design of the product or an alternative product that reduces the risks while providing much or all of the same benefits. One of the pathbreaking cases for products liability, *Greenman v. Yuba Power Products* (1963), illustrates a defect when there is an alternative design. Greenman, a home woodworker, received a Shopsmith from his wife for Christmas. The Shopsmith was a combination power tool that could be used as a saw, drill, and wood lathe. While he was working on a piece of wood on the Shopsmith, it suddenly flew out of the tool and struck him on the forehead, inflicting serious injuries. Greenman's expert testified that the Shopsmith was defective in using inadequate set screws to hold parts of the machine together, so that normal vibration loosened the screws, causing the part of the machine holding the wood in place to move out of position, allowing the wood to fly off. In the expert's opinion, the manufacturer could have used stronger screws or other, better ways of fastening the parts of the machine together to prevent this kind of accident. Because there was a readily available alternative design, the risk of making the machine this way (the possibility of injury) outweighed the benefit of doing so (the slight reduction in cost).

Many other products that have been involved in products liability litigation are defective because there is an alternative design of the product that serves the same purpose with less risk. Nightgowns and pajamas not treated with a flame retardant are defective relative to the slightly more expensive, treated garment, for example. An automobile with a gas tank situated where it will leak easily in a minor accident is too dangerous because the cost of prevention through relocating or lining the tank is relatively small.

Sometimes a product is defective because there is an alternative product that provides similar benefits at less risk. A famous example of this type involved the Dalkon Shield contraceptive device. The Dalkon Shield was an intrauterine device (IUD) that was highly effective as a contraceptive but had the tragic side effect of dramatically increasing the incidence of pelvic diseases among woman who used it. Even if the Dalkon Shield could not be redesigned to avoid this problem without losing its basic function, there are many other effective contraceptives available, so the risk of using the IUD far outweighed the benefits provided by it when considered in light of the available alternatives.

Determining whether there is an alternative design of a product or alternative product that functions as a substitute at less risk is not always easy. Large, heavy SUVs are safer in crashes than tiny subcompact cars simply because of their greater mass, but that doesn't mean that every vehicle has to be built like a behemoth; the tradeoff of a modest reduction in safety for a much cheaper price seems like a reasonable one. But what about a toy gun that shoots hard pellets at high speed—is a Nerf gun that shoots soft foam pellets a reasonable substitute or is the loss of realism too great a tradeoff?

The third type of product defect involves a failure to warn about the dangers of a product or how it can be used safely that renders the product unreasonably dangerous. Excessive warnings supposedly caused by the threat of litigation have become a staple butt of tort reform jokes: the label on a children's scooter that warned "This product moves when used," or the warning on an electric blender to "Never remove food or other items from the blades while the product is operating." In fact, manufacturers are not required to warn of obvious dangers—that scooters move, for example. But manufacturers do have to warn about foreseeable risks of a product that can be reduced or avoided if a reasonable warning is provided, where the failure to warn renders the product not reasonably safe. That way, a consumer can choose whether to use the product at all and, if so, can use it more safely.

A warning cannot always cure a design defect in a product. A label warning the operator of an industrial machine not to put his hands in the machine is not sufficient when the machine could easily be designed with a safety guard. But a product is not necessarily defectively designed because it is dangerous; instead, the danger may require a warning to render the product reasonably safe. Some products are defective because the manufacturer does not adequately warn of the risks of the product, as when the manufacturer of a household cleaning product does not warn users that it is caustic and might cause skin damage. Other products are defective because the manufacturer fails to provide proper instructions as to their use, as when a manufacturer does not warn that combining different household cleaners may produce toxic fumes.

The warning communicated to the user of a product must be reasonable in content, form, and location. In a particularly tragic case, Coy Carruth bought a Pittway smoke detector that failed to sound an alarm in a fire in which seven of his family members perished, arguably because the smoke detector was improperly placed. The box contained a picture of a smoke detector installed where the wall and ceiling met, but a more detailed explanation about not placing detectors in such "dead air" spaces was included in a pamphlet inside the box, buried among seven pages of fine print with no prominent warning of the danger. Given the obscurity of the warning, a jury reasonably could find that the warning given was inadequate given the risk (*Carruth v. Pittway*, 1994).

A traditional exception to the duty to warn concerns prescription drugs. Under the *learned intermediary rule*, the warning is properly directed to the patient's doctor—the learned intermediary—who is in the best position to evaluate the information and assess the risks and benefits of the product. In many jurisdictions, however, there are exceptions for mass inoculations, such as flu vaccine, and for oral contraceptives. There the patient exercises more choice in the process of choosing the medication than, say, when her physician prescribes an antibiotic for a sinus infection. The issue then arises whether the learned intermediary doctrine should be extended to the increasingly popular drugs advertised directly to consumers. Television ads tout the benefits of the latest drug for arthritis, allergies, or erectile dysfunction, encouraging consumers to ask their doctors to prescribe those drugs in particular; if consumers are exercising more choice, should that choice be informed by an appropriate warning?

What Damages Can a Plaintiff Get in a Tort Case?

Tort law cannot undo the consequences of an accident by healing a broken arm or taking away the pain of an injury. What it does instead is to award money damages in an attempt to compensate the injured plaintiff for the loss she has suffered at the hands of the defendant. The goal is to put the plaintiff in the position she would have been in if the accident had never happened, so far as it is possible to do so by giving her a sum of money to make up for her loss.

Because these damages are awarded to compensate the victim for the harm suffered, they are called *compensatory damages*.

Consider the tragic fate of Keva Richardson, whose car was struck from behind by a semi-trailer while stopped at a traffic light in Highland Park, Illinois. Richardson had just moved to the Chicago area from her native Texas to start her new job as a flight attendant for American Airlines; she planned to work for the airline for a few years and then return to school for a post-graduate degree in education, with the ultimate goal of becoming a teacher. Those plans were ended by the accident, which fractured her cervical vertebra and severely damaged her spinal cord. She underwent surgery to stabilize her spine and spent five months in a rehabilitation institute, with subsequent follow-up visits and occasional hospitalizations. As a result of her injuries, Richardson lost the use of her legs, has only limited use of her arms, with loss of control of her fingers and the fine muscles in her hands, is unable to control her bladder or bowel functions, is at risk for pneumonia, infections, and pressure ulcers, and can expect to be hospitalized periodically for the rest of her life.

The legal system cannot adequately compensate Keva Richardson for her injuries, just as medical science cannot cure them. The best it can do is attempt to measure her injuries and require the negligent truck driver who injured her, and his employer and their insurance companies, to pay money to ease the burden of those injuries.

Richardson suffered several kinds of losses. Up to the time of trial, she incurred medical expenses of $258,814, and she lost income from being out of work. But her losses did not end at the time of trial. Based on the testimony of her doctors and expert economists, the jury estimated that her total lost earnings would be $900,000 and her future medical expenses would be $11 million. All of these are elements of the financial loss inflicted on her by the defendant and are appropriately awarded as damages for *economic loss*.

The financial consequences of the injury are not even the whole story. Richardson suffers pain in her legs and shoulders. She is self-conscious about her appearance because of the facial injuries she suffered in the accident and because of being in a wheelchair. What she misses most, she testified, is "just being able to get up in the morning and begin her day" and then go through the day without assistance from others; she requires help to shower and dress, she can only push her wheelchair on a smooth, level surface, and she needs help to empty her bladder by catheterization every six hours and to empty her bowels every day. Of course, she also endured the pain of the accident and her operation and now is unable to carry out many of the activities she could do before, and she knows she is unable to return to her job as a flight attendant or achieve her ambition of becoming a teacher.

To compensate for losses like these, tort law gives *noneconomic damages*. The jury awarded Richardson $3.5 million for being disabled, $2.1 million for disfigurement, and $4.6 million for noneconomic loss. Although noneconomic damages are commonly referred to as *pain and suffering*, Richardson's case illustrates why they are broader than that. In addition to the physical pain caused by her injuries, she suffers a loss of quality of life in being unable to carry on her normal, daily activities, to enjoy life in the same way she could before the accident, and to fulfill her dreams.

The principle here is easy to state: Money damages are awarded to remove the economic consequences of an injury and to provide monetary compensation for the noneconomic consequences. The amount required to compensate the plaintiff is the measure of the harm done by the defendant. The defendant is responsible for these damages as a matter of fairness and social policy. (The rules are much more complicated in their application, of course, but we will not worry about the details here.) Notice several striking features of this seemingly simple system.

First, the system operates under a single-judgment rule. Tort damages are awarded only once, at the time of trial. At the time of trial the past damages are relatively straightforward. Richardson incurred medical expenses and presented bills to prove it, and she was out of work for a time and could prove what she would have earned for that time. Damages for pain and suffering are much hazier (more on that in a moment), but at least the plaintiff and other witnesses could describe how she had been feeling, how her activities had been limited, and so on.

The single-judgment rule also requires a prediction about the future, and the future is necessarily uncertain. The court must make a prediction about the plaintiff's future losses based on the evidence presented by both parties. The plaintiff's injury might get better or worse, requiring little more treatment or major surgery. Her pain and her ability to function normally might diminish or increase. Keva Richardson was working as a flight attendant, she had a bachelor's degree in elementary education, and she expected to return to graduate school and then teach. Predicting her future career path over several decades, and therefore her lost earning capacity, requires speculation.

The single-judgment rule is an instance in which serving the tort policies in a precise manner yields to administrative efficiency. The court could maintain control of the case into the indefinite future, requiring the defendant to pay the plaintiff's expenses as they arise and compensate periodically for noneconomic losses. The tort system does not do this because it would be too complicated and burdensome; to make things simpler, we accept the fact that many of the predictions about future damages will turn out to be wrong, with the plaintiff getting too little and the defendant not paying enough, or vice versa, as the facts turn out. In an increasing number of cases, the plaintiff does not receive the damage award in a lump sum. Instead, through a *structured settlement*, the award is paid out over time, much like an annuity. Sometimes the parties use a structured settlement to guarantee that the money will be available as it is needed in the future. In other cases, tort reform statutes require that a structured settlement be used, and even provide that benefits end if the plaintiff dies, which works to the defendant's benefit.

Second, the damage award is individualized to the particular accident and the circumstances of the particular plaintiff. Keva Richardson received the damages from her accident, not from the average rear-end car accident or the average person with a medical condition like hers. Or imagine a series of drivers, each of whom ignores a stop sign and drives into an intersection, hitting a pedestrian. Each driver commits an identical act of negligence but pays a very different damage award. The first driver delivers only a glancing blow, so the pedestrian is only slightly bruised. That driver's damages will be trivial. The second driver also delivers a glancing blow, but the pedestrian suffers from a degenerative bone disease, so the slight touch of the car causes major fractures of both legs. Under the rule that the defendant "takes the victim as he finds him," the defendant is liable for all of the plaintiff's huge medical bills and substantial income loss. The third driver runs over the pedestrian, seriously injuring him, but this pedestrian is an ailing, elderly person with a short life expectancy and no job, so the damages for future economic and noneconomic losses are small. The fourth driver also runs over the pedestrian, but the pedestrian happens to be basketball superstar LeBron James, so the driver is liable for James's lost earning capacity in the tens of millions of dollars.

As these hypotheticals suggest, the desire to compensate the plaintiff for her actual losses is in tension with the tort policy of providing incentives for proper conduct. The costs of a negligent act are hard to predict in advance and fortuitous in practice, making it difficult for defendants to assess how much to invest in reasonable care. They also suggest that tort damages, like so many other things, follow the existing distribution of wealth and income in society. Tort law compensates rich, highly paid plaintiffs more than poor plaintiffs with fewer economic prospects.

Third, the jury's award of damages is not the final word on the subject. The trial judge and, to a lesser extent, the appellate court can review the award and set aside the verdict. The usual standard for doing so is that the jury's award is "against the weight of the evidence"; this is a deferential standard of review, because damages are a fact within the jury's purview, and the award should be upset only if it reflects passion or prejudice rather than a reasoned assessment of the evidence. (This explains why the appellate court should be more circumspect in reviewing the verdict, because only the trial judge actually heard all the evidence.) Some state tort reform statutes have given the judges more power to review jury verdicts; in New York, for example, a verdict can be overturned if it "deviates materially from what would be reasonable compensation."

In the overwhelming majority of cases, judges review jury damage awards to determine if they are too high, not if they are too low. The traditional remedy for an excessive verdict is to award a new trial to the defendant. Sometimes, however, through a device known as *remittitur*, the court offers the plaintiff a choice between going to trial again or taking a smaller award without a new trial. In Keva Richardson's case, for example, the appellate court determined that the damages for future medical costs were higher than the evidence justified, so they ordered remittitur in the amount of $1 million, reducing the jury's award by that amount. Remittitur saves the expense of a new trial, but it also can put to the plaintiff a difficult choice: take less than the jury thought she was entitled to or undergo the delay and expense of a new trial and roll the dice on a second jury. The choice is particularly difficult if the plaintiff needs the money for ongoing care or living expenses. (The parallel procedure of *additur*, by which the court offers the defendant the choice of paying a larger award or going to trial again, is used much less often.)

Fourth, a substantial portion of many tort awards is for the victim's noneconomic loss. Noneconomic loss includes physical pain and suffering, anguish or depression resulting from an injury, emotional harm that accompanies disability or disfigurement, loss of enjoyment of life, inability to perform normal activities such as taking a walk in the park or enjoying sexual relations, and all other forms of emotional distress caused by an injury. There is no doubt that these are real losses, but there also is no doubt that money doesn't make up for them. Traditionally, courts have concluded that an award for noneconomic loss serves several purposes. It provides some measure, however inadequate, of the victim's loss, affirming the significance of her injury and requiring that the defendant bear the full cost of his wrongdoing (which encourages potential defendants to take those costs into account in calculating how much care to exercise). It also provides the victim a fund for activities and pleasures that can reduce her pain and make up for her loss of enjoyment; the victim who can build a new swimming pool may find a partial substitute for her lost ability to play tennis. Finally, damages for noneconomic loss provide a means of paying the plaintiff's attorneys' fees while allowing the award for economic loss to remain intact; otherwise, the plaintiff is not fully compensated for her economic loss because of the need to pay a lawyer.

These reasons have considerable power to them. Tort reformers think things have gone too far, however, and have enacted in many states legislation limiting damages for noneconomic loss. One widely adopted measure, first enacted in California in 1975 and popular among tort reformers ever since, imposes an absolute cap of $250,000 on noneconomic damages in medical malpractice cases. An absolute cap affects different victims in different ways. In California, for example, infants and women are among the groups whose damages are most often capped. Infants who suffer lifelong, disabling injuries at birth are likely to have huge noneconomic losses because of the extent of their injuries, but the damages for those losses are limited by the cap. Conversely, women on average have smaller economic losses relative to their noneconomic losses than men, because of their lower earning capacity, so they are also very likely to have their damages cut by the cap. A stay-at-home mom may suffer no income loss from a botched operation, for example, so her noneconomic loss will be a more important part of her award, compared to that of her high-earning husband.

Indeed, the effect of a cap may be to deny many victims a remedy at all. A damage cap reduces the potential recovery and accordingly reduces the potential contingent fee for the victim's lawyer. Therefore, lawyers are less likely to take cases in which liability is not clear or economic loss is not large; the mom who suffered from the operation may not be able to find a lawyer willing to take her case.

When Are Damages Awarded to Punish the Defendant?

The typical tort damages are purely compensatory. They may be burdensome to the defendant, even to the point of bankruptcy, but the measure of damages is the plaintiff's loss. In extreme cases, however, a different kind of damage is awarded with the sole purpose of punishing the defendant for doing wrong. These are called *punitive damages* or *exemplary damages*.

As a matter of law and practice, punitive damages are awarded in only a very small number of cases. The law on punitive damages varies from state to state, but everywhere something more than ordinary negligence or even the typical intentional tort is required before punitive damages can be awarded. The tests are stated in terms such as whether the defendant's conduct "shocks the conscience," is "outrageous," or demonstrates a "reckless indifference" or "willful and wanton disregard" for the safety of the plaintiff. Because of the narrowness of the standard, punitive damages are awarded in only 1 or 2 percent of the tort cases that go to judgment.

Punitive damages, especially large amounts of punitive damages, are most often awarded in commercial cases. A leading U.S. Supreme Court case on punitive damages, for example, involved a false advertising claim by the maker of the popular Leatherman multifunction tool against one of its competitors. Sometimes, though, personal injury cases produce substantial punitive damage awards. Asbestos manufacturers concealed the harmful effects of asbestos for decades and were held accountable through punitive damages in several cases; in one case, a worker recovered compensatory damages of $1.8 million and punitive damages of $31 million. A long-time smoker who contracted lung cancer sued Philip Morris for misrepresenting the dangers of smoking; a jury awarded him $3 billion in punitive damages, an amount that was reduced to $50 million on appeal. A. H. Robins Co. was held liable for $10 million in a Kansas case for "malicious silence" in concealing information about the dangers of its Dalkon Shield contraceptive device.

Punitive damages serve two purposes. As the name suggests, they punish the defendant for its wrongdoing. The law has different means of punishing wrongdoers; the criminal process is the most obvious. Administrative penalties serve a punitive function—such as when the motor vehicles bureau suspends a driver's license or the Securities and Exchange Commission suspends a stockbroker's license. But private civil litigation also serves public values, and plaintiffs who seek punitive damages become private prosecutors of the public good. The dangerous or wrongful behavior of defendants who intentionally manufacture dangerous products might not fit within a definition of criminal conduct or come to the attention of the public prosecutor. Punitive damages punish just as criminal penalties do, and the award of damages is a reward and incentive to the injured plaintiff to serve the public good in this way.

The second purpose is to enhance the deterrent effect of tort law. In some cases, the defendant's conduct is so outrageous that the award of compensatory damages seems insufficient to deter it. In other cases, compensatory damages are inadequate because all of the injured victims will not sue or recover. In both situations, punitive damages reduce the defendant's incentive to engage in wrongful conduct, acting as a big stick that requires a potential wrongdoer to think twice about the consequences of his or her actions.

Punitive damages are not numerically an important part of the tort system. Despite spectacular news reports, the proportion of cases in which punitive damages are awarded has not really increased in recent years, and most punitive damage awards arise out of wrongful business transactions, not personal injuries. Nevertheless, punitive damages have attracted the attention of tort reformers and are under attack in many jurisdictions. The key to the attack is the degree of discretion afforded to the jury in determining when to award punitive damages and how high they should be. As in setting pain and suffering damages, the judge gives guidelines to the jury, but the jury has leeway in determining what amount is necessary to punish the defendant.

As a result of these attacks, a number of state statutes have imposed restrictions on the award of punitive damages. Some statutes cap punitive damages, either at a flat dollar amount or as a multiple of the compensatory damages award. Others impose higher burdens of proof or set narrow limits on the kind of behavior for which punitive damages can be awarded. The U.S. Supreme Court also has developed constitutional limits on punitive damages. In a series of cases beginning in 1996, the Court defined a standard for the award of punitive damages beyond which they are constitutionally excessive. Courts reviewing jury awards of punitive damages have to weigh the degree of reprehensibility of the defendant's misconduct, the relation between the compensatory and punitive damage awards (with few awards exceeding a single-digit ratio of punitive to compensatory damages passing constitutional muster), and the difference between the punitive damages award and civil penalties in comparable cases. In *Philip Morris USA v. Williams* (2007), for example, a jury awarded compensatory damages of $821,000 and punitive damages of $79.5 million to the widow of a deceased smoker because Philip Morris knowingly and falsely led him to believe that smoking was safe. The Court recognized that conduct like that injures many people and so is especially reprehensible, part of the constitutional standard for assessing punitive damages, but it held that a punitive damages award cannot be based on harm to people other than the parties to the immediate litigation. As a result of the Court's rules, the largest awards, directed at the worst behavior, are the most likely to be cut.

6

A Deal's a Deal

Contract Law

In the novel and film *The Paper Chase*, the distant, forbidding Professor Kingsfield is the caricature of the law teacher who can both stimulate and terrorize his students. It is no accident that Kingsfield was portrayed as a professor of contract law. Contract law ought to be simple—a deal is a deal—but it often is regarded as the most challenging subject in the first year of law school, the subject that has tormented the most students. And with good reason.

What Is Contract Law?

Contract law concerns all aspects of the making, keeping, and breaking of promises and agreements. People make promises and agreements all the time. Dana asks Brian over to her apartment for dinner Saturday night; he says he will come and bring the wine. A consumer accepts a junk mail solicitation for a Visa card by signing a form with paragraphs of fine-print terms on the back or signs up for a Visa card by filling in a form online and clicking the "I accept" box. A worker takes a new job, with or without a written employment contract. A construction company contracts with a land developer for the erection of a large office building.

These promises and agreements, and the millions more that people make every day, are vastly different from each other. Agreeing to come to dinner is different from agreeing to build an office building. Agreeing to come to dinner on a typical Saturday night is even different from agreeing to go to the once-in-a-lifetime senior prom. Taking a part-time job flipping burgers at the local McDonald's is different from signing an employment contract to become president of McDonald's Corporation. Despite the differences, contract law deals with all of these events. If Brian stands up Dana, can she sue him for the money she spent on food and a new dress? Is the Visa customer bound by all the fine print he didn't read and wouldn't understand anyway? If the office building takes months longer to build and comes in far over budget, who is responsible—the developer or the construction company? Contract law provides the answers, or at least the vehicle through which we can argue about what the answers should be.

Contract law governs different types of agreements without regard for who made them or what their subject matter is, but some types of agreements are excluded from its scope. For example, contract law governs the employment contract between the president of Ford and the company, but a specialized body of law, known as labor law, governs the collective bargaining agreement between Ford and the United Auto Workers, the union that represents Ford's factory workers. The agreement among the partners in a law firm is a contract, but partnership law, rather than general contract law, controls the agreement. The rules and principles of contract law underlie labor law and partnership law, but they have been adapted to meet the needs of the specialized subject matter. In this way, contract law is residual—it deals with all those agreements that are left over after certain types of contracts are dealt with by other, more specialized areas of law.

Contract law's focus on promises and agreements distinguishes it from the two other major areas of private law: property law and tort law. Promises and agreements look to the future—the date on Saturday night or the building of an office building over a period of years. Contract law, therefore, is concerned with what *will be*. When someone makes a promise and fails to keep it, contract law makes her pay because she has failed to bring about a future state of affairs to which her promise committed her. Property law, on the other hand, deals with what *is*. When a trespasser enters someone's property without permission, the trespasser is liable for interfering with an existing state of affairs—the owner's right to use the property and to exclude others from using it. Tort law looks to what *was*—the past state of affairs before harm occurred. A driver who negligently injures a pedestrian is liable because he has made the pedestrian worse off than he was before by taking away something the pedestrian had before the accident, such as his health or earning capacity.

Why Do We Need Contract Law?

From the lawyer's perspective, contracts are the mechanism by which society works and contract law is the lubricant that makes the mechanism work better. In a market economy, work is done, goods are distributed, and specialization of labor and production is coordinated through contracts. People want a means of transportation, and Ford makes it available to them by offering for sale cheap subcompacts and large SUVs. If the cars are attractive and the price competitive, people will contract to buy them. Ford meets consumer demand by hiring workers, buying raw steel and finished tires, advertising the cars on television, franchising local dealers to sell its cars, and entering into a thousand other contracts. This complex system of production and distribution is not dictated by a Central Commissar of Automobile Production, as it might have been in the former Soviet Union; instead, it is organized through the interaction of many contracts.

These contracts benefit the participants: Ford hopes to make a profit, its workers get paid, Goodyear sells tires at a profit to Ford, and the car buyer gets a usable car at an attractive price. Economic theory asserts that everyone benefits from a contract-based market system because people get what they want and resources are used most effectively. If drivers want fuel-efficient cars that are easy to park, Ford will produce and sell more hybrids and subcompacts; if they want big gas guzzlers, Ford will provide SUVs. If Ford guesses wrong about what consumers want, Toyota will get their business instead. All of these economic effects are achieved by the coordination of individual choices through contracts.

The contract process provides more than products. People can fulfill their desires and achieve what they want in life through the agreements they make. Going to college, choosing one job over another, building a home, collecting art, and joining health clubs are all accomplished through contracts. Seen broadly, the contracting process is about the freedom and autonomy of each individual. In our kind of open, democratic society, according to this view, individuals are free to the extent that they can make choices.

Contracts, therefore, define what we mean by a society based on the market and individual choice. Contract law has two special functions in making this kind of society possible. It provides a dispute resolution mechanism for exchanges, and it demonstrates society's commitment to freedom and autonomy.

If the performance of both parties to an agreement could occur at the moment the contract is made, contract law would be unnecessary. Immediate, simultaneous performance is seldom the case, however. An agreement to buy a house must be made weeks or months before the deal closes to allow time for the buyer to obtain a mortgage and for the seller to prepare to move. Therefore, contract law provides security for exchanges that are projected into the future. Between the time of agreement and the time for final performance, many things can happen that may upset the relationship. The buyer may find a better house, have a change of heart, or be unable to get a mortgage. By providing an enforcement mechanism for agreements that are to be performed in the future, contract law assures contracting parties that they can make plans or investments in reliance on the promises others have made to them. The home seller can get ready to move, knowing that contract law deters the buyer from changing his mind and gives the seller a remedy if the buyer does try to back out.

Contract law also offers a mechanism for working out problems that arise during or after performance. The home seller and buyer may not have stated in their sales contract what happens if the house burns down before the time of closing, but the law will deal with that problem if it occurs.

While contract law is useful in performing these functions, lawyers are inclined to overstate its importance. Contract law is important—contracting parties consult their lawyers for help in planning and drafting agreements and resolving disputes—but when we look at the entire landscape of contracting in society, we see that contract law is only a small part of the picture.

Most agreements are made and performed with no trouble. Law students are trained to look on every deal as a potential disaster, so lawyers often lose sight of how well things usually work. For example, of the millions of contracts made each year by Ford, its suppliers, and its dealers, only a small number generate problems. Most of the time Goodyear delivers the tires on time and they are of the specified quality, and the car buyer gets the car from the dealer with no problem. In an economy based on private agreements, everything has to run smoothly most of the time or the system falls apart. Fortunately, everything usually does run smoothly, so contract law has to step in on relatively few occasions.

Even when trouble does occur in a contract, contract law is a remedy of last resort. When a dispute arises between Ford and one of its suppliers, neither of them will immediately call their lawyers. Instead, the purchasing agent for Ford and the sales manager for the supplier will get on the phone and try to work things out. The supplier wants to protect its reputation and the prospect of future sales to Ford, and Ford wants to keep its assembly line moving, so either or both of them may be willing to make concessions to resolve the problem. People enter into contracts to get things done, not to establish their legal rights in case of breach. If problems do arise, persuading the other party, appealing to reasonable standards of behavior, or threatening economic sanctions are remedies much preferred to calling in lawyers and engaging in expensive litigation.

Often, the size of the dispute does not justify litigation anyway. A homeowner who is dissatisfied with the job a plumber did replacing a faucet may complain to the plumber or post a negative rating online but is unlikely to sue for the hundred dollars it will cost to have the job redone.

The second and more general function of contract law is to honor individual freedom and autonomy. Contract law demonstrates the law's respect for these values by enforcing the agreements people make and by imposing obligations on people only when and to the extent that they consent to assume those obligations. This is what we mean by *freedom of contract*. Freedom of contract encompasses freedom to contract and freedom from contract. Freedom *to* contract is the ability to enter into any kind of agreement that you want. In theory, your ability to enter into contracts is unrestrained by contract law. Freedom *from* contract is your ability to not enter into an agreement unless you choose to do so. If you don't want to buy a car from Ford, the company cannot get a court to order you to do so.

For more than a century, freedom of contract has been both the central organizing principle of contract law and a rallying cry for an individualist philosophy of social organization. But freedom of contract is one of those great slogans in law and politics that captures an idea by ignoring any of the subtlety that implementation of the idea requires. Actually, freedom of contract reflects an important aspect of the idea of choice or consent that underlies contract law, but the principle can be misleading if not applied carefully.

To see some of the subtleties and weaknesses in freedom of contract, think about a classic case, *Hurley v. Eddingfield*, from the Indiana Supreme Court in 1901. George Eddingfield, a physician in the small town of Mace, Indiana, was the Burks' family doctor and attended Charlotte Burk during her pregnancy. When Charlotte went into labor she became seriously ill. Her family sent for Eddingfield, but he refused to come. Several times a messenger went to Eddingfield, told him that Charlotte and her unborn child were in danger and that no other doctor was available, and tendered payment of his fee. Nevertheless, Eddingfield refused to come to her aid "without any reason whatever," as the court said. Charlotte and her baby died because of the lack of medical treatment, and her heirs sued Eddingfield.

The Indiana Supreme Court held that Eddingfield had no duty as a licensed physician to come to Charlotte's aid. And the court could not even consider the idea that Eddingfield, as the Burks' family doctor, had a duty as a matter of contract law to come to the aid of his patient. The principle of freedom from contract speaks directly to this issue. Because contract law is based on consent, no one can be compelled to enter into a contract against his will, not even the only physician available to treat a dying patient whom he had treated previously.

Hurley v. Eddingfield illustrates some difficulties of freedom of contract and of the idea of choice or consent that underlies contract law. First, freedom from contract is not an absolute principle. Because our sentiments have changed since 1901, federal law today requires hospitals to treat patients in certain circumstances, including women in labor. Many other laws also require people to enter into contracts whether they want to or not, thereby limiting their freedom from contract. A prejudiced employer might want to refuse to hire blacks, Muslims, or women, but the civil rights laws bar him from doing so. A driver has to contract with an insurance company to obtain state-mandated auto insurance as a condition of driving a car.

Second, even when freedom of contract does apply, a person's freedom to contract is powerfully influenced by the practical circumstances of the situation. In *Hurley*, for example, the patient's choice of a physician is controlled by the system for the delivery of medical care. By the beginning of the twentieth century physicians had established themselves as a licensed profession, begun to severely limit entry into the profession, and engaged in a campaign to eliminate other types of health care practitioners. All of this may have left Burk with no source of medical care other than the single doctor in a small Indiana town. Her family's choices would have been very different if more doctors had been available or if medical care had been regarded as a public resource that was available to everyone through a government program.

We can see similar influences in many contemporary settings. Advertising shapes consumer preferences. Many communities have no adequate public transportation systems, so people need to buy cars. In a recession workers often have to take whatever jobs they can get on whatever terms are available. Thus the ideal of freedom of contract is always put into practice against a background of social factors and economic constraints. When the law defines the contours of freedom of contract, it has to decide the extent to which we want to consider that background.

Third, contract law is only partly about choice. Suppose that, because Eddingfield repeatedly treated Burk and her family, over time they thought of each other as "my doctor" and "my patient." Then we could assume that there was a relationship of family doctor and patient here. Can we infer from this that Eddingfield has agreed to come when called in emergencies? If so, we are moving away from consent as the basis of contract. The parties to a contract may be bound to a particular term—providing service in an emergency—even if they did not actually agree to it or never thought specifically about it. We could say that the patient has a right to expect that her doctor would treat her in an emergency because of the usual terms of the doctor–patient relationship. If that is so, then the basis of contractual liability is protecting the patient's expectation raised by the relationship of being a family doctor, rather than the intent behind it. But even that is not quite right. Just as Eddingfield may not have intended to provide emergency service, Burk may not have thought about the issue in advance either. In that case, she had no real expectations to protect. When the emergency does arise, though, we could still hold the doctor liable for failing to respond. The basis of liability in that case flows from our sense of the relationship itself. And, taking one more step away from consent, our sense of what those obligations are is not derived from some simple empirical survey about what doctors and patients think and how they ordinarily act. Each of us determines what we think the right answer should be based on evidence about the typical doctor–patient relationship, our own experience with doctors, and our sense of what kinds of duties people should owe to each other.

This decision about the extent of legal obligation in a case like *Hurley v. Eddingfield*, as in any other contract case, is a decision about what is the best social policy. The consent of the parties does not determine the scope of freedom to contract and freedom from contract; the legal system necessarily makes this judgment. When a court says that a doctor does or does not have to treat a patient in an emergency, we are making the same kind of judgment that the legislature makes when it says, for example, that an automobile driver must carry insurance or an employer cannot discriminate on the basis of race. Each of these rules rests on a decision about what is best for the interest of society as a whole. Thus choice in a contractual setting always operates against a background of legal policymaking.

How Do You Make a Contract?

You can make a contract almost any way you want.

The basic principles of contract law dictate what it takes to make a contract. We look to see whether a reasonable person would be justified in believing that a person has made a promise—that the person has chosen to commit to a future course of action. The two elements of promise—commitment and future—are the keys to contracting and contract law. When you promise to do something, you are saying that you really will do it, not that you will do it if you feel like it when the time comes or you will do it unless you change your mind.

The best way of determining if someone has made a promise is through words of commitment. When someone says, "I promise to pay $5,000 for your car," it is reasonable to believe that the person is committed to buying the car. But that is by no means the only way of finding commitment to contract. It's possible to make a contract by implication or with no words at all. At an auction, the auctioneer says, "We have this lovely Picasso." As in innumerable comedy sketches, if you raise your hand, nod your head, or scratch your nose, you may have obligated yourself to pay $20 million for the painting.

This area is called the law of *contract formation*—how a contract is formed. There are two questions in the law of contract formation: What are we looking for? Where do we look to find it? Proceeding from the idea that contract law is about manifested consent, we look to see if the parties have demonstrated their consent to enter into a contract. To determine that, we look at the words and conduct of the parties.

Consider a set of facts that illustrates a well-formed contract. An employee is working under an employment contract that expires on December 15. In early December the president of the company offers to renew the employee's contract for another year. The president and the employee discuss in detail the employee's duties, salary, health benefits, vacation, and sick leave and incorporate their understanding in a lengthy written document. With great ceremony they both sign the written contract, shake hands, and break out the champagne to toast the continuation of their relationship.

In this hypothetical, both of the contract formation questions can be answered easily. By executing a written document labeled "Employment Agreement" that contains the terms we normally see in such a document, the president and the employee have indicated that they intend to enter into the legal relationship called an employment contract; their handshake and champagne toast, while not necessary, also show their intent. The document is detailed and specific about the content of the contract; this is further evidence of their intent because people who write out and sign agreements at this length usually intend to be bound by them, and it gives the court somewhere to find the terms of the agreement in case a dispute arises.

This hypothetical illustrates a well-formed contract because the evidence of assent to contract is compelling and the resulting agreement is clear and complete. Here the contract is formed at the moment when both sign the document, but the agreement process can take other forms. Often formation occurs through *offer* and *acceptance*, in which one party initiates the agreement process and the other party then completes it. An email saying, "I will sell you my car for $5,000" is an offer that you accept by writing back, "I will buy it."

Unfortunately for contract law, the perfectly formed contract is elusive. Many contracts are not formed with this degree of precision or clarity. Consider the actual case on which the previous hypothetical is based, *Embry v. Hargadine, McKittrick Dry Goods Co.* (1907).

Embry was the manager of the samples department of a dry goods company. Although Embry's contract was due to expire on December 15, McKittrick, the president of the company, had put him off whenever he tried to raise the issue of a renewal. Finally, on December 23, Embry went to McKittrick and said he would quit then and there unless they agreed on a contract for another year. McKittrick asked him how his department was getting along, and Embry said they were very busy, as it was the height of the season for getting salespeople out on the road to see customers. McKittrick then said, "Go ahead, you're all right. Get your men out and don't let that worry you." Embry, assuming he had a new contract, worked until February 15, when he was told he was fired.

Was there a contract in this case? Embry thought so, but McKittrick said that he had just been busy and distracted so he tried to brush off Embry, not intending to bind the company to a new contract. Here again we have the issue of whether consent is the exclusive basis of contractual liability. If it is, then Embry is out of luck. Actually, the law says that if Embry was reasonable in believing that McKittrick was making a promise, we will protect his reasonable expectation. The test for contract formation is not whether someone actually intended to make a promise but whether their words and conduct as reasonably understood by the person to whom they were directed were sufficient to imply a promise. (We call the person who makes a promise the *promisor* and the person to whom the promise is made the *promisee*.) The law's term for this is *manifestation of assent*, and it gives us an *objective theory* of contract formation, focusing on objective, observable factors such as words and conduct, rather than a *subjective theory*, which would focus on the promisor's actual state of mind.

The purpose of looking at the words rather than the intention is to protect the reasonable expectations of the person to whom the promise is directed. As an old legal saying goes, "Not even the Devil knows the mind of man." Neither a person hearing a promise nor a court adjudicating a case has any way of judging another person's subjective state of mind except through the words he uses and the actions he takes. When Embry hears McKittrick say what sounds in the circumstances like a promise, he is entitled to believe that a promise is being made. Embry reasonably believes he has a contract and, relying on McKittrick's manifestation of assent, continues working. It would be unfair to disappoint Embry's belief, so McKittrick is bound even if he never intended to consent to the contract.

Lawyers often distinguish contract law and tort law by saying that contract liability is assumed by the exercise of choice while tort liability is imposed by law even in the absence of consent. What we have done by the objective theory is make contract law resemble tort law. Using words is very much like driving a car; if it is not done carefully, someone can be injured. McKittrick's words (and the conduct that accompanies them—a dismissing wave of the hand, a smile, a shrug) can raise an expectation in Embry and cause him to keep working at his job instead of taking another one. Whether or not McKittrick intends to be bound by his words, he should be careful in considering their effect on Embry. If he is not careful, he can be liable for "negligent promising," just as he would be liable if he physically injured Embry by negligent driving.

A common formation problem concerns indefinite contracts. Suppose a written agreement for the sale of a house doesn't state anything about when the closing of the transaction will take place (that is, when the buyer will hand over the money in return for the deed). Or suppose that it has all the other relevant terms but doesn't include the price because they haven't agreed on one. If the seller wants to get out of the deal, he might argue in either case that the agreement is too indefinite to enforce.

Definiteness is important in contract formation for two reasons. First, definiteness is evidence of consent; we ordinarily assume that a contract that dots all the i's and crosses the t's is better evidence of intent to contract than one that leaves large areas uncovered. Second, a definite contract gives the court a better basis for dealing with a breach. If the contract doesn't say when the parties will perform, the court cannot know when they are in breach; if it doesn't say what the price is, the court will be hard-pressed to prescribe a remedy.

Going back to the objective test, we can see these two cases are different. Proceeding from the reasonable expectations of the parties, can we fill in the gap in either agreement? Where they have not specified a date for the closing, we might say that the parties have a reasonable time to perform. We can determine a reasonable time by looking at similar real estate transactions and at what the parties have to do to prepare for closing—in this case, the buyer needs time to get a mortgage or otherwise raise the money. Based on all this information, we might conclude that sixty or ninety days would be a reasonable time. But what is a reasonable price where the parties have not specified one? Although we can look at the sale prices of comparable properties, we have the sense that every property is different and sellers and buyers usually negotiate about price on an individual basis. Accordingly, we might be more reluctant to impose a price term on the parties than a time of performance term, so where there is no price term here, there is no contract.

Does a Contract Have to Be in Writing to Be Enforceable?

Usually, a contract doesn't have to be in writing. As long as the parties sufficiently indicate that they intend to make a contract, oral promises are enforceable.

There are some kinds of contracts, however, that must be in writing to be enforceable. These are the promises governed by the Statute of Frauds. The Statute of Frauds originally was enacted in Britain in 1677 and was designed to cut down on widespread fraud and perjury at the time of the English revolution. The statute listed a number of kinds of contracts in which the problem of fraud was thought to be especially acute and required that there be written evidence of the agreement to make the contract enforceable.

The Statute of Frauds has been copied in every common law jurisdiction. (Oddly enough, Parliament repealed most of the British Statute in 1954.) The list of contracts required by the statute to be in writing varies from jurisdiction to jurisdiction, but there are a few that are commonly on the list:

- A contract to pay someone else's debt.

- A contract for the sale of an interest in land.

- A contract that is not to be performed within one year of the time it is made.

- A contract for the sale of goods for $500 or more.

To enforce one of these contracts, a plaintiff must produce a writing signed by the other party that contains evidence of the contract. Because of the ubiquity of email and Internet transactions, federal law and statutes in most states specify that an electronic record can substitute for a physical writing where the parties have agreed to do business electronically.

The Statute of Frauds expresses contract law's preference for formality in the execution of contracts. When contracting parties observe prescribed formalities such as signing a writing to enter into a contract, it brings home to them the seriousness of their actions, just as when children making a promise say "cross my heart and hope to die." Observing formalities also gives the court solid evidence of their intent to make a contract and of the terms on which they agreed.

Formality is a concern in other areas of the law for the same reasons. We regard some acts as sufficiently important to prescribe certain formalities that the participants must observe before the law will recognize the acts. A will must be in writing, signed, and witnessed. A deed transferring property must be signed, sealed, and delivered. The problem with required formalities, however, is that sometimes people just won't follow them. An ailing, elderly man will scribble a few notes about how he wants his property distributed after his death. A landowner will informally divide up her land among her children without giving them deeds. In each case, upsetting the transaction because the proper formality wasn't followed can create havoc in a settled relationship or go against the obvious intentions of the participants. On the other hand, recognizing the informal transaction undermines the strength of the formality requirement. In dealing with these cases, we are in the awkward but frequent situation of having created a policy (here formality) to prevent injustice but knowing that strictly applying the policy will cause injustice.

The courts' interpretation of the Statute of Frauds reflects the conflict between honoring the desire for formality and recognizing the need to loosen the requirements to do justice in individual cases. In determining whether a particular contract is covered by the statute, courts are more rigorous in areas in which they think formality is really important and more relaxed in areas in which it is not. The sale of land, for example, is usually an economically significant transaction and one in which it is important to have a written record to establish ownership. Therefore, courts broadly interpret the scope of the statute to cover most options, sales contracts, and other agreements concerning the transfer, leasing, or mortgaging of land. It is not as obvious why contracts that are not to be performed within one year are within the statute, so courts water down the scope of the one-year requirement, most importantly by reading the statutory requirement of "a contract that is not to be performed within one year" as "a contract that *cannot* be performed within one year." Thus a contract to build a skyscraper is not within the statute because it is theoretically possible (though physically impossible) to build a skyscraper within one year; if anyone were foolish enough to agree to build a skyscraper without signing a written contract, the agreement would be enforceable.

Courts also recognize the need for flexibility in the application of the Statute of Frauds by loosely interpreting the requirement that the contract be evidenced by a writing. As universally interpreted, the statute does not require that a single document signed by both parties be presented to prove the existence of the contract. The contract can be constructed from letters, emails, forms, checks, or receipts made by the parties. All of the terms do not have to be stated if there is sufficient evidence of the crucial terms. And the writings do not have to contain a full signature; initials, a rubber stamp, or a printed letterhead are sufficient to authenticate the document.

Can Anyone Make a Contract?

Almost anyone can make a contract, but two groups of people are specially protected by contract law: children who have not reached the legal age of majority (generally eighteen years old) and people operating under a mental disability. If a child or a person lacking mental capacity makes an agreement, it is voidable on her part. People like these are said to lack the *capacity* to contract.

At first glance this result seems to follow from the basic principle that drives contract law. Contracts are based on free choice, but some people are incapable of making a free choice. A child has not achieved the maturity necessary to exercise real choice. Some adults suffer from disabilities that deprive them of the cognitive capacity to make a meaningful choice, or they may attempt to make an agreement while under the influence of drugs or alcohol that have the same disabling effect.

Remember, though, the counterprinciple that the enforcement of contracts is based on the reasonableness of the expectations of the person to whom a promise is directed. What happens when someone contracts with a person who looks nineteen but is really only seventeen, or with a person who acts normally but is psychotic or drunk? Once again, we are faced with a conflict of principles. We want to protect someone who doesn't have the capacity to contract, but we also want to protect the person with whom she has contracted when that person has acted reasonably.

The law responds to these conflicts by sometimes trying to find a middle ground and sometimes flipping back and forth between the principles. In the case of the intellectually challenged, for example, courts often say that their disability allows them to get out of the contract only when the other party knows or has reason to know of their disability. When the person looks and acts as if he or she has contractual capacity, it is reasonable to rely on the appearance; on the other hand, when the contracting partner knows that the other has a history of mental illness and is making an irrational choice in the present transaction, the partner can hardly say he suffers by allowing the other out of the contract. In the case of minors, courts generally adhere to the rule that someone who has not reached the age of majority can avoid a contract; a minor who looks and acts mature is still a minor. But the courts have created a series of exceptions. The minor can ratify his contract after reaching the age of majority by recognizing it in words or accepting the other party's performance, and it then becomes a binding contract. The minor also is required to pay on his contract when he has received "necessaries." That old common law phrase once meant food, drink, and little else, but today it may bind a child to pay for medical services, education, or a car. In some states, a minor is obligated to pay for what he has received under the contract if he has misrepresented his age; the minor who lacks sufficient maturity to contract is held to a standard of maturity in telling the truth.

Once Two People Make an Agreement, Is It Always Enforceable?

Not always. (Do you sense a theme here? Law students get very frustrated because the answer to a question is more often "It depends" than "Yes" or "No.")

For a long time the great question of contract law was, "Which promises will the law enforce?" This area of contract doctrine is known as the *validation* of promises, and the main doctrine is *consideration*. The story of consideration is bizarre but intriguing. For about a hundred years, beginning in the late nineteenth century, consideration was nominally the central doctrine of contract law. It was so nonsensical in application, however, that courts routinely avoided it and have now discarded large portions of it. Today consideration doctrine only presents problems in unusual cases, but a discussion of the doctrine provides interesting insights into how lawyers think and how contract law has developed.

Consider two simple hypotheticals based on a favorite case of contract law teachers: (1) Uncle agrees to sell and Nephew agrees to buy Uncle's car for $5,000. (2) Uncle promises to give Nephew the car on Nephew's next birthday. In each case, if Uncle changes his mind, is his promise enforceable?

The first hypothetical is an easy one. Uncle and Nephew have each exercised their freedom of contract in an obvious manifestation of assent, so we are inclined to enforce the promise. The essence of consideration is the concept of exchange. Any exchange is an enforceable contract, because the parties are the only true judges of value. A car, a year's work, and a Picasso painting are worth what someone else is willing to pay for them. As long as there is manifested intention to enter into a bargain, there is a contract. The only measure of fairness in a market economy is the price arrived at by a willing buyer and a willing seller, so the court has no basis for second-guessing the parties' judgment.

Now consider the second hypothetical: Uncle's promise to give the car to Nephew. Here, too, we have a manifestation of assent. Is it enough? Although there is a promise, it is a promise to make a gift, not promise to enter into a bargain. Gift promises, especially between family members, often are more loosely made, with less deliberation, than promises to make commercial exchanges. This presents a problem because it is sometimes harder to figure out if a gift promise was seriously made and should be seriously understood and because we don't want to encourage people to make gift promises lightly. Nor is a gift an economically productive transaction. If the purpose of contract law is to promote exchange so that resources will be used most productively, gift promises are irrelevant. Perhaps the limited resources of contract law should be saved for the enforcement of commercial promises.

This is the approach taken by the doctrine of consideration. The corollary of the principle that any promise supported by consideration is enforceable is the rule that any promise *not* supported by consideration is unenforceable. A promise to make a gift is given freely and seriously, but because Uncle receives nothing in return for his promise, it is not legally binding. We might argue that Uncle does receive something—the psychic gratification he received from giving the gift. The law rejects that idea, though, because of its focus on exchange; even if Uncle feels good about helping out Nephew, Nephew has not given him that feeling in exchange for the promise. (Note, however, that once Uncle actually gives the car he cannot demand it back; although a promise to make a gift is unenforceable under contract law, an executed gift is a binding transaction under property law.)

On the other hand, consider the law professor's favorite, *Hamer v. Sidway* (1891). In this case Uncle promised Nephew that he would give Nephew $5,000 if Nephew refrained from smoking or drinking until his twenty-first birthday. Uncle derives no economic value from Nephew's performance of his side of the bargain by abstaining, but that doesn't matter; the promise is still supported by consideration and therefore enforceable. If it was worth it for Uncle to make the deal, because of his interest in his nephew's health or moral fiber, then that is reason enough for the court to enforce the exchange. Nor does it matter that Nephew is physically helped and not harmed by performing; because he gave something up, the resulting exchange is enforceable.

Consider some other traditional applications of the consideration doctrine. Two parties who have a contract modify its terms during the course of performance. Under traditional consideration rules, the modification may be unenforceable. If an employer agrees to give a current employee a higher salary or a lender agrees to forgive part of a debt, the promise is unenforceable because it is not part of an exchange. The employer or lender is not receiving anything in return for the new promise, because the employee is already legally obligated to work and the debtor to repay the loan. The rule is called the *preexisting duty rule*: Performance of a preexisting duty cannot be consideration for a new promise.

Or suppose the board of directors of a company informs a long-time employee that, in recognition of her years of faithful service, the company will pay her a lifetime pension whenever she chooses to retire. The employee, relieved at the promise of financial security, retires shortly thereafter. Inevitably, the company reneges. If the promise had been framed differently ("If you retire, we will pay a pension"), there would have been an exchange, but, as stated, the company's promise is essentially a promise to make a gift. Because the employee has promised or given nothing in return, the promise is unenforceable for lack of consideration.

Consideration doctrine presents a crabbed view of human nature and contracting practice. Everyone looks out for himself or herself; no one gives up anything without getting something in return; only economically productive exchanges are worthwhile. The limitations of that view make the results in each of these cases unpalatable. The preexisting duty cases and the employee reliance case invalidate ordinary, understandable commercial transactions.

The courts responded to these feelings about the consideration cases by developing rules that avoided the harshness of the doctrine. At an early stage of development these rules commonly took the form of manipulation or evasion of consideration doctrine to reach contrary results. For example, if a debtor rendered some performance in addition to repaying part of the debt—for example, he gave the lender $1,000 and a handkerchief to settle a $2,000 debt—the preexisting duty rule was satisfied because the debtor had done more than render the performance to which he was already obligated.

More recently, the courts have rejected consideration outright as a requirement for enforcement. Some of the moves have been based on fairness and public policy. A promise to make a gift to a charity is enforceable even though the donor receives nothing in return. Other rejections of consideration have been based mostly in commercial reality. The preexisting duty rule has been replaced by rules that enforce contract modifications that are made in good faith or in light of circumstances that were unanticipated at the time of contracting. And today the major counterrule to consideration is the reliance principle. A promise unsupported by consideration is enforceable if the promisee reasonably relies on it. When the long-time employee retires in reliance on the board's promise to pay her a pension, her retirement substitutes for consideration and validates the promise.

If a Contract Is Unfair, Can a Court Refuse to Enforce It?

This is a tough question for contract law. The emphasis on exchanges prohibits the court from upsetting a bargain, no matter how unfair it seems; the parties made the deal they wanted and now they are stuck with it. But some contracts just stink. In extreme cases, the court has a few other tools to avoid enforcing an unfair contract.

It is difficult to pin down what we mean by "unfair" in this context and to give the court a precise formula for determining when a contract is unfair. A court is supposed to decide each case according to a general principle that governs like cases, so it can't just go on a gut feeling that one party made a terrible bargain. Courts have developed two guidelines that suggest that a contract might need special scrutiny. First, there is something suspicious about the agreement process by which the parties arrived at their contract. The model of free contracting assumes two independent, informed parties each negotiating a deal in his or her best interest, but the process in a particular case doesn't measure up to that ideal in some important respect. Second, the resulting contract is too one-sided. One party—typically the one who had the advantage in the agreement process—ends up getting a lot more than seems justified in the circumstances.

Both of these guidelines are extremely problematic. If they are applied too generously, they will undermine the foundations of contract law. In many contracts one party or the other will have the advantage in bargaining and will end up with a better deal because of superior knowledge, skill, or economic position; contracting often is about trying to get the best deal possible. The tough question is where to draw the line between fair and unfair advantage. We can see the difficulties by briefly exploring two doctrines, duress and unconscionability.

The doctrine of *duress* allows a party to get out of a contract when he was forced to enter into the contract by threats from the other party. When the victim of a holdup agrees to give up his wallet to a robber or a parent agrees to pay ransom to the kidnapper of her child in exchange for the child's safe return, the resulting contract is unenforceable because it was entered into under duress. The same logic applies in a commercial setting in which one party extorts contract terms from the other. In a famous case, a one-time creditor who no longer had a valid claim against the debtor obtained a court order to seize the debtor's ice wagon after it had been loaded with ice. The debtor had to agree to pay the invalid claim or watch his business literally melt away, a payment that obviously was induced by duress (*Chandler v. Sanger*, 1874).

Of course drawing the line between extortion and permissible economic pressure is extremely difficult. When Walmart uses its economic muscle to get an advantageous price from a supplier, that's just hard negotiating and good business, not unreasonable bargaining that is the equivalent of extortion. The doctrine of duress is reserved for cases in which the contracting party has no reasonable alternative but to take the deal that is offered and the deal is really one-sided, as is the case with the victim of a holdup or the owner of the ice wagon.

Similarly, the doctrine of *unconscionability* allows a court to refuse to enforce a deal in which one party had limited choices and poor bargaining position and the deal seems grossly unfair. In a famous case, Ora Lee Williams, a low-income consumer in Washington, D.C., over a period of five years had purchased furniture and other household items on an installment plan from an inner-city furniture store. Each time she signed a form contract that included the following credit term:

> The amount of each periodical installment payment to be made by purchaser to the Company under this present lease shall be inclusive of and not in addition to the amount of each installment payment to be made by purchaser under such prior leases, bills or accounts; and all payments now and hereafter made by purchaser shall be credited pro rata on all outstanding leases, bills and accounts due the Company by purchaser at the time each such payment is made.

The effect of this obscure term was to keep a balance owing on every item purchased until the entire balance for all items purchased had been paid. When Williams defaulted on the payments for the last item she purchased, a stereo set with a price of $515, the store invoked the contract term to reclaim the stereo and all the other items she had bought over the last five years. The total price of those items was $1,800, of which Williams had paid $1,400.

In *Williams v. Walker-Thomas Furniture* Co. (1965), the U.S. Court of Appeals held that the credit term could not be enforced against Williams if it was unconscionable. The court identified two elements of a transaction that could render it unconscionable. One element relates to the agreement process: "an absence of meaningful choice on the part of one of the parties." The other element relates to the substance of the transaction: "contract terms which are unreasonably favorable to the other party." Because unconscionability depends on the particular facts in each case, the appeals court instructed the trial court to go back and see if these facts presented a case in which Williams lacked "meaningful choice" in entering the contract because of her economic circumstances and the legalese of the terms and whether the resulting deal was "unreasonably favorable" to the store.

This is a very sympathetic case for unconscionability: An exploitative merchant gets a poor consumer to buy things she may not be able to afford and then uses a contract chock-full of incomprehensible legalese to take back all the merchandise when she misses a single payment. But applying unconscionability in too many cases presents problems. Choosing among limited and often unpalatable options is the essence of contracting in a market economy. If Williams can't afford to pay cash, is it unfair for one of the few stores that is willing to extend her credit to require her to acquiesce to tough terms that protect the store's interest? If we go too far in upsetting contracts like this, the courts will see many more claims that contracts are unconscionable, and we may have to give up on the basic notion that a deal is a deal. For that reason, courts have been careful in striking down contract terms as unconscionable. Today one of the most important uses of the doctrine is to evaluate oppressive terms in standard-form contracts, particularly forced arbitration clauses that limit consumers' right to their day in court, which are discussed in the next section.

How Does the Law Treat Form Contracts and Online Contracts?

Today some of the most important issues about contract formation, enforceability, and fairness arise in the most common type of contract— a *form contract*, often called an *adhesion contract* (because one party just adheres to it, without negotiating terms). A form contract is a standardized agreement prepared by the dominant party to a transaction for that and many similar transactions, containing standard terms and usually presented to the other party on a take-it-or-leave-it basis. Insurance policies, credit card agreements, employment contracts, website terms of service and privacy policies, and purchase contracts are only some of the form contracts people encounter every day. If a friend told you *Law 101* is a wonderful book, you may have gone to Google to learn more about the book; if so, you agreed to Google's Terms of Service (1,900 words) and Privacy Policy (2,900 words), both including dozens of links to other documents. Among other things, you agreed to let Google track your searches, place digital cookies on your computer, and sell information about your online habits to other companies so ads targeted to you pop up in the future. Then you went to Amazon.com to buy the book, agreeing to its Terms and Conditions (3,400 words). By agreeing to those terms, you agreed that Amazon is not liable for any kind of financial loss you might suffer from using the site or from anything you bought on it. You may have used your Capital One credit card (the contract for which spans eight pages of fine print). If you read and understood your contracts with Google, Amazon, and Capital One, you are in the minority; even Supreme Court Chief Justice John Roberts admitted he doesn't read the fine print of online contracts.

Form contracts are essential to a modern economy because they allow large organizations to operate efficiently and reduce transaction costs for everyone. But they can be problematic, because they allow a dominant party to impose its will when the contract terms are presented in such a way that they are unlikely to be read or understood at the time of contract and there is no opportunity for negotiation. Because form contracts depart from contract law's ideal of two independent parties with full knowledge hammering out a deal, great controversy has arisen as to how the law should respond to them. In Professor Charles Knapp's colorful terms, should form contracts be treated as "sacred cows" or as "dangerous animals, likely to do harm unless confined and tamed"?

Courts apply the objective theory of contract formation and, in extreme cases, the doctrine of unconscionability to determine whether form contracts and terms within them are valid. Under the objective theory, the courts ask whether the party presented with a form contract has received adequate notice of the terms and has done something that shows assent to it. If a buyer signs a form presented by a seller, the seller can assume that the buyer has either read and agreed to the terms presented in a form or has acquiesced to them without reading. In situations in which that assumption is unrealistic, sometimes courts have created exceptions. A driver who receives a claim check in a parking garage may not be held to expect that the back of the check includes a limitation of the garage's liability for harm to the car, so no contract results.

Increasingly, however, courts have enforced even hidden terms. Eulala Shute, on a seven-day Carnival cruise with her husband, slipped on a deck mat during a guided tour of the ship's galley and subsequently sued Carnival for her injuries in federal court in Washington, her home state. Carnival successfully moved to have the case thrown out, pointing to a clause in the cruise contract requiring that all litigation be brought in Florida, where it was headquartered. On appeal, the majority of the U.S. Supreme Court felt no need to address whether the Shutes had actually agreed to the clause, because the Shutes "were given notice of the forum provision and, therefore, presumably retained the option of rejecting the contract with impunity." The "notice" of the provision was included only in fine print as the eighth of twenty-five numbered paragraphs on the ticket, a ticket they did not receive until after they had purchased their cruise. Moreover, another of the terms stated that the price of the cruise was nonrefundable, so even if the Shutes actually read the ticket and understood its import, the only way they could avoid the forum selection clause would be to give up their vacation plans at the last minute and forfeit the price they paid, or at least go to court in Florida from their home in Washington in an attempt to get a refund (*Carnival Cruise Lines, Inc. v. Shute*, 1991).

The *Shute* case is an example of a *pay now, terms later contract*, in which the boilerplate terms in a contract are not presented until after the transaction appears to have been completed. Courts differ on their approaches to contracts like these. Some take an approach like that of the court in the *Shute* case. In *Hill v. Gateway 2000* (1997), for example, Rich and Enza Hill called Gateway and ordered a computer system, giving their credit card number in payment. When the delivery arrived, the box included their new computer, the usual assortment of cables and manuals, and a sheet of paper with a set of boilerplate terms, including a statement that the Hills accepted the terms unless they returned the computer within thirty days. When their computer did not work some months later and Gateway would not repair it, they sued. Gateway defended by pointing to another boilerplate term that stated they had given up their right to sue Gateway and instead had to take any claims to arbitration. Even though the arbitration clause had not been presented when the Hills placed their order and Gateway accepted the order, the court held that it became part of the contract when the Hills failed to pack up their computer and ship it back (at their own expense), as Gateway's statement required. Other courts have reached different results, holding that consumers are not bound by terms presented after the contract has been made.

Online contracting has probably become the most pervasive form of entering into contracts, through what are known as *clickwrap* and *browsewrap contracts*. Clickwrap contracts arise when you click the "I accept" box on a website. In browsewrap contracts, the terms of use of the website are located somewhere on the site but the user does not have to click an "I accept" box before proceeding. And there are infinite variations depending on where the terms are located and what the user has to do to indicate assent. In *scrollwrap contracts* some of the terms are immediately visible but require scrolling down on the screen to read all of them. In *sign-in wrap contracts*, terms are visible at the sign-in or registration page for a website but the user does not have to specifically click to indicate agreement to them.

It is obvious that you are entering into a contract when making a purchase on Amazon.com because you have to click a box indicating that the transaction is complete. Most courts have held that clickwrap agreements are enforceable. Whether you are presented with the terms before accepting or given the option to go to another page of the website to read the terms first, you have been given notice of the terms and have the opportunity to read the terms (although almost no one does) and you have shown assent to the terms because if you don't like them, you don't have to click the box to purchase the product. Browsewrap agreements are more widespread because almost every commercial website has them, but they are more controversial. Even if you just look at TMZ.com or Yahoo! News, the terms of agreement somewhere on the site purport to control your use of the site. Courts have divided over the enforceability of browsewrap agreements; how obvious it is from the design and language of the website that the user is agreeing to terms and how readily the terms are accessible are key facts that move courts one way or the other.

One of the most common provisions in standard forms is a *mandatory arbitration clause*. These clauses dictate that if problems arise the consumer gives up the right to a day in court and require instead that all disputes be referred to a specified form of private arbitration. In arbitration, one person or a panel of arbitrators, who are not judges and may not even be lawyers, decide the case. Although the arbitrators are supposed to follow the same rules of law as judges and juries, their decision is not generally subject to review in court, even if they get the facts or law wrong. Arbitration clauses are often paired with a class action waiver, through which consumers give up the right to participate in class action lawsuits, effectively barring them from pursuing small claims altogether. Businesses prefer arbitration because it can reduce their litigation costs and shift cases away from courts and juries to a forum of their choosing that they expect will be more congenial.

The U.S. Supreme Court has broadly interpreted the Federal Arbitration Act to preempt state law that limits the scope of arbitration clauses and therefore to make many arbitration clauses enforceable. Judicial decisions and state law prohibitions on class action waivers, rules that require waiver of the right to a day in court to be explicit, and a prohibition on arbitration of personal injury claims in nursing home contracts are among the rules held to be invalid under this approach. But arbitration clauses can be held to be unenforceable under the doctrine of unconscionability. Zenia Chavarria was hired as a deli clerk at a

Ralph's Grocery store. Subsequently she sued Ralph's on behalf of herself and other workers for failing to pay for overtime and meal breaks as required by California law. The company pointed to a mandatory arbitration clause and class action waiver—its "Mediation & Binding Arbitration Policy" referred to but not included in its employment application, one of twenty-two different forms and manuals Chavarria had received at a new employee orientation. The court held that the policy was procedurally unconscionable as a take-it-or-leave-it contract that Chavarria had to agree to but could not review before she was hired. The policy also was substantively unconscionable because it always allowed Ralph's to pick the arbitrator, who is likely not to be neutral, and allowed the arbitrator to split the costs between the parties regardless of who won. Typical fees would be $7,000 to $14,000 per day, which would likely be more than the value of Chavarria's claim and would make it impossible for many employees to hold Ralph's responsible for violations of the law (*Chavarria v. Ralph's Grocery Company*, 2015).

Given how ubiquitous form contracting is, relatively few judicial opinions explore its contract law dimensions. In consumer cases the stakes are typically too small and the costs of litigation too high, and arbitration clauses and class action waivers bar much litigation. Outside of traditional contract law, however, federal and state law regulate many elements of form contracts. There are two approaches to regulation. The first approach regulates how terms in form contracts must be disclosed, requiring the party presenting the form to try to make clear its essential terms. Plain language laws require sellers and lenders to write contracts in plain language, without legalese, using short sentences and paragraphs, and in readable type. Laws regulating credit cards require standard-form disclosures of interest rates and fees. Disclosure regulation aims to improve the process of contracting by giving consumers better information about their deals, but it often fails because more disclosure becomes too much disclosure, overwhelming consumers, and no matter how clear or prominent the terms, consumers often won't pay attention to them. Therefore, the second approach is direct regulation of the terms of form contracts. Federal law limits when and why credit card companies can increase interest rates, and state laws prohibit product sellers from including in sales contracts a term saying the seller is not liable if the buyer is injured because of a defect in the product. Direct regulation is more effective than disclosure regulation but limited in scope; form contracting takes myriad forms and direct regulation only addresses specific problems.

Once You Make a Contract, Can You Ever Get Out of It?

The easiest way to get out of a contract is to have the other party let you out. Even though the other party may have a legal right to have you perform the contract, she may not insist that you perform. Most people in business are reasonable and understanding. They want to do the right thing, which is not always to pursue their legal rights to the full extent. In many settings people would say it is not nice to make the other person do something he doesn't want to do. In addition, many contracts arise out of long-term relationships, and it may be more important to preserve the relationship than to obtain the benefit of a single performance. Often it may not be worthwhile to make a federal case out of a small contract.

Someone who has made a contract can invoke the law in a number of ways to get out of it, too. We have already seen that many agreements are not enforceable because of a defect in the agreement process or a doctrine such as duress or unconscionability. In addition, one party to a contract may be excused from performance because of a mistake in the formation of the contract, because his performance has become impossible, or because a condition of his duty to perform has failed to occur.

Many contracts involve a prediction about the future, but the prediction may turn out to be wrong. An investor contracts to buy a company's stock in the expectation that the company's business will expand and the price of the stock will go up. If the investor is mistaken and the value of the stock plummets, she can hardly get out of the deal (or undo it, if the transaction has already been consummated) because of her mistake. The possibility that the stock price might fall is one of the risks that she took in entering into the contract, and the law will not relieve her of that risk because of her mistake.

Sometimes, though, the mistake doesn't involve one of the risks the parties were bargaining about. Suppose a contractor, in preparing a bid on a construction job, makes a clerical error in figuring the cost of the materials needed at $1,000 instead of $11,000. The contractor submits a bid for $15,000 instead of $25,000 and the owner accepts the bid. If the contractor discovers the error immediately, courts would be inclined to let him out of the contract because of the mistake. The owner is not much prejudiced by letting the contractor out if the mistake is discovered right away, compared to the burden on the contractor of performing at the lower price, and the owner should be aware of the mistake if the other bids come in around $25,000. On the other hand, if the contractor makes an error in judgment—predicting it will take two weeks to do the job when it actually takes a month—the court will not excuse him. The contractor takes the risk that the job will take longer than two weeks when he makes his bid on that assumption at a fixed price.

Sometimes the mistakes parties make concern the state of facts at the time the contract is made rather than predictions about the future performance. This is what happened in one of the great cases of contract law, *Sherwood v. Walker* (1887), the "barren cow" case. The buyer, wanting to buy some Angus cattle, contacted the seller, who had some cattle on his farm. The seller warned the buyer that in all probability the cows were sterile and would not breed. The buyer picked out a cow named Rose 2d of Aberlone, and they agreed on a price of 5.5 cents per pound, on the assumption that the cow was incapable of breeding so her only value would be as beef. When the buyer tendered $80 after the cow was weighed, the seller refused to turn her over, because he had discovered that Rose was bearing a calf, making her value as a breeder between $750 and $1,000. The court said the seller did not have to go through with the deal because the parties had been mistaken about the substance of what they were buying and selling.

The decision in *Sherwood v. Walker* is based on the concept of the risks of the contract. Surely the buyer and seller knew they were bargaining with respect to a particular cow, Rose 2d, but they were bargaining about her on the assumption that she was useful only for butchering and not breeding. Their mistake about her condition went to a basic assumption of the contract, would have a significant effect on the value of the contract, and was not a risk that either of them took, because (the court assumed) they were both sure she could not breed. When the assumption outside the risks of the contract turned out to be incorrect, the seller could get out of the contract. The case would have been different if one of the risks of the contract had been whether the cow could breed, with the buyer thinking she might and the seller guessing she probably wouldn't. Then they both would be stuck with the deal whichever way things turned out.

The concept of the risks of the contract extends to another class of excuse cases involving what are known as *impossibility* and *frustration*. Sometimes the performance that a party has promised to render is impossible to achieve when the time comes. In the classic case of *Taylor v. Caldwell* (1863), for example, the owner of a music hall had agreed to rent it out to a local promoter for a series of concerts over four days. Between the time they made the agreement and the time scheduled for the performances, the music hall burned down. The promoter asked for damages because the owner of the hall couldn't make the music hall available for use on the days promised. The owner of the hall responded that he should be relieved of his contractual obligation because the performance had become impossible; he could not make the music hall available when it no longer existed.

This is an appealing argument; if you cannot do something, how can you be held responsible for failing to do it? Note, however, that there are several intermediate steps we need to take to reach that conclusion. The owner cannot provide the hall, but that does not mean that he cannot be held liable for damages for failing to do what he promised to do. The issue is whether he should be relieved from liability, not whether he should be compelled to do the impossible.

Courts resolve this issue exactly the way they resolve other contract law issues. When the parties have not clearly said what should happen if the music hall burns down, the court has to determine what they intended, which really means what they reasonably should have intended, which really means what is the fair result given the court's views of what parties ordinarily do and should expect in this context. Following this analysis, courts generally conclude that impossibility of performance does constitute the kind of excuse that lets a person out of a contract, so the music hall owner, for example, doesn't have to pay damages for failing to have the hall available for the promoter's use.

There is a parallel doctrine from the other side of the contract, known as *frustration of purpose*. In 1902 a great procession was scheduled in London to mark the coronation of Edward VII as King of England. Owners of apartments along the parade route rented out their rooms to prospective spectators at rates much higher than the normal rental value. Unfortunately, Edward became ill and the coronation was postponed. The persons who had taken the rooms in anticipation of the procession sought to be excused from their contracts. Their performance was neither impossible nor impracticable. It was perfectly possible for them to pay the money and sit in the rooms on the appointed date. What had happened, though, was that their purpose in entering into the contract had been frustrated; although they could rent the rooms, they could not use them to watch the now nonexistent procession. The court granted an excuse in this circumstance, for the same reason that an impossible performance is excused. The court determined that postponement of the coronation was not one of the risks that the renter should bear under the reasonable understanding of the contract.

What Happens if One Party's Performance Depends on Something Happening and It Doesn't Happen?

The most common way to get an excuse for not performing a contract is because you have a duty to perform that arises only if something happens and the something never happens. Lawyers call the something a *condition* of your duty. Returning to *Hamer v. Sidway*, suppose Uncle promises to give Nephew $5,000 if Nephew refrains from smoking and drinking until his twenty-first birthday. At Nephew's twenty-first birthday party, he tells Uncle that he has been hitting the bottle and smoking a pack a day, but he wants the money anyway. Is Uncle obligated to give it to him? Of course not. Uncle's promise to give $5,000 was conditional on its face: If you refrain from smoking and drinking, then I will give you the money. Because the condition of Uncle's duty to pay never occurred, he is not obligated to follow through. This follows even though Nephew never promised to refrain. Because Nephew never promised to refrain, Uncle can't sue him—a condition is different from a promise—but unless the condition comes about, Nephew can't collect on Uncle's promise.

That was an easy case because the terms of the promise expressly stated that it was conditional. Suppose instead that Uncle agrees to sell and Nephew agrees to buy Uncle's car for $5,000. Nephew shows up at the appointed time and place, informs Uncle that he still wants the car but doesn't want to pay for it, demands the keys and title, and says he will sue if Uncle doesn't hand them over. Can Nephew sue for the car?

This case is as easy as the first one. Even though the agreement did not expressly state that Uncle has to deliver the car only if Nephew pays, we are sure that is the right result. How do we know that? Here we use the same process of constructing the meaning of the promises that we used to determine if there were promises at all, when we considered contract formation. It would be unreasonable to allow Nephew to get the car and leave Uncle with nothing but a lawsuit for the price, so Nephew has to fulfill the implied condition of Uncle's promise—coming up with the money—before he is entitled to the car. In this case, the condition is also a promise; if Nephew doesn't pay, Uncle can refuse to turn over the car (because the condition of his duty to do so has failed to occur) and sue Nephew for breach (because Nephew has broken his promise to pay for the car).

This does create a dilemma though. Presumably the condition runs in the other direction, too. Nephew is not required to pay the money unless Uncle gives him the car; Nephew is buying a car, not a lawsuit. We can end up with the absurd situation of Uncle holding the keys and Nephew holding the cash, each demanding that the other perform before he will perform. Are both in breach for failing to perform, or is neither in breach because the condition of his performance has not occurred? Here again we have to use our experience and judgment to construct a reasonable solution. Uncle does not actually have to give Nephew the keys before the condition of Nephew's duty to pay has occurred. If he did, Nephew might drive off without paying. Instead, Uncle only has to *tender* performance, by showing he is ready, willing, and able to perform, and Nephew has to do the same.

Many contracts contain conditions that do not depend on the performance of the other party. An insurance policy is an everyday example. The insurance company promises to pay on a homeowner's policy for damage to the insured's house if the house is damaged. If the house is never damaged, the condition of the company's duty never arises, so the company never has to pay.

When the court decides that a contractual duty is conditional, must the condition be fully met before the duty becomes binding? In some cases, certainly; if Nephew only has $2,000 of the $5,000 price, he can't demand the keys to the car. But in other cases conditions can be satisfied by something other than strict performance. Consider *Jacob & Youngs, Inc. v. Kent* (1921), an opinion by the great judge Benjamin Cardozo.

Kent hired Jacob & Youngs, Inc., a construction company, to build his custom-designed country residence. The construction contract specified in detail how the house was to be built, including a requirement that the cast iron pipe used for part of the plumbing be "of Reading manufacture" (made by the Reading Pipe Company, a reliable manufacturer). When construction was almost finished, Kent learned that Jacob & Youngs had used some pipe manufactured by the Cohoes Company instead of Reading pipe. Kent's architect ordered Jacob & Youngs to tear the offending pipe out of the walls and replace it with Reading pipe, even though the two were of identical quality.

Most reasonable homeowners would have excused Jacob & Young's failure of condition by not insisting on strict performance. Kent, however, was known as a man who would "chase all over town for a dollar," so he pointed to the contract and demanded strict performance, regardless of the expense, or else he would not pay Jacob & Youngs the amount he still owed on the contract.

This is an intriguing case. Jacob & Youngs has not performed; does its failure to perform operate as a failure of condition in the same way that Nephew's failure to tender the price of the car does? It seems unfair to make the builder do a lot of useless work in replacing the perfectly functional Cohoes pipe with Reading pipe. (And we suspect that Kent anticipates that the contractor won't do it, so Kent can keep whatever payments he still has to make under the contract and do nothing about the pipe.) On the other hand, the parties have made a deal that specified Reading pipe, and a deal is a deal.

But what was the deal? Here the court decided that the deal was not that Jacob & Youngs had to build the building exactly as specified in order to be paid but only that it build substantially in accordance with the plans. Minor deviations, like a difference in pipe that has no functional effect, don't matter; the builder is still entitled to be paid. If Jacob & Youngs leaves the house half-finished, it may not get anything on the contract, but if it does nearly all of the work, Kent has to pay. As Judge Cardozo wrote in this case,

> Those who think more of symmetry and logic in the development of legal rules than of practical adaptation to the attainment of a just result will be troubled by a classification where the lines of division are so wavering and blurred. Something, doubtless, may be said on the score of consistency and certainty in favor of a stricter standard. The courts have balanced such considerations against those of equity and fairness, and found the latter to be weightier.

A related issue concerns conditions of satisfaction. Suppose Kent hires an interior decorator to prepare a plan for decorating the country residence. Kent is fussy, so he promises to pay the decorator twice her normal hourly fee if he likes the design and nothing if he doesn't. The decorator works furiously and comes up with a plan that wins prizes and is applauded by art critics and other designers. Unfortunately, Kent hates it and refuses to pay. Will we say that the design is much like pipe—everyone else agrees it is good so the owner should be satisfied, too? Not here. Satisfaction with pipe ought to be based on purely functional characteristics, but satisfaction with an artistic design is personal. Kent's freedom to make a deal on his terms leads the court to conclude that if Kent really does not like the design, the condition of his duty to pay has failed to occur. (Kent really has to not like the design, though; he can't use his purported dissatisfaction to get out of the contract for some other reason.)

Will a Court Order Someone to Perform a Contract?

If someone doesn't do what she has promised to do, she is in breach of contract. One common consequence of breach is that the other party does not have to perform its side of the bargain. One party's breach constitutes a failure of a condition of the other party's duty to perform, as when Uncle doesn't have to hand over the keys to the car if Nephew refuses to pay. Not being required to perform and perhaps being able to keep part of the other party's performance (such as a down payment) is often the greatest advantage that a contracting party can have.

The other consequence of breach is that the injured party is entitled to a legal remedy for breach of contract. We might think that the injured party should be able to demand that the other party perform, by delivering the goods or performing the job that was promised. Ordering the breaching party to perform would affirm the importance of keeping one's promises and make sure that the other party is not harmed by the breach.

In contract law, however, ordering the other party to perform (called *specific performance*) is an exceptional remedy that is ordered only in unusual cases. Ordinarily, the injured party is entitled only to money damages as a substitute for the promised performance, not the actual performance itself.

There are three reasons that courts treat specific performance as an extraordinary remedy. The first and probably most important is historical. Money damages were the usual remedy in law courts. Ordering someone to do something as a remedy was generally available only in equity courts. As a result of the political conflict between the law courts and equity courts, equitable remedies such as specific performance became regarded as exceptional. (See Chapter 4.)

The second reason is practical. In many cases it would be difficult for the court to order someone to do something and then to determine whether he or she has complied. If the contract requires a builder to construct a house, some of the terms of performance will be easy to determine—whether the house meets the physical dimensions described in the plans—but many of the other terms will be difficult to supervise—whether the carpentry has been done in "a workmanlike manner." The court does not want to have to supervise a complex performance and listen to the parties as they repeatedly run into court to complain about some aspect of it.

The third reason is conceptual. The basic principle of contract remedies is that the typical contract has a monetary value. Contract law serves to protect people who rely on promises, but they can be adequately protected by giving them the monetary equivalent of the performance promised to them instead of the actual performance itself. Money damages are thought to be as good as performance because the injured party can use the money to procure a substitute on the market. If the contract is to build a house and the builder refuses to perform, the owner can hire another builder and sue the builder for the higher cost, if any; if the owner breaches, the builder can get the profit it would have made on the job.

The principle that money damages are an adequate substitute for a contractual performance is so strong that there are very few exceptions to it. Only where money damages cannot substitute for the performance is the injured party entitled to specific performance of the contract. This usually occurs only when the item sold is unique so that no market substitute is available. If a buyer contracts to buy a new Cadillac from a GM dealer and the dealer breaches, the buyer is not entitled to specific performance because she can get an identical car elsewhere. If a buyer contracts to buy a used 2014 Cadillac and the seller breaches, it may be hard to find the exact model in the same condition elsewhere, but even then the court will say that money damages are enough because the buyer should be able to get a similar car. However, if the buyer contracts to buy a 1966 gold Cadillac driven by Elvis Presley, she will be entitled to specific performance. Elvis's Cadillac is unique, so no damage remedy can make up for the loss.

How Much Does Someone Have to Pay for Not Keeping a Promise?

Contracts are enforceable because people expect that someone who makes a promise will carry through on it. When the promise is broken, the injured party's expectation is the usual measure of contract damages.

Take a simple example. A farmer agrees to sell a truckload of pumpkins to the owner of a roadside produce stand for $100. When the farmer fails to deliver the pumpkins, the stand owner buys a substitute truckload from another farmer for $120. The owner expected to have paid $100 to receive a truckload of pumpkins, so requiring the breaching farmer to pay $20 damages would satisfy that expectation. If the owner buys substitute pumpkins for $100 or less, the farmer owes nothing, because the owner is in as good a position as if the farmer's promise had been performed even without the payment of damages.

Similarly, if the stand owner refuses to take the pumpkins and the farmer resells them for $90, the owner should pay $10 to put the farmer where he would have been if the promise had been performed: no pumpkins in his truck and $100 in his pocket. If the pumpkin market doesn't fall and the farmer resells for $100 or more, the stand owner owes nothing.

In all of these cases we assume that the injured party has no expenses in either buying substitute pumpkins or reselling the pumpkins that were contracted for. If there are such expenses, they will be added to the damages. If, for example, the farmer has to truck the pumpkins some distance to resell them after the stand owner's breach, the farmer could recover the cost of transportation; if he cannot recover those costs, his expectation from the contract has not been fully satisfied.

Suppose when the farmer breaches the stand owner doesn't buy any substitute pumpkins. The law says he is still entitled to his damages, measured by what he would have paid for substitute pumpkins. If the market price has risen to $120 per truckload, the owner is entitled to $20 even though he does not have any tangible loss. Contract remedies are based on the expectation of performance, not actions actually taken in reliance on the expectation of performance. The reasons for this are obscure, but it has something to do with the difficulty in many situations of proving that one actually relied on a specific contract. If the buyer is not the owner of a small roadside stand but Libby's, buying thousands of truckloads of pumpkins to process into pie filling, it would be hard to link a particular broken contract and a particular substitute, but we imagine there must be a loss there anyway.

Contract law imposes some limitations on expectation damages. One is that damages must be foreseeable. Suppose the pumpkin contract called for delivery on October 15 and the stand owner had made special arrangements to resell the pumpkins at a premium to school groups to make into jack-o'-lanterns for Halloween. When the farmer fails to deliver, it is too late for the stand owner to get pumpkins from anywhere else, so he loses more than the ordinary resale markup for pumpkins. Here the owner's expectation is higher than usual, and the issue is which party should bear the burden of this loss. The owner will point to his expectation of higher profit, but the farmer will respond that he did not know about the special arrangements. The law states that only where the farmer knows or reasonably should know of the owner's special loss will he be liable for it. This provides an interesting contrast with the tort law damage rules, under which the party causing the harm is responsible for all the consequences, foreseeable or not, because fault is more important in tort than in contract law.

A second limitation is that the nonbreaching party cannot recover damages that it could have avoided through reasonable efforts. This rule operates most frequently in employment cases. If a corporate executive is fired with six months remaining on her employment contract, can she just sit home watching reality television shows and drinking margaritas while collecting her salary? Not necessarily. If she does not look for another job or take a comparable job if one is offered, her damages will be reduced by what her former employer can prove she could have earned in the substitute employment. The standard is reasonableness; she is not required to move across the country to take a position, nor does she have to take a minimum-wage job at McDonald's.

A third limitation is that damages must be proven with reasonable certainty. This limitation can be particularly troublesome in the case of new businesses. Suppose an entrepreneur plans on opening a new restaurant on March 1, but the opening is delayed for two months because the kitchen equipment supplier fails to deliver the ranges and refrigerators on time. The entrepreneur may have difficulty proving with reasonable certainty what the restaurant's profit would have been during those two months; the patronage of a new restaurant is highly speculative, and it is hard to draw inferences from the experience of other restaurants.

This hypothetical suggests the need for other types of remedies to supplement expectation damages. *Reliance damages* are awarded when expectation damages are unavailable, to compensate the injured party for expenses incurred in reliance on a contract. The restaurant owner may not be able to recover for lost profits, but if she has spent hundreds of dollars buying newspaper advertising and printing invitations for the March 1 opening, those expenses are wasted and the supplier is liable for them as reliance damages. *Restitution damages* are the recovery of benefits conferred on the other party. If the owner cancels the contract with the supplier and gets equipment elsewhere, the owner is entitled to get back the down payment made to the supplier.

If the contract damage rules worked really well, people would seldom break their promises. Unless someone could get a much better deal by breaking a contract and going elsewhere, it just wouldn't pay once the breaching party had paid the other party's damages. But contract damage rules don't work very well. Aside from the foreseeability, avoidability, and certainty limitations on expectation damages, it costs money to get damages. The injured party has to hire a lawyer and pay litigation expenses to recover the damages. These costs are also damages caused by the broken promise, but they are not recoverable as contract damages. So if the injured party has a loss of $10,000 she might have to pay $2,000 in attorney's fees and other expenses to get it back, meaning she has been undercompensated to that extent. It also takes time and aggravation to litigate, and the financial and psychic burden cannot be recovered either. Therefore, many valid breach of contract cases are not worth pursuing.

From a different direction, though, recall that contract remedies, like the liability rules of contract law, are residual. The threat of legal remedies is not as important in deterring people from breaking their promises as are other factors. People will avoid breaking their promises because they think that it is wrong to do so. Other people may think badly of them if they do, and reputation is a valuable commodity in business. Their contracting partner may refuse to deal with them in the future if they breach. So contract remedies, like the rest of contract law, are only part of the story.

7

You Are What You Own

Property Law

The fundamental principle of property law seems obvious: If you own something it's yours, and you can do what you want with it. But more than any other subject, property law is burdened with a thousand years of legal history and a plethora of technical distinctions. Did you know you probably own your house in *fee simple absolute*—unless you have a *fee simple subject to an executory limitation*? And if you plan to leave property to your grandchildren, do you need to be concerned about the Rule Against Perpetuities? Both of these vestiges of feudalism, and many others, still have bite in the modern day.

At the same time, property law concerns issues of great social policy and cutting-edge technology. Should the government be able to construct dunes to prevent beach erosion even if the dunes block the ocean view of beachfront homes? If a research physician develops a commercially valuable product from a patient's cancer cells, who owns the rights to the product—the physician or the patient? Can a music fan make a mash-up video and post it to YouTube? If so, who owns the rights to the video?

This chapter begins with some basic principles and then examines some of the most important issues in property law from medieval times to the present. The subject is so large that we can only hit some highlights.

What Is Property Law?

People in our culture have an intuitive notion of what property is, and part of the task of this chapter is to explore the extent to which the law's idea of property differs from that intuitive notion. Let's begin with intuitions about property, which we can see from the ideas children absorb from their parents.

A small child has a very clear concept of property: "Mine!" Little Suzie's toy, doll, or favorite blanket is her property. Implicit in "mine" is a concept of ownership, the same concept of ownership that her parents may have about their house, car, or investment accounts, which are other examples of property. The core of this concept is what Sir William Blackstone, author of the definitive eighteenth-century treatise on English law, called "sole and despotic dominion . . . over . . . things . . . in total exclusion of the right of any other individual in the universe." Ownership, or dominion, is the ability to control the use of the property. Suzie can pretend that her doll is a guest at a tea party, a superhero, or her mother going off to work, just as her parents can paint their house orange, put their bed in the dining room, or hang posters of Adolf Hitler on the walls. She can allow a friend to play with her doll, or she can prevent her friend from playing with it, just as her parents can invite neighbors over or keep them out. She can give it to her friend for keeps, she can trade with her friend for a different toy, or she can refuse to do so, just as her parents can sell their house at any price they can get or keep it for themselves.

In our culture, this concept of the ownership of things has been central to the idea of property. Property law concerns the different things people can own and the ways in which they can own them. Both elements of the concept—things as the subject of property law and absolute ownership—are deficient, however, and property law is more diffuse.

Think first about things, or the subject matter of property. Suzie's doll and her parents' house are things that can be someone's property. Almost anything tangible can be the subject matter of property. We have to say "almost," because whether some tangible things can be property is controversial. Suzie "belongs" to her parents, but she is not their property. (This shows that definitions of property change; if Suzie is African American, prior to the Civil War she could have been someone's property.) What about Suzie's father's kidneys? They are property in the sense that no one else can take them away, but are they property in the sense that he could sell one to someone who needs a transplant? (In Iran the answer is yes; in other countries, the answer is no, at least to date.)

Property isn't limited to tangible things either. If Suzie's father is an author, he has a copyright in the novels he writes. This is an intangible form of *intellectual property*; he doesn't own the books, but he does own the right to produce the books. Suzie's parents also may own stocks, bonds, and mutual fund shares. Financial instruments like these are the most prevalent form of property in our society, even though they are intangible.

Once the law goes down the path of recognizing intangible property interests, the core conception of property as involving "things" comes apart. Does an employee have a property right in her job? Is the right to receive or maintain government benefits or privileges, like a television broadcast license, property? Is every kind of privilege or entitlement potentially the subject of property?

The move from tangible to intangible property presents a problem for property law. If property cannot be confined to things, then what is the scope of property law? If it extends to every potentially valuable resource, then everything is subject to property law. But if everything is part of property, then there is nothing really special about property law.

Raising these questions also illustrates the deficiency of the second element of property, the concept of absolute ownership. Suzie's parents own their house, but the ownership falls far short of Blackstone's conception of absolute dominion. They cannot use their property for anything they want. If they want to put a store on the property, local zoning regulations may prevent it. If they host loud parties or leave garbage piled on the lawn, the neighbors or local officials may bring legal action to stop them. Nor can they prevent all others from using the property. They own the sidewalk in front of their house, but they cannot exclude pedestrians from using the sidewalk. And others may have ownership interests in the property, too. When they borrowed money to buy the house, they gave the bank a contract right (a promise to repay the money) and a property interest (the mortgage that secures the loan).

When we put together the extension of property to intangibles and the collapse of the idea of absolute ownership, we see that property is not really about the ownership of things. Instead, property is about relationships among people with respect to valuable resources. Those relationships are not defined by Blackstone's—or Suzie's—concept of absolute ownership but instead vary depending on the context. Property law is often described as involving a *bundle of rights*; no single concept of ownership prevails. Instead, there are a variety of legal relationships that people can have with respect to valuable interests.

The bundle of potential rights defines what interests an owner can have in an item of property. Think of the bundle of rights as a bundle of sticks. If an individual is holding all of the sticks with respect to a certain subject of property, tangible or intangible, then we think of that person as the owner of the property. Even if they do not hold all of the sticks, if they hold most of them, or some particularly important sticks, we might still think of them as owning the property. Here are the most important sticks, or interests in property that one might have. Because property is not absolute, all of these are subject to limitation.

- *Liberty to use.* Suzie's parents can do pretty much what they want with their house without anyone else's permission.

- *Right to exclude.* No one else has a right to use the house unless Suzie's parents let them.

- *Power to transfer.* Suzie's parents can sell or give away the house. They also can determine what happens to it upon their deaths, by leaving it in their wills to Suzie or to the SPCA.

- *Immunity from damage.* Just as no one else can use the property, no one else has a legal power to damage the property. If a neighbor chops down his own tree and it falls through their roof, Suzie's parents can recover money damages from the neighbor for the cost of repairing the roof.

The extent to which property law is relational rather than absolute is evident by looking at a few examples of the ways in which one of these fundamental interests is defined and limited. Often the most important of the bundle of rights is the right to exclude others from the use of one's property. Some aspects of the right to exclude are obvious; a homeless person can't come sleep in your living room without permission. Any entry upon your land without your permission or without a legal privilege to enter is a *trespass.* If someone drives across your land, throws garbage on it, or even walks a dog on your lawn, it technically is a trespass. Traditionally, a landowner was thought to own not only the surface of the land but also all property extending down to the center of the earth and up "to the heavens." The former is still true; your neighbor cannot dig a tunnel under your land or dig diagonally to extract minerals under your land. The latter concept has been eroded, however; it is not a trespass for an airplane to fly over your house at 30,000 feet, or for a satellite to orbit the Earth above your property.

Some entries on other people's land are privileged, though, and therefore are not trespasses. For example, the seller of a house has a reasonable time after the sale to remove items that have been left there, unless the parties have agreed that all of the seller's property will be removed before the sale. Public officials such as the police, firefighters, and health inspectors can enter property under some circumstances to protect the public safety. If Suzie's parents operate a business on their property, antidiscrimination laws prevent them from excluding customers on the grounds of race.

Suppose there is not a physical invasion of the property but some other type of entry. Does a property owner have the right to exclude noise, smells, smoke, or vibrations? If you live near a fertilizer plant and the plant emits unpleasant odors and occasionally dust that settles on your land, have your property rights been invaded? The law's answer is yes, if the infringement on your enjoyment of your property is deemed to be unreasonable. These invasions of your property are called *nuisances*. They also may violate local ordinances or state law specifically directed at these kinds of problems.

The tricky part, of course, is figuring out when something like dust, odors, or noise are unreasonable. Think about noises that might constitute nuisances: Your neighbor's kid practicing the piano (badly) for an hour after school? The kid's teenage brother's rock band practicing at full volume for an hour after school? For three hours? At midnight? As you can see, there are judgment calls to be made here. The court will look at the kind of invasion, when, where, and how frequently it occurs, and how much impact it has on the enjoyment and economic value of your property in deciding whether to label a certain activity a nuisance. These judgment calls are part of the courts' task of defining the relationships that constitute the law of property.

So property law is not about things, or even in a simple sense about the ownership of things. Instead, property law—like all other law—is about the allocation of value in society. It is inevitably tied to questions about economics, politics, and our vision of the good society. We need to explore, then, what qualifies as property, what it means to say something is property, and how the answers to those questions tie in to social relations, power, and justice.

Why Do We Need Property Law?

The first question, as with any body of law, is why do we need property law at all? In particular, why do we need a system of private property and what does it do for us? What would be wrong if instead everybody "owned" everything in common, or if there were no legally enforceable rights to own anything?

Lawyers, judges, and scholars have grappled with these questions from the time of Blackstone and John Locke to the present. The answers are not entirely satisfactory, and this lack of clarity is one source of the confusion in the law. Here we focus on three types of arguments that have dominated the debate over property: First, property encourages productive activity. Second, property protects political liberty. Third, property contributes to human flourishing.

Property arguably encourages people to engage in productive activity by providing them some security in knowing that their property will be protected and by creating a system in which property can be transferred to those people who will use it most effectively. The same parables have been used from the time of Blackstone to modern law and economics scholars to illustrate the point. Suppose you decide to grow crops on a piece of land. You till the soil, plant seeds, and water and fertilize your crops. When the day comes for your crops to be harvested, however, you find that your neighbor has been there the night before and has taken for himself all of the food you have grown. If you don't have a legally enforceable property right in the crops, your only recourse is to use force against your neighbor, which you may not be inclined to do if he is bigger and stronger than you are. In the future, you won't have much of an incentive to work hard growing crops if you won't be able to enjoy the fruits of your labor.

Suppose also that you are not a very good farmer, compared to some of your neighbors. You can only produce 100 bushels a year of corn on the land, while a better farmer could produce 200 bushels. If you can sell your land to your neighbor, or sell the right to use the land to grow corn, you and your neighbor both will be better off. But you cannot do so unless you have property rights in the land, to use it exclusively and to transfer the right to use.

In short, property law serves an economic function. If people have legal protection for the use of property, the legal ability to exclude others from using it, and the capacity to transfer property to others, they are more likely to invest labor and capital in the development of resources, and resources will flow to the hands of those who can use them most effectively. These consequences benefit the individuals who use resources and they benefit society as a whole because, as the economists say, they encourage people to put resources to their "highest and best use."

Whether private property really does encourage productive activity in these ways depends on the validity of the implicit assumptions underlying the economic argument. Many books have been devoted to examining these economic arguments, and they cannot be explored in depth here. Consider, however, that the economic argument translates a theoretical analysis into a broad empirical assumption: that a person will do anything not prohibited by law, and that a person will only do things protected by law. It is not necessarily true that the strong will steal from the weak, nor that farmers will farm only to the extent that they have legal protection for their efforts. In both instances, social constraints or different perceptions of self-interest and community interest may cause people to act in ways that the economic argument does not predict. Anthropologists have described many societies and situations in which collective ownership of resources rather than private property was economically productive.

Moreover, today the debate about the economic function of private property takes on a different form when considering intellectual property in electronic form, such as movies, music, and online content. Providing strong protection may encourage producers to create more such content—rock groups will record more songs and recording companies and iTunes will distribute more of them—but it also prevents or discourages other people from building on that content—hip-hop artists will be less able to remix the songs, and fans will be less able to create tribute websites containing the songs.

There also is a political dimension to private property. The ability to own property and thereby to establish a means of independence from others makes it possible for the property owner to assert political independence. Sometimes it is said that property is a precondition of democracy, because property enables a citizen to speak freely and participate in public affairs without concern that political participation will undermine one's economic well-being. For Thomas Jefferson, this meant that everyone (or at least every adult white male) should have the opportunity to own land and that land ownership should not be concentrated in a few wealthy families. "Dependence begets subservience and venality," he wrote, while independent ownership contributes to democracy.

In the 1960s the political argument for property was applied to the many people who in one way or another depend on the government for their livelihood. In a much-celebrated law review article titled "The New Property," Yale law school professor Charles Reich argued that welfare recipients, government employees, and the holders of public franchises and licenses needed property rights in their benefits to establish themselves as politically independent of the state.

Lately we have come to recognize the limits of the political argument for private property. As Jefferson noted, it is not just property but the distribution of property that contributes to democracy. When property is concentrated in large corporations and super-rich individuals, and when wealthy institutions dominate the political process, the ability of individuals to participate and influence affairs declines.

Finally, there is a strong personal dimension to property. Things can be very important to people because they contribute to creating a sense of self, a sense of place, a sense of being and belonging. It is not too far a stretch to say that the importance of a favorite doll or a treasured blanket to little Suzie is analogous to her parents' ownership of a house, or other cherished items, from family heirlooms to an expensive car. These elements of property define, in part, who Suzie and her parents are, and without the ability to own them they would not be the same persons. The point can be seen by looking at environments in which people have little access to property. In prisons or psychiatric hospitals, inmates collect a few belongings, hide them, or carry them around to establish a personal space and a sense of self. And an important demonstration of selflessness in a religious order is abandoning property: not just taking a vow of poverty but giving up the ability to own more than a few necessities as personal property.

What Kinds of Property Are There?

Property covers a lot of ground. (Forgive the pun.) As we have seen, Suzie's doll, her parents' house, and her father's copyright are only some of the subjects of property. The law treats different kinds of property differently, so it is helpful to sort out the kinds of property that one can own.

Perhaps the most basic distinction is between *real property* and *personal property*. Real property is land and things permanently attached to the land. (Thus the origin of terms such as "real estate" and "Realtor.") Personal property is everything else. Furniture, jewelry, and cars are personal property but so are intangibles such as copyrights, patents, and stocks and bonds. Some types of property present difficult definitional issues—growing crops are sometimes real property, sometimes personal property—but for the most part the distinction between real and personal property is easy to understand.

Why we have the distinction and what it means are more complicated, though. In medieval times, land was not only an object of wealth but also the basis of a system of social organization. After the decline of feudalism, land still merited special treatment because it was the most widespread and important form of wealth and, as such, was subject to special procedural forms. For example, when Thomas Jefferson argued for the distribution of property as protection against tyranny, he meant the distribution of land among small farmers, in opposition to large dynastic landholdings.

Today the historical distinction between real and personal property, combined with the functional differences between property that doesn't go anywhere and property that does, is seen in the different treatment of the different kinds of property. Separate bodies of law regulate each type of property and many subcategories within each type. Selling a piece of land is governed by one body of law; selling a car is governed by another. The ways in which a landowner can use a piece of land is governed by several overlapping bodies of law, while the rights an owner has in a car or a copyright are different still.

As should be evident, some property is tangible and some is intangible. Indeed, land once was the most prevalent form of property, but now intangible property dwarfs real property in value and importance. The average family may own a car and a house, but they also may own mutual funds, bank accounts, and retirement accounts that exceed the value of their tangible property.

A particular kind of intangible property is *intellectual property*, or property created through intellectual work rather than physical work. Patents and copyrights are intellectual property. A *patent* is the exclusive right to use, license, or sell an invention. When an inventor designs a better mousetrap (or, more realistically these days, when the research department of a large pharmaceutical company creates a new drug), the inventor can apply to the government, proving the originality and usefulness of the invention, and be granted a patent that makes the invention the inventor's property for a term of years. Patent law originally protected mechanical innovations, like mousetraps, but it now extends to other types of inventions; controversies have arisen over how far it should go in covering business methods (such as Amazon.com's one-click ordering system), living organisms (such as microbes used for cleaning up oil spills), and even scientific discoveries (such as the decoding of the human genome).

Similarly, when a novelist writes a book, she acquires a property interest in the work known as a *copyright*. Copyright covers many kinds of creative works, including works of fiction and nonfiction (such as this book), photographs, songs, movies, and websites. Copyright protects the expression of ideas rather than the ideas themselves; Disney cannot prevent you from creating a cartoon with an amusing mouse as the protagonist, but it can prevent you from depicting its particular mouse, Mickey.

Trademarks are a kind of property related to intellectual property. Patents and copyrights are protected because they are original creations; trademarks are protected because they have commercial value. The name "McDonald's" and the golden arches symbol have value because people associate them with McDonald's fast food and all of the convenience, quality, and fun that the company tries to evoke with the images. Accordingly, the McDonald's Corporation has a property interest in the name and the symbol, although the extent of the interest is different from other forms of property.

Intellectual property illustrates some very important points about property in general. First, when we think of property, it is easy to think that property is somehow naturally occurring and the only issue is to how to allocate it. Land, trees, and even manufactured products have an existence that predates their allocation as property. But the nature of copyrights and patents should make clear that property is a product of the law. Without law, there would still be inventions and novels, but there would be no property rights in them. Because intellectual property is created and regulated by law, it may be easier to see this than with property that has been allocated by centuries of common law rulings.

Second, intellectual property makes clear that there is no single conception of the ownership of property. Patents, copyrights, and trademarks are all forms of intellectual property, but the law governing them creates different interests with respect to each—a different bundle of rights. The duration of the property interest, for example, is twenty years for a patent, the life of the author plus seventy years for a copyright (or up to 120 years for copyrights held by companies), and as long as it is commercially valuable for a trademark. Congress changes these terms from time to time—in 1998, it extended copyright terms, notably protecting Disney's Mickey Mouse copyright, which was about to expire. After those periods, the property goes into the *public domain* and can be copied or used by anyone. In each case, the law constructs what it means to own property, and the definition differs with respect to different kinds of property.

Third, intellectual property, like all other property, is a product of the law's balancing of the interests of owners, nonowners, and society at large. The Constitution empowers the federal government to grant patents and copyrights "to promote the progress of science and useful arts," and intellectual property law both creates and restricts the owner's rights in order to achieve that objective. In return for the grant of exclusive patent rights by the government, the inventor has to disclose what the invention is and how it works; other inventors can then build on that knowledge in making discoveries of their own. Copyright includes a concept of *fair use*, so that the copyright owner's interest is not exclusive; a reviewer can quote part of a novel in a review, or a college professor can use a portion of it to illustrate a point in an English course without infringing the copyright. Some of the most heated intellectual property debates of recent years have involved this kind of balancing, such as whether copyright terms should be extended for longer periods and to what extent producers of online content can use songs and images created by others.

Who Owns the Internet?

The Internet is a particularly good illustration for thinking about property because the explosion of new technologies and new uses presents many different puzzles for the law to solve. The beginning of this chapter explained that property law does not follow the intuitive understanding of the absolute ownership of things. The Internet is made up of many kinds of things, information that is like things, and some things that are hardly thing-like at all, and deciding who has what rights requires creative analysis and not just intuition.

The easiest part of the Internet to understand in property terms is its physical infrastructure. The Internet is a network of computer networks. You own your computer at the very end of the network. Your Internet service provider owns the wires that go into your house and connect to your computer. Starbucks owns the router that broadcasts a Wi-Fi signal to its customers. Innumerable other routers, access points, satellites, computers, and miles of cable are owned by somebody.

When we talk about the Internet, however, most of the time we are talking about the information that flows through the physical infrastructure: emails, YouTube videos, blogs, Wikipedia, movies, celebrity gossip websites, and more. The law, including contract and tort law as well as property law, has had some difficulty adapting to the production and distribution of this wealth of information.

A basic principle is that everything on the Internet is owned by someone. The Fox television network holds the copyright in episodes of *The Simpsons* posted on its website. Google owns the trademark in the multicolored "Google" that resides on its search home page. A news organization that puts an article on its websites, a college student who uploads a wacky video on YouTube, and a blogger who posts musings about her dog each has property rights in the content they have created.

Because everything online is owned by someone, the owner can assert the ordinary rights of a property owner. The content is intellectual property, so the owner possesses a copyright that others cannot infringe. A music company that copyrights a song has the same rights to distribution of the song on the Internet as it does in distribution on a CD. Therefore, when Joel Tenenbaum, a Providence, Rhode Island, graduate student, used file-sharing sites like Napster to post and download thirty songs by Nirvana and other groups, a jury ordered him to pay $675,000 to the groups' recording companies for copyright infringement. Similarly, if you post an entire *Simpsons* episode on your website, prepare to hear from Fox's lawyers.

But copyright, like all property, does not give the owner absolute rights to control its use. Other people can make "fair use" of the owner's work, including use that is "transformative"—not just copying, but adding something new that presents a different expression or meaning than the original work. If transformative uses of other people's copyrights were not permitted, the Internet would hardly work at all. Google constantly crawls the web, collecting information on text, images, and video on millions of websites. When you Google "Kardashian" and click "Images" on the search results page, you will see countless thumbnail images of members of the celebrity family. Each of those images is the property of a copyright holder—*People* magazine, a photographer, the E! television network, or the celebrities themselves. Does Google infringe on copyrights when it shows you the thumbnails? No, because Google's use of the photos is transformative; showing a photograph is one thing, but showing many thumbnail photographs as a search result is something else entirely, and something that has enormous public benefit in giving everyone access to the vast resources of the Internet in a way that otherwise would be unavailable. The purpose of the copyright law is to promote creativity; search engines serve that purpose by making it easier to find information online.

Protection of trademarks on the Internet similarly is available but limited. Congress enacted the Anticybersquatting Consumer Protection Act to enable trademark owners to protect their marks. John Zuccarini registered the domain names electronicboutique.com, ebwold.com, and ebworl.com to take advantage of misspelling by web users trying to go to electronicsboutique.com and ebworld.com, the sites of video game retailer Electronics Boutique. Electronics Boutique sued and the court, applying the statute, ordered Zuccarini to turn over the domain names and to pay damages (*Electronics Boutique Holdings Corp. v. Zuccarini*, 2000). But when Andrew Faber created a website called Bally Sucks to post complaints about Bally Total Fitness health clubs, the site did not infringe or dilute Bally's trademarked logos and names because no one could confuse the complaint site with the real Bally's (*Bally Total Fitness Holding Corp v. Faber*, 1998).

Internet intermediaries such as YouTube or Comcast are stuck in the middle of disputes like these, because they are potentially liable for secondarily infringing the rights of a copyright owner by hosting the offending website. The Digital Millennium Copyright Act immunizes them from liability if they comply with the act's requirements and attempts to balance the interests of owners of intellectual property and others who use it in new and creative ways. If the owner of a song discovers that a video containing it is posted on YouTube without her permission, the owner sends a takedown notice informing YouTube of the potential infringement, and YouTube responds by removing the offending material. But the original poster then can request that YouTube put the material back up, which shifts the burden back to the copyright owner. When Stephanie Lenz uploaded a YouTube video of her thirteen-month-old son bouncing along to "Let's Go Crazy" by Prince, Universal Music sent a takedown notice to YouTube demanding that the video be taken down because it infringed their copyright in the song. YouTube notified Lenz that it was removing the video. Exercising her rights under the statute, Lenz filed a protest claiming that her use of the song was fair use permitted under the copyright law, so YouTube reposted the song and Lenz went one step further, suing Universal for misusing the statute. The court, recognizing the conflicting interest at stake in property law, concluded that Universal had to consider whether Lenz's inclusion of their song in her video constituted fair use (*Lenz v. Universal Music Corp.*, 2015).

One instinct about information on the Internet is to analogize it to traditional forms of property, but sometimes the analogy is hard to draw. In the physical world the tort of *trespass to chattels* provides a remedy for interfering with the interest of an owner of personal property (a chattel), as where a teenager takes a neighbor's car for a joyride. Can someone trespass on a computer system? When Bidder's Edge's software robot accessed eBay's auction website 100,000 times a day to collect information to aggregate on Bidder's Edge's own site, thereby raising the possibility that other auction aggregators would do the same thing and overwhelm eBay's servers, the court ordered Bidder's Edge to stop (*eBay, Inc. v. Bidder's Edge, Inc.*, 2000). But when Kourosh Hamidi, a disgruntled former employee of Intel Corporation, sent six emails over two years to some 35,000 Intel employees, the court found there was no trespass because the impact of Hamidi's emails on Intel's system was trivial (*Intel Corp. v. Hamidi*, 2003). To deal with the broader problem of invasion of everyone's email accounts by spam, Congress enacted the cleverly named Controlling the Assault of Non-solicited Pornography and Marketing Act of 2003—the CAN-SPAM Act. The act prohibits the sending of fraudulent email and requires unsubscribe procedures, but as your daily email demonstrates, enforcement has been limited.

The Internet is governed by contract law as well as property. Websites restrict how people can use the information they contain through terms of service, whether agreed to through an "I accept" box or not; Chapter 6 discusses the enforceability of these terms. But some owners of intellectual property on the web have taken a different approach and expanded rather than restricted the rights of other people to use their property. Blizzard Entertainment gives users of its hugely popular World of Warcraft role-playing game a blanket license to use screen-shots from the game on their personal websites. Creative Commons is a nonprofit group that offers standard forms for licensing intellectual property that make it easy for web users to allow others to use their works. Creative Commons licenses include forms that, for example, allow others to use their work in any way as long as they credit the original owner, to "share alike" by using property as long as they then allow others to use their own works, and to use it in any way but only for noncommercial purposes.

The most provocative challenge the Internet presents to law arises in virtual worlds, including the Necromancers, Paladins, Shadowknights, and other avatars who stalk EverQuest, and Second Life with its millions of inhabitants and its own economy. Assets in virtual worlds have real-world value; Linden dollars, the currency of Second Life, are bought and sold for real U.S. dollars. Avatars in virtual worlds acquire property the same way as their real-life counterparts, through work, trade, and ingenuity, and the property is as important to the virtual persona as traditional property is to physical people. Should the law therefore recognize virtual property rights? Or can the company that produces and hosts a virtual world use the terms of service to exercise control over everything that happens there? Marc Bragg sued Linden Research, the producer of Second Life, after Linden froze his account, depriving him of virtual property worth $4,000 to $6,000 in the real world; Bragg and Linden eventually settled the case. And what law should be used to resolve the disputes that arise? If a virtual world is a community with its own norms and rules, should it have its own legal system as well, or should the existing legal system at least recognize the norms and rules as binding in real-world courts? As these environments have evolved from games to worlds, they challenge our notions of property and law.

How Can Someone Acquire Property?

A crucial issue for the law of property is under what circumstances the law will recognize that someone has come to own an item of property. In making that determination, the law has to grapple with the potentially inconsistent policies that underlie property law. We want to encourage people to engage in productive activity. We want to recognize the personal value property holds for people. We want a system that will provide clear indications of who owns what. And so on.

A person can come to own a piece of property in a number of ways. The most common way to acquire property, of course, is to buy it. Two ways that were of historical importance but don't happen much anymore are discovery and conquest. Discovery means finding previously unknown territory and doing something to take possession of it, such as planting a flag and establishing a settlement. Today the whole world has been charted, so discovery is irrelevant. The only remaining unoccupied land is in outer space, but, by virtue of an international treaty, the United States doesn't own the moon, even though it was the first nation to land there. Historically, conquest has been closely related to discovery. European powers such as Holland, England, France, and Spain acquired ownership of America by establishing the first non-native settlements, conquering the indigenous peoples who lived here, and mapping the new territories.

A means of acquiring property related to discovery and conquest is by being the first person to possess or use it, giving rise to the saying "first in time, first in right." The principle is illustrated by the struggle, physical and legal, for the baseball that Barry Bonds hit for his record-setting seventy-third home run. The San Francisco Giants slugger crushed a homer into the right-field stands of Pac Bell Park on the last day of the 2001 season. Fan Alex Popov caught the ball in his glove, but a melee ensued, and another fan, Patrick Hayashi, came up with the ball. Popov sued Hayashi, claiming the ball was rightfully his because he was the first to possess it. By convention, the Giants, the original owner of the ball, yielded ownership to whichever fan came up with it. After a three-week court battle that involved viewing videotape of the event, hearing more than a dozen witnesses, and soliciting the opinions of legal experts, Superior Court Judge Kevin McCarthy found that Popov had momentarily caught the ball but had not held it long enough to establish control. Hayashi also was involuntarily knocked to the ground, where he picked up the loose ball. Each had a type of possession, neither was a wrongdoer, so each had rights in the ball which, according to Judge McCarthy's Solomonic ruling, would be realized if the ball was sold, with each of them getting half of the proceeds. (When the ball was sold at auction, it fetched a price of $450,000, disappointing Popov and Hayashi because of earlier estimates up to $1.5 million.)

What about property that is discovered after someone else already has established ownership of it? Suppose you find a ring on the sidewalk and take it to a jeweler to determine its value. The jeweler tells you that the ring contains valuable diamonds but refuses to return it to you, arguing that you are not the true owner. Who is entitled to the ring? Recall that property is not a relationship between people and things but among people. It is true that you are not the owner of the ring, but you do have a superior right of ownership to the jeweler because you found and possessed the ring, so you are entitled to have it returned to you.

But now suppose that the jeweler recognizes the ring as belonging to one of his customers and calls the customer who comes to the store to reclaim the ring. Who gets the ring, you or the customer? The customer—the original owner—does. You, the finder, have a right of ownership that is superior to the jeweler and everyone else, except the true owner. Thus the maxim "finders keepers, losers weepers" is not good law. This explains the general rule about lost items: Turn them in to the police, and if the original owner does not claim them within a specified time period, the items belong to you, because your claim is superior to everyone except the owner.

Another way to acquire ownership to property is by *adverse possession*. Adverse possession is an odd concept because it allows someone to acquire ownership by taking it away from the rightful owner.

Suppose you own a cabin in the backwoods, but, intent on seeking your fortune, you move away from it to live in an apartment in the big city. The move is successful and you enjoy urban life. Meanwhile and unknown to you Zeke, who likes to live off the grid, moves into the cabin and for all practical purposes treats the cabin as if he actually owned it. If you return to the cabin in a couple of years and discover that Zeke has been squatting there, you can order him out and, if he refuses to leave, bring a legal action to have him ejected. But if you wait too long, your legal claim to the property will be lost and Zeke can become the legal owner through the doctrine of adverse possession.

Adverse possession is, as property scholar Joseph Singer notes, a "magical rule [that] mutates a wrong into a right." Why should the law favor Zeke, a trespasser and wrongdoer, over you, the true legal owner of the cabin? In part the doctrine is an application of the principle of a *statute of limitations*, which requires that a claim be brought within a certain period of time after a harm occurs, or else the claim is lost forever. Moreover, although ordinarily the law does not reward someone for doing a wrongful act, such as occupying someone else's land, here the law rewards Zeke for his industriousness and penalizes you for your lack of diligence in failing to attend to your property and to assert your rights for so long. Although possession isn't always nine-tenths of the law, as the maxim says, here possession is rewarded and used as the basis for clarifying ownership.

The jurisdictions vary in the precise requirements for adverse possession, but generally an adverse possessor can claim ownership if for the statutory period (from ten to twenty-one years, depending on the state) it has made open and continuous use of the land without the owner's permission. In essence, the adverse possessor has to have acted like the owner, making use of the land as an owner would, in such a way as to put the real owner on notice that someone has effectively taken the land for its own. This is just what Zeke did, and the doctrine of adverse possession means that if you snooze, you lose.

Someone also can acquire property by gift. A gift is a present transfer of a property interest. For a gift to be legally effective, the donor must intend to make a gift, the property or evidence of it must be delivered to the recipient, and the recipient must accept it. The law is wary of purported gifts, presuming perhaps that people are more self-interested than altruistic, so it requires clear evidence of the intention and delivery. (Acceptance is presumed where the gift is beneficial to the recipient.) Requiring delivery is particularly important because it brings home to the donor the fact that he or she is relinquishing the property and provides evidence of the gift, in case there is a subsequent dispute. Therefore, if I hand you a ring, saying, "I want you to have this," the gift is effective. If I say, "I want you to have this ring, and I will give it to you after I wear it to dinner," the gift is not effective. There is no present delivery, and a promise to make a gift is usually unenforceable. (See Chapter 6.)

What about an engagement ring? When a man gives an engagement ring to his fiancée, there is intention to make a gift, delivery, and acceptance. If the engagement is broken off, is he entitled to get the ring back? This is a unique situation that most courts characterize as a conditional gift. The ring is given in contemplation of marriage, so it is unlike a sweater, a book, or even another piece of jewelry that he gives her during the courtship. If the marriage is off, he has a right to ask for the ring to be returned.

How Is Property Purchased and Sold?

The most common method of acquiring property is by purchase. People buy and sell property every day, of course, from a morning cup of coffee to the family car. Most of the legal issues that arise from these transactions are governed by contract law, not property law. Here we discuss what is for many people the most economically significant purchase they will ever make, the purchase of a home. The purpose is not to provide a legal checklist for the home buyer but to illustrate some of the important issues in property law as they arise in real estate transactions.

First consider why home purchases are worth examining separately at all. One reason obviously is the amount of money at stake. A family's home is likely to be one of their largest assets, perhaps along with a retirement fund and other investments. Where more money is at stake, the law tends to be more complicated. But the sale of real estate is also more complicated because of the bundle of rights concept of property. With most forms of personal property, only one person has an interest in the property at a time, and that person usually is the one who possesses the property. Real property is different. Several different persons are likely to have an interest in the property, and possession is not as good an indicator of ownership. The same piece of property will have been transferred many times over the years, with careless indications of ownership, the property boundary between two neighbors' yards may not be well established, and a bank, a home equity lender, and the grandparents who helped with the down payment all may have an interest in a piece of property. Therefore, some special principles of law have grown up around real estate transactions.

Let's describe the elements of a typical home sale and then focus on two of the elements as particularly pertinent to our examination of property law. The transaction involves both property and contract concepts. The contract issues arise sufficiently frequently that they tend to be treated a little differently from contract law issues arising in other contexts. And custom, local practices, good faith, and cooperation, more than law, are what carry many of these transactions through to completion; only where problems come up that cannot be resolved by other means do the parties resort to the legal system.

A homeowner and a purchaser can arrange the sale themselves, but very often a real estate broker is the intermediary in the transaction. Although the broker often works with both seller and buyer, helping the seller get the house ready for sale, setting the price, advertising, and helping the buyer find the perfect house, by contract the broker often is the agent of the seller, not the buyer. (Sometimes there is a separate buyer's agent, or the agent acts as a dual agent, representing both parties.) Under the brokerage contract, the seller's broker has the obligation to help the seller get the highest price possible and to otherwise serve the seller's interests. The law also defines certain obligations that the broker owes to the buyer, however, such as a duty to fairly represent the condition of the house.

Once the buyer has focused on a house, she makes an offer to buy. Local practice dictates whether the offer is oral or in writing, whether it must be accompanied by an earnest money deposit, and how the subsequent negotiations will be carried out. When the buyer and seller have agreed on a price, they proceed to enter into a written purchase and sale agreement. The agreement includes all of the terms of the transaction, including the price, closing date, and conditions to the closing; the buyer's right to inspect the property; and the seller's duty to deliver good title to the property. The closing date is set several weeks or even months away, enabling the buyer to do what she needs to do to get ready to close, especially obtaining a mortgage. Once this interim period is concluded, the parties close the transaction by exchanging numerous pieces of paper, including the money from the buyer to the seller and the deed in the other direction.

Consider two elements of this transaction. First, the essence of the transaction is the seller conveying to the buyer its interest in the land. What exactly is the seller transferring, and what happens if questions arise concerning who owns what? Second, in most cases the buyer has to borrow money to meet the seller's price, typically from a bank or mortgage company. What kind of property interest is a mortgage, and what does it mean to the buyer and the bank?

When land is sold, the seller delivers to the buyer a deed, a formal written document embodying the conveyance of the property. (Deeds are used in all transfers of land, even if the property is given away rather than sold.) In medieval times the means of transfer was not by document but by *livery of seisin*. The buyer and seller would meet on the property, in the presence of witnesses, and the seller would state that he was transferring ownership and would hand the buyer a twig or a clod of dirt to symbolize the transfer. Today a deed serves the same formal purposes; it makes clear to all that a transfer has taken place and, through the document rather than the witnesses, establishes a record of the transfer. The deed identifies the parties and the land and expresses the seller's intent to convey the property. The deed must be signed by the seller and delivered to the buyer (or to the buyer's agent); this is the origin of the phrase "signed, sealed, and delivered," though most jurisdictions have abolished the need for a seal.

The homeowner who receives the deed acquires title to the house. Title is the formal concept of ownership in real property law. Typically, a seller is required to deliver marketable title to a buyer. The full legal meaning of this definition is complex, but think about what the buyer expects to be getting: full ownership of the property, without any conflicting interests such as other claims of ownership, leases, or mortgages (called *encumbrances*) and without any problems in the record that substantiates the title (called *chain of title defects*). One of the reasons that the sale of real property generates such a complicated body of law is that it is not easy to guarantee that there are no encumbrances or chain of title defects on a piece of property. After all, the land has been there for hundreds of years, during which time many people have owned it, used it, borrowed money against it, conveyed it, let their neighbors use it, and so on. Any of these acts could affect the current state of the title. How do a seller and buyer make sure that the seller is giving the buyer the kind of title the buyer is paying for?

Every state has addressed this problem by enacting a recording act, which establishes a governmental repository of land records. Often the acts establish the Recorder of Deeds or Clerk of the Court in a county as the place where deeds, long-term leases, mortgages, and other documents pertaining to land transfers are maintained. Since in many states the recording acts have been in existence for centuries, the land records provide a comprehensive history of the recorded interests in the land. There is a record of the deed the seller received when he bought the land, and a record of the deed the person who sold to the seller received when she bought the land, and so on back into history.

The recording acts also establish priority among successive purchasers of a piece of land. Suppose an unscrupulous seller sells a piece of land to two different people. Who actually owns the land? In a few states, the first person who records a deed wins, even if that person knows that the property was sold to someone else previously. This system encourages a race to the courthouse, so it is not much used. More common are statutes that specify that the second purchaser has superior title only if she purchases the property without notice of the prior conveyance, or that the second purchaser has priority if she has no notice and records before the prior purchaser.

The recording system can't prevent all title problems. First, there are records besides those in the recorder of deeds' office that must be searched to establish all of the interests in the property. If real estate taxes have not been paid, for example, the government may have a tax lien on the property, and the lien will appear only in the tax records. (A *lien* is a claim against the property that has effect only when the property is sold; at the time of sale, the lien holder can get its money out of the proceeds of sale.) Other problems don't appear in any record at all; a neighbor may have acquired an easement to use part of the property, but that right will be apparent only (if at all) from an inspection of the property itself.

Different practices have grown up to deal with problems of title. The two main kinds are title abstracts and title insurance. Both begin with a search of the records. Lawyers or professional title abstracters examine the available public records to trace back the chain of title. They also look for tax liens and other potential problems, and they check to see if, for example, some prior owner conveyed the property twice or failed to pay a mortgage. When the title abstract is complete, the buyer's attorney can determine if the title is marketable or, if it is not, what it would take to clear up the problems (for example, paying off a lien). When title insurance is provided, the title insurer provides a guarantee against defects that eventually may cloud the buyer's title or even cause it to lose the land.

Few home buyers can afford to pay cash for such an expensive purchase, so many buyers borrow a large portion of the purchase price. Most often they borrow from a lending institution, such as a bank or mortgage company, but they may also borrow from a relative or from the seller. The transaction has two elements, one contractual and one property based. Since the money to buy the house is not a gift, the lender expects to be repaid. To enforce that expectation, the lender makes the borrower promise to repay the money. Usually the borrower signs a note, a document that states the terms of the loan and the obligation to repay. If the borrower doesn't repay the money according to the terms of the loan (such as by making monthly payments of specified amounts), the lender can sue for breach of the promise to pay.

The lender's breach of contract action for the borrower's failure to repay the loan does not provide much security for the lender though. The borrower could sell the house and squander the proceeds of the sale, and the lender would have nothing but a worthless lawsuit to recover its money. So lenders typically back up their contract interest with a property interest as well. The property interest is the *mortgage* (in some states called a *deed of trust*). The mortgage document contains many of the same terms as the note, such as the promise to repay, but its key is the pledge of the house as collateral to secure the repayment of the loan. If the borrower doesn't repay the loan, the lender can pursue its property interest by selling the house and taking what it is owed out of the proceeds. (Security interests in property also are used in many other contexts, including personal property. When a bank extends credit to a business, for example, the bank may take a security interest equivalent to a mortgage in the inventory of the business.)

The mortgage is an example of concurrent interests in property. As long as the homeowner (called the mortgagor) keeps up payments on the loan, the lender (the mortgagee) can't do anything to assert its interest in the property. But when the borrower defaults, the lender's property interest moves to the fore, and it can claim its share of the property.

As with other concurrent interests in property, the mortgage presents conflicts between the interests of the borrower and lender. Suppose the borrower has paid off half of her debt and then fails to make some payments. Can the lender take the property because of the default? If so, the lender gets a windfall, since it has the property and partial repayment. In most states, if the lender wants to pursue its interest in the property after a default it has to bring a court action. The borrower can still keep the property by satisfying the debt. If she does not, the court will order the property sold under supervision of a court official. If the proceeds of the sale are less than the amount the borrower owes, the lender gets a deficiency judgment for the balance. If the proceeds are greater than the outstanding debt, the borrower gets the difference.

What about the reverse situation? Suppose the borrower wants to stop making payments and let the lender just take the house; can she do that, or does she still owe the balance of the loan? This became a widespread issue in the housing crisis that began in 2008. Many homeowners were "under water" on their mortgages—because of the collapsing real estate market, many homeowners owed more on their mortgage loans than their houses were worth. Under the traditional rules, in some states homeowners could default on their mortgages, walk away from the house, and owe nothing more; in other states, they still owed the balance of the loan. As often happens in times of crisis, the law accommodated economic reality, and the federal government developed plans that allowed at least some homeowners to refinance their loans with lower payments or to walk away altogether.

How Is Property Transferred on Death?

A separate body of property law deals with the disposition of property on death. This is the law of wills, intestate succession, and trusts. Much property is transferred between spouses or between generations on the death of the owner, or through planning mechanisms that anticipate the owner's death, or is dedicated to charitable purposes on death or through trusts.

First a note about procedure: Every state has a separate division of its court system to deal with wills and trusts, called generically *probate courts*. When someone dies, his or her will is presented to the probate court and an *executor* is appointed to administer the person's property, collecting amounts owed, paying debts, and disposing of the property as directed in the will. If the person has no will, the probate court appoints an *administrator* to dispose of the person's property. Probate can be a cumbersome process and, because it is administered by a court, it is public, so there has been something of a movement to avoid the process. Some people establish living trusts for this purpose (which have their own problems), others use nonprobate devices such as life insurance, and most states permit small estates to be administered through a less time-consuming, less expensive, summary procedure.

A person who dies without leaving a will is said by the law to have died *intestate*, and the law specifies how that person's property will be distributed. Intestate succession is governed by statute in every jurisdiction. The predominant purpose of these statutes is to dispose of the property as most people would want. In constructing that assumption, the law also takes account of views about how people should want their property distributed, as well as how they generally do want it distributed. Therefore, the law assumes that most people would want their property to be distributed to those family members who most rely on them for economic support. If the decedent (the deceased person) is survived by a spouse and no descendants (children or grandchildren), the spouse receives the entire estate. If the decedent leaves descendants but no spouse, then the descendants get the estate. If both a spouse and one or more descendants survive, the property is divided among them, typically with the spouse receiving a third to a half of the estate (perhaps more if it is a small estate) and the descendants receiving the rest.

The rules of intestate succession are one-size-fits-all. A surviving spouse who was married to the decedent for fifty years and has no independent means of support is treated the same as a spouse who was married only for a day and has her or his own profession. Adult children, minor children, loving children, and estranged children all are treated the same. To avoid the intestacy laws and dispose of property in a different way, many people make wills.

There also are at least two other reasons to make a will. First, if parents die with minor children, the children and their property have to be cared for. If both parents die, the court will appoint a guardian for the children, who may or may not be the person the parents would have chosen. In a will, a parent can appoint someone to be the guardian of minor children, and the court usually will confirm the choice. Even if only one parent dies, if the children inherit property by intestate succession then a guardian of the property must be appointed, which requires a degree of court intervention and again may not accord with the parents' wishes. Second, the federal estate tax laws and inheritance and estate tax laws in some states can take a bite out of the estate. Various devices can be used in a will to reduce or minimize the tax burden on the estate.

Therefore, many people make wills to dispose of their property. The power to dispose of one's property by will is one of the basic bundle of rights that accompanies the ownership of property. Just as a person can sell, give away, destroy, or otherwise dispose of his property while he is alive, so, too, he can direct who is to receive it after his death.

There is an important exception to the principle of freedom to dispose of property by will. In general, a married person cannot give away all of his or her property by will, leaving nothing for a spouse. Marriage is seen as an economic partnership. While spouses are alive, they have a duty to support each other, a right to share property and income on divorce, and, in some cases, the right to share property owned by the other. The obligations of the economic partnership are not extinguished upon the death of a spouse. The law has the concept of an *elective share* in the property of a deceased spouse. If, for example, a wife's will leaves all of her property to her children by a prior marriage and to the SPCA, her surviving spouse has a statutory right to claim a portion of the estate despite the will. Although the jurisdictions vary somewhat, some typical statutes entitle the spouse to take one-third of the estate despite a contrary disposition in the will, and others graduate the surviving spouse's share according to how long they have been married and take the survivor's assets into account in determining the elective share.

Note two things about the elective share statutes. First, the share is optional; the surviving spouse can claim or decline the share. If the survivor has enough money set aside so that he is happy to see the wife's money go to the SPCA, or if the will sets up elaborate trusts for estate planning purposes that he does not want to upset, he can refuse to claim his share and let the will operate. Second, it may seem odd that elective share statutes guarantee a portion of the estate to a surviving spouse but not to the decedent's children, who are even more likely to be economically dependent. The assumption of the statute, however, is that the surviving spouse will support the couple's children, and passing the money to the spouse avoids the need to have a guardian appointed to manage the children's property.

Most Americans who are middle-aged and older and most people with a substantial amount of property have a will, so devise of property according to the terms of a will is the most common means of transmission of property at death. The basic form of will must express the intent to dispose of property in writing, signed by the testator, and attested to by witnesses.

The purposes served by the required formalities can be seen by contrasting the formal will with a possible substitute. Suppose after Jane Doe dies her nephew comes into court and says that his beloved aunt told him that he could have $100,000 of her money after she died. How can we be sure that Doe actually said that? Now that she is no longer around, the nephew is the only witness, and, given the temptation to be overly optimistic or unscrupulous, his testimony is suspect. Second, how can we be sure that she meant it? Did she really understand that she was giving away a portion of her property, or was she just making conversation? Third, how can we be sure what she meant? Were there any conditions attached to the gift? Fourth, how can we be sure she didn't change her mind, with or without telling the nephew of the change? Formal wills provide evidence of the intent to make a gift and make clear to the testator and the court that a gift was seriously considered.

The question is how formal is formal enough. Over time the essential requirements of writing, signature, and witnesses have remained relatively constant.

The requirement of a written will establishes a permanent record for the court to consider and brings home the seriousness of the endeavor. The signature requirement demonstrates seriousness, and it also shows finality. (Another function—providing evidence that it actually was the testator who made the will—is probably less important than it used to be.) The law assumes that if someone is merely making notes about the disposition of property, or doing a draft of a will, the document will not be signed; only a final, complete version of a document is usually signed, so the signature shows that the testator has fully and finally expressed his or her wishes. The requirement of witnesses serves similar functions.

Whenever the law requires certain formalities, the question arises as to what happens in a case in which the formalities are not complied with but the purposes behind the formalities are served. Suppose, for example, during the execution ceremony of her will, the testator goes to the bathroom while one of the witnesses is signing. The will does not comply with the statutory requirement that the witnesses sign in the presence of the testator; should the probate court refuse to enforce it for that reason? If it doesn't enforce the will, it will be denying effect to the wishes of the testator over a technicality. If the court does enforce the will, it begins the process of chipping away at the formalities, little by little, raising the possibility that eventually they will be cut away altogether. Some states are stricter than others, but there has been a tendency in recent years to relax the requirements for insignificant errors such as this.

Now take a more extreme case. An accident pinned Cecil George Harris underneath his tractor. With his leg trapped but his hands free, Harris scratched a message into the tractor's fender: "In case I die in this mess, I leave all to the wife. Cecil Geo Harris."

Here we have a document that expresses a testamentary intent but is not witnessed. Should it be accepted as a will despite the lack of formality? Once again, the law faces a tough choice. Recognizing the validity of a *holographic will* (from holograph, meaning a handwriting) undermines the required statutory formalities for a will and the purposes those formalities serve. But failing to recognize its validity would undermine what in this case is the obvious intention of Harris, that his wife be the beneficiary of his estate. It also would introduce a bias in the law against people who can't afford to hire a lawyer to draft a will. About half the states recognize holographic wills, with some of them recognizing such wills only if they are made by members of the Armed Forces serving overseas, under the assumption that service members in combat are less likely to have access to lawyers, or if they would be valid in the state in which they were written.

In probate court procedure, someone in possession of a will submits it for probate, to be accepted as the effective will. Someone else who believes that the will that is proffered should not be effective can challenge the will; the challenger will do this because he or she stands to take part of the estate, either by intestate succession or under another will, if the will does not go into effect. Aside from a defect in form, the most common bases for challenging a will (which are still not very common) are because the testator lacked sufficient mental capacity to make a will or was subject to undue influence.

The law uses different definitions of mental capacity for different purposes. Here the question is: Did the testator understand what he or she was doing with respect to the will? This involves understanding the nature of the property owned, the people who are to receive it or are being excluded from it, and the relationship among the people and the property being given away. Thus even if the testator is unable to carry out normal business affairs or suffers from the delusion that he is haunted by evil spirits, he still may have testamentary capacity if the deficiencies or delusions do not interfere with the understanding necessary to dispose of one's property reasonably. Difficult cases concern testators who feel resentment because their children or grandchildren have placed them in hospitals, nursing homes, or psychiatric institutions; does this resentment have a reasonable basis, even though the testator needs the care, or is it delusional?

Undue influence is sometimes alleged, either as to the entire will or as to a particular bequest. Undue influence is particularly likely to be presumed where the person who benefits from the will is in a position of superiority over the testator, such as an attorney and her client, a doctor and her patient, or someone who manages the affairs of an aged relative. The question, which depends heavily on the facts, is whether the will is actually the product of the testator's volition or that of the person exerting the influence.

What Is a Trust?

A trust is a division of the bundle of rights in property in an unusual way. First, the management of the property is separated from the benefit of the property. The property is managed by a trustee, who usually has the authority to invest the property, collect income, rent, or sell, but who is paid a fee for its services, rather than receiving any income from the property itself. The beneficiary of the trust owns the right to receive the benefit from the property, such as the income it produces. Second, the beneficiary's rights are defined when the trust is established by the grantor, the person who gives the property that becomes the principal (or corpus, meaning body) of the trust. The grantor can, for example, specify that the beneficiary can receive the income from the trust but no payments from principal, that one beneficiary receives the income for life and then the principal goes to someone else, or, in the case of charitable trusts, that the income should be devoted to seeking a cure for cancer or the care and feeding of stray cats.

As the last examples suggest, some trusts are devoted to charitable purposes, but in the context of wills and family property, private trusts are more important. Trusts are used for many purposes. Living trusts can be used to keep property out of probate, which minimizes publicity and may save fees, although the advantages of a living trust have been lessened by recent reforms in probate laws. Trusts created either during the grantor's lifetime (inter vivos trusts) or in a will (testamentary trusts) can protect the property of a person who is unable to manage the property, either because of a legal disability (a minor child, for example) or because of practical inability to do so (someone who is unsophisticated in financial matters). Probably the most prevalent use of trusts is for tax purposes, particularly in estate planning. Currently the federal estate tax law imposes a tax on the amount of an estate above a certain minimum amount. When the husband dies, for example, his property can pass to a trust, rather than to the surviving wife, to avoid having her estate exceed the minimum amount when she dies later.

How Do People Own Property Collectively?

So far we have been thinking of property that one person or company owns. In many cases, though, property interests—different elements of the bundle of rights—are held by more than one person. For example, property rights can be shared by several people or divided over time.

In property law, there are three kinds of *concurrent estates*, or forms of co-ownership at the same time: *joint tenancy, tenancy in common,* and *tenancy by the entirety*. In all three forms of co-ownership (or cotenancy), each tenant has the right to possess and use the entire piece of property. Tenancy by the entirety is unique in that it is available only to married couples, so there can only be two co-owners of a piece of tenancy by the entirety; a joint tenancy or tenancy in common can have an unlimited number of co-owners. Joint tenancy and tenancy by the entirety are like each other and unlike a tenancy in common because the cotenants have a *right of survivorship*. When one owner dies, the property automatically passes to the surviving tenant. When a tenant in common dies, by contrast, his or her interest in the property goes to his or her heirs, not to the surviving cotenant. Finally, joint tenants and tenants by the entirety always have equal shares in the property; the interests of tenants in common can be split up in different ways (with one owning one-third and the other owning two-thirds, for example).

Today concurrent ownership is used in many situations. Spouses may have a joint checking account and a mutual fund account and may own their house jointly. (In jurisdictions that allow tenancies by the entirety—about half the states—that would be the form of ownership; otherwise, these would be joint tenancies.) Two siblings may own the family farm together. The copyright in a song may be held by the person who wrote the lyrics and the one who wrote the music.

Let's take one example to see how the different forms of co-ownership work. This example focuses on joint tenancies and tenancies in common; for most purposes, a tenancy by the entireties is treated the same as a joint tenancy. Assume that two siblings inherited the house their parents had lived in. The first question in dealing with these instances of co-ownership is: What kind of co-ownership is it? The mother was the later of the two parents to die, and her will said, "I leave my house to Juan and Maria, my children." Are Juan and Maria joint tenants or tenants in common? Put more generally, in the absence of a designation by the original property owner, which form of co-ownership should the law prefer? The answer depends on the structure of property law and the underlying social conditions.

From the Middle Ages to modern times the law shifted its preference for concurrent estates from joint tenancies to tenancies in common. The traditional preference for a joint tenancy arose partly from the logic of the property system and partly from practical concerns. Under the estates system, joint tenants were seen as owning a single estate; when one of them died, the estate remained unchanged, and it was simply held by one fewer owner. Probably more important, the traditional property system favored concentrating ownership in a smaller number of large landowners, a purpose that joint tenancy served well. Joint tenancies also became effective estate planning devices, avoiding some of the feudal taxes that otherwise would be due on the transfer of property at death. By the eighteenth century, though, the presumption was otherwise. With the rise of a market economy and land viewed increasingly as a commodity and an object of wealth like any other, it made more sense to the legislatures and courts to prefer tenancies in common, which made property more freely transferable; a co-owner could transfer his share in property at death, and he could use it as collateral for debts, with creditors secure in the knowledge that they would not lose their interest if the debtor died. Therefore, today Juan and Maria would be presumed to be tenants in common.

Of course, as in many legal situations, the best approach to this problem is to avoid it by advance planning. The law permits people to specify what kind of relationship is being created, and good lawyers typically do so. If you open a bank account with a family member, for example, you will see that one of the boxes that can be checked to indicate the form of ownership is labeled "Joint tenant with right of survivorship," a clear indication that the intention is not to create a tenancy in common. Scrupulous belt-and-suspenders lawyers may add "and not as tenants in common," to remove any doubt. The attorney drafting the mother's will likewise could have expressly provided for a joint tenancy, if that is what the mother intended.

What is it that a cotenant owns? Joint tenants and tenants in common hold substantially the same bundle of rights in the property. In either case, each cotenant possesses an undivided interest in the entire property. "Undivided" means that Juan and Maria each have a right to use the entire house; they do not have to physically divide the house, so that Juan has use of the kitchen and Maria the living room. If they rent out the house rather than live in it, they share in the rent paid equally (if they are joint tenants) or according to their ownership interests in the property (if they are tenants in common).

If Juan and Maria are tenants in common, on Juan's death his heirs will inherit his interest in the property. If they are joint tenants, however, Maria owns the entire property on Juan's death. If Juan wants to prevent this, so that his children can inherit his share of the property, for example, he can, by various means, sever the joint tenancy, converting it into a tenancy in common and thereby destroying Maria's right of survivorship. Tenancies by the entirety are different in this respect, however. Because one of the purposes of this form of co-ownership is to protect the surviving spouse, the right of survivorship cannot be destroyed in a tenancy by the entirety.

Tenancy by the entirety is one form of property ownership between a married couple. Beyond that, a special set of rules has been applied throughout history to marital property, and again the rules change as the social system changes.

In the old common law a husband and wife were treated as one person in the eyes of property law, and that person was the husband. The husband controlled all property owned by either of them, so he could sell land owned by the wife or control its use without her consent. The wife's only protection was a right in the husband's property on his death. Under the rule of *dower*, a widow had a claim for as long as she lived to one-third of all of her husband's real property that otherwise would be inherited by the children. A widower had a parallel, and greater right, called *curtesy*, which granted him a life interest in all of the lands owned by the wife.

In the middle of the nineteenth century all of the states passed Married Women's Property Acts, which granted married women the same rights to manage their property as possessed by single women and married men. Today marital property is governed by one of two systems of law, called *separate property* (in effect in most states) and *community property* (which controls in a few states, mostly those which in colonial times were governed by the civil law, such as California, Texas, and Louisiana).

In separate property jurisdictions, the property of a husband and wife is, naturally, separate. If a wife owns a piece of land or some stock, she can use or dispose of it as she wishes, without the consent of her husband. During the marriage, the only limitation on her bundle of rights is the duty of one spouse to support another; the wife cannot enjoy her own property and leave her husband destitute (and vice versa). Spouses can, of course, choose to own property jointly. Upon divorce, the property of each spouse is subject to *equitable distribution*. The court granting the divorce has great discretion to divide the property between the spouses on an equitable, or fair, basis, taking into account who contributed to the property and who needs it after the divorce.

In community property jurisdictions, property owned by each spouse before the marriage, or property acquired during the marriage by one of them by gift or inheritance, is separate property of each spouse and is treated the same as property in a separate property state. Property otherwise acquired during the marriage, though, including property that is derived from the earnings of either spouse, is community property. Community property is much like property held in joint tenancy. Each spouse has an independent right to use the community property without the consent of the other spouse. Either spouse can also convey the property, except for land and certain business assets, which requires the consent of both spouses. Upon divorce, some community property states divide the community property evenly between the two spouses; others use equitable distribution principles to divide the property.

An important limitation on a spouse's bundle of rights is a restriction on the ability to dispose of his or her property upon death. In most states, the ability of a spouse to dispose of property on death is limited by the rule of an elective share, discussed in the section above on property transfers on death. The elective share operates somewhat like dower and curtesy at common law. No matter what a will says, the surviving spouse may claim a certain portion of the deceased spouse's assets to provide the surviving spouse a measure of protection against being deprived of the financial benefits of the marriage.

How Else Can Ownership of Property Be Shared?

In joint tenancy and tenancy in common, each person is the owner of the property, though he or she shares that ownership with someone else. There is another way in which people can share interests in real property, which falls under the legal category of *servitude*. The concept is most easily understood with a few examples. To provide telephone service, the phone company has to run its cables across many people's land, either underground or on poles. Two neighbors share a wall that straddles both their property at the border line, and each contributes to the cost of maintaining the wall. Homeowners in a subdivision purchase by deeds that prohibit them from building more than one home on their lot, even though there is no zoning that prevents subdividing. A patron at a movie theater occupies some of the theater owner's property—a seat—for the duration of the movie.

What all of these examples have in common is that one person has an interest in someone else's property. The interest may attach as a result of property ownership (the neighbor who shares a wall) or not (the theatergoer). The interest may allow the person to do something (sit in the theater), require someone else to do something (help maintain the wall), or prevent someone else from doing something (subdividing a lot). In each case the landowner who is subject to the obligation has had one element of the bundle of rights of full property ownership taken away and transferred to the other person.

As a doctrinal matter there are important differences among these kinds of rights. We say that the theatergoer has a *license* to use the theater owner's property because she has permission to enter the property for a limited time and purpose. Licenses are revocable; look on the back of a ticket stub for a movie and you may see language to the effect that the management can revoke the license at any time. The telephone company has an *easement*, a durable right to use someone else's property. The subdivision owners have *real covenants* or *equitable servitudes* that restrict each other's use of their lots; these are devices that grant control over the use of someone else's property rather than the right to use it oneself.

We won't try to understand the law of servitudes in any great detail here. It has been described as "an unspeakable quagmire" full of archaic terms, fine distinctions, and confusing rules that bedevil even the most diligent law students. But we can use the topic to illustrate a few basic points about property law.

First, servitudes are a form of private regulation of property and land use. People begin by holding the entire bundle of rights that constitute property ownership and then cede some of those rights in the form of easements, covenants, and so on. (Sometimes servitudes don't arise from express agreements but from implication of an agreement, although that is less common.) The ability to act this way is an element of both the ownership of property and the ability to contract. Each gives the individual a sphere of autonomy to create this kind of obligation and to define its content. Servitudes have been valuable in controlling land development and creating particular types of residential environments through private action, particularly in suburban subdivisions and planned communities.

Second, the law of servitudes is not the law of contracts. The development of a distinct body of law illustrates the power of the concept of property, especially real property. Because these obligations are not unique to the parties but attach to their land, and may benefit or burden subsequent owners of the land, they are burdened by history and the trappings of property law.

Third, as contract and property, the ability to do what one wants with one's property is not absolute. Servitudes are subject to direct and indirect public policy restrictions. The best-known direct restriction is the prohibition on discriminatory covenants. Through the mid-twentieth century it was common for deeds to contain covenants prohibiting any future owner from selling the property to nonwhites. The courts eventually declared the enforcement of that type of restriction unconstitutional; a private owner's right of property was limited by the paramount social concern against racial discrimination. Limits on the use of servitudes are still frequently litigated, as in cases in which a homeowners' association enforces draconian building restrictions, or a covenant requiring single-family houses is claimed to prevent the establishment of a group home for the intellectually challenged.

One other way that property ownership can be shared occurs when different people can own different interests in a piece of property at the same time but their interests are divided over time. The issue is steeped in medieval history, most of which we can ignore, but it is an interesting illustration of the conflicts that underlie all of property law.

Suppose that Gerald O'Hara wants to preserve Tara as his family's ancestral plantation. In his will, he gives the land to Scarlett for her life, and then, on her death, the property would pass to her children, and then her children's children, and so on as long as O'Hara had heirs. Or suppose that O'Hara bequeaths his plantation to the state of Georgia, on the condition that the state is to use the property as an arboretum, planting at least two of every variety of tree native to Georgia. If the state met the condition for 99 years, the property would go to the state outright; if it did not, ownership would revert to O'Hara or his heirs.

In both of these examples we can see that different people have different temporal relationships to the property. In the first example, when O'Hara dies, Scarlett has ownership of the property for her life, but a kind of ownership that is limited by the condition that the property would pass to her child upon her death. In the second hypothetical, he gives up ownership of the plantation to the state, but his heirs still have an interest in it: the possibility that, if the state fails to maintain the arboretum, the property will revert back to them.

The examples are related to the fundamental issue of how much we will let owners control their property over time. O'Hara owns Tara in *fee simple*, which means that he owns as many of the rights as anyone can have in the property. Clearly he can give away his land, during his lifetime or upon his death, so one might think that he could perform the lesser act of giving it away with a condition attached (that it be used for an arboretum) or give away only a part interest (to Scarlett for her life, then to her child).

But we want current owners of property to be able to use it productively, too. How much should we let the dead hand of the past control the present use of property? Imagine what might happen if we let owners impose lasting restrictions on the use or disposition of property. Some property owners would dream of family dynasties and would attempt to keep property in the family by imposing the kind of restriction O'Hara did in his will. Over time, this would tend to concentrate property in fewer and fewer hands, rather than making it available to a wider population. Or the opposite might occur; several generations down the line, tiny pieces of Tara might be owned by dozens of O'Hara's descendants.

The same problems arise with restrictions outside a family. Conditions change over time, and it may not always make sense to honor restrictions placed on property by a previous owner. After twenty or fifty or seventy years, the state of Georgia may decide that Tara could better be used as a playground, a library, or a hospital instead of an arboretum, but enforcing O'Hara's restriction would prevent such a use.

Accordingly, courts have had to balance the desire to let people do whatever they want with their property against the unfortunate consequences that would result from enforcing all such restrictions. They have done so in a number of ways. Often a grantor will not be clear about what kind of interest is being created or what kind of restriction is being imposed. In those cases, courts develop presumptions, assuming for example, that grantors do not intend to encumber their land with restrictions unless they do so clearly.

A second technique of dealing with arguably outmoded restrictions is through the use of the *cy pres* doctrine (meaning "as near as"). Under the doctrine, when a charitable bequest cannot be fulfilled in exactly the way the donor intended, the court will find a way to carry it into effect as nearly as possible to effectuate the donor's intention.

A third technique is to use certain substantive rules that simply prohibit certain kinds of dead hand restrictions. An example is the *Rule against Perpetuities*, a major step in the law's effort to control dynastic wealth. The Rule states that a future interest in property must vest—must become final—within twenty-one years of the death of someone who is alive at the time the interest is created. The Rule against Perpetuities has tormented law students for generations; the California Supreme Court once stated that the rule is so complicated that it is not malpractice for a lawyer to fail to understand it, and its strictures have been modified by statute in most states. But the basic concept is simple. A landowner cannot tie up the land forever by creating interests that will not arise for generations to come. Under the rule, O'Hara's attempt to have successive generations of his heirs each hold only a life interest in Tara would be invalid.

What Are the Property Rights of a Landlord and a Tenant?

Leases are a very common form of holding property, from a short-term lease of an apartment to a long-term lease of commercial office space. A lease is a particular form of shared use of property in which the owner, known as the landlord or the lessor, permits the tenant or lessee to use the property for a period of time. Everyone is familiar with the practice of leasing, but the concept presents particularly interesting property law issues. What are the relations between landlord and tenant? How much are those relations prescribed by law? And to what degree can the parties direct those relations by agreement?

Landlord and tenant law has seen some historic shifts concerning the answers to those questions, with some of the most important shifts occurring relatively recently. Let's consider two of the shifts and some of their implications for current law: the change from a property-based conception of the lease to a conception that incorporates elements of contract, and the increasing regulation of the relationship between landlord and tenant.

From an early point in English law, a lease was considered to be a conveyance of a property interest. The owner would, in effect, give up ownership for a period of years to the tenant, who became, in a sense, the new "owner" for that time, subject to the promise to pay rent and to perform certain other limited obligations. Although the lease relationship originated in the agreement between the landlord and tenant, it was essentially a property relationship, not a contract. Therefore, the basic duty of the landlord was to transfer the property for the specified time, and the basic duty of the tenant was to pay rent and return the property at the end of the lease. The law placed few other obligations on either party.

This model fit the traditional lease of agricultural land very well, but it became outmoded. Beginning in the nineteenth century, the renting of residential or commercial property became much more common than the lease of farmland. In a residential lease, especially in a crowded urban apartment, the tenant relied on the landlord for maintaining the condition of the premises, controlling the behavior of other tenants, and providing services such as heat and hot water. In many urban housing markets, the tenant's options and bargaining power were limited. Meanwhile, parties to commercial leases increasingly negotiated the precise terms of the lease, spelling out the obligations in much greater detail than the law had previously. These changes encouraged courts and legislatures to think differently about the landlord–tenant relationship. The changes were further spurred in the 1960s by the availability of legal services to the poor, the activism of the civil rights movement, and the perception of a housing crisis, among other social factors. As a result, the legal view of a lease shifted from the pure transfer of a property interest to a relationship that had many contractual aspects, and, at least with respect to residential leases, the content of the contract was more closely regulated by the law.

Probably the most important area in which the changed thinking was felt concerned the landlord's obligation concerning the condition of the premises. Traditionally, the lease was seen as a conveyance of a property interest, so the conveyance was complete when the landlord gave the tenant possession of the premises. The landlord was obligated to turn the premises over to the tenant but was not obligated to deliver or maintain them in a livable condition. If the landlord failed to provide heat or hot water, for example, the tenant was out of luck.

The leading case shifting the conception of landlord and tenant rights was *Javins v. First National Realty Corp.*, a 1970 decision of the U.S. Court of Appeals for the District of Columbia. The case was part of a litigation campaign by tenants' attorneys to advance tenants' rights. First National, the landlord, sought to evict the tenants for nonpayment of rent. The tenants admitted that they had not paid rent but responded that housing code violations in their apartments entitled them to a setoff in damages equal to the rent due. The court first noted the changes in the situation property law faced. Treating a lease as a conveyance of property made sense in an agrarian society, but the apartment-dwellers were seeking something more than a conveyance of farmland:

> When American city-dwellers, both rich and poor, seek "shelter"
> today, they seek a well-known package of goods and services—
> a package which includes not merely walls and ceilings, but
> also adequate heat, light and ventilation, serviceable plumbing
> facilities, secure windows and doors, proper sanitation and proper
> maintenance.

Accordingly, it was appropriate to treat a lease more as a contract. In contracts cases, consumer protection had been expanded by, for example, implying that the manufacturer of a product guaranteed its safety and effectiveness. The same principle controlled with residential leases. The court implied a *warranty of habitability*, which required that the landlord keep the premises in compliance with the housing code.

Following *Javins*, the implied warranty of habitability in residential housing became well established in most jurisdictions, either through judicial decision or legislation. In some states the warranty adopts the local housing code as the standard for the landlord's performance; in other cases the warranty is more general, requiring perhaps that the dwelling be "fit and suitable for human habitation." Sometimes any residence is covered; in other places, only multiunit apartment buildings are covered.

Since the move to an implied warranty is in part a recognition that the lease is as much a contract as a transfer of a property interest, the logical question is how much freedom the parties have to define the terms of their relationship. Can the lease include an agreement by the tenant to waive the implied warranty of habitability? Under modern contract and property principles, the answer is usually no. Otherwise, landlords could negate the effect of the implied warranty by including a broad disclaimer in a form lease, and few tenants would be knowledgeable enough or have enough bargaining power to demand that the disclaimer be excluded.

Because the implied warranty is in part contract-based, the remedies available to the tenant have been expanded. Many remedies are available. As with any contract, the tenant can sue for money damages for breach of the warranty. Or the tenant can repair and deduct, fixing the apartment to correct the landlord's violation and then deducting the cost of doing so from the rent. The tenant also can use the damage claim defensively, refusing to pay rent and, if sued by the landlord, asserting the breach of warranty as a defense; if the court agrees that the apartment is uninhabitable, the tenant can remain without paying rent until the violation is repaired.

When Can the Government Take Your Property?

Inherent in the idea of property is that property is private; your property is yours, you can do what you want with it, and the government can't take it away from you. But that's not entirely true. Suppose the state is planning to build a highway which, unfortunately, is going to be routed through your backyard. Can you refuse to allow the highway to come through, causing the state to reroute it at great expense and inconvenience? No. If the state insists, it can build the highway through your property even over your objection, by taking the property from you. However, because it is your property, the state has to pay you for it.

Short of actually taking your property away from you, the government has the authority to regulate your use of the property. But how much? Many municipal zoning laws prevent the operation of a factory in a residential area. Some suburban communities require homeowners to keep their grass neatly trimmed. Wetlands, pinelands, and beachfront preservation regulations may prevent construction altogether in environmentally sensitive areas. Can the government lawfully regulate property to this extent?

Let's begin with the most extreme limitation on private property, the government's ability to take private property. This ability is known as the power of *eminent domain*. When the government determines that it needs private property for a public purpose, it can condemn the property—in effect purchasing it from the owner whether the owner wants to sell or not. The eminent domain power is an inherent power of government; the federal and state governments possess the power to condemn property as an essential part of being a government. Indeed, in the early Republic it was often held that private property could be taken without even paying for it. Federal and state constitutions do provide a limitation on the power, however. The Fifth Amendment to the U.S. Constitution states: "Nor shall private property be taken for public use without just compensation." The government may condemn land, but it must pay a fair price for it.

The degree to which eminent domain has long been accepted as an inherent power of government makes clear that property is never wholly private. There is a public interest in the ownership of property, but when the public interest requires that property be taken, there is no barrier to doing so.

The typical condemnation case—the homeowner whose yard will be the site of a new highway—is legally simple. The state brings a condemnation proceeding to take the land and to establish the just compensation. Determining what is just compensation in a particular case may be factually complex, but it basically means establishing the market value of the property. But other cases present tough issues. To exercise the eminent domain power, the property taken must be used for a public purpose. Building a highway for everyone's use obviously serves a public purpose, but what about less traditional activities of government? In a series of cases, the Supreme Court has shown great deference to the legislative determination of what is a public use or purpose justifying eminent domain. In *Berman v. Parker* (1954), the Court allowed the District of Columbia to take by eminent domain a department store located in a blighted area, even though the store itself was economically viable and not blighted, because of the validity of the redevelopment plan for the area as a whole. In *Hawaii Housing Authority v. Midkiff* (1984), it upheld legislation by the state of Hawai'i that allowed tenants to petition the housing authority to have the land they rented taken away from the private landlord and sold to them, in order to promote more equitable distribution and an open market for land. In both cases, the Court said, "Subject to specific constitutional limitations, when the legislature has spoken, the public interest has been declared in terms well-nigh conclusive."

As states' use of the eminent domain power expanded, the question of how far a public purpose extended became more controversial, and the Court returned to the issue in 2005 in the much-debated case of *Kelo v. City of New London*. New London, Connecticut, embarked on the economic revitalization of its Fort Trumbull area, with its efforts managed by the private, nonprofit New London Development Corporation (NLDC). After an extensive planning process, NLDC finalized a development plan for the area that included a hotel, shops, and restaurants in an "urban village," a Coast Guard museum, new residences, office and retail space, and a marina. The plan required NLDC to acquire the property of 115 owners in the area, most of whom sold at negotiated prices. Nine owners refused to sell at the prices offered by NLDC, or perhaps at all, including such long-time residents as Wilhelmina Dery, who was born in her Fort Trumbull house in 1918 and had lived there her entire life. The owners challenged the exercise of eminent domain, claiming that the redevelopment plan did not constitute a public use because the area was not blighted and the plan would simply transfer their property from one private owner to another, without being open to a public use as constitutionally required. The Court rejected their challenge, holding that community economic development is a valid public purpose. The constitutional requirement of "public use" did not mean that the property physically be open to the public. Instead, the requirement long had been interpreted to mean that the legislature had determined that the public would benefit from the new use of the land, as when courts upheld statutes that allowed mill dams to flood upstream landowners or a mining company to transport ore buckets over other owners' property, or, as in *Berman* and *Hawaii Housing Authority*, when land was redeveloped or even simply transferred to a new owner. According to the Court, it was the task of the legislature, not the courts, to draw the lines about what constitutes a public purpose: "For more than a century, our public use jurisprudence has wisely eschewed rigid formulas and intrusive scrutiny in favor of affording legislatures broad latitude in determining what public needs justify the use of the takings power." Four justices dissented, arguing that the majority had effectively deleted the public use requirement from the takings clause. As Justice O'Connor stated, "All private property is now vulnerable to being taken and transferred to another private owner, so long as it might be upgraded—i.e., given to an owner who will use it in a way that the legislature deems more beneficial to the public—in the process." Most of the states enacted legislation in response to the Court's decision in *Kelo*. Most statutes ostensibly prevented the exercise of eminent domain for economic development or the transfer of property to private developers, but many contained exceptions that limited their effect, permitting, for example, takings of "blighted" property or those that are in the way of "sound growth."

Suppose that instead of taking the property of one of the complaining landowners, New London had passed an ordinance stating that the property had to be used as parking lots for some of the new retail shops. Then the landowners could complain that the government had taken their land in reality, if not in form, and the state should be required to pay just compensation for doing so. In that kind of case, the landowners could bring an *inverse condemnation* action complaining about a *regulatory taking* and require the government to pay. Most cases are less egregious than that, but where do we draw the line?

The Supreme Court has tried to draw the line in a series of cases from the early part of the twentieth century. Its basic principle was that regulating the use of land is a valid exercise of the police power; if the legislature determined that regulating even to the extent of practically eliminating its value was necessary to prevent public harm, its decision would be respected; only taking away all the value of land without a corresponding public benefit is a taking. In the *Penn Central* case in 1978, for example, the Court allowed New York City to prevent the construction of an office tower atop Grand Central Station in order to preserve the station's historic architecture (*Penn Central Transportation Co. v. City of New York*).

Beginning in the late 1970s, however, conservative activists pressed litigation that challenged the long-standing rules, and the changing membership of the Court sometimes provided a responsive audience. The activism arose as conservatives challenged environmental protection legislation and as home builders and other developers challenged zoning and other land-use regulations.

In *Lucas v. South Carolina Coastal Council* (1992), a majority of the Court adopted what it called a categorical rule: When a property owner is deprived of the economically beneficial use of his property, even if the regulation is crafted by the legislature to prevent harm to the public, the regulation constitutes a taking of property unless it falls within the traditional common law category of nuisance. Thus the state had taken the property of an owner of two lots on a barrier island when it enacted a statute that prevented development too close to the shoreline, in order to prevent erosion and other damage. While the decision raised as many questions as it answered, it did signal the Court's willingness to expand the takings doctrine into the realm of what traditionally had been valid police power regulation.

The Court also changed traditional rules defining what kind of burdens could be imposed on new development. Often when a landowner seeks approval for a new development, the government requires in return some dedication of land to the public or some land improvements to support the development, such as parkland or streets. Traditionally, as long as there is a reasonable relation between the exaction and the development, the government's action is a valid exercise of the police power, not a taking. In *Nolan v. California Coastal Commission* (1987) and *Dolan v. City of Tigard* (1994), however, the Court held that unless there was a close link and a rough proportionality between the burden imposed by the development and the exaction, the regulation was a taking. In *Dolan*, for example, a store owner had applied for a building permit to expand the size of her store. The city conditioned the permit on the store owner's dedicating a strip of land as a pedestrian and bicycle pathway. The Court invalidated the condition because the city had not demonstrated that the pathway would be needed for the additional customer traffic generated by the new construction.

Since *Lucas*, however, the Court has been ambivalent about how far to alter the traditional rules. For example, activists argued that *Lucas* should be applied to any part of an interest in property, so that if the government prevents the use of property for a period of time, that is a deprivation of all economically beneficial use for that time and therefore a taking. In *Tahoe-Sierra Preservation Council v. Tahoe Regional Planning Agency* (2002) the Court disagreed, holding that a two-and-a-half-year moratorium on land development for planning purposes did not constitute a taking because it was only a temporary regulation of all of the rights in the property. On the other hand, in *Horne v. Department of Agriculture* (2015), the Court held that compensation is required whenever personal property is taken, and the prospect of the owner receiving some payment for the property taken did not change the situation. New Deal legislation authorized the secretary of agriculture to issue orders requiring growers of certain agricultural products to set aside a portion of their crops for the government, free of charge, in order to stabilize the markets for those products. The Hornes refused to give the government a portion of their raisin crop and were fined. The Court regarded a fine as equivalent to a physical appropriation of their raisins and the fact that they would receive proceeds from the government's sale of their raisins was irrelevant, so the order constituted a taking.

8

Crime Doesn't Pay
Criminal Law

Criminal law absorbs our attention in a way that no other body of law does. Horrific crimes, juicy tales of passion, and mundane muggings occupy the news media and public attention. Criminal law is a hot political topic that has immediate personal dimensions. But, as elsewhere in the law, the issues are more complicated than they seem. This chapter is designed to help you think in different, more broad-ranging ways about criminal responsibility.

What Is Criminal Law?

Criminal law is, of course, about punishing the bad guys. To define criminal law, we need to distinguish it from other bodies of law that do something like that and to distinguish the substantive criminal law from the process that applies it.

Suppose three teenagers (call them Tom, Dick, and Harry) go on a minor crime spree at the mall, shoplifting in some stores, writing graffiti on the walls, and rudely bumping into other customers. Have they committed any crimes? Think about why their conduct may be criminal and how else we might characterize it.

Shoplifting is certainly a crime. A state statute defines theft as, roughly, taking something that doesn't belong to you. Tom, Dick, and Harry can be prosecuted for the crime. By *prosecuted*, we mean that a state official (commonly the district attorney) will bring a proceeding in court to have them found guilty of criminal conduct and punished for their acts, typically by being fined or sent to jail.

The criminal prosecution is not the only proceeding that can be brought, however. First, the store owner can bring a civil action against them because the same conduct constitutes the tort of conversion— taking someone else's property. In the civil action, the store owner receives money damages from the defendants—not a fine, but compensation for her lost property. Second, if Tom is only fourteen years old, the district attorney might decide to proceed against him as a juvenile. A juvenile proceeding is not a criminal proceeding. It is not designed primarily to punish Tom but to provide for the correction of his behavior; even if he is sent to a juvenile detention facility, the law doesn't think of that as criminal punishment. Third, and similarly, if Dick is found to be suffering from mental illness that causes him to uncontrollably assault mall patrons, a family member or the district attorney might bring an action to have him committed to a psychiatric institution for treatment. In this action, the question is not whether Dick has committed a crime but whether he is dangerous to himself or others. Even though he may be involuntarily deprived of his liberty, he has not been found guilty of a crime. All of these are noncriminal sanctions because only—and always—criminal law involves a determination of guilt, or criminal responsibility, in a proceeding brought by the state, for which legally defined punishment may be imposed.

What if Harry receives a speeding ticket on his way to the mall? Is that a crime? Speeding is an offense for which Harry can be prosecuted, and he can receive a public punishment (a fine) for committing the offense. But we usually distinguish relatively minor violations of the law, like speeding, from more serious offenses, like drunk driving, and label only the latter as crimes.

Next, suppose that Harry is prosecuted for the crime of battery for rudely bumping into Jill, a mall patron, and knocking her to the ground. At trial Jill testifies that although she didn't know Harry she really didn't mind being knocked down, she wasn't hurt too badly, and she thought teenagers ought to be able to have some fun. Does that get Harry off the hook? No; he still can be convicted. Harry's behavior, like all crimes, is criminal not because it is a wrong against another person but because it is a wrong against the public good. The state has determined what behavior is wrongful, and the state can punish that behavior even if the victim doesn't care.

Now suppose that the district attorney decides to prosecute Tom, the fourteen-year-old, as an adult for shoplifting. (In most states, the prosecutor has that choice.) At trial the store's video security camera tape reveals that Tom didn't actually mean to steal the DVD that he is accused of taking. Instead, he bumped into a store counter and, without his knowing it, the DVD fell into a bag he was carrying. Tom would be acquitted—found not to have committed a crime. Why? In nearly every case, criminal law has a *culpability* requirement: Someone must intend to commit a crime or at least be very careless (as in running someone over when driving drunk). One of the distinctive features of criminal law is that it embodies an idea of *blameworthiness*. Someone must have done something wrong, something that deserves moral condemnation, before a criminal sanction may be imposed. To deserve condemnation, it's not enough that someone commit a bad act; he or she also must have done so with a bad state of mind.

When we put all of these hypotheticals together, we see that it is actually harder to define the scope of criminal law in a systematic way than it first appears. Violations of criminal law are prosecuted by the government, but the government brings other types of actions as well. Violations result in negative sanctions but so do civil lawsuits, prosecution of minor infractions, and administrative proceedings, and not all negative sanctions in criminal cases are that harmful to the recipients.

The core of criminal law, then, is moral condemnation and punishment based on blameworthiness. A crime is a wrong that deserves punishment because the criminal has violated public standards of morality. Even this definition is not perfect, but it captures the essence of what distinguishes criminal law from other bodies of law.

The hypotheticals also suggest what the issues are in any criminal case. First, has the defendant committed an act that is prohibited by the criminal law? The crime of theft requires that someone take property that does not belong to him or her. To convict Tom of shoplifting, the prosecutor would have to prove that Tom did that. If he had not walked out of the store with an item, or if he had paid for it, he would not have performed the prohibited act. Second, has the defendant performed the act with a culpable state of mind? Theft requires not only that the defendant take someone else's property but that he do so with knowledge that the property belongs to someone else. If Tom believes that a bin near the front of a music store contains free DVDs, he does not commit theft if he takes one without paying for it. Third, if the defendant has committed a criminal act with a culpable state of mind, does he have a defense? Dick's mental illness might be a defense. Fourth, if the defendant has not committed a prohibited act with the requisite state of culpability, might he still be criminally liable? Suppose Tom, Dick, and Harry agree to go on a shoplifting spree but Harry doesn't actually steal anything. Could he be liable anyway for agreeing to be part of the gang?

There is one other essential distinction between *substantive criminal law* (which is the subject of this chapter) and *criminal procedure* (which is examined in Chapter 9). Criminal law states general principles of criminal liability and defines what behavior is criminal. It helps answer questions such as: What's the difference between murder and manslaughter? What constitutes legal insanity? Criminal procedure concerns the process by which criminal behavior is investigated and adjudicated. When must the police read a suspect his *Miranda* rights? What does it mean to have a fair trial?

The substantive criminal law often is divided into two parts: general principles of criminal liability and definition of specific crimes. The general principles of criminal liability cut across all of the definitions of specific crimes. First, if criminal law prohibits wrongful acts of various kinds, what do we mean by an "act"? Specific crimes prohibit specific acts (such as taking someone else's property), but what are the basic requirements for the kind of conduct that is criminal? Second, because criminal acts are culpable only when accompanied by a blameworthy mental state, how do we define the mental states that will lead to criminal liability? The law defines a range of relevant mental states, and the courts apply those definitions in interpreting criminal statutes. Third, when is someone justified or excused in doing an act that otherwise would be criminal? A criminal act might be justified if doing the act avoids some greater harm. Self-defense, for example, is a principle of justification. Similarly, an act is excused when for some reason the actor is blameless in performing it. A person suffering from a mental disease or defect may intend to kill someone else but still lack the blameworthiness necessary to declare his behavior criminal. Fourth, when may someone be liable for acts that are preliminary to a crime, or further a crime, but may not fit the elements of a specific offense? One who attempts to commit a crime but fails is generally liable for the attempt, but how close does she have to come before she has committed a crime? Similarly, if a group of criminals participate in a conspiracy to rob a bank and one of them shoots a guard during the robbery, are all of the others liable for murder?

The definition of specific criminal offenses obviously concerns what acts and accompanying mental states are necessary to convict a person of a crime. For example, what are the differences among murder, voluntary manslaughter, and involuntary manslaughter?

Creating the general principles of criminal law and defining the specific offenses was once the province of the courts. In the twentieth century, however, legislatures began to enact comprehensive codes of criminal law. In the 1950s and 1960s the American Law Institute, a private body of lawyers, judges, and professors, drafted a Model Penal Code to serve as a guide to state legislatures in adopting criminal legislation. The effort was very successful; about three-fourths of the states have adopted codes based on this guide. Each state has departed from the model in some ways, and legislatures keep rewriting the law as issues continue to arise, but the Model Penal Code provides a useful takeoff point for discussion of the state of the criminal law generally.

The sections that follow discuss the general principles of criminal liability and the definition of some of the most important and most interesting specific offenses. But before getting into the details, consider the most fundamental issue of all: Why do we need criminal law?

Why Do We Need Criminal Law?

This should be obvious. We need criminal law to punish criminals and prevent crime. But as we've seen with the other legal concepts in this book, it's not that simple.

The first purpose criminal law serves is to define what behavior society regards as wrongful. It is wrong to murder your neighbor, set fire to her house, or steal her lawnmower. The acts defined as criminal often (but not always) have the most serious consequences for others; murder and arson are very harmful, but stealing your neighbor's lawnmower probably is less of a social evil than manufacturing lawnmowers without adequate safety devices, which is only a civil wrong. What distinguishes criminal offenses from other wrongful acts is that, as a class, they are particularly worthy of social condemnation. Just because an act is not criminal does not mean that it is not wrongful; we condemn other behavior in other ways, such as through the imposition of tort liability or simple social disapproval.

Condemnation of wrongful behavior isn't enough for criminal law. Criminal acts are so wrongful that when someone commits a criminal act as distinguished from some other type of wrong, she is not just made to pay damages or snubbed at the country club; she is punished. So in considering why we have criminal law, the real question is why we have criminal punishment. Answering this question is supremely important for criminal law; figuring out why we punish will also tell us who we should punish, how, and to what degree.

Criminal law theorists offer two kinds of justification for punishing criminals, called the *utilitarian* and *retributivist* positions. Utilitarians view criminal law as useful, in that punishing criminals benefits society. Retributivists see the primary role of criminal law as retribution; in other words, criminals are punished because they deserve it.

Utilitarianism is the theory that society ought to be organized to promote the greatest good for the greatest number of people. Criminal law, in the view of the utilitarian, serves the social good primarily by preventing crime. Punishing criminals may prevent crime in several ways. Imprisoning a criminal prevents him from committing another crime while he is incarcerated; executing a criminal prevents him from ever committing another crime. (This is commonly called *restraint* or *incapacitation.*) *Individual deterrence* or *specific deterrence* assumes that once someone has been punished for a crime, he or she may be less likely to commit another crime. The threat of punishment in general—*general deterrence*—discourages people from committing crimes. Placing criminals in a restrictive environment where they can receive treatment, counseling, and education may lead them away from a life of crime; it may *rehabilitate* them. And public knowledge of criminal punishments reinforces people's sense of the importance of the standards of behavior of the criminal law, by *denunciation.*

Let's begin with rehabilitation. Criminal punishment can prevent crime by changing criminals. Once someone has been convicted of a crime, he or she can be given counseling, psychological treatment, education, or moral examples, either in prison or while on probation, to turn the person from a life of crime to law-abiding behavior. The rehabilitative ideal was extremely important, perhaps dominant, in criminal law through most of the twentieth century. With rehabilitation as a goal, criminal law and punishment focused on the criminal, not the crime. Judges attempted to individualize sentences to meet the rehabilitative needs of an individual criminal, prisons offered a wide range of opportunities for education and reform, and release from prison on parole was based on evidence that the convict had been rehabilitated. Of course, prisons were never really treatment centers, and the resources that might have been needed to fulfill the rehabilitative ideal were never provided, but at least the concept was an important part of the system.

Rehabilitation as a purpose of the criminal law has declined in recent years because its critics argued that we don't have a good sense of what works. A series of widely publicized studies in the 1970s asserted that all of the efforts at rehabilitation had little effect on rates of recidivism, or criminals' tendency to repeat their crimes. Some rehabilitative programs might work under some circumstances, but we have no firm basis for knowing which is which, so constructing a system of criminal punishment on rehabilitation is arbitrary at best and irrational at worst. In the face of that criticism and the growing public concern that we needed to get tough on crime, rehabilitation has faded as an objective of criminal law.

Incapacitation ought to have an obvious effect on crime: If we put criminals in prison where they cannot commit more crimes, crime will be reduced. The underlying assumption is that at least some criminals are prone to commit more crimes. We may not be able to rehabilitate these repeat offenders, but we can prevent them from committing crimes by removing them from society, at least for a time.

The problem with incapacitation is an empirical problem akin to the problem with rehabilitation. We would find it unjust to sentence all criminals to long prison terms just because some of them will commit more crimes, so incapacitation demands the ability to predict who is likely to be a repeat offender. For a time the law attempted to individualize this judgment; judges in sentencing, for example, would consider a criminal's background, education, social circumstances, and even psychological profile in an attempt to determine how likely he was to commit another crime, and thus craft an appropriate sentence. More recently the attempt has been made to predict future criminality on a large-scale or systematic basis, focusing more on the nature of the crime and objective factors in the offender's background. But as with rehabilitation, the system's reach may exceed its grasp. The evidence suggests that we are not in a good position to predict future behavior; in fact, the tendency is to overpredict criminality, so that people who are not likely to commit future crimes are held in prison for unnecessarily long periods of time.

Denunciation reduces crime by reinforcing people's views of the wrongfulness of criminal behavior. Declaring an act criminal and punishing an offender does more than make a moral statement; it strengthens the public's tendency to be law-abiding. Most people want to do what is right, and public knowledge of criminal punishment reinforces the perception of what is right. Most people also want to be treated fairly; if they have the sense that many other people are getting away with breaking the law, they may be more likely to break the law themselves. In this indirect way, the criminal process reduces the incidence of crime.

Rehabilitation, incapacitation, and denunciation have their adherents, but the main utilitarian justification of criminal law is deterrence. Deterrence assumes that people act rationally, weighing the potential costs and benefits of what they do. If society wants to prevent people from acting in certain ways, it only has to increase the cost of acting in those ways. Making robbery a crime punishable by imprisonment discourages people from robbing. For behavior that is more wrongful, we have only to increase the penalty to increase the deterrent—burglary may be punishable by five years in prison, robbery by ten years, and murder may involve capital punishment.

The threat of punishment is general deterrence. Some people just don't get the message, though. If the threat of punishment doesn't deter someone from robbing a bank, actually spending time in prison for the crime might do so. And if that doesn't work, increasing the punishment the second time might deter a third robbery. This is the logic behind "three strikes and you're out" laws, mandating life terms for criminals convicted of three serious crimes. Focusing on the potential repeat offender in this way is specific deterrence.

Deterrence as a basis of criminal law makes intuitive sense. If a mother tells her children that if they don't stop fighting she will send them to their rooms, the threat of the punishment may be enough to deter the kids' conduct. Although the world at large is more complicated, the same principle seems to hold; the threat of criminal punishment has a deterrent effect. But the effect depends on a number of factors. First, although criminal law in general deters crime, the choices that lawmakers have are narrower than whether or not to have a criminal law. Instead, the choices are whether to criminalize a particular act, how severely to punish it, and how much to invest in enforcement of the law. Then the results of those choices—the definition of crime and the threat of punishment—must be communicated effectively to potential criminals. Second, some criminals and some crimes cannot easily be deterred: psychopaths, mentally ill persons, people acting under the heat of the moment, criminals who think they can escape detection, and gang members who have few other opportunities or who regard arrest and punishment as an accepted part of their life cycle are not likely to be deterred. Third, the likelihood and severity of punishment affect deterrence. If prostitution is criminalized but the police regard it as a trivial offense or can't easily track down prostitutes and seldom arrest them, or if the police do enforce the law but judges routinely impose only a minor fine on prostitutes, the law will have little effect.

These issues about deterrence are empirical questions—what works and what doesn't. There is also an ethical question about deterrence as a reason for having criminal law that goes to the heart of the utilitarian approach. The utilitarian objective of criminal law is to reduce crime, and it does so by deterring criminal behavior. But deterrence also must accord with our nonutilitarian conceptions of justice. Suppose we are concerned that drivers aren't being careful enough about pedestrians. The legislature might respond by enacting a statute requiring that drivers yield to pedestrians in marked crosswalks. (Many states have such a law.) But if we really want to deter drivers from being careless, we could make the penalty for failure to yield a prison term of twenty years to life. That's extreme, of course. Our desire to deter has to be tempered by a sense of proportion.

As this hypothetical suggests, even though deterrence has been the most important utilitarian justification for criminal law, it is not the whole story. The other important element, which has gained increasing support in recent decades, is a retributivist approach. Retributivists argue that retribution through the criminal law is not vengeance but justice.

Someone has committed a wrong, and wrongs should be punished. A famous hypothetical was posed by the philosopher Immanuel Kant. Imagine an island society that was about to disband, with all the inhabitants departing for other places. Someone who commits a murder on the eve of departure still ought to be punished. There is no utilitarian justification for punishment; the islanders never will see each other again, so punishment will not prevent a future crime. But justice demands that the society redress the wrong by punishing the murderer.

Retributivist theory requires that we know which acts are wrong. In many cases we are confident about this; an intentional killing without justification or excuse is always wrong. Retribution also requires us to grade wrongs, so that a crime is punished in accordance with its severity, and that can be more complicated. Which is worse, arson or armed robbery? Prostitution or drunk driving?

The deterrent approach to utilitarianism and the retributivist approach interact at this point. Deterrence is a basis for criminalizing behavior to prevent crime, but retributivist principles require deterrence that is just. Imposing a long prison term for failing to yield to a pedestrian may deter bad driving, but it is unjust on a retributivist basis, in that it is out of proportion to the harm sought to be prevented. Similarly, it would certainly deter crime if punishment were imposed not only on the criminal but also on all members of his or her family, but that would violate a basic retributivist principle. Just as criminal liability is imposed if someone has violated the law, liability may not be imposed unless the person to be punished has violated the law. The retributivist check on deterrence may also enhance respect for the law and encourage law-abiding behavior; a law that is seen to be just is more likely to be obeyed than one that is unjust.

What Is a Criminal Act?

Every criminal offense requires both a criminal act (often still referred to by the Latin phrase *actus reus*) and an accompanying state of mind (*mens rea*). The requirement of a criminal act is easily understood and is contested in only a few cases, but it reflects interestingly on the purposes of criminal law. The *act* element of the requirement refers to a voluntary action of the defendant, and the *criminality* element refers to the harm that ensues from the act.

An act is simply a movement of a part of the body. The criminal's finger pulls the trigger on the gun or her hand takes a wallet out of the victim's pocket. At this point we are not concerned with the consequences of the act—the death of the victim or the value of the wallet—but only with the defendant's physical act itself. It's enough that there be an act and that the defendant voluntarily performed it.

The element of voluntariness is essential. Suppose John Doe is quietly peeling an apple when he suddenly has an epileptic seizure. During the seizure, an involuntary muscle contraction causes his hand, which is holding the knife he was using, to jerk out, slashing the throat of Jane Roe, who was sitting next to him. Or suppose one night Doe gets out of bed and, in an unconscious, sleepwalking state, picks up a knife and slashes his wife to death. Has Doe committed a criminal act in either case? The law says no, because Doe's conscious mind has not directed a voluntary act.

How does requiring a voluntary act fulfill the purposes of criminal law? Sometimes it is argued that we can't deter involuntary acts, so there is no point in punishing them; the threat of a criminal sanction cannot prevent the epileptic from having a seizure. But that's not exactly right. We can't prevent the somnambulist from sleepwalking, but we can provide a disincentive for him to be in potentially dangerous situations when he might do so; perhaps the threat of criminal punishment will encourage sleepwalkers to keep their bedroom doors locked and keep sharp objects out of reach, or even to seek treatment for the affliction. An even more important reason to require a voluntary act is retributivist. Criminal punishments are exacted because the criminal has done something wrong in a moral sense. Only where the criminal has chosen to commit harm—that is, has acted voluntarily—is it just to punish him.

Voluntariness as an issue arises in a few cases more common than sleepwalking. Suppose a deeply fatigued truck driver continues to drive at the end of a very long day, falls asleep at the wheel, and runs over a pedestrian. Has the driver committed a criminal homicide? Running over the pedestrian was not a voluntary act, but continuing to drive while tired was, so the act requirement has been satisfied. The issue then becomes the degree of homicide. The driver might argue that he should only be liable for negligent homicide (manslaughter) because he didn't intend to hit the pedestrian, even though he may have been reckless in driving in the first place.

The U.S. Supreme Court constitutionalized the doctrine of voluntariness in a pair of cases in the 1960s, *Robinson v. California* (1962) and *Powell v. Texas* (1968). California enacted a statute making it a criminal offense to be a narcotics addict, but in *Robinson* the Court held that the statute violated the cruel and unusual punishment clause of the Eighth Amendment. A state cannot constitutionally punish someone for having the status of being an addict; addiction is an illness, so one who suffers from it has not committed a voluntary act. *Powell* suggested the limit of the principle, however. Leroy Powell was convicted of being intoxicated in a public place and pleaded the disease of alcoholism as a defense. This was different, the Court said. Powell had committed an act—being drunk in a public place—so he was not simply being punished for his status. Although he was an alcoholic, he should take measures to control the conduct that flowed from his disease.

If the law requires an act, is failure to act enough? In a notorious incident in New York City in 1964, Kitty Genovese, a twenty-nine-year-old woman coming home from work, was brutally attacked and murdered over the course of a half hour; residents in nearby apartments saw or heard parts of the attack, but most did nothing to help. Are any of them criminally liable for failing to come to her aid? The law's answer is no. Traditionally two reasons are offered for this position. One reason is practical. It's hard to prove how much each of the bystanders contributed to Genovese's death; subsequent reports presented conflicting evidence on what the bystanders saw, heard, or did. The other reason is principled and is based on the right to be left alone from demands by the government. The government may be able to punish you for doing harm, but it should not apply the extreme measure of a criminal sanction for affirmatively failing to do good.

There are exceptions to the rule that one is not liable for failing to act. Most prominently, some statutes create duties to act. Failing to pay your taxes or to stop at the scene of a traffic accident in which you are involved may be characterized as inaction, not action, but it still is criminal. Also, people in certain status relationships have to fulfill the responsibilities of the relationship. A parent cannot allow his child to starve and then defend a prosecution of criminal neglect by saying all he did was fail to act.

The "reus" portion of "actus reus" requires that the act be of a criminal nature. This expands the requirement beyond act and voluntariness to include harm. The law doesn't punish all acts, only those that are criminal in that they are wrongful and cause harm to society. In some cases the harm is immediate and obvious; in a homicide case, the harm is the death of a human being. In others the harm is potential rather than immediate. A driver who is intoxicated may not injure someone the first time, but the potential for harm is sufficiently great that it is useful and fair to punish the conduct before the harm occurs.

Does Someone Have to Mean to Commit a Crime to Be Guilty?

An ancient maxim states, "An act does not make a person guilty unless the person's mind is guilty." To be guilty of a crime, a person must commit a prohibited act and must do so with a certain specified state of mind.

Suppose, for example, that a group of hunters are in the woods hunting on the first day of deer season. Hunter #1 (call him Cain) is about to shoot at a deer when he sees his worst enemy, Victim #1, also out hunting. Cain shifts his aim from the deer to Victim #1, shooting and killing her. Meanwhile Hunter #2 (Abel) aims, fires at a deer, and misses; his bullet travels past the deer and strikes and kills Victim #2, who was walking in the woods near the deer but out of sight of Abel. The classic definition of murder is "the unlawful killing of a human being with malice aforethought." Are Cain and Abel guilty of murder?

Cain has committed the prohibited act—the unlawful killing of another human being. (The act is unlawful because he wasn't a police officer or soldier killing in the line of duty.) He has also satisfied the mental element of the crime, or the *mens rea*, because he intended to kill his victim. Note that the mental requirement is intention, not motive. Cain had a motive to kill his victim—she was his worst enemy—but he would have been just as guilty if he didn't know the victim and had shot her on a whim, or even if he had killed with a good motive, which is why euthanasia can be punished as homicide.

What about Abel, who didn't even know his victim was there? He, too, has committed the prohibited act by unlawfully killing another human being, but he lacks the required mental state; he didn't act with the intent to kill.

Think about the culpability requirement in light of the purposes of criminal law. Requiring that someone have a "guilty mind" to be a criminal does not necessarily serve utilitarian objectives, the most important of which is deterrence. Some people argue that the law cannot and should not deter people who didn't mean to do anything wrong; we cannot deter Abel, for example, from causing a result that he never intended. But that's not quite right. Even if Abel did not mean to shoot his victim he may have been careless, and the threat of a criminal penalty can encourage people to be more careful. Moreover, prosecuting Abel generally deters criminality in that the more people are prosecuted for homicide, the fewer homicides there are likely to be.

But it seems unjust to punish Abel when he didn't mean to do anything wrong. A criminal conviction is a serious thing, because a stigma attaches to labeling someone as criminal and a severe punishment is likely to follow. We want to preserve that stigma and punishment for situations in which the criminal has acted wrongly in a moral sense. Even if punishing the innocent would deter crime, retributive theory places a limit on deterrence; even if we punish the guilty for utilitarian and retributive reasons, punishing the innocent is prohibited.

Cain meant to kill his victim, and Abel was completely blameless because he didn't know his victim was in the area, but in many cases determining the mental state that is required to make someone a criminal is a much more complicated thing. Definitions of criminal offenses traditionally drew on a confusing range of words describing mental states: *with malice aforethought, with intent to, willfully, maliciously, carelessly,* and so on. Many jurisdictions have followed the Model Penal Code's attempt to clear up this confusion by limiting the definitions of mental states to four: *purposely* (sometimes called *intentionally*), *knowingly, recklessly,* and *negligently.* A series of hypotheticals helps us explore the differences.

Someone acts purposely when it is their "conscious object to engage in conduct of that nature or to cause such a result." Cain kills his victim purposely because that is what he wants to accomplish by firing his gun. Suppose, though, that he sees his enemy among a group of bystanders and opens fire with an automatic weapon, spraying the group with bullets and killing them all. Cain has purposely killed his enemy but only knowingly killed the others. To act knowingly means that Cain is "practically certain" his conduct will cause a prohibited result, or that he is aware of the nature or circumstances of his conduct. Even though it is not his "conscious object" to kill the bystanders, since he is of normal mental faculties he knows that some of them will be killed when he fires on the group. There may not be much of a distinction between purposely or knowingly, but it permits the legislature in defining crimes to punish more severely someone who wants to accomplish a criminal act from someone who just knows that criminal harm will follow from his act.

In our original hypothetical Abel was in a well-known hunting area in the woods, looked around carefully before he fired, but still did not know his victim was near the deer. Suppose instead that he saw the victim standing near the deer and knew he wasn't a very good shot but fired anyway. Then he would have acted recklessly. Someone who acts recklessly "consciously disregards a substantial and unjustifiable risk." He knew he might hit the victim and not the deer; because he knew he might, he consciously disregarded the risk, but because he wasn't practically certain that he would, he did not act knowingly. The risk of doing so was substantial because he was not a good shot and unjustifiable because there was no compelling reason why he couldn't have waited to shoot.

Finally, suppose Abel didn't see the victim standing near the deer because he rushed into the clearing and, although he should have known that other hunters might be in the area, failed to look around before shooting. He did not consciously disregard the risk of hitting someone else, so he wasn't reckless; he should have been aware of the risk, however, so he was negligent, or careless.

The four mental states are in descending order in terms of the social harm to be prevented and the moral wrongfulness of the conduct. From the utilitarian perspective, it is more important to prevent and punish deliberate killers rather than reckless ones and reckless killers more than careless ones. From a retributivist perspective, someone who means to kill is more worthy of moral condemnation than someone who kills when disregarding the risk to others, who is in turn more blameworthy than someone who doesn't know of the risk she is creating. Distinguishing these mental states allows us to define which behavior is more criminal than others and to punish more severely the more serious behavior.

Return to Abel in the original hypothetical, in which he was not even careless in seeing the person he shot. Most people would say Abel has not committed a crime because he didn't mean to do anything wrong. Suppose that en route to his hunting trip Abel was stopped for speeding, going 80 mph in a 65 mph zone. Abel goes to court to fight his speeding ticket on the basis that, unknown to him, his speedometer was defective so that it read 15 mph too low. Can Abel successfully argue that he lacked the required mental state for the crime of speeding, because he did not act purposely, knowingly, recklessly, or carelessly?

This is an issue of statutory interpretation. What mental state did the legislature intend to require when it enacted the traffic laws? Generally, we would be much less offended if proof of one of the four mental states was not required to convict someone of speeding than of some other crime, such as homicide. Although on retributive grounds Abel may not have done anything wrong by failing to notice that his speedometer was broken, on utilitarian grounds it makes sense to sanction that behavior anyway. It would be impossible for the prosecutor to prove in every case that a traffic offender knew he was speeding, that his speedometer was working, or that he knew or should have known it was not working. Accordingly, we might find Abel *strictly liable*, or liable without being at fault, because only a minor violation is involved and not a serious crime.

Another form of strict criminal liability is *vicarious liability*, in which one person is liable for a crime committed by another person. The owner of a business often is vicariously liable for acts committed by her employees in the scope of their employment. If an employee mislabels packaged meat, sells cigarettes to a minor, or dumps toxic waste, the employer may be subject to the criminal penalty as well as the employee. (Note that the fact that the employer is vicariously liable does not relieve the employee of primary responsibility. As a matter of law, both employer and employee are liable, but as a practical matter, often the employer is the only one prosecuted.) Similarly, the owner of a car is liable for any parking tickets it receives, whether she was operating the car at the time or not. As with strict liability, vicarious liability is more often imposed for relatively minor, regulatory offenses than for major crimes.

Can a corporation be liable for a crime? In the early common law, the answer was no. In an old phrase, the corporation had "no soul to damn, no body to kick," and therefore lacking the attributes of a human being, it could neither form criminal intent nor be punished. Over time the courts have increasingly recognized that corporate criminal liability is a special form of vicarious liability. Because authority is so diffused in a large corporation, for some crimes only the corporation itself is liable, not any individual employees, and it would be unfair to single out one employee for an act participated in by many. Making the corporation the criminal also provides an incentive to top management to control the actions of their underlings, and it stigmatizes the proper entity—the corporation on whose behalf the criminal acts were carried out.

Suppose that a defendant argues that he has made a mistake about the state of affairs that negates one of the elements of the crime, typically one of the mental elements. Where the effect of the mistake is that the defendant did not have the mental state required to violate one of the elements of the offense, the defendant has not committed the offense. If Abel is hunting and shoots a person in a brown coat, mistakenly thinking the person is a deer, Abel has not committed intentional homicide because he did not intend to kill a human being. Here even if his belief is unreasonable, he has not committed a crime that requires intent or knowledge; the only issue is his subjective mental state. However, he may have been careless in thinking the person was a deer, in which case he could be convicted of negligent homicide. And the reasonableness of his belief is relevant to determining what his state of mind really was. If Abel testifies that he thought the person wearing a bright orange coat was a deer, the jury may well be highly skeptical of his testimony— especially if the victim turns out to be Abel's worst enemy.

When Is Self-Defense Justified?

When someone is put on trial for a crime, the prosecution presents its side of the case first. During the presentation of the prosecution's case, the defendant has a chance to poke holes in the prosecution's case by cross-examining the prosecution's witnesses. Then the defendant has the opportunity to present her own side of the story. In short, the prosecution is saying, "You did it." The defendant can respond in one of two ways: By saying "No" or by saying "Yes, but." (As we will see in Chapter 9, the defendant can be acquitted without offering any evidence if the prosecution has failed to prove her guilt beyond a reasonable doubt, which is a requirement of our adversary process with its presumption of innocence.)

The defendant's "No" in response to the prosecution's case essentially means that the defendant didn't commit the crime charged. "Yes, but" responses are different. Instead of rebutting the prosecution's claims, the defense introduces some new factor that exonerates the defendant. Criminal law has identified two types of "Yes, but" defenses, or reasons that we might not want to punish someone who has satisfied the elements of an offense: *justifications* and *excuses*.

Criminal law defines an act as criminal because it is wrong, both in terms of moral fault and social harm. But sometimes committing a crime doesn't seem wrong; because of special circumstances, doing something that otherwise would be criminal is an act that we are willing to tolerate or even want to encourage. When this occurs, we say that the act is justified and the defendant is not guilty of a crime. Usually justifications involve a choice among evils, and when someone chooses the lesser of two evils, she should not be punished for doing so. Justifications include self-defense, acting under official authority, and other circumstances that involve a choice of evils.

At other times a criminal act is not justified, but there is still something about the case that makes us uneasy about imposing criminal liability. What the offender did was not the right thing to do, but some special circumstances suggest that she couldn't be expected to do any better. In those circumstances the offender is excused. Excuses include mental disorders, intoxication, and duress.

To understand when self-defense is justified, consider the story of the "subway vigilante," Bernhard Goetz.

On a Saturday afternoon just before Christmas four youths—Darryl Cabey, Troy Canty, James Ramseur, and Barry Allen—boarded a New York City subway train. The four were not sweet young boys; all were high school dropouts with criminal records. Goetz boarded the train at the 14th Street Station. He was not a complete innocent, either; he was carrying a loaded .38 caliber pistol in a waistband holster, and he did not have a license for the gun, which he had been carrying illegally for three years since he had been injured in a mugging. Twice before he had successfully warded off attackers simply by displaying the gun.

Canty and Allen approached Goetz and said, "Give me five dollars." Neither Canty nor any of the others displayed a weapon. Goetz said that he "knew" from the smile on Canty's face that they wanted to "play with me." (All of this is from Goetz's subsequent confession.) When Canty asked for money again, Goetz stood up, pulled his gun, and established "a pattern of fire" from left to right. He shot each youth in turn, aiming for the center of their bodies. After Goetz had shot each one, he checked on their condition. Seeing that Cabey seemed not seriously hurt, Goetz said, "You seem to be doing all right, here's another," and fired another shot that severed Cabey's spinal cord. Goetz later said that he wanted "to murder them, to hurt them, to make them suffer as much as possible."

Goetz was charged with attempted murder, assault, reckless endangerment, and illegal possession of a firearm and defended on the basis of self-defense (*People v. Goetz*, 1986). Let's first consider a hypothetical set of facts. Suppose first that one of the youths had pulled a gun out of his pocket, pointed it at Goetz, and shouted, "I'm going to blow your head off!" Reacting quickly, Goetz pulls out his own revolver and shoots and kills the attacker. Goetz has satisfied all of the elements of the crime; he has purposely killed another human being. On these facts, however, we would say that Goetz was justified because he acted in self-defense. It may be useful to allow people to protect themselves because it could deter punks from assaulting subway riders. It also seems right from a moral point of view. Goetz has a right to personal safety, and he should be able to protect that right when it is threatened. The threat to him was imminent and serious, and he had no reasonable alternative except to defend himself or die. If the threatened harm had been less severe ("Give me your money or I'll slap you") or less imminent ("The next time I see you on this subway, I'll kill you"), Goetz's use of deadly force would not have been justified.

The facts of Goetz's case were much more complicated, however. The first troubling issue in the case concerns the standard to be applied in evaluating Goetz's claim of self-defense. Self-defense requires that Goetz believe that the four were going to imminently attack him and that shooting them was necessary to prevent that. Is the issue Goetz's belief, or whether his belief was reasonable? Is it enough that Goetz thought he was going to be attacked and the only way to prevent that was to fire, or are we going to evaluate his beliefs by determining whether a reasonable person would have thought that? If the latter, then Goetz's overreaction would not give him a valid claim of self-defense.

The Model Penal Code applies its general principles concerning state of mind and focuses on the actor's subjective belief. If Goetz believed that he was justified, then he did not purposefully attempt the unlawful killing of the four, so he is not guilty of attempted murder. If his belief was unreasonable, he may be guilty of negligent homicide or even reckless homicide, but he did not have the intent required for the more serious offense of attempted murder. A belief in the necessity of self-defense, even an unreasonable belief, rendered Goetz less culpable.

The New York law was different, though, requiring that Goetz's belief be reasonable. If the standard were wholly subjective, then someone who is unusually fearful or hot-tempered might have a claim of self-defense where an ordinary person would not. Under this view, criminal law wants to discourage those people from acting rashly, so it holds everyone to the same standard—the standard of the reasonable person. Applying this view, the court upheld the indictment for attempted murder against Goetz.

If we are going to require that someone acting in self-defense act like a reasonable person, what characteristics does the reasonable person have? Ordinarily we take into account some of the actor's physical conditions but not his mental state. A weak person reasonably may believe that he has to use deadly force to repel the attack of a much stronger person, but a fearful person cannot claim self-defense in every unpleasant encounter.

In the Goetz case the issues of reasonableness were very pointed. Is it relevant that Goetz had been mugged before? Is it relevant that Goetz was white and the four youths were black, and that many white city-dwellers think that all tough-looking black teenagers are potential muggers? The jury obviously thought so, because it acquitted Goetz of all charges except possession of an unregistered firearm, which was practically impossible to dispute. In the jury's view, perhaps, those generalized factors made Goetz's belief understandable and even typical. But is typical reasonable? If many people are afraid of crime, should criminal law bend to those beliefs or try to shape them? If it is typical for a white subway rider to be afraid of black teenagers, should the law say that it is reasonable to act on that fear?

These issues about self-defense and its racial overtones also played out in the killing of Trayvon Martin by George Zimmerman in 2012. Zimmerman, a neighborhood watch volunteer, called 911 in Sanford, Florida, to report "a real suspicious guy" who "looks like he is up to no good or he is on drugs or something." The "guy" was Trayvon Martin, a seventeen-year-old who had gone to a local 7-Eleven to buy a bag of

Skittles. Zimmerman followed Martin and an altercation and struggle ensued, during which Zimmerman shot and killed Martin. When tried for homicide, Zimmerman pleaded self-defense, arguing that Martin had punched him and was hammering his head to the ground; although the prosecution disputed Zimmerman's account, the jury concluded that Zimmerman reasonably believed that he had to shoot Martin and acquitted him as acting in self-defense. Even if Zimmerman started the tragic chain of events by following Martin after the 911 dispatcher told him not to and then approaching Martin, at the moment he used deadly force, he met the requirements of self-defense.

Zimmerman's case also provoked discussion about Florida's "Stand Your Ground" law, even though Zimmerman's defense ultimately did not rely on it. Under the common law, the use of deadly force in self-defense was not available to someone who could retreat safely from a dangerous situation, because the use of deadly force was not really necessary in that situation. Therefore, if Zimmerman could have run away from the altercation, he would not have been justified in shooting Martin in self-defense. (Following the maxim that "a man's home is his castle," the retreat doctrine does not apply to someone attacked in his own home.) But Florida, like more than twenty other states, had abolished the retreat rule to allow the use of deadly force to meet an attack even if retreat is possible, as long as the actor is not engaged in an unlawful activity and is in a place where he or she has a right to be.

When Are the Police Justified in Using Force?

If a police officer tackles a fleeing bank robber, can he be convicted of an assault? Of course not. The officer's exercise of government authority justifies what otherwise would be a criminal act. The police are authorized to use force in the performance of their duties to serve the public interest in enforcing the law and in protecting people and property. When the police can act and how far they can go produces enormous controversy, however.

While arresting Eric Garner for selling cigarettes without a tax stamp, New York City police officer Daniel Pantaleo restrained him with a choke hold that resulted in his death; while being restrained by other officers on the sidewalk, Garner repeatedly said, "I can't breathe." Ferguson, Missouri, police officer Darren Wilson approached Michael Brown following the robbery of a convenience store, a struggle took place between Brown and Wilson, and then Brown fled; witness accounts were in conflict about just what happened next, but in the end Wilson shot the unarmed Brown at least six times, killing him. Garner and Brown were

African American, and the incidents contributed to the spread of the Black Lives Matter movement. These events and numerous widely reported police-involved shootings raised public visibility of the dilemma in the justified use of force by police. We want the police to be able to use force, even sometimes deadly force, so they can do their job, but we also want them not to go too far and not to have their judgments about when and how to use force affected by racial bias. How can the law help resolve these conflicting aims?

Criminal statutes such as the Model Penal Code provide that a police officer is justified in using force when making an arrest if the officer "believes that such force is immediately necessary." Several requirements are built into this type of provision. First, the justification is available to an officer authorized to enforce the law; a private citizen who tackles a criminal while helping an officer make an arrest also may have a justification defense, but its scope is more limited. Second, the officer must have reasonable grounds for believing that a crime has been committed and this person has committed it. A police officer certainly is justified in tackling the fleeing bank robber; if the person tackled is actually a bank customer carrying a sack of money who was frightened by the robbery and running away, the officer's reasonable belief still provides a justification. Third, the force must be "immediately necessary"; the officer may be justified in shooting an armed bank robber who is spraying bullets while fleeing the scene of the crime but not a thief who has tricked a bank teller into giving him money and is giving herself up to the officer. Often this requirement is qualified by focusing on whether the officer believed that he had to use force, even if the belief was not fully supported by the facts. Fourth, "*such* force" must be necessary; the amount of force must be proportional to the need to protect the public interest that gives rise to the justification in the first place.

The controversies about police-involved shootings especially raise the proportionality requirement. The law allows the use of deadly force by police but it puts special restrictions on its use. Statutes vary, but often deadly force only is permitted if two conditions are met: First, the crime for which the suspect is being arrested itself involved the use or threatened use of deadly force or there is a substantial risk that the suspect will cause death or serious bodily harm if not arrested, and second, the officer's use of force doesn't create a substantial risk of harm to innocent bystanders. There is even a constitutional dimension to these requirements; the Supreme Court has held that the Fourth Amendment permits the use of deadly force only where the officer has probable cause to believe that a fleeing suspect poses a threat of serious physical harm to him or others, although the Court has been forgiving of officers' judgment about probable cause in some circumstances, such as when they are engaged in high-speed car chases.

Other bodies of law in addition to criminal law are available to evaluate police conduct. The federal government can bring criminal charges and victims themselves can bring civil actions against the officers and cities under the federal civil rights acts; the unlawful killing of a suspect is a denial of life without due process performed "under color of state law." Or victims can bring tort actions for intentional or negligent conduct that results in physical harm. But the most urgent focus in these cases has been on criminal law, which suggests its unique importance. People invest great weight in the judgments that the criminal process makes. When grand juries refused to indict the police officers involved in the killings of Eric Garner and Michael Brown, outrage increased because many members of the black community thought the system had failed; in one survey, two-thirds of African Americans reported little confidence in the criminal process's investigations.

High-profile events demonstrate that the principles and rules of criminal law can frame our understanding of issues such as when police use of force is justified but they cannot resolve those issues. The Model Penal Code has an elegant and well-organized provision that defines when police use of force is justifiable, with two main sections, two subsections, six sub-sub-sections, and two sub-sub-sub-sections. This complex provision is used to judge the behavior of a police officer making a split-second judgment on the street while his life may be in danger. The judgment is based on evidence and witness testimony that often is vague and conflicting, and it is carried out by lawyers, judges, and jurors who bring their own backgrounds, beliefs, and biases to the issue. And the criminal law's judgment is judged again by segments of the public with their own understanding of the prevalence of crime, the behavior of police, and America's troubled history with race. The police and the courts have to act and the people have to judge, but we ought to keep in mind the ways in which our judgments are colored and incomplete.

In What Other Circumstances Is Someone Justified in Committing a Crime?

Self-defense and the exercise of law enforcement authority are justified because the actor is choosing the lesser of two evils. It's not good to kill someone who attacks you, but it is justified to avoid being killed yourself. Is there a general principle of *choice of evils* or *necessity* that justifies other kinds of conduct? The issue pushes our understanding of criminal law to the limit and is posed by one of the most famous cases in criminal law, *Regina v. Dudley and Stephens.*

In July 1884, Dudley, Stephens, Brooks, and Parker, the crew of an English yacht, were caught in a storm and forced to cast themselves off in an open boat containing no water and no food except for two pounds of turnips. Dudley, Stephens, and Brooks were seamen; Parker was the cabin boy. For three days they had only the turnips to eat. On the fourth day they caught a small turtle. They had no water except for rainwater they caught in their raincoats. On the eighteenth day they had been without food for seven days and without water for five, and Dudley and Stephens proposed to Brooks that one of them—meaning Parker—should be sacrificed to save the rest. Brooks did not agree, but on the next day Dudley and Stephens, first offering a prayer for forgiveness, told Parker that his time had come and slit his throat. The three sailors survived on Parker's blood and body for four days, until they were rescued, barely alive, by a passing ship.

When they returned to port Dudley and Stephens were put on trial for Parker's murder. If they had not killed and eaten Parker they probably would have died before being rescued, and Parker, being the weakest, was likely to have died before them anyway. In the face of this necessity, was the murder of Parker by Dudley and Stephens justified?

The court held that it was not. First, preservation of life is a high value but not a supreme value:

> To preserve one's life is generally speaking a duty but it may be
> the plainest and highest duty to sacrifice it. War is full of instances
> in which it is a man's duty not to live, but die. The duty, in case of
> shipwreck, of a captain to his crew, of the crew to the passengers,
> all these duties impose on men the moral necessity, not of the
> preservation, but of the sacrifice of their lives for others, from which
> in no country least of all, it is to be hoped, in England, will men ever
> shrink.

And second, establishing a principle of necessity would open the floodgates:

> It is not needful to point out the awful danger of admitting the
> principle which has been contended for. Who is to be the judge of
> this sort of necessity? By what measure is comparative value of lives
> to be measured? Is it to be strength, or intellect or what? It is plain
> that the principle leaves to him who is to profit by it to determine the

necessity which will justify him in deliberately taking another's life to save his own.

Is this expecting too much of Dudley and Stephens? The court thought it was not: "We are often compelled to set up standards we cannot reach ourselves, and to lay down rules which we could not ourselves satisfy." Thus even though no ordinary person would be able to resist the temptation to act as the defendants did, the law required them to resist anyway.

Some modern jurisdictions depart from the rule of *Dudley and Stephens* and permit a defense of choice of evils where "the harm or evil sought to be avoided is greater than that sought to be prevented by the law defining the offense charged" (Model Penal Code) or where the action is necessary to "avoid an imminent public or private injury . . . which is of such gravity that, according to ordinary standards of intelligence and morality, the desirability and urgency of avoiding such injury clearly outweigh the desirability of avoiding the injury sought to be prevented by the statute defining the offense in issue" (New York law). These standards vest the ultimate decision-making authority about the necessity of acting and the relative weight of the evils in the court, not the actor. Even if Dudley and Stephens believe it is necessary and right to eat Parker, the court subsequently may reject their defense if, for example, the court finds that the chances of rescue in time were sufficiently great, or that, as seamen, they owed a higher duty.

The choice of evils defense also arises in other circumstances. During his first six months as an inmate in a Missouri prison, John Charles Green was gang raped twice. When he reported the attacks to prison officials, they told him to "fight it out, submit to the assaults, or go over the fence." One day at lunchtime, a group of inmates told him that they would visit his cell that night and he would submit to them for sex or they would kill him. At 6:00 that evening he escaped. At trial for his escape, he attempted to plead necessity but the court excluded the defense. The majority of the appellate court also rejected the defense because he was not avoiding imminent harm and he could have reported the threats to the authorities, but the dissenting judge pointed out the unreality of that choice; if he reported the incident he would be targeted for retaliation as a "snitch" and would have been "as good as dead."

Or consider the hypothetical case of torturing a suspect to reveal the location of a ticking time bomb and its real-world parallel in the controversy surrounding the Bush administration's program of "enhanced interrogation" of detainees at Guantanamo and elsewhere. Torture is a federal crime. If waterboarding and other harsh techniques are torture, could the agents who engaged in them be prosecuted? In an infamous memorandum in August 2002, the Justice Department's Office of Legal Counsel advised that torture would be justified to prevent a terrorist attack on the United States. (The authors of the memo also creatively argued that torture could be justified as a matter of self-defense—the defense of the nation itself from a potential terrorist attack.) The Justice Department subsequently withdrew the memorandum, and to date the question has not been presented to the courts.

Cases like these raise the most challenging issues about criminal responsibility and about the purpose of the criminal law. In some cases the law might deter, discouraging all but the most committed abortion protestors from illegal activity. But in extreme situations, is that realistic? Would Dudley and Stephens sacrifice their own lives and refrain from dining on Parker for fear of criminal punishment, or because a court had pronounced it wrong to do so? Probably not. The law seems to recognize its limits, too. Dudley and Stephens were sentenced to death, but the sentence subsequently was commuted to six months imprisonment. An important function of the criminal law is to declare what is right and wrong, to develop and reinforce people's moral fiber, and these cases may serve this purpose more than any other.

Why Are Criminals Allowed to Plead Insanity as a Defense?

The insanity defense has been part of the criminal law for centuries, and a classic hypothetical explains why the defense makes sense. A man acting under an insane delusion strangles his wife, all the time thinking that he is squeezing a lemon. How can someone who did not even understand the physical nature of his act be held criminally responsible for it?

In recent years, though, the insanity defense has become enormously controversial as it has become more widely used in a number of high-profile, often bizarre cases. John W. Hinckley Jr., who shot and wounded President Ronald Reagan and three other people in an assassination attempt, was found not guilty by reason of insanity. Andrea Yates drowned her five children, ages six months to seven years, in the bathtub of their home, had her first conviction reversed on appeal, and was found not guilty by reason of insanity at her retrial because she was suffering from severe postpartum psychosis and delusions that made her believe she was saving her children from hell. John DuPont, an eccentric multimillionaire who proclaimed that he was the Dalai Lama, Jesus, and the last of the Romanovs, shot Dave Schultz, an Olympic wrestler and member of DuPont's personal Foxcatcher wrestling team, and was found guilty but mentally ill. What should the criminal justice system do with people who commit horrific crimes under the influence of mental illness?

The defendant's mental health is relevant for several purposes. First, someone who is mentally ill and is found to present a serious danger of causing injury to himself or other people can be involuntarily confined to a mental institution through a noncriminal process known as *civil commitment*. A person who has been civilly committed has not been found guilty of a criminal act (indeed, the mental illness may involve noncriminal behavior) and can be held only as long as his mental illness presents a continuing danger.

Second, a criminal defendant who is mentally ill at the time of trial may be found *incompetent to stand trial*. Here the issue of mental illness is unrelated to the crime itself. Instead, the question is whether the defendant is able to understand the charges against her and to participate in her defense. It would deprive a defendant of the constitutional right of due process of law to try her when she could not understand what was happening or aid her attorney in presenting a defense. When someone has been found incompetent to stand trial, the state must determine whether she probably will become competent and either provide treatment or begin civil commitment proceedings.

Third, at the other end of the process, a defendant convicted of a capital crime may not be executed if he is mentally incompetent. Courts have always refused to allow the execution of a person who cannot understand that he has been convicted of a crime and sentenced to death, and the Supreme Court has held that it would violate the Eighth Amendment's prohibition of cruel and unusual punishment to execute an insane person. Various reasons have been offered for this position, but it likely comes down to the belief that it is unfair and even inhumane to put to death someone who cannot comprehend why it is being done to him. This humane instinct creates an anomaly, however. The mentally ill person on death row can be given treatment to restore his mental competence—at which point he is killed.

The insanity defense is different from civil commitment, incompetence to stand trial, or incompetence to be executed. Insanity in criminal law is an excuse. Someone intentionally commits an act prohibited by a criminal statute—say, attempting to assassinate the president. He has satisfied all of the elements of the crime: firing a gun at the president, knowing that he is doing so, and realizing that it will likely result in the president's death. Nevertheless, his lawyers argue, he should not be held criminally responsible for his act because he was mentally ill at the time of the crime. If their argument is successful, as John Hinckley's was, he will not be convicted of the crime and cannot be punished, although he will be held for psychiatric evaluation and released only if he is found not to pose a continuing danger—a process that may still keep the defendant in psychiatric confinement for many years.

Why are criminals allowed to get off because of mental illness? Think about the purposes of criminal law and criminal punishment. A major objective of criminal law is retribution, the moral condemnation and punishment of those who are responsible for committing seriously wrongful acts. The insanity defense distinguishes between those people who are responsible for their acts and those who are not. In a well-worn phrase, the insanity defense distinguishes "the mad from the bad, the sick from the wicked." Someone who commits an act that otherwise would be criminal because he is psychologically ill does not deserve the condemnation or punishment that criminal law usually metes out. The offender may need to be treated or even confined if no treatment is available, but as a sick person, not as a criminal.

Criminal law also aims to deter crime and incapacitate offenders. The mentally ill person who meets the legal definition of insanity typically does not engage in a calculation of the consequences of his acts that can be deterred, so the threat of a criminal sanction is useless. And because the result of a verdict of not guilty by reason of insanity is to commit the offender for treatment as long as he presents a danger, the offender is incapacitated and prevented from committing another crime to the extent it is necessary to do so.

Although medical testimony at trial is necessary to establish insanity, insanity is a legal concept, not a medical one. The issue of insanity is whether, according to the purposes and principles of criminal law, the defendant had a mental state that is appropriate to hold him criminally responsible for his acts. In most cases of the insanity defense, the defendant had the mental state defined in the offense, but his mental condition was so clouded as well that we think it unwise to hold him criminally responsible anyway. Over time, and especially since the Hinckley verdict, the definition used to determine legal insanity has changed. The basic question is whether we can formulate a test for insanity that satisfies those purposes and principles and is attuned to our understanding of mental illness and its effect on behavior.

The first great insanity case was *M'Naghten's Case*, a British decision from 1843. Daniel M'Naghten shot and killed Edward Drummond, private secretary to Prime Minister Sir Robert Peel. M'Naghten was under the delusion that Peel was involved in a conspiracy to kill him, so he shot the unfortunate Drummond (who was wearing Peel's overcoat) thinking that he was shooting at Peel. The jury acquitted M'Naghten because of his delusion (which today would be described as the product of paranoid schizophrenia), and the resulting uproar matched that which followed the Hinckley verdict. The House of Lords debated the issue and sought an advisory opinion from the justices of the Court of Queen's Bench. That advisory opinion included what became known as the *M'Naghten* rule:

> [T]o establish defense on the ground of insanity, it must clearly be proved that, at the time of committing the act, the party accused was laboring under such a defect of reason, from disease of the mind, as not to know the nature and quality of the act he was doing, or if he did know it that he did not know he was doing what was wrong.

The *M'Naghten* rule was widely adopted and is in effect in one form or another in most American jurisdictions. The rule focuses on cognition: the ability to know, understand, and think about one's actions. As a threshold requirement, the defendant must suffer from a mental disease or defect, although what type of disease is sufficient is seldom defined. As a result of the disease, the defendant must fail to comprehend either the nature of the act or that it was wrong. One can either know something at an intellectual level or can have a deeper appreciation of it; someone might know that killing is wrong, in the sense of being able to relate that fact, but still lack any emotional awareness of the wrongness of killing. Courts often fail to instruct the jury on which of these meanings is intended, although modern federal law requires that the defendant have been "unable to appreciate" the nature of his acts.

Similarly, failing to understand the "nature and quality" of an act, or that it is wrong, are subject to differing definitions. Usually nature and quality is taken to refer to the physical consequences of an act—that the defendant was strangling a person rather than squeezing a lemon and that strangling will result in that person's death. And wrong may mean either that it is a legal wrong or that it is wrong in a moral sense.

The *M'Naghten* rule makes sense in light of the purposes of criminal law. People who do not understand what they are doing or that it is wrong cannot be deterred from their conduct and are therefore not morally culpable for it. But mental health professionals complain that it is based on outmoded ideas about people's mental processes, focusing on cognitive defects when mental pathology often affects a person's entire personality.

The *M'Naghten* rule is limited in an important respect. Suppose John Hinckley knew that shooting Ronald Reagan would kill him, knew that it was legally and morally wrong, but heard voices in his head commanding him to shoot, commands that Hinckley was unable to resist because of his mental illness. Under the *M'Naghten* rule, Hinckley would not be excused because he appreciated the nature and wrongfulness of his act. In response to this limitation, some states supplemented the *M'Naghten* rule with an *irresistible impulse* test. If a defendant had a mental disease that prevented him from controlling his conduct, he could not be deterred and was not culpable, so he should be found not guilty by reason of insanity.

The irresistible impulse test has not been widely adopted for two main reasons. First, it attempts to draw a line that is very hard to draw—the line between an impulse that *could not* be resisted and one that simply *was not* resisted. Second, we may not want to draw the line here; providing a criminal penalty may serve an important deterrent effect in strengthening the resolve of someone who is subject to such impulses.

The major competitor to the *M'Naghten* rule has been the Model Penal Code formulation. The Model Penal Code revises the *M'Naghten* rule and the irresistible impulse test to allow broader evidence of the effect of mental illness on conduct:

> A person is not responsible for criminal conduct if at the time
> of such conduct as a result of mental disease or defect he
> lacks substantial capacity either to appreciate the criminality
> [wrongfulness] of his conduct or to conform his conduct to the
> requirements of law.

The Model Penal Code adds the irresistible impulse test's awareness of the importance of volition (the ability to control one's behavior) to *M'Naghten*'s emphasis on cognition (understanding one's behavior). And it takes a more flexible approach to the role of mental illness, allowing an excuse where the mental illness causes the defendant to lack substantial capacity, rather than lack an entire understanding of the nature or wrongfulness of his acts or lack any control over his impulses.

The Model Penal Code also defines "mental disease or defect" to exclude "an abnormality manifested only by repeated criminal or otherwise antisocial conduct." Under this rule, a sociopath who suffered from a disease that caused him to commit horrible crimes—such as a Jeffrey Dahmer, who killed repeatedly, then refrigerated and ate the body parts of his victims—could not be acquitted because of insanity. This provision was adopted to prevent the insanity defense from overwhelming the concept of criminality. Could a repeat offender claim that he lacked substantial capacity to conform his conduct to the requirements of the law, presenting as evidence the fact that he continued to commit crimes?

The yes or no quality of the verdict of not guilty by reason of insanity can be troubling, so courts and legislatures have taken two steps to supplement it. One problem is that a defendant who obviously committed a serious crime could be found not guilty by reason of insanity, temporarily held for psychiatric evaluation and treatment, and then released in a relatively short period of time after trial. A few states have responded with a middle-ground alternative: the verdict of *guilty but mentally ill*, when the jury finds that the defendant was mentally ill at the time he committed the offense, though not legally insane. The effect of the verdict is that the defendant is found guilty, not acquitted, so the judge can sentence the defendant to incarceration. The statute provides, however, that while in prison the defendant be given appropriate treatment for his mental illness.

A different problem of the insanity defense is that it is designed only for the most extreme kinds of mental abnormality. Many criminals have some degree of mental illness but not to such a degree that they cannot distinguish right from wrong or substantially control their conduct. Should we take account of this degree of mental illness or impairment? And if we are willing to take account of it, should we allow the presentation of expert testimony on the defendant's mental condition not to establish insanity but to suggest that the defendant is less responsible for his act?

The issue has been controversial, but courts and legislatures have attempted several solutions. First, the court can exclude evidence of the defendant's mental condition in the determination of guilt or innocence and then consider it as relevant to sentencing. Where a judge has discretion in sentencing, one of the factors that might mitigate a harsh sentence is that the defendant's mental state at the time of the crime rendered him less responsible than a normal person might be.

Second, the defendant's mental condition might be considered to negate one of the required mental elements of the crime. This applies especially to mental elements that require *specific intent*, such as the intent to kill for first-degree murder, but some jurisdictions apply it more broadly to any crime. If a defendant knew he was killing someone but lacked the mental ability to plan the crime, he would still be guilty of homicide but of a lesser degree, such as manslaughter instead of murder. On the one hand, this *diminished capacity* defense allows the jury to make more individualized culpability judgments, attuned to the degree of responsibility in each case. On the other hand, it immerses them in a confusing maze of psychiatric testimony. Once again, the mental health professionals have difficulty distinguishing "normal" from "abnormal" behavior, and the jury is more likely to be confused than aided by the testimony.

What Other Defenses Are Available?

To complete our study of defenses, consider intoxication and duress. Being drunk is something like being temporarily insane, but can it be used as a defense? In many cases, it can. Suppose Doc Holiday is charged with first-degree murder for shooting Billy Clanton at the OK Corral. At trial Doc testifies that he was present at the time of the shooting, wanted to shoot Billy, but was so drunk that he couldn't get his gun out of his holster, so he did not commit the crime. If the jury believes Doc's story, obviously he is not guilty, because he had not committed the act prohibited by the offense (i.e., killing Billy). But suppose instead that Doc's defense is that he did in fact shoot Billy, but he was so drunk he didn't realize what he was doing. If the jury believes Doc's story, is his intoxication still a defense?

Although some states refuse to recognize intoxication as a defense, most states would give Doc a defense, at least to first-degree murder. When he is too drunk to pull out his gun, his intoxication negates the act element of the offense. When he is too drunk to know what he is doing, his intoxication negates the mental element of the offense. First-degree murder requires that he have intended to kill Billy. If he does not have that intent, he has not committed the crime, even if the reason he does not have the intent is because he was drunk. Criminal offenses are defined to punish offenders who deserve blame. Doc may deserve some blame for getting drunk but not the degree of blame that is associated with first-degree murder.

Whether Doc gets off the hook altogether depends on whether there is some other offense available for which intoxication would not be a defense. If Doc is charged with stealing a horse but his defense is that he was too drunk to know that the horse on which he rode away was someone else's, his intoxication is a complete defense. In the case of killing Billy, however, the intoxication may negate the intent requirement of first-degree murder, but he may still be guilty of a lesser degree of homicide, which only requires that Doc have been reckless.

But why is this so? Recklessness requires a conscious disregard of a substantial and unjustifiable risk—for example, wildly shooting in the direction of a crowd is reckless. If Doc was very drunk, he may not have been conscious of the risk he was creating. Many courts draw the line at this point, though. Even if Doc was not aware of the risk he was creating by shooting, he was (or is presumed to be) aware of the risk he was creating by getting drunk. As a matter of policy, the possibility of criminal penalties for acts committed while intoxicated may discourage people from drinking excessively; as a matter of fairness, it is not unreasonable to hold people responsible for the risk they incur when they get drunk.

Next, consider duress. Suppose three men brandishing guns enter a taxi and threaten to shoot the driver unless he drives them to a bank they intend to rob and waits for them to aid in their getaway. The driver has technically satisfied all of the elements of the offense of robbery: He has committed the act by participating in the robbery, and he had the required mental state; even though he didn't want to take part, he did so purposely (that is, he meant to participate). But he doesn't seem morally responsible for the robbery. Or, put another way, it seems as if he ought to be excused from responsibility because he was committing one wrongful act—aiding a robbery—only to avoid a more wrongful act—being killed by the three bank robbers.

This excuse is known as *duress*. Where people commit a crime only because they reasonably believe that doing so is the only way to avoid imminent death or serious bodily injury, they have an excuse and are not guilty of the crime. The law recognizes that a person may be forced to choose between two evils and it does not punish someone if he or she chooses the lesser of the two evils. An actor is excused if he does something that is wrong, but we can understand the reasons for doing so and forgive him for it; it wasn't good that the driver aided the bank robbers, but we would be hard-pressed to say he should have sacrificed his life instead. He only participated in the robbery because the robbers said they would kill him if he didn't, a threat they were apparently ready, willing, and able to carry out. It would do no good to punish his action because we couldn't deter anyone from acting this way; any person would go along with the robbery even if it meant criminal punishment, because the possibility of punishment is not as bad as the imminent threat of being killed. And what he did was wrong but not too wrong; it would be a different case if the driver, under duress, had shot someone during the course of the robbery.

Defenses such as insanity, intoxication, and duress have been recognized for a long time, but the list of excuses is not closed. As our understanding of the social, biological, and psychological factors that influence criminal behavior expands, lawyers argue that new defenses should be recognized.

Millionaire heiress Patty Hearst was kidnapped by the militant group Symbionese Liberation Army; subsequently she participated with the group in a bank robbery. When she was arrested and tried, she claimed that it was not she, Patty Hearst, who had committed the robbery, but "Tanya," the revolutionary she had become after being brainwashed by her captors. Benjamin Murdock, an African American who was raised in a low-income neighborhood, deserted by his father, and preoccupied with unfair treatment of black people, killed two unarmed Marines after one directed racial epithets at him; his lawyer argued the jury should be able to consider as a defense equivalent to insanity that his "rotten social background" gave rise to an irresistible impulse to shoot in response to the epithets. Conversely, Ethan Couch, sixteen years old, was speeding in his father's truck while intoxicated and plowed into two cars stopped on the side of a two-lane road, killing three people. After his conviction for manslaughter, Couch's lawyer argued he should be sent to a cushy rehabilitation facility instead of being sent to prison because of his "affluenza"; having been raised in a home that taught him wealth buys privilege, he was unable to link his actions and their consequences.

Critics deride defenses like these as a denial of personal responsibility and the desperate tactic of creative lawyers using junk science. Advocates argue that at least some of these defenses are legitimate, because the criminal law's traditional distinctions are too rigid: sane or insane, subject to immediate provocation or not. As we come to understand the complex factors that contribute to criminal acts, they say, the law needs to make more nuanced judgments about free will and blameworthiness. Some of these defenses have been accepted and others have not, but the debate is certain to continue.

Can Someone Be Convicted for Almost Committing a Crime?

Most of the time a person can be convicted of a crime only if he or she has satisfied all of the elements of the definition of the crime. Murder, for example, is an intentional killing. Think about the attempt on Don Vito Corleone's life in *The Godfather*. The upstart mobster Salazzo and the Tattaglia family have two hit men shoot Don Corleone while he is buying fruit. If the Don dies, the hit men have committed murder; but since he doesn't, have the hit men only committed an aggravated battery? Or can they be prosecuted for what they intended to accomplish but failed to do—that is, for the attempted murder? Furthermore, if the Don dies, what about Salazzo and the Tattaglias? They didn't do the shooting, but they were the brains and the money behind the operation. Can they be convicted for their role—that is, for soliciting the crime or conspiring to commit it?

These issues involve what are known as *inchoate crimes*, because the criminal acts are incomplete or imperfect. The hit men's crime of murder is incomplete because the Don did not die, and Salazzo and the Tattaglias' crime is imperfect because they did not actually pull the trigger. Criminal law punishes three inchoate crimes: *attempt*, *solicitation*, and *conspiracy*.

Criminal law punishes inchoate offenses for two simple reasons. First, people who engage in attempts, solicitations, or conspiracies are about as dangerous as those who actually commit the crimes. The hit men who don't shoot accurately, the bosses who plan the hit, and the intermediaries who hire the hit men all are about as culpable as a hit man who actually succeeds. "About" as culpable is a necessary qualification, because there is much debate about whether someone who commits an inchoate offense should be punished as severely as someone who finishes the job. On the one hand, they have the same degree of moral culpability; a gunman who shoots but has bad aim is morally as responsible as one with better aim. On the other hand, they have not caused the same degree of harm, and the law usually doesn't punish people just for the level of their intent without resulting harm.

Second, establishing inchoate crimes is necessary for law enforcement. If attempted murder was not a crime, a police officer who observed the hit men pulling out their guns and approaching Don Corleone could not arrest them until shots were fired. And many crimes, including so-called victimless crimes, depend on attempt and solicitation prosecutions. The police usually cannot prove prostitution because it is extraordinarily difficult to catch a prostitute and her customer in the act, but they can use decoys and undercover agents to reach agreement with the prostitute or the customer, who then may be prosecuted for solicitation.

The use of inchoate crimes as a law enforcement tool raises the central problem in this area. A person has not satisfied the elements of an offense, such as murder or prostitution, but she has done something else that suggests that she ought to be punished. But what exactly is that something else? If we define the something else too narrowly, the inchoate crimes will lose their effect. If we define it too broadly, we will criminalize behavior that is far removed from causing harm.

Begin with the law of attempt to see how this problem works out. An attempt in criminal law is defined much like an attempt in any other sense of the word: Someone attempts something when he or she tries to accomplish it. Therefore, the mental element of an attempted crime is the intent to commit the crime. The complications arise with the act element. Most crimes involve a chain of events, beginning with formulating the intention to commit the crime through getting ready for it to committing the act itself. The hit men in *The Godfather* first agree to murder the Don, then they stake him out for several days to find a time in his schedule when he is most vulnerable; they obtain guns, wait outside the fruit store, get out of their car when they see the Don coming, pull their guns, and finally fire at him. At which of those points have they gone far enough along to punish them for attempted murder? Suppose the police catch wind of the plan. How long do they have to wait before they can arrest them and get a conviction for attempted murder?

Courts and legislatures have constructed a variety of tests to determine when a would-be criminal has done enough so that a criminal attempt has been committed. The tests illustrate something important and ubiquitous in law. If the test is relatively clear and easy to apply, it produces wrong results in many cases—wrong in the sense of not adequately balancing the need to prevent criminal behavior and the desire to only punish the guilty. To balance those policies, it takes a vaguer, more open-ended test, but any test like that becomes difficult and unpredictable to apply. Consider just one of the tests.

The Model Penal Code punishes an attempt if the defendant has committed an act that is "a substantial step in a course of conduct planned to culminate in his commission of the crime" if the substantial step "is strongly corroborative of the actor's criminal purpose." This allows the jury to assess all the facts and determine whether the defendant in some meaningful way attempted the crime, but it requires a highly individualized, unpredictable determination on the facts of each case. To make things more predictable, the Code lists some actions that constitute substantial steps, such as lying in wait for the victim or possessing near the crime scene the tools to be used.

A second inchoate crime is solicitation. Solicitation involves trying to get someone else to commit a crime. Like attempt, if the crime is completed, the solicitation merges with the substantive offense. If the Tattaglia family gets the hit men to kill Don Corleone, they may all be liable in some way for the murder. If the hit men refuse the job, then Tattaglia may still be liable for solicitation.

Defining solicitation presents the same problem as defining attempts. Someone who asks or induces someone else to commit a crime is a dangerous person, and the police ought to be able to intervene and the courts able to punish before the crime is committed. But asking someone to commit a crime lies at some distance from the harm caused by the crime itself, so if the standard for solicitation is too broad, we come close to punishing someone for thinking about a crime or only engaging in preliminary acts.

Attempt and solicitation aim at almost-crimes, acts that are dangerous but that have not yet culminated in a defined offense. Attempt and solicitation have their limits, though, and legislatures have responded to those limits by creating new classes of offenses, designed to make conduct criminal even before it comes to fruition. An example is stalking. Suppose a man is angry at his ex-wife and sits in his car outside her house, follows her to work, and hangs around when she goes out on dates. None of this behavior is criminal, but it might result in actions that are; the ex-wife is afraid that he might attack her. Some legislatures have responded by criminalizing stalking. A California statute, for example, punishes "Any person who willfully, maliciously, and repeatedly follows or harasses another person and who makes a credible threat with the intent to place that person in reasonable fear for his or her safety." Such statutes raise all the problems of inchoate crimes. How early can we punish someone before he has committed a clearly criminal act? If we wait too long, we may be too late to prevent the harm from occurring; if we act too early, we may criminalize too much behavior, including behavior that isn't harmful.

Conspiracy is the third inchoate offense, and the one that is most widely used by prosecutors. A conspiracy is an agreement among two or more persons with the purpose of committing an unlawful act. The bosses of the Tattaglia family hire the hit men and don't themselves kill Don Corleone, but they can be liable for the hit men's acts because they are all part of the same scheme. More broadly, all of the members of the Tattaglia family might be liable as conspirators because they engage in a broader criminal enterprise that involves gambling, drug dealing, prostitution, and general thuggery.

Conspiracy not only punishes near-crimes, like attempt and solicitation, but it also deals with the broader problem of group criminality. A criminal group, whether the Tattaglia family or a drug cartel, is more dangerous than just the cumulation of the crimes that its members actually commit; the group holds the potential of committing more crimes over a longer period of time, becoming more effective at crime through the division of labor among its members (bosses and hit men using their respective talents, for example) and providing mutual support and encouragement for criminal activity by its members. At the same time, conspiracy is an even more problematic inchoate crime than attempt or solicitation. What does it mean to agree to commit a crime, and to what extent is one of the agreeing parties liable for the acts of others? Is the lowliest soldier in the Tattaglia family criminally responsible for all of the acts of crime and violence committed by any member of the family?

Conspiracy has been called "the darling of the prosecutor's nursery" precisely because of its potential breadth. The substantive law of conspiracy and the procedures at trial carry a number of advantages for the prosecution.

First, the essence of conspiracy is agreement, so conspirators can be convicted for acts that are much more remote from actual criminal consequences than are required for the law of attempts. But punishing the agreement alone is very much like punishing an intention without an act, which criminal law never does. Most jurisdictions have responded to this problem by requiring proof of an overt act by one co-conspirator in furtherance of the conspiracy in addition to the agreement, but that is not much of a burden for prosecutors, for almost any act will do.

Second, unlike other inchoate offenses, in some jurisdictions conspiracy does not merge into the completed crime. If the hit men succeed, they can be charged with murder but not also with attempted murder. However, if the hit succeeds, they and everyone else involved can be charged with murder and conspiracy to commit murder and sentenced independently for each. Conspiracy therefore has the effect of increasing the punishment for the crime.

Third, every participant in a conspiracy is potentially liable for a criminal act committed by any other member of the group. This dramatically expands the scope of liability of any particular participant, which not only leads to more convictions but also allows prosecutors to exert considerable leverage on one participant to cut a deal to testify against others, at the risk of being liable for far-flung acts in which he did not take part. A traditional rule imposed liability broadly: A conspirator is responsible for any reasonably foreseeable crime committed by a co-conspirator in furtherance of the conspiracy. Today most jurisdictions, following the Model Penal Code, apply a narrower rule, making defendants responsible only for crimes which they solicited, aided, or agreed to.

Fourth, a conspiracy case is different from any other crime in that normal procedural rules are relaxed in favor of the prosecution. All the conspirators can be tried together. This seems efficient; much of the evidence will be the same against all of them. But it also creates massive, complex trials that disadvantage the defendants. There is the danger of guilt by association, when evidence against one blends into an inference of evidence of all. Defense lawyers also have a problem: If it is apparent that a crime has been committed, it may make sense for each defendant to try to get off by accusing the others, with the consequence that all end up being implicated. Moreover, hearsay evidence normally is not admissible, except for an incriminating statement made by the defendant. In a conspiracy case, though, hearsay that ordinarily would be admissible only against one defendant can be admitted against all the defendants.

There is one other circumstance in which someone can be liable for a crime she didn't commit. This is called *accomplice liability*, when the accomplice doesn't perform the criminal act but helps the criminal do so. Accomplice liability is somewhat like conspiracy, but it focuses on the act rather than the agreement. The driver of the car who takes the hit men to the scene of the crime and helps them with their getaway afterward has not killed Don Corleone, but he still is liable for the murder. On basic principles of criminal responsibility, the driver has participated in the act of killing with the intent that it occur. Someone who helps a criminal conceal the crime or escape prosecution after it has been committed also is liable as an accomplice.

What Is Homicide?

An introductory book can only define and discuss a few crimes. New Jersey statutes, for example, define more than 200 separate offenses, from murder to fixing a baseball game. The legislatures keep adding to the list, making some conduct criminal in response to a particular social problem or political demand. So we consider a few crimes that are very important and that illustrate general issues about criminal law, starting with the most serious crime: *homicide*, or the killing of a person.

Homicide is the perfect place to start not only because of the importance of the crime but also because the development of the law of homicide exemplifies the basic operating principle in the history of criminal law: the drawing of increasingly fine distinctions between crimes and the difficulty of doing so. Five hundred years ago English common law defined only one kind of homicide—murder—and only one punishment—death. Since then courts and legislatures have separated many different kinds of homicide and defined the degrees of punishment that are appropriate to each. At each step they have to distinguish more serious from less serious crimes, based on the purposes of criminal law.

First, a preliminary matter: Homicide entails the killing of a human being. A few cases have grappled with the question of when a human's life begins and ends, and the issue resurfaces in modern controversies. The common law rule was that a fetus becomes a human being for this purpose when it is born alive. Some legislatures also have defined late stages of fetal development as within the definition or have enacted special statutes to deal with the killing of a fetus (subject, of course, to the constitutional protection of a woman's decision to have an abortion). At the other end of life, developments in medical technology have complicated the decision of whether someone near death is still alive. Most states have adopted a definition that focuses on the death of brain function, so that removing a respirator from a person in a severe, irreversible coma is not murder.

The proliferation of degrees of homicide proceeded in roughly the following manner. First, manslaughter was distinguished from murder. The traditional definition of murder, still used in many states, is the killing of a human being with malice aforethought. The legal definition of malice aforethought is quite different from the obvious meaning of the words and has nothing to do either with malice or forethought. Instead, as the law developed it became a code, standing for a list of states of mind, one of which was required to convict a defendant of murder. Manslaughter includes every other type of homicide. Next, murder was separated into degrees, commonly first-degree and second-degree murder. First-degree murder basically included willful killings; second-degree included other kinds. Finally, voluntary and involuntary manslaughter were distinguished. Manslaughter under provocation is the typical instance of voluntary manslaughter, and reckless or negligent killing is involuntary manslaughter.

Let's start with some hypotheticals based on the bombing of the Murrah Federal Building in Oklahoma City in 1995. Timothy McVeigh, an anti-government terrorist, was convicted of the crime. In the prosecution's account, McVeigh acquired the materials for a huge homemade bomb, constructed the bomb in a rental truck, and parked the truck outside the building on the anniversary of the tragedy in Waco, Texas, in which government agents battled the members of an antigovernment cult to which McVeigh was sympathetic.

First take the facts as presented, and assume further that McVeigh wanted to kill scores of government workers to make a political statement. This exemplifies the first category of malice aforethought, known as *intent to kill*. McVeigh meant to bring about the deaths of government workers, so this is the most serious kind of homicide. Note that we do not care about his motive—why he wanted to kill them—but only his intention—that he wanted to kill them. If a killer acts out of a laudable motive, he still has the intent to kill; if a man shoots his aged wife who is suffering from a painful, terminal disease, the fact that he only wanted to end her misery is irrelevant to the determination of his guilt, although it may be relevant to his punishment.

Suppose that McVeigh wants to make his political statement by damaging the Murrah Building but doesn't particularly care about killing anyone. He parks the bomb-laden truck outside the building. When people in the building are killed, McVeigh is still held to have acted with malice aforethought, under either of two theories. If he was substantially certain that some people would die, because he knew he had constructed a bomb that would cause a huge blast, he is just as guilty; he didn't necessarily want to kill anyone, but he knew it was going to happen. If he didn't know how strong the blast was going to be and didn't care, either, then he didn't intend to kill in the sense that he knew his actions would result in someone's death, but he is still regarded as acting with malice aforethought because he acted with extremely reckless disregard for human life—what the common law colorfully called a "depraved heart." (Something like the same principle made homicide committed only with the intent to commit serious bodily injury murder; it is reckless to attempt to injure someone so severely.) This reflects the value placed on human life, and it also shows that malice aforethought really has nothing to do with premeditated murder.

Hypothetically, let's go back in time to illustrate the final branch of malice aforethought. McVeigh constructed his bomb of fertilizer, fuel oil, and chemicals triggered by blasting caps. Suppose he obtained the blasting caps by robbing a construction site. A construction worker, alarmed during the robbery, accidentally triggers a blasting cap, which explodes, killing her. Under the ordinary rules of murder, McVeigh has not acted with malice aforethought because he did not intend to kill the worker and robbing a construction site does not in itself display a reckless indifference to human life. Nevertheless, traditionally McVeigh would be responsible for murder under the *felony murder rule*. A death caused in the course of committing a felony (such as robbery) automatically becomes murder whether or not the killer intends to kill.

The felony murder rule makes a killing in the course of a felony a strict liability crime. Even if the criminal did not intend to kill, or was not even careless in that respect, he is still liable for murder. The principal justifications for the rule are to provide an added deterrent for those who might commit serious crimes and to recognize the seriousness of the consequence even in the absence of the specific intent to kill. But the courts have been uneasy with that logic, particularly as the doctrine was extended to less obvious cases. Suppose that McVeigh attempts to secure the blasting caps by forging the federal license that is required to purchase explosives. When he presents that forged license to a manufacturer, the manufacturer's stock clerk drops the blasting caps, which explode, killing him. Assuming it is a felony to forge the federal certificate, has McVeigh committed felony murder? This seems to go too far, so most jurisdictions now limit the application of the felony murder rule either to violent felonies that are dangerous to life or even a specified list of the most serious felonies, such as rape, robbery, kidnapping, arson, and burglary. Many jurisdictions limit which killings in the course of a felony count as felony murders; if McVeigh and an accomplice were robbing a construction site and a police officer coming upon the crime shot the accomplice, who was fleeing, McVeigh would not be guilty of felony murder. And the Model Penal Code's provision on felony murder only creates a presumption that a killing in the course of a dangerous felony is reckless (and therefore murder), allowing the defendant to try to rebut the presumption.

Moving from intent to kill to substantial certainty to extreme recklessness to felony murder as a basis for including a killing within the definition of murder expands the scope of responsibility by a process of analogy. Acting with extreme recklessness isn't quite the same thing as acting with intent, but it is still pretty serious, so the courts made it punishable as murder. The next step, though, is to make distinctions among the different kinds of murder. Are some more serious than others, and therefore deserving of more serious punishment? In particular, should the death penalty be imposed for all types of murder or only for some of the most serious?

The classic formulation separated murder into first-degree and second-degree murder, with only first-degree murderers capable of being sentenced to death. Based on a 1794 Pennsylvania statute, first-degree murder had to be "willful, deliberate, and premeditated"; that is, the killer must have coolly and consciously arrived at the decision to kill. The Pennsylvania statute suggested the kinds of murder that would fall within the definition: "all murder which shall be perpetrated by means of poison, or by lying in wait." The statute also punished as first-degree murder killings committed in the course of the most serious felonies. All other kinds of murder are classified as second degree. Thus intentional killings without premeditation and deliberation, extremely reckless murder, and other forms of felony murder would be murders of the second degree, which, historically, were not punishable by death.

Someone who kills by poison or lying in wait obviously has calculated his act and deserves a special kind of condemnation, more so than one who kills intentionally but without the same degree of reflection. Once the deliberate and premeditated formula was established, however, its limits became hard to define. A wife who wishes to poison her husband so she can collect life insurance and marry her lover might plan the murder for weeks by calculating the proper dosage, illegally obtaining the poison, figuring out how to disguise its taste, and looking for an opportunity to administer the fatal potion. Suppose instead that the same wife, who has not previously considered the scheme, is about to make supper when she realizes she could easily do away with her husband by slipping some rat poison into his meatloaf. Has she deliberated and premeditated? Most courts would say yes. Suppose she is about to place the food on the table when she realizes she could kill her husband by handing him the wrong plate, since her food contains an ingredient to which he is highly allergic. Increasingly, courts have required planning and deliberation over a period of time to find first-degree murder.

The Model Penal Code addressed the difficulty of distinguishing between first- and second-degree murder by abolishing the distinction. It first defines murder as a killing caused purposely, knowingly, or recklessly "under circumstances manifesting extreme indifference to the value of human life." It then states *aggravating and mitigating factors* that are to be taken into account in determining whether the death penalty should be imposed. The aggravating and mitigating factors address the nature of the crime—whether it was "committed for pecuniary gain" or was "especially heinous, atrocious or cruel, manifesting exceptional depravity," or "was committed under circumstances which the defendant believed to provide a moral justification or extenuation for his conduct." They also consider facts about the criminal, such as whether he has committed previous crimes, his age, and his capacity to appreciate the wrongfulness of his act. In this respect, the Code exemplifies a further extension of the refinement of criminal categories, drawing distinctions not only among crimes in general but also among their individual circumstances and the persons who commit them.

The next level of distinction among criminal homicides is between murder and *manslaughter*. Some killings are severe enough to merit punishment but not so severe that they deserve to be classified as murder. These are killings without malice aforethought. As we saw, that phrase is a catchall for various types of extremely bad acts, and manslaughter, too, comprises a number of different types of killings. And within manslaughter there is a further distinction between *voluntary* and *involuntary* manslaughter.

The major type of killing falling within voluntary manslaughter is killing under the heat of passion caused by a sufficient provocation— killing in hot blood, rather than the cold blood required for murder. One of the classic illustrations of voluntary manslaughter is the man who comes home, finds his wife in bed with another man, and, in a jealous rage, shoots the paramour. Traditional judges understood how the husband could be so shocked by his wife's infidelity or inflamed by the affront to his dignity that he lost control; though killing the paramour is not a praiseworthy act, it is at least understandable and so constitutes a lesser degree of criminality than murder, even though there was an intent to kill.

Essentially, allowing provocation to reduce a crime from murder to manslaughter recognizes human frailty; under extreme circumstances, people simply cannot be expected to conform their conduct to the requirements of the law. Once we start down this path, though, many killings might be excused, so criminal law recognizes only reasonable provocation. Once again we see the conflict between attending to individual circumstances and making rules that cover classes of cases. At common law, the courts tended to develop categories of provocation that were reasonable. The husband who discovers his wife's infidelity was a classic instance. Other groups included people engaged in a fight and the victim of a serious assault. Traditionally, "mere words" did not constitute a reasonable provocation; someone insulted, threatened, or told by his wife of her infidelity could not kill in response, for example. More recently there has been a tendency to individualize the inquiry; the Model Penal Code permits murder to be reduced to manslaughter if the defendant killed under an "extreme emotional disturbance" caused by a "reasonable explanation or excuse."

Involuntary manslaughter is the final category of homicide. Malice aforethought for murder can be satisfied by extreme reckless indifference to the risk created to human life—such as driving a car wildly onto a crowded sidewalk. In tort law, civil liability is imposed for ordinary negligence or carelessness—causing an accident by eating your Egg McMuffin on the way to work and not paying sufficient attention to the road. Somewhere in between extreme recklessness and ordinary negligence lies another type of recklessness and criminal negligence, and this gives rise to involuntary manslaughter. The issue is particularly controversial in cases involving car accidents that result in death. Historically courts and juries were reluctant to convict reckless drivers of murder, perhaps under the instinct that "there but for the grace of God go I," so legislatures created a crime of vehicular homicide, either as a free-standing offense or a variety of involuntary manslaughter. The recent activism against drunk driving has increased the willingness to criminalize drunk driving, as involuntary manslaughter or even second-degree murder.

Why Is Rape Law So Controversial?

Rape has been one of the most highly publicized and controversial areas of criminal law in recent years and an area that has seen the greatest transformation. High-profile cases capture the media's and the public's attention. How are men, women, and criminal law to cope with changing patterns and perceptions of sexual behavior and gender roles? Does "no" always mean "no"? Is sex without overtly expressed consent rape?

The law on rape has many dimensions, from the elements of the crime to the kind of proof admissible at trial, and every element has been in a state of flux. As with any other legal issue, the decision in a particular case often turns on the precise wording of a statute or the authority in the jurisdiction. Keep that in mind as we examine here more general questions about where the law has been, where it is now, and where it might be going.

We begin with an extremely controversial Pennsylvania case from 1994, *Commonwealth v. Berkowitz*. The complainant, a female college student, left her class, went to her dormitory room where she drank a martini, and then went to a lounge to await her boyfriend. When her boyfriend failed to appear, she went to another dormitory to find a friend, Earl Hassel. She knocked on the door but received no answer. She tried the doorknob and, finding it unlocked, entered the room and discovered a man lying on the bed. The complainant at first thought the man was Hassel, but it turned out to be Hassel's roommate, Robert Berkowitz. Berkowitz asked her to stay for a while and she agreed because she "had time to kill." He suggested that she sit on the bed, but she declined and sat on the floor.

Berkowitz then moved to the floor beside her, lifted up her shirt and bra and fondled her breasts. He then unfastened his pants and unsuccessfully attempted to put his penis in her mouth. Berkowitz locked the door and pushed her onto the bed, and the complainant described this as, "He put me down on the bed. . . . He didn't throw me on the bed. . . . It was kind of like a push but not." Then he removed her sweatpants and pulled her underpants off one leg. Berkowitz did not restrain her in any way, other than lying on top of her, nor did he threaten her. Berkowitz then penetrated her vagina with his penis. The complainant said "no" throughout the encounter. After withdrawing and ejaculating on her stomach, he stated, "Wow, I guess we just got carried away," to which she responded, "No, we didn't get carried away, you got carried away."

Rape? The Pennsylvania Supreme Court, following the traditional law, said no. The Pennsylvania rape statute made it a crime for a man to engage in sexual intercourse with a woman other than his spouse "by forcible compulsion." In the court's view, the complainant's testimony did not establish the use of force or the threat of force. Berkowitz had not knocked her down or physically restrained her. Saying "no" throughout the incident may show lack of consent, but it does not show that Berkowitz used force.

In a similar case, *State in the Interest of M.T.S.* (1992), the New Jersey Supreme Court disagreed. Fifteen-year-old C.G. lived in a townhouse with her mother, her siblings, and several other people, including M.T.S. (Initials are often used in cases involving juveniles to avoid identifying the parties.) Each disputed exactly what had happened, but the trial court concluded that early one morning C.G. had consented to kissing and heavy petting with M.T.S. but had not consented to intercourse and, when M.T.S. thrust his penis into her vagina, she pulled him off of her and said "Stop, get off." The key issue for the New Jersey court was consent, not force. Without "affirmative and freely given permission," the act of unconsented sexual penetration itself satisfies the requirement of physical force. Permission does not have to be verbal or announced, but the evidence must be sufficient to demonstrate to the reasonable person that consent has been given.

How do we explain the difference between the two results? The wording of the Pennsylvania and New Jersey statutes differed, but not so significantly that it should have made such a difference in the result. One way of understanding the difference is that the Pennsylvania court applied a traditional conception of the crime of rape and the New Jersey court applied a more modern one.

The traditional conception of rape requires force or the threat of force in its commission. The definition of rape as forcible even gave rise to a requirement that the victim had to resist her attacker "to the utmost." The resistance requirement did not apply, however, where resistance would be obviously futile in the face of an overwhelming threat. If the rapist holds a gun to the victim's head, she is not required to resist.

The resistance rule reflects traditional perceptions about men, women, and sexual behavior, and as perceptions have changed, the law has changed too. Everyone understands what legal scholar Susan Estrich labeled "real rape": "A stranger puts a gun to the head of his victim, threatens to kill or beat her, and then engages in intercourse." But most rape cases differ in some respect from this model, as Estrich explains: "Where less force is used or no other physical injury is inflicted, where threats are inarticulate, where the two know each other, where the setting is not an alley but a bedroom, where the initial contact is not a kidnapping but a date, where the woman says no but does not fight." In those cases the decision about whether what has happened deserves to be called rape depends on one's perceptions. The traditional law is motivated by perceptions such as men are sexually aggressive and women are passive, women have a responsibility to avoid stimulating men or creating compromising situations if they do not wish to have intercourse, a woman's resistance to a man's sexual overtures is part of the routine of sexual behavior, and "no" doesn't always mean "no." The modern law is motivated more by the perception that a woman has a right to personal autonomy, and a man has the responsibility to be sure that a woman consents to a sexual encounter. (Traditionally rape could only be committed by a man against a woman, but some recent statutes are gender neutral, protecting men from forcible sexual assault, too.)

Under the modern approach, many states have abolished the resistance rule and redefined the definition of rape. Some require both force and the absence of consent, and others specify that the essential element of the crime is either force, the absence of consent compelled by force, or the absence of consent alone. The exact terms of the statutes matter, but the persistence of traditional perceptions of gender norms and sexual conduct matter too. The *M.T.S.* case changed New Jersey law to focus on consent rather than force, and other states have done the same. Despite the change in the law, even in those states police, prosecutors, judges, and juries are more likely to look for force and even resistance as evidence of rape.

Sometimes there is consent to sexual relations but the law concludes that the consent is ineffective so the perpetrator is still guilty of rape. (Often statutes define degrees of sexual assault and these offenses may be lesser crimes than forcible rape.) A high school principal threatens a student that he will prevent her from graduating unless she submits to intercourse with him; under the traditional law, the absence of force or threat of physical harm prevents this from being rape, but the Model Penal Code criminalizes the principal's conduct as achieved by coercion. A man slips a date-rape drug into a woman's drink and has intercourse with her, or a man's date becomes so intoxicated that she can't think clearly or communicate resistance and they engage in sex; the first case obviously is more blameworthy, but many states declare the second to be criminal misconduct as well. A person who has a mental disability that renders her incapable of understanding the nature and risks of sexual relations cannot effectively consent. The law also provides special protections for minors by limiting the effectiveness of their consent. The statutes vary, specifying different ages of consent or taking account of the age difference between the defendant and the victim. If an adult man believes the woman with whom he has intercourse is eighteen when she is actually only fourteen, has he violated the statute? Traditionally the rule was yes. Statutory rape laws were strict liability offenses enacted to protect innocent girls who were not mature enough to consent to sex, and a mistake about the girl's age was not a valid defense. More recently a number of jurisdictions have changed the law to allow a defense of reasonable mistake.

The different perceptions of sexual behavior have also colored evidentiary issues in rape cases. The traditional conception was suspicious of rape complaints and reflected that suspicion in three rules that made the prosecution of such complaints more difficult. First was the *fresh complaint* rule, which required that the victim had to report a rape promptly after its occurrence. Second was the *corroboration* rule, which required that the defendant could not be convicted solely on the uncorroborated testimony of the victim. Third was the admissibility of evidence of the victim's prior sexual history. These rules reflect antiquated attitudes and have been abolished in many jurisdictions.

9

Protecting the Innocent, Freeing the Guilty

Criminal Procedure

You may know more about criminal procedure and the criminal justice system than any other branch of the law. News reports of notorious trials and police dramas bring the criminal process into the American living room every night. Even small children can recite a *Miranda* warning, hardly knowing that they are paraphrasing a U.S. Supreme Court opinion: "You have the right to remain silent. Anything you say can and will be used against you in a court of law."

Criminal procedure has become the most-discussed area of the law, and it also is one of the most important. Half of the rights enumerated in the Bill of Rights are directed at the criminal process because it is the area in which the greatest power of the state can be brought to bear: the power to take a person's liberty or even life. This chapter explores that process and comes to grips with how that power is regulated.

What Is Criminal Procedure?

Criminal procedure, also called the *criminal process* or the *criminal justice system*, is the mechanism through which crimes are investigated, the guilt of criminals adjudicated, and punishment imposed. It includes the police, prosecutors, defense attorneys, and courts; the practices and procedures observed by them; and the legal rules that ostensibly govern them. In the criminal process an individual is pitted against the government, with all of its resources and authority, and only through the criminal process can the state's most serious sanctions—imprisonment or even death—be applied.

Criminal law, discussed in the previous chapter, defines what conduct is criminal and prescribes the punishment for criminal conduct. Criminal procedure makes the criminal law work; the sanctions defined by criminal law are effective only because the criminal process can bring the sanctions to bear on individuals who violate the law. At the same time, criminal procedure aims to make sure that criminal sanctions are applied only to those who are guilty and only through procedures that are recognized as fair. One goal of the criminal process is to punish the guilty, but other goals are to protect the innocent and to ensure that even the guilty are protected from abuse by the government.

Although we talk about "the" criminal process, different systems are in place in each state and in the federal courts. Each system is controlled by several overlapping bodies of law. Most states have enacted comprehensive codes of criminal procedure that structure the process from arrest through appeal. To supplement these codes, the state supreme courts often exercise their authority to adopt rules of criminal procedure that further specify how the criminal process is to be conducted. Similarly, criminal cases in the federal courts are conducted in accordance with statutory requirements set by Congress and the Federal Rules of Criminal Procedure adopted by the U.S. Supreme Court.

In a most important respect, however, all state and federal criminal justice systems are alike: They all are required to adhere to the requirements of the federal Constitution. The federal courts have always been subject to constitutional requirements, of course, but especially since the 1960s the law of criminal procedure has been constitutionalized. This criminal procedure revolution involved two steps: The Supreme Court applied the due process guarantees of the Bill of Rights to the states and, in the process, interpreted those guarantees in a more expansive manner than it had done previously.

The Supreme Court originally had held that the Bill of Rights was a restriction on the powers of the federal government, not the states. The Reconstruction Amendments, particularly the Fourteenth Amendment, radically changed the situation. In addition to granting citizenship and equal rights to former slaves, the Fourteenth Amendment expressly prohibited "any state" from depriving "any person of life, liberty, or property, without due process of law" or "the equal protection of the laws." The task that then faced the Court was to determine which of the protections of the Bill of Rights were included within these vague commands. Over time, the Court settled on a standard of *selective incorporation*. The Fourteenth Amendment did not incorporate all of the guarantees of the Bill of Rights; it selectively incorporated those protections that are "necessary to an Anglo-American regime of ordered liberty." The fact that a protection is included in the Bill of Rights is strong evidence that it has that status. In fact, selective incorporation has not been all that selective. Virtually all of the protections in the Bill of Rights have been held to be fundamental under this standard, with the notable exception of the right to indictment by a grand jury.

Applying the Bill of Rights guarantees to the states would not be particularly significant unless those guarantees had broad meaning. In *Boyd v. United States* (1886) the Court recognized its obligation to "liberally construe" constitutional protections such as the Fourth and Fifth Amendments in order to ensure "the security of person and property." The movement beyond a narrow interpretation of criminal procedure rights gained strength in the 1920s and accelerated rapidly in the 1960s.

State constitutions have also played an increasingly important role in criminal procedure. State courts often interpret their constitutions to provide more extensive rights for citizens and criminal defendants than are guaranteed by the federal Constitution.

Criminal procedure codes and constitutional law make up only one dimension of the criminal justice process, however. The actions of the participants and the culture of the local system are crucial in determining how the process will actually work. Who is selected to be a police officer? How does the officer act during a traffic stop, when called to a domestic dispute, or when interacting with drug dealers, teenagers, and persons being interrogated? Does the officer's behavior differ if a potential offender is black or white? What are prosecutors' practices about charging minor offenses, bail, and plea bargaining? Who are the judges and what are their backgrounds? How well-funded and aggressive is the public defender's office? The answers to questions like these tell us at least as much about how the system works as does the latest Supreme Court decision. The law of criminal procedure is designed to regulate the behavior of these actors, but there are limits to the law's ability to control conduct.

Why Do We Need Criminal Procedure?

Suppose that we had statutes that proclaimed certain conduct to be criminal but no police, prosecutors, or courts to implement the statutes. If criminals were not afraid of being caught and prosecuted, it would hardly deter them from committing crimes, and it would send a powerful message that, as a society, we were not serious about punishing wrongdoers.

Suppose, by contrast, that we were determined to crack down on crime. We could establish a criminal process that would go as far as possible in investigating crimes and punishing criminals. The police could wiretap everyone's phone, stop and search anyone walking down the street who looked suspicious, come into any home or office without knocking, and beat confessions out of suspects. In court, the defendant would not be allowed a lawyer, only the prosecutor could present a case, and a judge could convict the defendant on flimsy evidence.

Obviously, neither of these situations would be tolerable. We need a criminal process to investigate and apprehend people who may have committed crimes and to adjudicate their guilt or innocence in order to control crime, but the process has to be consistent with our values and traditions as a free society. This conflict of objectives produces great controversy about the content of the law. How far should we allow the police, prosecutors, and courts to go? To think about that question, we need to spell out in more detail the conflicting values inherent in criminal procedure.

A first value of criminal procedure is truth-seeking. The criminal process should identify, apprehend, and punish persons who have committed crimes, but it also should exonerate those who have not committed crimes. Truth-seeking is an important value at every stage of the criminal process. It certainly is important in the final determination of guilt or innocence at trial, but it also applies at earlier stages of the process. Police need to make accurate determinations of when there is sufficient reason to investigate a crime or arrest a particular person, and prosecutors need to decide correctly when charges should be brought against someone.

The system also needs to seek the truth efficiently. We want the system to work reasonably well in implementing the criminal law, given that resources are limited and mistakes inevitable. Because resources are limited, we cannot have a perfect system, but the police have to solve a reasonable number of crimes and the courts cannot make too many mistakes in convicting those who are brought to trial.

A focus on efficiency might suggest that police, prosecutors, and courts are pretty good at separating the innocent from the guilty. It would make sense, therefore, to let the agents of the process do their job through procedures that are informal and routine. Police, for example, should not be burdened with cumbersome procedures or hypertechnical requirements about what they must do in investigating crimes, seizing evidence, or interrogating suspects, burdens that would only diminish the system's ability to determine the truth.

But the system must not be too efficient. Truth-seeking is an imperfect process, and efficient truth-seeking can be a dangerous process. Resources are limited, and limited resources for police, investigators, lawyers, and judges means that mistakes will be made. Indeed, even the best-designed and most fully funded system will produce mistakes. The people operating the system are just people, and people have prejudices and can exhibit bad judgment. If mistakes are to be made, therefore, they should be made in the direction of making sure that an innocent person is not convicted, which necessarily means that some guilty persons will be set free, too.

From this perspective, informal, routine procedures are particularly dangerous. Police, prosecutors, and criminal court judges see a lot of crime, so they tend to see crime everywhere. We need rules to control their conduct, judges to carefully apply those rules, and other judges to review those decisions. This perspective leads us to value an adversarial system, with substantial legal protections that can be applied to correct errors and abuses, even if those protections lead to the release of persons who actually have committed crimes.

This conflict is not only about truth-seeking and efficiency. In the criminal justice system, the government brings its power to bear against an individual. But people are not simply problems of crime control to be dealt with by bureaucratic procedures. The dignity and the status of the individual are essential values of criminal procedure. A criminal sanction can be imposed only after a process that respects that dignity and status, even if the process is slow, cumbersome, and likely to err on the side of the individual.

To limit mistaken convictions and to respect the dignity of the individual we have a presumption of innocence. It may be factually true that someone who has been investigated and arrested by the police and charged by the prosecutor is probably guilty, but that probability is legally irrelevant. Just the opposite; all through the process, up to the moment of conviction, the accused is presumed to be legally innocent. The state must meet a heavy burden to overcome this presumption, and it must follow all the rules in doing so.

The adversary process and presumption of innocence serve another purpose. We are justifiably afraid of the wrongful exercise of the great government power in the criminal process, and there is a particular concern that the power will be applied unequally. Police, prosecutors, and courts have a great deal of discretion in how they exercise their power, and American history is full of incidents in which the power has been exercised to the disadvantage of the poor, minorities, or other unpopular groups.

How do we balance these conflicting objectives in criminal procedure? Do we want the process to look more like an assembly line or an obstacle course? The conflict between these objectives generates all of the arguments about what kind of criminal procedure we should have, just as it generates the body of law we do have. There is widespread agreement among participants in the system and scholars of criminal procedure that things are a mess. The conflict has created a body of law that is inconsistent and unpredictable. In this chapter, as you think about what the rules should be, consider as well whether, given the conflicting objectives of the criminal process, it is possible to have clear rules at all.

What Are the Steps in the Criminal Process?

Before exploring the details of criminal procedure, let's look at a quick overview of the steps of the process. The process works differently in different states and the federal system, and not every case proceeds through the system in the same way, but this description is a good approximation of the path of a typical case.

The criminal process begins, of course, with a crime, or, more accurately, the suspicion of a crime by the authorities. A 7-Eleven convenience store is robbed, and either a police officer witnesses the crime or, more commonly, the victim (here the owner) reports the crime to the police. The first step is for the police to investigate the crime: interview potential witnesses, look at video from the security camera, collect other evidence from the crime scene, and compare this crime to similar incidents. The investigation may focus suspicion on an individual—call him Buggsy—and the police might question him. They might stop him on the street, or go to his home, and temporarily detain him to conduct the questioning. If the 7-Eleven was held up by an armed robber, or if they have other reasons to suspect Buggsy might have a gun, the police might frisk him—pat down his clothing to make sure he is not concealing a weapon that could immediately endanger them. These kinds of encounters with the police can be annoying, intrusive, or even harassing, but they are permitted as steps short of arrest or taking someone into custody.

In other types of cases the investigation may be more complex. In a homicide, for example, the scientific investigation of the crime scene may be more extensive, and an autopsy will be performed on the victim. Informants, wiretaps, and even sting operations may be used in investigating more complex criminal enterprises.

From this point on, several screens are applied to determine whether Buggsy will be formally brought into the criminal process and, once he is in it, whether he will be able to get out. (As long as Buggsy remains in the system, the investigation of the crime may be ongoing; the police and prosecutors may gather further evidence to be used against him at trial.) Once the investigating officer is satisfied that there is probable cause to believe that Buggsy held up the 7-Eleven, he will arrest him. Buggsy will be taken into custody (except in the case of very minor offenses) and *booked* by having his name and other information recorded, being fingerprinted and photographed, searched, and locked up (again, except for certain minor offenses, for which he will be released and told to appear before a judge at a certain time).

The next step is to determine whether to formally charge Buggsy with a crime, and, if so, which crime. Charging is normally done through the filing of a *complaint*, a document that sets forth what offense Buggsy has been charged with and the facts underlying the charge. The charging decision is typically made by a higher-ranking police officer, a prosecutor, or both. The person making the charging decision might decide not to charge Buggsy or to charge him with a different crime for a number of reasons. She might decide that the matter can be better handled in another way; if Buggsy is a kid who has stolen a candy bar from the 7-Eleven, for example, the police may release him to his parents with only a stern lecture. Or she might decide that the arresting officer's determination of the charges was incorrect; depending on what kind of weapon Buggsy had and how much he stole, the charges might be increased or reduced accordingly.

After Buggsy is charged, his status changes from arrestee to defendant, and the focus shifts from the police station to the court system. Shortly after the charge is filed, the defendant is brought before a judge (often a lower-level magistrate) for an initial appearance. Most jurisdictions impose a time limit on how long a defendant can be held (often 24 hours) before being brought before a judge. At the first appearance, the judge will inform Buggsy of the charges against him and will advise him of his basic rights, such as the right to remain silent and the right to counsel. If Buggsy is indigent, the judge will take steps to have a free attorney provided for him; the Supreme Court has interpreted the Sixth Amendment to the Constitution to require the appointment of counsel for an indigent defendant at critical stages of the proceedings, from interrogation and pretrial through an appeal. The judge will also set bail. The amount set will depend on the seriousness of the crime, Buggsy's background, and the perceived risk that he will fail to appear for trial. If the defendant cannot make bail, he remains in jail awaiting trial. In many cases, the judge will release the defendant on his own recognizance, not requiring any bail at all.

Following the initial appearance, a defendant in a felony case may be entitled to a preliminary hearing. In misdemeanors (minor crimes) the preliminary hearing and some other intermediate steps usually are not necessary. The preliminary hearing is the first independent review of the charges by a judge, who must determine whether probable cause exists that the defendant committed the crime charged. The prosecutor presents witnesses to establish the basic elements of its case, and Buggsy's defense attorney can cross-examine those witnesses and even present defense witnesses, although for tactical reasons that opportunity is seldom taken. If the judge determines that there is sufficient cause to hold the defendant, the case proceeds; if not, the case may be dismissed, unless the prosecutor is able to file reduced charges that are supported by the evidence.

The traditional means of giving further review to felony charges is by the *grand jury*, which decides whether there is sufficient evidence to *indict* the defendant. The prosecutor can also use the grand jury as an investigatory body before bringing charges. The grand jury, like the trial (or *petit*) jury, brings laypeople into the criminal process as decision makers. The grand jury proceeding is secret, and only the prosecutor presents evidence. Witnesses brought before the grand jury are not allowed to be assisted by counsel during their testimony. Accordingly, the grand jury's historic function of reviewing the prosecutor's case and screening out unsupported cases has significantly declined. As the saying goes, a competent prosecutor can persuade a grand jury to indict a ham sandwich. In many jurisdictions, there is no longer a requirement that the grand jury review the charges.

If the grand jury has indicted, the indictment is filed with the court. Where grand jury review has not occurred, the prosecutor files a comparable document known as an *information*. Like the complaint, the indictment or information lays out the charges against the defendant and the factual basis for them. Buggsy is brought back to court and *arraigned* on the indictment or information. At the arraignment, he is again informed of the charges and asked to plead either guilty or not guilty. Here (or sometimes earlier, sometimes later) *plea bargaining* enters the picture; Buggsy may decide to plead guilty in exchange for reduced charges or favorable sentencing.

A defendant who pleads not guilty looks ahead to the trial. Before the trial, however, the defense attorney may make a series of procedural or substantive motions to the court. Typical procedural motions will challenge some defect in the charging process. The most important substantive motions concern discovery of the prosecution's case and suppression of evidence. Buggsy has a right to know what evidence, favorable and unfavorable, the prosecutor has against him prior to trial, so that a defense can be better prepared. If there were defects in the process of collecting evidence, such as an interrogation of Buggsy without adequate warning of his constitutional rights, the defense can make a motion to have the evidence excluded from the trial.

The formal centerpiece of the criminal process is the trial. The defendant has a right to a jury trial in felonies and in serious misdemeanors, although the right can be waived so the case will be tried to a judge (called a *bench trial*). If the defendant is acquitted, the case is over. If he is convicted, the judge or jury, as directed by statute, will determine the sentence—the punishment that is to be applied.

The trial is hardly the end of the story. The defendant has a right to appeal, to ask a higher court to review the trial for errors. (If the defendant is acquitted, the prosecution cannot appeal, because of the constitutional prohibition on *double jeopardy*, or being tried twice for the same crime.) If errors are found, the defendant may be entitled to a new trial. Even after the normal appeals are concluded, the convicted defendant can pursue collateral postconviction remedies. Sometimes the defendant will petition a federal court, alleging some constitutional error in the trial, even if the trial initially was in state court.

When Can the Police Conduct a Search and Seizure?

The law of *search and seizure* governs some of the most basic police investigative techniques, including wiretapping and other electronic surveillance, examination of business records, and going through people's trash, in addition to more traditional techniques such as stopping suspected criminals and searching their clothes, cars, or other belongings. If criminal procedure was focused entirely on finding the truth and solving crimes, the police would be given wide latitude to engage in searches and seizures. But giving them that latitude would infringe on people's rights of property, privacy, and personal security. Therefore, the police's ability to engage in these activities is regulated by the Fourth Amendment to the U.S. Constitution:

> The right of the people to be secure in their persons, houses, papers, and effects, against unreasonable searches and seizures, shall not be violated, and no Warrants shall issue, but upon probable cause, supported by Oath or affirmation, and particularly describing the place to be searched, and the persons or things to be seized.

The Fourth Amendment applies to searches and seizures conducted by any government official, not just a police officer. A public school principal who wants to search a student's locker or a Food and Drug Administration meat inspector who wants to inspect a packing plant has to abide by the Fourth Amendment, although the standards of what constitutes an unreasonable search are different in those contexts than with a police officer stopping someone on the street. Conversely, the constitutional safeguards only protect against actions by government officials. A private employer who wants to monitor employees' email or a department store that installs security cameras in its dressing rooms is not subject to constitutional restrictions. (In some cases, statutes or the common law right of privacy provide some protection.)

Although the Fourth Amendment applies to all government activities, how it applies is less clear in cases of investigations involving national security. A series of statutes have expanded the government's investigatory powers beyond what is permitted in ordinary criminal investigations. Under the Foreign Intelligence Surveillance Act (FISA), for example, federal agents can apply to a special court that meets in secret to approve wiretaps, search warrants, and other investigative tools. The USA PATRIOT Act, enacted in the wake of the September 11 attacks and amended since then, introduced new measures such as *sneak and peek* warrants, under which agents conduct a search without notifying the subject of the search and have the power to demand library and bookstore records in the course of an investigation without notice to the person being investigated. As was revealed by massive leaks of National Security Agency data in 2013, the FISA court authorized the NSA to collect information on millions of telephone calls and emails without obtaining warrants, an extension of authority that was limited by the USA Freedom Act in 2015. The rest of the discussion of search and seizure law in this section only concerns traditional criminal prosecutions. (For more on the constitutionality of government actions taken in the war on terror, see Chapter 2.)

The first question in this area of law is: What is a search or a seizure? Let's focus on searches first. Is it a search if a police officer peers inside your car to look for drug paraphernalia? If she goes through your garbage? Has a trained dog sniff your luggage? Taps your telephone to hear if you talk about drugs? The question of what is a search is an important one because the Fourth Amendment provides protection only when there has been a search or seizure. If it is a search, then the court goes on to determine whether the amendment's other requirements have been satisfied.

Originally the Supreme Court held that only a physical intrusion into one of the areas enumerated in the Fourth Amendment—persons, houses, papers, and effects—counted as a search. In *Katz v. United States* (1967), the Court broadened the scope of protection to encompass a justified expectation of privacy with respect to the scope and manner of the search, without the necessity of a physical intrusion of a particular kind. Today the Court uses both approaches. In two majority opinions Justice Scalia held that physical invasion of property—by installing a GPS tracking device on a suspect's car (*United States v. Jones*, 2012) and bringing a drug-sniffing dog onto the porch of a suspect's house (*Florida v. Jardines*, 2013)—violated the Fourth Amendment; in each case other justices concurred in the result but argued a violation of privacy, not just a physical trespass, was key to the decision.

Under the expectation of privacy standard, some cases are easy to decide. A person who walks down the street openly smoking a crack pipe is exposing his illegal activity to the public, so a police officer's observation of the activity is not a search. A person who smokes crack at home, behind closed doors with the curtains drawn, has a legitimate expectation of privacy and the police cannot peer through the keyhole or break in to discover the criminal activity.

Beyond those easy cases, defining the expectation of privacy becomes very confusing, and many of the Court's decisions seem odd. For example, the interior of a house is protected from a police officer peeping through a keyhole or scanning by a thermal imaging device to detect high-intensity lamps used for growing marijuana, but the backyard or a greenhouse is not protected from aerial photography that detects marijuana plants, because the plants would be evident to anyone who happened to be flying over. If someone abandons property, no expectation of privacy exists, and the concept extends to one's garbage, even if it has been "abandoned" by being left in opaque containers on the sidewalk on garbage pickup day. So, according to the Supreme Court, there is no expectation of privacy in credit card bills, love letters, or other personal or revealing items left in the trash. (In an example of broader protection under a state constitution than under the federal Constitution, several state courts have held that people do have an expectation of privacy in their abandoned garbage, so the police need a warrant before searching it.) Finally, obtaining a person's bank records from the bank or a record of telephone calls made from the phone company is not a search. Because the information is available to the bank or phone company, there is no expectation that the information will be kept private.

Even if a search has occurred, it does not mean that the police have violated the Fourth Amendment. Notice that the amendment contains two independent clauses. The first clause prohibits unreasonable searches, and the second prescribes requirements that search warrants must meet, notably the requirement that there be *probable cause* for the search. What the amendment does not tell us is which of these clauses is primary.

For a long time the Court has considered the warrant requirement to be primary. To obtain a search warrant, the police have to establish probable cause that the search would turn up evidence of criminality, in an orderly procedure before a neutral magistrate. Requiring a warrant places a significant check on police activity and so provides considerable protection for personal liberty. Of course, sometimes it is impractical to obtain a warrant because of the need to act quickly to find evidence that otherwise would be removed or destroyed. Therefore, some searches can be made without warrants, but only in narrowly defined circumstances so that the search is not unreasonable.

The Court also has expressed a second approach to the amendment that inverts the order of the requirements. In this view, the essential command of the Fourth Amendment is that searches not be unreasonable. A search may be unreasonable for a number of reasons, only one of which is that it was not conducted pursuant to a warrant. The warrant clause states what is required to get a valid warrant, but it does not render unreasonable searches conducted without a warrant. Instead, the Court has to construct a general standard to evaluate the reasonableness of warrantless searches.

It is tempting to regard the first theory as more consistent with an approach to criminal procedure that focuses on the protection of rights and the second theory as allied with one that focuses on letting the police do their job. The primacy of the warrant requirement might be read to severely limit the situations in which police will be able to search, while reasonableness is a more flexible standard. But the case law has not come out that way. Instead, the conflict of values that underlies criminal procedure is expressed in each view. The exceptions to the warrant requirement have proliferated, and standards of reasonableness have not been completely open-ended.

Begin with the warrant requirement. A warrant is an authorization from a judge or comparable official to the police to search for and seize evidence of a crime. Requiring a warrant separates the decision of whether a search is appropriate from the person whose job it is to do the search; presumably, an independent magistrate can more coolly assess the evidence of alleged criminality and decide whether it meets constitutional standards. But the warrant process as actually conducted in many jurisdictions is paradoxical. The judge seldom takes more than a few minutes to review the evidence in support of an application, most warrant applications are granted, and the police can even request a warrant by telephone, simply reciting the facts underlying their request. Given this situation, can the warrant requirement act as an effective check on police behavior? To some extent, it still does; the knowledge that the request will have to be submitted to the judge disciplines police and prosecutors to adhere more closely to legal standards.

The key task for the magistrate issuing the warrant is to determine whether there is probable cause to believe that the search will find particular evidence of a crime at the place indicated. In this context "probable" does not mean it is more likely than not that a suspect is guilty or that a search will turn up evidence of a crime, and how probable the cause must be sets the balance between allowing police the discretion to fight crime and protecting people's privacy interests entailed in the Fourth Amendment. For example, in two cases during the Warren Court era, the Supreme Court held that in the common situation in which the police present information obtained from an informant as the basis for a warrant, the magistrate must be provided with sufficient facts about the reliability of the informant and the basis for the informant's conclusions so that the magistrate can make an informed judgment about whether probable cause exists (*Aguilar v. Texas*, 1964, and *Spinelli v. United States*, 1969). A Burger Court decision, *Illinois v. Gates* (1983), explicitly abandoned this test. If, looking at the "totality of the circumstances," the magistrate could arrive at a commonsense judgment that probable cause existed, a warrant could be issued even if the magistrate could determine neither the credibility of the anonymous informant nor the basis for the informant's knowledge.

Even under the view that the warrant clause of the Fourth Amendment is primary, some searches do not require a warrant. Under the view that the reasonableness requirement of the Fourth Amendment is primary, of course, searches can be conducted without warrants if they are reasonable; the key indicator of reasonableness is probable cause to believe that evidence of crime will be found. In general, we might say that warrantless searches are valid when stopping to get a warrant would unduly frustrate the goal of controlling crime or when the privacy interests protected by the Fourth Amendment are not seriously infringed by the search. But that general proposition hides much controversy about how far we should let the police go.

Consider the exception for the seizure of items that are discovered in *plain view*. If a police officer has lawfully entered a house or stopped a car, for example, and suddenly notices a pile of drugs on the floor, he may seize the drugs even if he lacks a warrant and did not have probable cause to suspect the drugs were there. It would frustrate the purposes of law enforcement if an officer, while engaged in a permissible act, was unable to seize the evidence of criminality that came to his attention. But the exception creates two temptations for the police: to make stops, obtain warrants, or conduct searches under a pretext, with the expectation of finding in plain view items that they suspect are present but for which they do not have probable cause, and to testify falsely that items were found in plain view when they were actually discovered by going beyond the authorized search. The Supreme Court initially responded to the first temptation by permitting the plain-view exception only when the discovery of the items was inadvertent. Ultimately, however, the Court rejected that requirement; once the officer is lawfully conducting any search, the Court stated, there is little more invasion of a protected privacy interest by allowing him to seize items found in plain view in the course of the search, and the court can evaluate the reasonableness of the search by considering objective standards (whether the item was in plain view) that do not depend on the officer's intention. The second temptation still exists, and some defense attorneys suggest that police officers routinely testify falsely that the product of a search was discovered in plain view.

Another example of a search that may be conducted without a warrant is a search incident to an arrest. When a police officer makes an arrest, it is reasonable for the officer to search the suspect and the area right around him for weapons and for evidence. Otherwise, the officer's safety might be endangered and the suspect may conceal or destroy evidence of her crime (*Chimel v. California*, 1969). If the officer finds the suspect's cell phone, he can seize it because it might be used as a weapon or it might contain evidence that the suspect would like to destroy. But the concerns for safety and preservation of evidence do not permit the officer to access the information on the phone, scroll through text messages or a contacts list, or examine the call log to find more evidence of a crime (*Riley v. California*, 2014). Similarly, police reasonably can require someone arrested for drunk driving to take a breathalyzer test and require any arrestee to submit to a cheek swab for a DNA sample because the public's interest in safe driving and proper identification of arrestees outweighs the minimal invasion of the arrestee's person and privacy, but they cannot require the greater personal invasion of a blood test without a warrant.

The use of objective standards such as these for assessing reasonableness has become increasingly favored by the Court as providing a basis for striking the balance between allowing the police to do their job and protecting Fourth Amendment liberties. For example, if the police have probable cause to believe a crime has occurred, they may stop the person who committed the crime; this is a reasonable seizure of the person under the Fourth Amendment. But suppose the crime is only a traffic offense and the stop is a pretext for searching for evidence of drug dealing by an African American driver in a high crime area. Then the threat of unreasonableness is real, but the Court has held that as long as probable cause exists, even if the probable cause of a minor traffic violation is established only on the testimony of the officer, the stop is reasonable. And even if the initial stop is unreasonable and therefore unconstitutional, if the officer checks and finds an outstanding traffic warrant for the person, the officer may arrest and search the person and use any evidence he finds in a subsequent prosecution. As Justice Sotomayor noted in dissent in *Utah v. Strieff* (2016), this approach vastly expands the power given to police, and "it is no secret that people of color are disproportionate victims of this kind of scrutiny." The Justice Department has found that African American drivers are three times more likely than white drivers to be searched during traffic stops.

In one type of situation, police do not need either a warrant or probable cause to engage in search and seizure. This is the *stop and frisk* situation, where an officer detains a person briefly to talk to the person, usually about some suspicious activity, and pats down the person's clothing to make sure that the person has no weapons that might pose an immediate threat to the officer. In *Terry v. Ohio* (1968) the Court recognized that "a police officer may in appropriate circumstances in an appropriate manner approach a person for purposes of investigating possible criminal behavior," and then may "conduct a carefully limited search of the outer clothing of such persons in an attempt to discover weapons which might be used to assault him." Subsequently the Court held that requiring a suspect to identify himself during a *Terry* stop violates neither his Fourth Amendment right against unreasonable search and seizure nor his Fifth Amendment privilege against self-incrimination (*Hiibel v. Sixth Judicial District Court*, 2004).

What are the appropriate circumstances that permit a stop? The key here is letting the police do their job while avoiding the arbitrary exercise of discretion. There must be some factual basis for suspecting the particular person stopped of criminal activity, but what constitutes an objective basis is not clear, and the courts often give deference to the officer's judgment.

Finally, there are some encounters between police and individuals that do not even rise to the level of a *Terry* stop, so no Fourth Amendment concerns are implicated. The Court in *Terry* struck the balance "when the officer, by means of physical force or show of authority, has in some way restrained the liberty of a citizen." In the Court's view, therefore, when police board a bus and ask to see each passenger's ticket and identification and to search his or her luggage, or when the police chase a youth who panicked and fled at seeing the arrival of a patrol car, no seizures have occurred.

What Is the Privilege Against Self-Incrimination?

The Fifth Amendment to the Constitution provides in part that "No person . . . shall be compelled in any criminal case to be a witness against himself." This *privilege against self-incrimination* is fundamental to our criminal justice system. In our accusatorial system, the prosecution has the burden of proving its case through its own efforts, not through an inquisition of the accused. If a defendant was compelled to speak, she would be faced with what has been called the "cruel trilemma of self-accusation, perjury, or contempt"—being forced to choose among confessing to a crime, lying and being punished for perjury, or keeping silent and being punished for contempt of court. This violates our notions of fair play, the balance between the individual and the government, and the dignity of the individual. The privilege also protects an individual's privacy and reflects a mistrust of the police practices that may be used to extract confessions.

But there is a cost to the privilege. In many cases a confession, or information obtained from the defendant that will lead to other evidence, is the only plausible means of proving the defendant's guilt. In cases in which there are no witnesses and little or no physical evidence, only intense questioning of a suspect will provide evidence of guilt. Excluding the defendant's testimony, therefore, means that some crimes will go unpunished.

What does it mean for a person to be compelled to be a witness against himself in a criminal proceeding? The privilege relates to testimonial evidence from a defendant, not to other types of evidence. As long as proper procedures are followed, the prosecution can force a defendant to appear in a lineup, give a voice or handwriting sample, or even give a DNA sample that may be incriminating. The prosecution also can compel the production of records that were prepared for other purposes, such as business records in the course of a prosecution for tax fraud.

Read literally, the language of the Fifth Amendment might only prevent the government from forcing a defendant to testify at his trial but permit any other kind of government compulsion that produces evidence against the defendant. But the Supreme Court always has read the privilege more broadly. It would undercut the policies behind the privilege if the police could coerce a confession or the prosecutor could compel grand jury testimony and then use the evidence at the trial.

Consider what happens when the prosecutor is using the grand jury to gather evidence and calls one of the targets of the investigation as a witness. The witness is given a subpoena that requires her to testify. If she fails to appear or fails to answer questions put to her, she can be held in contempt of court and sent to jail. If she testifies falsely, she can be prosecuted for perjury. If she wants to avoid either of those consequences and testifies truthfully, and her testimony is later used against her at her trial, she has, in effect, been compelled to testify against herself. The key is the use of the compelled testimony, not the place where it is given.

The prosecutor can avoid the exercise of the privilege against self-incrimination, at the grand jury or elsewhere, only by guaranteeing that the testimony will not be used in a subsequent criminal prosecution. This is commonly done by granting immunity from prosecution on the basis of the testimony. Immunity can be of two kinds. *Use immunity* means that the prosecution cannot use the witness's testimony or any evidence derived from it in a subsequent trial. If the prosecutor has evidence against the witness that is not the product of the witness's testimony, though, that evidence can be used. *Transactional immunity* means that the prosecution may not subsequently prosecute the witness for any crime that is discussed in the witness's testimony, even if the prosecutor independently discovers evidence of the witness's guilt.

A more common and controversial issue is how the privilege against self-incrimination applies outside of formal judicial proceedings, particularly to police interrogations. In many cases, the most important questioning of the defendant does not take place in the courtroom or the grand jury room but rather in the police station. The Supreme Court has recognized that interrogating a suspect in the police station is sufficiently intimidating that it threatens to undermine the privilege against self-incrimination.

In *Miranda v. Arizona* (1964), after examining police practices about interrogating suspects, including the tricks and other psychological devices it believed were commonly used, the Court concluded that "the very fact of custodial interrogation exacts a heavy toll on individual liberty and trades on the weaknesses of individuals." It is necessary to use "adequate protective devices . . . to dispel the compulsion inherent in custodial surroundings." These protective devices must be used in every case and include the now-famous *Miranda* warnings. First, before a suspect in custody can be questioned, he must be informed "that he has the right to remain silent . . . that anything said can and will be used against the individual in court . . . that he has the right to consult with a lawyer and to have the lawyer with him during interrogation . . . [and] that if he is indigent a lawyer will be appointed to represent him." Second, if the suspect "indicates in any manner, at any time prior to or during the questioning, that he wishes to remain silent, the interrogation must cease . . . [and if he] states that he wants an attorney, the interrogation must cease until an attorney is present."

Although the Court suggested that other procedures that would effectively protect a suspect's rights could substitute for the *Miranda* safeguards, no other procedures have been offered or approved, so

Miranda remains the controlling authority for interrogation procedures today. Interestingly, as police have adapted their procedures to include these easily administered warnings, the incidence of confessions has not declined. Nevertheless, the decision remains controversial because in some cases, the failure of the police to adhere to its requirements leads to the exclusion of confessions from evidence.

The privilege of self-incrimination under *Miranda* attaches when police conduct a *custodial interrogation*. Custody means that the suspect has been deprived of his freedom of action in any significant way that creates an intimidating situation, even if the suspect has not been formally arrested. Thus when IRS agents interview a suspect in his home or office, he is not in custody, unless something about the situation is particularly intimidating; asking questions in the living room is not inherently intimidating, but being questioned by four police officers in one's bedroom at 4:00 a.m. has elements of compulsion. When the police ask a suspect to come to the police station and specifically tell him that he is not under arrest, he is not in custody. If he unwisely confesses to a crime in those circumstances, the privilege against self-incrimination is not violated. But when they pick him up in a police car, take him to the station, and do not tell him that he is free to go, he is subject to compulsion, even if he is not arrested.

The question of what constitutes an interrogation also can produce difficult cases. Obviously, when officers question a suspect, that is interrogation. Further, the intent of *Miranda* is to prevent unconstitutional compulsion, so other kinds of words or conduct by the police that they should know are likely to elicit an incriminating response also should be considered to be interrogation. But extending the privilege that far will exclude credible evidence. For example, sometimes police may carry on a conversation in the presence of the accused, which has the intent or effect of inducing the accused to confess. In *Rhode Island v. Innis* (1980) the defendant was arrested for murder and robbery with a shotgun. As the police were taking him to the station in their cruiser, they talked about how important it was to find the gun, lest it be found by a child from a nearby school for handicapped children who might be injured by it. The defendant volunteered to show the police where the gun was, and the Court ruled that the statement and the evidence could be used against the defendant, since the police had not interrogated him. On the other hand, in *Brewer v. Williams* (1977), a case concerning what constitutes an interrogation for purposes of the Sixth Amendment right to counsel, Williams was arrested for murder. During a trip from Davenport to Des Moines in a police car, an officer said that because the weather was worsening, it would be difficult to find the victim's body and give her a "Christian burial." Williams then directed the police to the body. Here the Court held that there was an interrogation because the officer's remarks were directed specifically at Williams, who was known to be deeply religious.

Suspects can waive the privilege against self-incrimination and its associated right to counsel. *Miranda* itself states that the waiver must be voluntary, knowing, and intelligent and that a waiver cannot be presumed from a suspect's silence after receiving the warning or from a confession itself. More recently, however the Court has held that the privilege can be waived if not unambiguously invoked. In *Berghuis v. Thompkins* (2010), for example, Thompkins was held not to have invoked the privilege by failing to respond when read his rights and staying silent during three hours of subsequent questioning; when he finally answered "yes" to an officer's question, "Do you pray to God for shooting that boy down?," the statement was admissible at trial. Here the Court held paradoxically that being silent is not enough to invoke the right to silence.

What Happens if Police Violate a Defendant's Rights?

The constitutional protections of the Fourth, Fifth, and Sixth Amendments are not self-executing. Although the Fourth Amendment prohibits unreasonable searches and seizures, for example, it does not tell us what happens if an unreasonable search occurs. Much of the controversy about the Supreme Court's decisions in this area have come on this issue of the remedy for violations of constitutional rights. Beginning in *Weeks v. United States* (1914), the Court has formulated the *exclusionary rule*, which states that evidence obtained by the government in violation of the Constitution may not be used against the defendant whose rights have been violated. If the police find incriminating evidence during the course of an illegal search or obtain a confession in violation of *Miranda*, the evidence or confession may not be used to convict the defendant.

There has been vociferous criticism of the exclusionary rule because it appears to undermine the objectives of law enforcement. Does it make sense, as Justice Cardozo wrote, that "the criminal is to go free because the constable has blundered"? The exclusionary rule favors the guilty, by putting in their hands the ability to exclude evidence of their guilt through the assertion of constitutional rights. To the extent that it prevents evidence of guilt from being admitted at trial, it subverts the search for truth and the imposition of criminal punishment.

Several reasons lie behind the exclusionary rule. If the courts allow the use of illegally obtained evidence, they are in effect approving the unconstitutional conduct of the police. As Justice Clark wrote in *Mapp v. Ohio* (1961), acknowledging Cardozo's epigram, "The criminal goes free if he must, but it is the law that sets him free. Nothing can destroy a government more quickly than its failure to observe its own law." In *Mapp*, which made the rule binding in all state prosecutions, the Court also added the rationale of the rule's deterrent effect, a rationale that has been emphasized increasingly since then. The rule discourages police from conducting illegal searches or illegally obtaining confessions because it would be fruitless to do so, since the evidence so obtained could not be used to convict the defendant.

Since *Mapp*, much of the debate about the exclusionary rule has focused on its deterrent effect. Does the rule have a significant deterrent effect, and does the deterrence of unconstitutional police behavior outweigh the cost to law enforcement? Supporters of the rule point out that through deterrence, the rule that seems to favor the guilty actually protects the innocent. The rule does much more than serve as a safeguard against unlawful police action in an individual case. It also serves as a warning to all police officers and encourages police departments to improve training and supervision; as a result, there are fewer invasions of constitutional rights of all of us. The costs of this deterrence are not too great.

Critics suggest, however, that the rule is largely unnecessary. Like the *Miranda* warnings, the exclusion of illegally seized evidence may have been a useful prophylactic in an era of abusive police practices, but today a greater concern is the need to fight crime. Exclusion of evidence unduly rewards the criminal and sabotages law enforcement. To the extent that illegal police practices occur, they can be dealt with by other means, such as a tort remedy or civil rights actions against the police. Both the innocent and the guilty would have their constitutional rights protected; either could bring an action against the police and recover damages for an illegal search.

But proponents of the rule question whether such a remedy would be effective. For modest violations of constitutional rights, the victim would have little incentive to sue; where the police conduct random traffic stops and illegally search cars, for example, the inconvenience, annoyance, and frustration at the practice might be great, but the damages would seldom be worth going through a protracted lawsuit. More serious violations that turned up evidence of criminality could theoretically bring larger damages, but it would be hard to translate the theory into reality. Officers often are immune from suit for their actions, and juries are likely to be very unsympathetic to the convicted criminal bringing a tort claim for damages against a police officer.

This conflict over the exclusionary rule has played out in court decisions as well. One development is the "fruit of the poisonous tree" doctrine, originating in *Silverthorne Lumber Co. v. United States* (1920). Federal agents unlawfully seized incriminating documents from the defendant. After the court ordered that the documents be returned, the prosecutor had the grand jury issue a subpoena to the defendant to produce the same documents. The Supreme Court invalidated the subpoena because it was the ultimate product of the illegal seizure. Justice Felix Frankfurter subsequently coined the colorful "fruit of the poisonous tree" language to indicate that the result of an illegal search could not be admitted into evidence. The doctrine extends the exclusionary rule by discouraging the police from making an illegal search in the expectation that it will produce leads to evidence that subsequently could be legally obtained. But the Court has cut back the doctrine as well; where the link between the fruit and the original illegal action is attenuated, where knowledge of the fruit came from an independent source, or where it would have been the subject of an inevitable discovery even without the illegal activity, it may be admitted. For example, the Court has found the link between the fruit and the illegal action to be too attenuated to exclude evidence where a police officer unconstitutionally stops a person, fortuitously discovers an outstanding traffic warrant against him, and then discovers drugs while arresting him on the warrant (*Utah v. Streiff*, 2016).

A second development concerns the proceedings to which the exclusionary rule applies. Obviously, it bars use of illegally obtained evidence as part of the prosecution's case at trial. To obtain the maximum deterrent effect, the police should be denied all use of the evidence. But that has not happened. Instead, the Court has balanced the incremental deterrent effect of the exclusion of illegal evidence in settings other than the trial against the cost to truth-seeking and conviction of criminals. Therefore, it has held, illegal evidence may be used as the basis of a grand jury indictment, to impeach the defendant's testimony at trial, in a sentencing hearing, in a prisoner's habeas corpus proceedings challenging a conviction, and in a proceeding by the IRS to levy against illegally obtained funds.

A third development, and the most important, is the *good faith exception* to the exclusionary rule. The rule is primarily intended to deter unconstitutional police conduct, and, the Court has concluded, it cannot have that effect where the police do not intentionally violate a defendant's constitutional rights. Where they conduct an illegal search in a good faith belief that their acts are constitutionally permissible, the criminal process should not be denied the benefits of using the evidence, even though it was illegally obtained. Suppose when a police officer stops a driver for a traffic violation, the computer terminal in his patrol car indicates that there is an arrest warrant outstanding for the driver. The officer arrests the driver, searches him and the car, and discovers drugs and a handgun. The warrant had actually been quashed but, due to negligence in entering information into the computer system, that information did not appear on the computer terminal. The drugs and guns are the products of an illegal search because the search was not incident to a valid arrest warrant, but, the Court ruled, it was not excluded from evidence because the officer acted in good faith in relying on the computer system.

The good faith exception makes significant inroads to the exclusionary rule. It gives police less incentive to exercise caution in cases in which they obtain warrants, and it gives magistrates little incentive to closely scrutinize the basis for the warrant; in either case, error is cured by the police officer's good faith in carrying out the warrant. In cases involving warrantless searches, it has further eroded the rule; a good faith exception encourages police to err on the side of invading constitutional rights because it permits the use of evidence obtained through good faith invasions. The Court concluded that the benefit of the exclusionary rule in deterring improper police behavior was modest when their error was in good faith and only negligent, not intentional; that modest benefit would be outweighed by the cost of setting a criminal free (*Herring v. United States*, 2009).

What Is Plea Bargaining?

Television programs portray the trial, with its battle between prosecution and defense, as the central feature of the criminal process. Actually, 95 to 98 percent of criminal cases are disposed of without a trial when the defendant pleads guilty, often through a plea bargain. A plea bargain is a deal: an agreement between the defendant (through her attorney) and the prosecutor that the defendant will plead guilty in exchange for the prosecutor's reducing the seriousness of the charges against the defendant, dismissing some of the charges pending against the defendant, refraining from bringing other charges, or helping the defendant obtain a lenient sentence.

Suppose Sara is arrested in a drug bust in which she is found in possession of ten bags of cocaine and an unregistered handgun. Attempting to flee the site of the bust, she tussles with a police officer. The prosecutor charges Sara with possession of drugs with intent to distribute (because of the quantity involved), possession of an illegal firearm, resisting arrest, felonious assault, and, because she threw one of the bags onto the street, littering. This is typical prosecutorial behavior; the prosecutor incurs no greater burden in bringing every charge imaginable, and it improves his leverage at the time of negotiating a plea agreement. Given the likelihood of conviction, Sara's attorney negotiates a plea bargain. In exchange for her agreement to plead guilty, the prosecutor agrees to reduce the distribution charge to simple possession, dismiss the weapons, assault, and littering charges, and recommend to the judge that she be diverted into a drug treatment program rather than be sent to jail. In addition, although the prosecutor has evidence that Sara has been involved in other drug transactions, he refrains from bringing any charges in those matters.

From this simple hypothetical we can see why plea bargaining is such an important part of the system. For the prosecutor, Sara's case is routine, and he has too many such cases to be able to bring them all to trial. Even if he could, the judges before whom he practices would be unable to try them all; underfunded courts face a huge backlog of cases. Moreover, even though Sara's case looks airtight, no case is a sure thing. So a plea bargain gives the prosecutor an efficient and certain disposition of her case. Sara may also be willing to implicate her drug supplier in exchange for a plea bargain, so the prosecutor can leverage the charge against her into a conviction of an even worse criminal.

A plea bargain works to Sara's advantage, too. The panoply of charges brought by the prosecutor threatens her with a lengthy prison term if she is convicted. No matter how good she thinks her chances are at trial (and for many defendants, the chances are not very good), if she loses she faces a heavy penalty. Depending on the charges and her criminal history, a charge reduction might be particularly important to her; if she is a prior offender, a third felony conviction might subject her to a mandatory sentence under a "three strikes and you're out" law, which she can avoid by pleading guilty to a misdemeanor. If she cannot make bail, she does not have to stay in jail for several months waiting for a trial. And she dramatically reduces the hassle and aggravation of being subject to the criminal process.

In some cases, usually involving white-collar crimes, the defendant doesn't even have to plead guilty to fulfill her part of the bargain. She instead may enter a plea of *no contest* or *nolo contendere*, which is a statement that she does not contest the charges against her but is not technically an admission of guilt. This plea has the same effect as a guilty plea in the defendant's case; the court will treat it as a plea of guilty and sentence accordingly. But there is an important difference in subsequent proceedings. Unlike a guilty plea, nolo contendere cannot be used as an admission against the defendant in civil litigation. When a company is prosecuted by the government for criminal antitrust violations, for example, it may agree to plead nolo contendere to prevent establishing its liability in subsequent civil suits by businesses or consumers it has injured.

Plea bargaining is usually seen to be a response to congested courts and long delays in the criminal process; the prosecutors have a huge caseload to move, the defendant doesn't want to wait for a trial, and the judges are happy to have the cases out of the system. But plea bargaining has been a prominent feature of the criminal justice system for at least a century, and it commonly occurs in small towns and rural areas as well in crowded metropolitan trial courts.

There is something unseemly about plea bargaining being a central feature of our criminal justice system. Isn't achieving justice supposed to be different from haggling over the price of a used car? The whole process breeds disrespect for the law, and it has very practical consequences. Critics point out that plea bargaining produces unjust results, results that are sometimes too lenient and sometimes too severe. Victims of crime and crime control advocates complain that plea bargaining lets criminals off too easily; defendants get a discount on their punishment not because they show remorse and accept responsibility for their conduct but because they are doing the system a favor. At the same time, plea bargaining places pressure on defendants who are innocent or at least not deserving of conviction on the charges against them to plead guilty. Doing so means a quicker exit out of the system, lighter punishment because judges sentence more harshly those defendants who insist on their right to trial, and avoidance of the risk of doing worse at trial. And because it is a low visibility process, it diminishes the ability of the courts to supervise the behavior of police and prosecutors.

Plea bargaining has its defenders, too. They argue that most defendants are guilty—if not guilty of all they have been charged with, then at least guilty of something. Plea bargaining ensures that the guilty will be punished, and it enables those who may know the most about the case—the prosecutor and the defense attorney—to agree on an appropriate punishment, given all the variables involved. Particularly as mandatory sentencing schemes have become more common, plea bargaining preserves a necessary element of discretion in fitting the punishment to the crime. And just as a practical matter, the system would grind to a halt if all cases went to trial.

Whatever the debate about plea bargaining, it is here to stay. The Supreme Court has not only sanctioned the system of plea bargaining; it has applauded it (in *Santobello v. New York*, 1971):

> The disposition of criminal charges by agreement between the prosecutor and the accused, sometimes loosely called "plea bargaining," is an essential component of the administration of justice. Properly administered, it is to be encouraged.

The Constitution regulates the practice of plea bargaining to a limited extent. First, the Sixth Amendment guarantees the right to be represented by an attorney. This right applies at the plea bargaining stage as well as at trial. Unless the defendant waives the right, she must be allowed to have her attorney bargain for her and must be provided an attorney if she cannot afford to hire her own.

Second, the defendant cannot be coerced into pleading guilty but, applying the kind of distinction only lawyers can love, she can be *induced*. Inducement, of course, is the key to plea bargaining, but the question is when inducement turns into coercion. Basically, as long as the defendant has a choice among alternatives, unpalatable though they may be, she is not compelled to plead guilty. For example, when the prosecutor in a check forgery case threatens to prosecute under a habitual criminal statute when a conviction would result in life imprisonment but offers instead to recommend a sentence of five years in exchange for a plea, the law sees the defendant as induced but not compelled.

Third, the defendant's plea must be *voluntary, knowing, and intelligent*. This does not mean that the defendant must make a good choice, but only that she be informed about the basis and consequences of her choice, including the charges against her and the rights she is waiving. Typically the intelligent and voluntary requirement is satisfied by the judge and the defendant engaging in a scripted, formulaic, often surreal colloquy, in which the judge inquires whether the defendant understands what is going on and the defendant responds briefly and affirmatively.

Fourth, there must be some factual basis for the defendant's plea but, strangely, the defendant does not actually have to be guilty in order for the court to accept her plea of guilty. In *North Carolina v. Alford* (1970), Alford entered into a plea bargain whereby he would plead guilty to second-degree murder to avoid a possible death penalty. At the arraignment, however, he testified that he was not guilty and was simply pleading guilty to escape the risk of capital punishment. Nevertheless, because there was evidence that might have supported a conviction, it was permissible to allow him to plead to a crime while denying his guilt.

Finally, a deal is a deal, at least in part. The prosecutor and defendant each must abide by the deal they have struck. If the prosecutor has promised to recommend a certain sentence in exchange for the plea, he must do so. Similarly, if the defendant has promised something in addition to the plea—such as testimony against a codefendant—she must keep her side of the bargain, too. Unless the judge has taken part in the plea negotiations, he is not obligated to abide by the understanding reached or the prosecutor's plea negotiations. In many cases, though, unless and until the judge accepts the plea agreement, the defendant will be allowed to withdraw her plea and go to trial.

Why Do We Have Juries?

A distinctive feature of the criminal process in common law countries is the jury. Recall from the earlier survey of the criminal process that there are two kinds of juries. The grand jury indicts, or brings charges against, a defendant. The trial jury, or petit jury, decides the issue of guilt at trial. (The grand jury is grand and the trial jury petit—French for "small"—because of their sizes. Historically the grand jury had twenty-three members and the trial jury had twelve.)

The jury has been the deciding body in criminal trials in English law for 800 years and in American law since the founding. It assumed particular importance in colonial times when it functioned as a guardian of the colonists' liberties against the impositions of royal judges. The Supreme Court described the jury's historic functions in *Duncan v. Louisiana* (1968):

> Those who wrote our constitutions knew from history and experience that it was necessary to protect against unfounded criminal charges brought to eliminate enemies and against judges too responsive to the voice of higher authority. . . . Providing an accused with the right to be tried by a jury of his peers gave him an inestimable safeguard against the corrupt or overzealous prosecutor and against the compliant, biased, or eccentric judge. . . . Beyond this, the jury trial provisions in the Federal and State Constitutions reflect a fundamental decision about the exercise of official power— a reluctance to entrust plenary powers over the life and liberty of the citizen to one judge or a group of judges. Fear of unchecked power, so typical of our State and Federal Governments in other respects, found expression in the criminal law in this insistence upon community participation in the determination of guilt or innocence.

More recently, the jury has come under attack. The criticisms have come in part because the jury has been fulfilling its historic functions, but critics believe those functions no longer fit our modern world. Jurors bring too much community sentiment into the courtroom. Under this view, the role of the jury is not to protect the defendant's liberties but simply to find the facts without error or prejudice, a task for which they are less well equipped than a professional judge. These criticisms expose an inherent conflict in the jury's role. The jury is the ultimate fact finder and, as such, should be neutral, detached, and objective. At the same time, the jury is the conscience of the community in the courtroom and, in a democracy, a form of citizen participation in governance. By bringing in the community's perspective, the jury may do something other than simply determine the facts and apply the law in a neutral way.

An extreme example of this conflict is found in the debate over *jury nullification*. At trial, the judge instructs the jury on the relevant law, and the jury determines the facts of the case and applies the law it has been given to the facts. But because a jury's decision to acquit is for all practical purposes unreviewable, it can, if it chooses to do so, refuse to apply the law and acquit a defendant or convict on lesser charges in spite of the judge's instructions. If the jury finds the law or its application to the defendant to be unjust, too harsh, or out of line with the values of the community, it can, in this way, nullify the law. As one court stated, the jury can act as a "safety valve" for exceptional cases without being a "wildcat or runaway institution" (*United States v. Thomas*, 1996).

For all of the criticisms of juries, the social science evidence suggests that in most cases they do a good job, or at least as good a job as a judge would do. In a large majority of cases, when judges are asked what verdict they would have arrived at, they come to the same conclusion as the jury, and in the cases in which they differ, judges are probably less likely to convict.

Some attributes of the jury system have remained constant, while others have changed over time. Two stable features are its availability to the defendant in all serious cases and its finality. At least where the possible punishment is more than six months' imprisonment, the defendant must be afforded the option of trial by jury. The source of the jury's great power is its finality. In a civil case, either party can appeal a verdict. In a criminal case, a defendant can appeal a conviction because of an error committed during the trial, but if the defendant is acquitted, the prosecution cannot appeal the decision. Two changing features of the jury are its size and decision requirement. Historically juries were composed of twelve persons and were required to reach a unanimous verdict. The Supreme Court has held that neither of those attributes is constitutionally required. A state can have a criminal jury as small as six members, at least in a noncapital case, and can permit juries to decide cases on less than a unanimous verdict, but most states have retained the historic position of twelve-member juries and unanimous verdicts in criminal cases.

Since the historic purposes of the jury are to inject an element of community participation in the criminal process and to forestall abuses by providing an unbiased decision maker, the jury needs to be representative of the community at large and to be impartial. Juries are selected through a process that begins with the construction of a large list of potential jurors. Depending on the practice in the jurisdiction, the list may be constructed from voter registration lists, telephone books, tax rolls, or drivers' license records. Forms are mailed out to people on the list, either to establish eligibility for jury service (excluding, for example, people who cannot speak English or those in essential occupations such as physicians and firefighters) or to summon members of the list for service. As many potential jurors as may be needed are summoned for a day or week, constituting the *venire*, or panel from which the jury eventually will be selected.

Since not every jury can be representative, the test of representativeness is applied to the jury list as a whole. The Sixth Amendment guarantees the right to a fair cross-section of potential jurors. No significant, distinctive group in the population of the district from which the list is drawn may be systematically excluded from the list without a valid justification. Under this requirement, rules that caused systematic underrepresentation of racial or ethnic minorities or women, for example, have been invalidated.

Impartiality is more a characteristic of the particular jury than of the whole jury list. Impartiality is a requirement of the criminal justice system as well as a right of the defendant, but the way impartiality is sought often allows the prosecution and defense to try to achieve what they each want: a partial jury, one that is likely to be predisposed to favor their respective cases. Once a panel of prospective jurors is chosen, *voir dire* is conducted. The jurors are questioned about their knowledge of the parties, lawyers, or facts of the case and about any background factors, experiences, or predispositions that may not render them impartial. In some jurisdictions the judge questions the jurors on voir dire; others allow the lawyers for each side to do the questioning, under the supervision of the judge. Where the lawyers conduct the voir dire, they use the opportunity to begin to persuade the jurors, through artful questioning that builds trust while it foreshadows the case that is to come. In the typical case, voir dire focuses on the facts of the individual case and can be accomplished quickly. In high-profile cases, jury selection may take days or even weeks, as the attorneys probe the nuances of the jurors' beliefs. This has become especially true in large cases in which the lawyers retain jury consultants, psychologists, or other purported experts who analyze the pool, describe model jurors, suggest questions to ask, and evaluate jurors' responses and even their body language.

As a result of the voir dire, the prosecution and defense lawyers can challenge jurors and exclude them from the jury. Some challenges are for *cause*, where the lawyer can persuade the judge that there is a factual basis for presuming that the potential juror may not be able to render an impartial verdict (for example, because of pretrial publicity, the juror has already concluded that the defendant is guilty). Each side also has a number of *peremptory challenges*, which it can exercise to exclude a juror without giving a reason. A prosecutor may not exercise a peremptory challenge for an impermissible reason, however, such as if a prosecutor in a case involving an African American defendant systematically excluded all African Americans from the jury.

The voir dire process takes on a distinctive cast in cases in which the death penalty can be imposed. The Supreme Court has held that a jury from which all persons were excluded who had "conscientious scruples against capital punishment" did not arise from a fair cross-section of the community. Such a jury was too likely to be predisposed to convict and sentence to death. But a jury can be death-qualified, or composed of those willing to return a guilty verdict and a death penalty. If a juror's view on capital punishment would make it hard for him to impose the death penalty, he may be excluded from the jury for cause. The result is that death-qualified juries are more likely to convict and impose the death penalty than truly representative juries, but, in the opinion of the Supreme Court, not unconstitutionally so.

Because the jury is required to reach its verdict only on the evidence presented in court, publicity about the case before or during the trial presents a problem for the defendant's right to a fair trial. The court can, when necessary, impose a gag order on the lawyers, preventing them from making public statements about the trial, but the media has a First Amendment right to report the news, and, except in limited cases, the court cannot close a trial to the public nor prohibit the media from reporting information about a crime or a trial. (The exceptions arise where the state has a compelling interest in closing the proceedings or otherwise limiting the reporting, as in allowing minors who are victims of sex crimes to testify in private or prohibiting the disclosure of jurors' names in high-visibility cases.) The courts have to balance the right to a fair trial against the right to report proceedings.

In extreme cases, the balance can be struck by moving the trial outside the venue where it would normally be tried. If many potential jurors in an area have seen television reports that might prejudice their view of the case, the trial can be moved to another county. Sometimes the change works in reverse, inconveniencing the jurors rather than the lawyers, court personnel, and witnesses; instead of moving the trial to another venue, a jury is brought in from another venue.

In less extreme cases, prejudicial publicity is dealt with during voir dire of the jury and by prophylactic measures during trial. The key is whether jurors are able to put aside what they have heard and consider only the evidence in court. The Supreme Court has held that even if a juror has formed a belief about the guilt of the defendant, that juror is not necessarily disqualified if he can put aside his previous beliefs in deciding the case. When the trial begins the judge will admonish jurors who have been exposed to pretrial publicity to ignore it in their deliberations. As with instructions from the judge in other circumstances, this is based on the belief that jurors will listen to what the judge says and will be able to suspend their preconceptions. The judge will instruct the jury not to read or listen to news accounts of the case or to do research online about its subject matter, and, in unusual situations, may order the jury sequestered, or housed in a hotel under the supervision of court personnel with limited exposure to news reports. A great hardship to jurors, sequestration is reserved for cases with the greatest potential for prejudice.

What Is the Adversary Process?

Once the jury is impaneled, the trial begins. We speak of the trial as a search for truth, but the law places restrictions on the search and assigns everyone in the courtroom a different role in conducting the search. The criminal trial, as a reflection of the entire system of criminal justice, is an adversary process in which the adversaries have different objectives, and the means they can employ to achieve those objectives are limited by the rules of law and professional ethics.

Begin with the prosecutor. The prosecutor's job, obviously, is to obtain a conviction of the defendant. In concept, this is not a personal triumph for the prosecutor. The prosecutor is an agent of the government, and, by obtaining a conviction, the prosecutor serves the government's interest: punishing the criminal and preventing future crime.

But because the prosecutor is an agent of the government, his task is not limited to obtaining a conviction. The government's job is to do justice, and that is the job of the prosecutor, too. Doing justice means that the prosecutor should attempt to convict only those who actually are guilty, not simply those against whom a conviction can be obtained. It also means that the prosecutor is required to uphold the law, including all of the laws that make it difficult to obtain a conviction.

Of course, in the press of business and the heat of battle, prosecutors sometimes focus on the first objective—obtaining a conviction—at the expense of the second—doing justice. In part this is just human nature, but it also reflects two features of the criminal process. First, prosecutors, as repeat players in the system, just assume that most defendants are in fact guilty. Second, the incentives of prosecutors favor achieving convictions. District attorneys are elected in most jurisdictions, and it is much easier to campaign on a platform of being tough on crime and getting convictions than on being protective of defendants' rights and dismissing cases against the innocent. This imperative filters down to prosecutors on the line, who are typically judged by conviction rates.

The defense attorney has a different role in the trial. The defense attorney is the client's advocate, putting the government to its proof, requiring that the case against the defendant be proved beyond a reasonable doubt. (More about reasonable doubt shortly.) In doing so, the defense attorney attacks the state's evidence, questions the credibility of its witnesses, and presents contrary evidence that tells a different story or at least casts doubt on the government's story. The defense attorney also protects the rights of the defendant. The protections of the Bill of Rights have meaning only because the defense attorney is there to enforce them. If the government is to convict the defendant, it must do so according to law. The defense attorney's role is so important that the Sixth Amendment guarantees an accused "the Assistance of Counsel for his defence." The Supreme Court has given this guarantee teeth by requiring a lawyer to be appointed to represent a defendant who cannot afford one and by providing that "ineffective" assistance of counsel renders the process constitutionally defective. If a defense attorney operates under a conflict of interest, fails to conduct any pretrial discovery where doing so would have revealed exculpatory evidence, doesn't know the relevant law, or otherwise is incompetent, the accused has been denied his right to counsel in function if not in form.

People generally seem to understand what prosecutors do, but the defense attorney's role is more troubling. Most of the defendants in the system undoubtedly are guilty. Therefore, to quote the title of James Kunen's book on his career as a public defender, "How can you defend those people?" The answer is a cliché based in the conflict of values underlying criminal procedure but, like most clichés, is basically accurate. In the criminal justice system, the power of the state is brought to bear against an individual. A basic principle of our government structure is that great power is subject to abuse. That is why Congress ordinarily can't pass a law without the approval of the president and why elaborate procedural and substantive rights protect criminal defendants. The defense attorney's role is to check the application of government power, by ensuring that the defendant's rights are protected. It would be convenient if we could only protect the rights of innocent people, but we can't, so we use an adversary process that empowers a defense attorney to assert the rights of any defendant.

Does this kind of system produce abuses? No doubt. Advocates can be overzealous, and all of the protections of defendants' rights almost guarantee that some guilty defendants will go free. What we need to decide, ultimately, is whether the abuses outweigh the advantages and whether the system can be modified without being scrapped.

Consider two of the ways that the adversary system is limited in the interest of protecting the defendant against abuse of power by the government. On television the trial often turns on a surprise witness or an unexpected tactic by which a clever advocate defeats his opponent. In real life, the opportunity for surprise is drastically limited by discovery rules. The Supreme Court has held that the prosecutor has a constitutional duty to disclose material evidence to the defense, particularly evidence that tends to exculpate the defendant. Conversely, the defendant's privilege against self-incrimination prevents the court from requiring the defendant to turn over incriminating evidence. And the imbalance of power is such that it seems fair to require the prosecutor to disclose more information; the Federal Rules of Criminal Procedure and most states require prosecutors to disclose potential evidence and other information beyond what is constitutionally required.

A second means of protection is the prosecutor's burden of proving guilt *beyond a reasonable doubt*. A jury verdict of acquittal does not mean that the defendant is innocent, and the defendant never has the burden of proving his innocence. The burden is entirely on the prosecutor, and if the prosecutor fails to carry that burden, an acquittal is required. The defense attorney may choose as a matter of trial strategy to try to convince the jury that the defendant is innocent, but it is equally appropriate simply to cast sufficient doubt on the prosecutor's story so that the burden is not met.

Reasonable doubt is a much higher standard than the burden of proof elsewhere in the law. In civil cases, the standard is *preponderance of the evidence*, which only means that the conclusion is more likely than not. Reasonable doubt is a doubt about guilt that remains after the jury has weighed all of the evidence and seriously considered the matter. This has long been the standard for conviction in criminal cases, and the Supreme Court has held that it is a constitutionally required element of due process. The criminal sanction should be reserved for cases in which there is the utmost certainty that the defendant has committed a crime.

Moreover, because of the imbalance in the criminal justice system in which the weight of the government is arrayed against an individual, the reasonable doubt standard provides further protection against government oppression.

How Does Sentencing Work?

When a defendant is convicted of or pleads guilty to a crime, sentencing is the process through which his punishment is meted out. Of all the steps from the definition of crimes through the stages of the criminal process, sentencing is where the rubber meets the road; to a large extent, all of the other activity is directed at punishment of the guilty, and sentencing is the step that determines the punishment.

The first step in sentencing is legislative. Judges are allowed to impose only sentences that have been authorized by statute. The legislature determines what types of punishments will be imposed in what type of cases and the procedure by which they will be imposed. Although the legislature's ability to prescribe sentences is limited by the Constitution, the Supreme Court has held that the limits are very broad. It would violate the Eighth Amendment's ban on the infliction of "cruel and unusual punishments" to provide flogging as a punishment, for example, but the Court held that a sentence of life imprisonment without parole for possession of 672 grams (about a pound and a half) of cocaine for an offender with no prior convictions might be cruel but was not constitutionally unusual (*Harmelin v. Michigan*, 1991).

The legislature has a great deal of latitude to determine the types of sentences to be imposed. The most severe sanction, of course, is the death penalty. Incarceration and probation are much more common. The variations among crimes, criminals, and jurisdictions make it hard to generalize, but about 70 percent of convicted felons are sentenced to imprisonment and about 30 percent to probation. For less serious crimes, the proportion receiving probation is much higher. For minor offenses or first-time offenders, community service, youth boot camp, home confinement, or other intermediate sanctions are common.

Criminals who receive probation actually often receive a jail sentence, too, but execution of the sentence is suspended while they are on probation. While he is on probation, an offender usually must meet a set of requirements, such as finding a job, reporting regularly to a probation officer, and staying out of further trouble. If he violates the conditions of probation, the probation may be revoked and the suspended sentence takes effect, sending him to jail.

Until recently, the typical procedure for sentencing a convicted offender required the judge to exercise discretion within a considerable range prescribed by the legislature. For example, the statute might prescribe that robbery is punishable by a sentence of five to fifteen years in prison. The judge would receive a presentence report from the probation office, relating important information about the offender, such as criminal record, family and employment history, and psychological profile. The victim of the crime or his family may make a *victim impact statement* to tell the court about the effect the crime has had on them and may provide more details about the crime than came out at trial. Combining this information with the perceptions gained at the trial, the judge would sentence within the permitted range, with the possibility of suspending the sentence and putting the offender on probation.

The defendant might actually serve much less than the stated sentence, however—often a half to two-thirds less. Under an indeterminate sentencing system, the parole authorities have considerable discretion in deciding when, if at all, a prisoner is sufficiently rehabilitated to be released before his sentence is completed. Most states also have "good time" practices, under which prisoners can earn a reduction in their sentence, at the discretion of prison authorities, for serving "good time," or time in prison on good behavior, sometimes with participation in educational, work, or other rehabilitative programs.

The traditional model is still widely used, but, beginning in the late 1970s, there began a concerted effort to restructure the system to rein in the judge's discretion in sentencing. The effort arose from a perception that judges were exercising their discretion in such a way that there was wide disparity among sentences, producing arbitrariness and unpredictability in the system. Two judges might sentence similar offenders in different ways because one judge was more lenient than another or emphasized different factors in sentencing. As doubts arose about the system's ability to rehabilitate offenders, moreover, confidence declined in judges' ability to determine appropriate sentences and in parole boards' ability to determine when a prisoner had been rehabilitated. A variety of measures were enacted to limit discretion in sentencing.

The first measure is the use of sentencing guidelines. The objective of sentencing guidelines is to take much of the discretion in sentencing away from the trial judge and place it in the hands of the legislature or a legislatively created sentencing commission. A set of guidelines prescribes how the trial judge must arrive at the sentence. Usually the guidelines include a *presumptive sentence*, a sentence that is presumed to be appropriate given the severity of the crime for which the defendant has been convicted and characteristics of the defendant, notably his criminal history. For example, a robbery will have a designated base level sentence that the judge is directed to reduce by a certain amount if the particular defendant was a minor participant (if he only drove the getaway car, for example) and increase by a certain amount if the defendant has a prior criminal history of a specified type. Sometimes the guidelines will simply prescribe an enhancement of a sentence when particular facts are present, such as the crime's being racially motivated. Depending on the system, the trial judge may have limited discretion to depart from the presumptive sentence, but if he does so, he must issue an opinion explaining why, and the departure is subject to review on appeal. Sentencing guidelines reduce the degree of variability in sentencing, but many judges complain that they prevent judges from individually tailoring the punishment to fit the crime and the criminal.

The use of sentencing guidelines and judicial enhancement of sentences was disrupted by a series of Supreme Court opinions beginning in 2000, which held that under the Sixth Amendment's right to a jury trial, facts that are used to increase a defendant's sentence must be submitted to the jury and determined beyond a reasonable doubt, unless the defendant admitted them. In *Blakely v. Washington* (2004), for example, Ralph Blakely pleaded guilty to second-degree kidnaping, which was ordinarily punishable by a sentence of forty-nine to fifty-three months. The judge, acting under Washington's guidelines, sentenced him to ninety months because Blakely had acted with "deliberate cruelty." Because "deliberate cruelty" was not part of the statutory offense of second-degree kidnaping, the Court held, his sentence could not be increased unless a jury found that factor beyond a reasonable doubt. Washington's sentencing guidelines were, therefore, unconstitutional. Then in *United States v. Booker* (2005) the Court held that it was unconstitutional for the trial judge rather than the jury to determine a fact that required an enhanced sentence under the federal sentencing guidelines and that the guidelines would thereafter be advisory rather than mandatory. Some jurisdictions now require that juries determine whether factors that will affect the sentence are present, and others have followed the Court's lead in *Booker* by giving judges more discretion to depart from the guidelines, an exercise of discretion that the Court has viewed favorably.

Another measure to limit discretion in sentencing—and to increase punishment for certain types of crimes—is mandatory sentencing for particular types of situations. Under these statutes, the judge has little or no discretion in meting out a sentence. In Florida, for example, pulling a gun during the commission of a crime carries a mandatory minimum sentence of ten years. Weldon Angelos was sentenced to fifty-five years in prison for selling $350 worth of marijuana to a police informant because he possessed a gun during the sale, even though he had not used or even shown the gun. Federal law required the minimum sentence, which the sentencing judge denounced as "unjust, cruel, and irrational" and which could result, the judge noted, in Angelos being in prison longer than another defendant he sentenced on the same day, a lifelong criminal with sixteen convictions who most recently had broken into the house of a young woman, held her at knifepoint, and forced her to drive him away from the scene of his crimes (*United States v. Angelos*, 2004). Mandatory sentencing avoids the Sixth Amendment problem but can violate the Eighth Amendment's prohibition on cruel and unusual punishment; a mandatory life sentence without the possibility of parole for a juvenile defendant was struck down in *Miller v. Alabama* (2012).

A different type of mandatory sentencing is the "three strikes and you're out" law. Upon a defendant's third conviction of a crime of specified seriousness, the defendant must be sentenced to a long prison term or, in some states, life imprisonment without the possibility of parole.

The purpose of three strikes statutes is to deter criminals from repeating their crimes by raising the stakes for a second and third offense and to make sure that the most serious criminals—repeat offenders— are sentenced severely and prevented from committing future crimes. As sometimes happens, three strikes laws have had unintended consequences. Because the statutes often are sweeping in their definition, some of the criminals sentenced under them are not the hardened threats to society imagined by the drafters, as in a notorious California case in which the defendant's third offense was stealing a pizza. In addition, the threat of being sentenced under such a law may affect the behavior of offenders potentially subject to it, making them less willing to plea bargain to a first or second felony and, if facing a third strike, more willing to violently resist apprehension. Three strikes and other mandatory sentencing laws have also contributed to a vastly expanded prison population. Public awareness of the draconian consequences of three-strikes laws has led some states to reduce their impact; California voters, for example, passed a ballot proposition that restricted life sentences for repeat offenders.

Finally, parole release has been severely restricted through "truth in sentencing" statutes under which the sentence handed out by the judge represents the time the defendant actually will serve. A few states have abolished parole altogether, and many more have restricted it to defendants convicted of nonviolent crimes. Most states also have limited credit for good time by requiring that violent offenders serve at least 85 percent of their sentence before they can be paroled.

What About the Death Penalty?

The death penalty may be the most hotly contested area of criminal procedure. All the other arguments about crime control, justice, fairness, and rights coalesce in the debate about whether the state may put someone to death. Some advocates of capital punishment cite the biblical injunction of "an eye for an eye, a tooth for a tooth" and see the possibility of a death sentence as the ultimate deterrent for violent crime. Opponents characterize capital punishment as an outdated barbarism, abolished in every other Western nation and having little real effect on the incidence of crime.

The debate about capital punishment is too complicated to do more than capture its intensity in this brief survey of criminal procedure. In a debate too often dominated by slogans, this section shows how complex the issue is. There are two issues, really: whether the death penalty should be applied at all and, if so, how it can be applied fairly.

The argument about whether we should have a death penalty has two strands. The first strand concerns the morality of the death penalty: Is it morally justified, without regard to its social consequences? The second strand addresses those consequences directly: Does the death penalty serve important social goals, especially the deterrence of crime?

Supporters of the death penalty argue that executing those who have killed is just. It is just in that their crime deserves the most extreme punishment, and imposing deserved punishments is an accepted function of the criminal law. Capital punishment is retribution rather than vengeance; the state weighs the criminal's culpability and imposes the penalty only on those most deserving of it.

Critics respond that there is no necessary connection between executing criminals and doing justice. Certainly many of those sentenced to death are culpable and dangerous, worthy of punishment and confinement, but most of them do not fit the model of a calculating killer who deserves to be executed. Instead, most are the product of a horrific upbringing, deprived of normal nurturing to an extent that they have become pathologically asocial. Moreover, it is not obvious that executions are necessary for retribution; we do not cut off the hands of thieves or castrate rapists, so why execute murderers?

Supporters also argue that the death penalty affirms the value society places on human life, reserving its most severe sanction for those people who have taken another life. Critics respond that capital punishment cheapens our regard for life, brutalizes us, and inures us to killing. As the U.S. Conference of Catholic Bishops wrote, "Increasing reliance on the death penalty diminishes us and is a sign of growing disrespect for human life. . . . The death penalty offers the tragic illusion that we can defend life by taking life."

The moral argument is linked to the policy argument; probably few people would argue for the death penalty, even if it is morally justified, if it did not also do some good. Deterrence is an important function of the criminal process, and the threat of capital punishment, supporters contend, is the ultimate deterrent.

Critics respond that the death penalty is not much of a deterrent. Many people who murder are under the influence of drugs or alcohol, psychologically disturbed, or in an emotional state so that they cannot stop and coolly reflect on the consequences of their acts. Other murderers believe, as most criminals do, that they will never be caught or, if they are, that they will somehow escape the maximum punishment.

The deterrent effect of the death penalty is an empirical question, but one that is hard to answer. Numerous studies have been conducted comparing, for example, homicide rates in neighboring states with and without the death penalty, or homicide rates in a state before and after the death penalty is introduced. As one might expect on such a hotly contested issue where clear data are difficult to gather, the studies report varied results. Some scholars find no deterrent effect; others have argued that each execution prevents as many as eighteen murders; still others have concluded that executions have a brutalizing effect on the public so that they actually increase the murder rate. At this point, we can only conclude that there is no convincing evidence of a deterrent effect.

An issue that overlaps the moral and deterrent arguments concerns whether the death penalty is applied fairly and consistently. Relatively few criminals who commit murder are ever sentenced to death—about one in a hundred—and even fewer of those ever are actually put to death. The effectiveness of counsel, economic resources, and personal characteristics all influence who will be sentenced to death and who will die. Even more troubling are patterns of racial bias. In Louisiana, for example, a defendant convicted of killing a white person is fourteen times more likely to be sentenced to death than one convicted of killing a black person, and in Washington, juries are four times more likely to sentence black defendants to death than white defendants in similar cases.

Advocates of capital punishment respond that inconsistency and discrimination are problems, but the real problem is that there are too few executions, not too many. On the issue of racial bias, for example, the problem is not that murderers of white people are executed at too high a rate but that murderers of black people are not executed frequently enough. The cure is to increase the application of the death penalty, not to abolish it.

Critics also question whether the death penalty can be applied without error, which is an important issue because the death penalty is final. Since 1976, when the Supreme Court reaffirmed the constitutionality of the death penalty, about 1,500 people have been executed and over 150 individuals have been set free from death row after further investigation revealed that they were wrongly convicted because of police or prosecutorial misconduct, ineffective lawyering, mistaken witness testimony, or the lack of DNA evidence. That is, for every ten people who have been executed, one person facing the death penalty has been exonerated. Groups such as the American Bar Association have called for a moratorium on executions until procedures are in place to ensure that fair and effective procedures are in place so that the innocent or the undeserving are not sentenced to death.

Whether or not the application of the death penalty is wise public policy, the Supreme Court has declared it to be constitutional, and thirty states have a death penalty, although one state (Texas) accounts for about a third of the recent executions and at least ten states with the death penalty have not executed anyone in a decade or more. The central constitutional issue is whether the death penalty violates the Eighth Amendment's prohibition on punishment that is cruel and unusual. Applying this standard raises an interesting theme in constitutional law. Capital punishment was practiced at the time of the enactment of the Bill of Rights in 1791, so how can it violate a constitutional amendment drafted and ratified by people who practiced it? The answer came in the Supreme Court's first major Eighth Amendment case, *Weems v. United States* (1910). The Court invalidated a punishment of being shackled while at hard labor. "Time works changes," wrote Justice Joseph McKenna, "[and] brings into existence new conditions and purposes. Therefore, a principle, to be vital, must be capable of wider application than the mischief which gave it birth." As Chief Justice Earl Warren later expressed the principle, the prohibition of cruel and unusual punishment "must draw its meaning from the evolving standards of decency that mark the progress of a maturing society."

There is a second anomaly here. The death penalty is prescribed by the legislature, the representative of the community. How can it then violate contemporary standards of decency? The answer, of course, is that the will of the majority (or, more realistically, the majority's representatives) is not conclusive as to community standards. Under our constitutional system, the courts possess the power of judicial review of legislation precisely to check the majority in cases where its actions exceed constitutional boundaries.

The constitutionality of the death penalty came to the Supreme Court in the 1960s, raised in a series of cases by a campaign of lawyers spearheaded by attorneys associated with the NAACP Legal Defense Fund. The decisive case was *Furman v. Georgia* (1972), which involved three persons under death sentence and, indirectly, more than 600 prisoners on death row. In the longest set of opinions published in a single case in the history of the Court, five justices invalidated the death penalty as then applied and four dissented, with each of the nine writing a separate opinion. Justices Brennan and Marshall held the death penalty to be inherently cruel and unusual, focusing on factors such as the arbitrariness of application (as shown in the cases under review), the cruelty, and the lack of deterrent effect of the death penalty. The three other justices in the majority focused on the arbitrariness of application. The dissenters did not all disagree that the death penalty was in some respects abhorrent, but they suggested that the Court should defer to the legislature's judgment about "evolving standards of decency." Subsequently in *Gregg v. Georgia* (1976) the Court in a set of similarly fractured opinions held that the death penalty does not invariably violate the Constitution and established standards for reducing the arbitrariness of its application.

Because the focus in *Furman* and *Gregg* was on the arbitrariness of the death penalty as applied, state legislatures rewrote their sentencing laws to conform to the Court's opinion. One proposed cure for arbitrariness is to make a death sentence mandatory in all cases of specified types of murder, such as all murders committed by prisoners under life sentence. The Court, however, subsequently rejected mandatory sentences, in the view that, because every person is a unique individual, particularized consideration of individual factors relating to the crime and the defendant is constitutionally required. A different cure for the problem of arbitrariness is to guide the discretion of the decision maker, and the Court has adopted this approach. Most states that have a death penalty allow the jury to impose the sentence, and a first step in guiding the jury's discretion is to bifurcate the trial. At the first stage of the trial the jury renders a verdict on the defendant's guilt. If the defendant is found guilty, additional evidence is presented at a second stage of the trial, at the conclusion of which the jury decides whether a death sentence will be imposed. Because the trial is bifurcated, the jury in the sentencing phase can hear evidence of *aggravating* and *mitigating factors* relevant to sentencing that would not be admissible during the guilt phase. This is important, because the Court has held that the jury must be allowed to consider all factors that mitigate the defendant's guilt so that it is free to decide that the death penalty is not appropriate. Typical factors to be considered include the particularly heinous nature of the crime as an aggravating factor and that a young defendant was influenced by someone else to commit the crime as a mitigating factor.

The Court has also narrowed the class of cases in which the death penalty can be imposed at all. In some circumstances the penalty is disproportionate to the crime, so, for example, it may not be imposed as a punishment where the defendant was only an accomplice to a crime or where the defendant has been convicted of rape but not murder. In other circumstances the situation of the defendant precludes execution; for example, the Court has held that to execute a mentally challenged person or a person who was under eighteen years old at the time he committed his crime would be cruel and unusual.

Why Does It Seem That Criminal Appeals Go on So Long?

In appeals, as elsewhere in the criminal process, we have to balance conflicting purposes. Trial judges can make mistakes, and when those mistakes prejudice a defendant's rights, we want to make sure that the mistakes are corrected. Otherwise, the rights guaranteed by the Constitution may be subverted and an innocent person may go to jail. But enough is enough. Finality is important, too. Just as we are unwilling to invest unlimited resources into the investigative and trial processes to make sure no mistakes are made, so, too, at some point, when a defendant's trial has been reviewed by an appellate court once, twice, or more, we conclude that the defendant has gotten as much review as he is entitled to.

Note that the discussion in this section is about appeal of a conviction by the defendant. In civil cases, either party may appeal an adverse decision and in criminal cases, the defendant can always appeal a conviction or an error in the conduct of the trial. The double jeopardy clause of the Fifth Amendment prevents the government from repeatedly prosecuting someone for a crime until, after a string of acquittals, it finally obtains a conviction. Therefore, the prosecution cannot appeal an acquittal. The clause's scope is broader than that, though. Jeopardy attaches once the jury is impaneled, so the prosecution cannot decide to stop a trial if it is not going well and try again with a different jury. It also bars prosecution for different statutory offenses arising out of the same set of facts, when the proof required for one is the same as the proof required for another. For example, if a driver is convicted of driving while intoxicated, she cannot subsequently be prosecuted for negligent homicide for running over a pedestrian during her drunken-driving spree, where the proof of her negligence is her drunk driving. The state could bring both charges against her at the same time, but sequential prosecutions constitute double jeopardy. However, the double jeopardy clause does not bar two prosecutions by state and federal courts, when the crime is a violation of the law of each authority. A bank robber may be prosecuted both under state law for robbery and under federal law for bank robbery, a federal crime. Nor does it bar a civil action that has some punitive effect following a criminal conviction for related conduct. When an inmate is about to be released from prison after serving time for sexual contact with a child, the state can institute proceedings to have him civilly committed to a state institution under a sexually violent predator statute without violating the double jeopardy clause.

There are two separate kinds of challenges that a defendant can make to a conviction or an error by the trial court. An *appeal* is a request for a direct review of a trial court error, directed to a court higher up in the system than the trial court. A *collateral challenge* is an attack on a trial court decision that is, as its name indicates, collateral, or out of the normal chain of review; a collateral challenge usually comes after all appeals have been exhausted. Most of the criticism of endless appeals by defendants is actually criticism of collateral challenges.

First, let's consider appeals. In every case, a defendant has a right to appeal to a higher court to correct errors made by the trial court. This makes sense; it would be grossly unfair if the trial judge improperly admitted evidence or erroneously instructed the jury on the law and there was no way for the defendant to have the mistake corrected. Beyond this first level of review, appeals are often discretionary with the reviewing court. In a typical state system, for example, the defendant has a right to appeal to the intermediate appellate court, but the state supreme court has some discretion to decide whether or not it wants to take the case. The U.S. Supreme Court exercises more discretion than almost any other court; most defendants who want their cases heard by the Court must petition for a *writ of certiorari*, asking the Court to decide to hear the case.

Suppose a convicted defendant could bring to the appellate court's attention any mistake that had been made below, and the appellate court would reverse and order a new trial if it discovered a mistake. Since no trial is ever perfect, a defendant always could have a second, third, and fourth bite at the apple; no conviction could ever withstand review. The courts have developed two doctrines to prevent this situation, one dealing with what may be reviewed and the other dealing with how it is reviewed.

The first doctrine states that an appellate court will only consider on appeal an issue that the defendant raised at trial. The rationale is simple;

it is unreasonable to go to the trouble and expense of a new trial that could have been avoided if the defendant had raised the issue initially and the trial court had an opportunity to correct its error. For example, a defendant cannot claim on appeal that she was convicted using illegally obtained evidence unless her attorney had moved to exclude the evidence from the trial.

In law, however, every rule has its exception. One exception to the failure-to-raise rule is the *plain error* rule. The appellate court can correct plain errors or "defects affecting substantial rights" that occurred at the trial, even if the defendant did not raise the issue below.

The second doctrine states that not every error gives cause for reversal. The rule, almost literally, is "no harm, no foul." Under the *harmless error* rule, only important errors justify reversing a conviction. When the error complained of does not concern the defendant's constitutional rights, the question is how much the mistake contributed to the conviction. For instance, when the judge admits inadmissible evidence on a point but there is plenty of other evidence substantiating the point, the erroneous admission is, in the scheme of things, harmless.

One might think that mistakes that implicate the defendant's constitutional rights should always give rise to a reversal. How can the violation of a constitutional right be harmless, either in its effect on the defendant or in the prophylactic effect in preventing constitutional violations? But the Supreme Court has distinguished constitutional errors that are harmless from those that require automatic reversal. For example, if a confession obtained in violation of the right to counsel is admitted into evidence, only the harmless error standard applies, but if a defendant is indicted by a grand jury from which members of his race are systematically excluded, any resulting conviction must be reversed even if there is overwhelming evidence of his guilt.

The appeals process should be enough to correct most errors, but for centuries there has been an alternative, collateral means of attacking a conviction: the *writ of habeas corpus*. "Habeas corpus" in Latin means "you have the body"—the initial words of the court order directed to a government official holding someone prisoner, in effect saying "you have the body of this person and you must bring him to court." Habeas corpus, known as the Great Writ, is an all-purpose proceeding for challenging the legitimacy of one's confinement. A convicted prisoner who is in custody (actual or constructive) can petition a federal court for habeas corpus directed at the federal or state authority holding him, claiming that the confinement is illegal because of a legal error in the proceeding that led to confinement. (As discussed in Chapter 2, the Supreme Court also held that habeas was available to challenge the legality of the detention of prisoners captured during the war in Afghanistan and held as enemy combatants in military prisons in the United States and at Guantanamo Bay, Cuba [*Hamdi v. Rumsfeld* and *Rasul v. Bush*, 2004, and *Boumedienne v. Bush*, 2008].)

Habeas corpus is a powerful remedy. It expresses some basic principles: An individual can be criminally punished only in accordance with law and especially constitutional law, and that requirement is so important that a judicial remedy exists in addition to the ordinary right of appeal. But once again there is a conflict. If a defendant can use habeas to challenge a conviction, can she use it over and over, to challenge one error after another, even errors that have not been considered on direct appeal? The courts and legislatures have attempted to balance the rights protected by habeas against the desire for finality and the practical concern of punishing criminals.

Since the 1970s, the balance has shifted in favor of limiting the habeas right. First, under current law a number of constitutional violations may not be raised at all in habeas proceedings. In particular, Fourth Amendment claims that a defendant was convicted on the basis of illegally seized evidence are precluded where the defendant had a "full and fair opportunity" to litigate the claims in the state proceeding. If the defendant had such an opportunity, the courts have said, whatever deterrent effect the Fourth Amendment was designed to have on illegal police conduct has already been felt, so there is no point in allowing the defendant to litigate the claims again.

Second, before invoking habeas a defendant must exhaust other remedies available. If the defendant's rights have clearly been violated, she must raise the issues first in the state court. The only exceptions to this rule are when the defendant can show a reason for failing to raise the claim and actual prejudice as a result, when there was a fundamental miscarriage of justice, or when there is no effective opportunity to obtain redress in state court. Remarkably, though, even when the defendant attempts to show that she actually is innocent of the charges of which she was convicted, the court is unlikely to allow the habeas petition.

Third, the federal habeas corpus statute permits courts to refuse habeas petitions if the issues have been dealt with in previous petitions and "the ends of justice will not be served" by further review. The statute also authorizes courts to deny petitions for abuse of the writ; where a defendant has once sought habeas, the court will deny successive petitions, even those that raise different grounds, unless the defendant can provide an explanation for failing to raise the issue previously and can prove the prejudice that will result.

Fourth, whether the defendant was actually innocent of the charges of which she was convicted is almost always irrelevant to the granting of habeas corpus. Habeas will be denied if, viewing the evidence most favorably toward conviction, any rational jury could have convicted beyond a reasonable doubt.

Conclusion

By reading this book, you have learned about the basic principles and issues of American law. Judges, lawyers, and law students use these concepts every day. Let's see if you can use this knowledge to do what a judge does when deciding a case, a lawyer does when solving a client's problem, or a law student does on a final exam.

Find a story in today's news or an incident in everyday life that has something to do with the law. That should be easy to do; as you now know, legal issues are everywhere. Then do what judges, lawyers, and law students do: Identify the issues involved, consider the arguments on both sides, and come to a conclusion about how the issues should be resolved.

Here are some questions for you to think about:

- What area or areas of law are relevant? Is there a constitutional question involved or is it an issue of private law? Does it involve procedure or substance?

- What rules and principles apply? What specific legal doctrines relate to the problem? What general principles, theories, and policies apply?

- Is your problem like any of the cases discussed in the book? In what respects are the facts similar or different? Do the similarities and differences suggest how the case should be decided under the rules and principles you have identified?

- What is really at stake? What economic, social, and political interests are involved? Who would benefit and who would suffer if the matter were resolved one way or another?

- What is the best argument you can make for resolving the issue one way, using the rules, principles, authorities, and facts you have identified? What is the best argument you can make for resolving the issue a different way?

- What do you think would be a just result? Would it require a change in existing law? What would be the consequences of such a change?

How did you do on your final exam? Were you able to use what you have learned from this book? Did you see different sides of the question? Did it seem as if there was not an easy answer? Were you better able to articulate your sense of justice? If so, congratulations—and welcome to the law.

Index of Legal Cases

Index of Subjects